D1117127

SEAL OF THE PRESIDENT OF THE UNITED STATES
E PLURIBUS UNUM

Debrett's
PRESIDENTS
OF THE UNITED STATES OF
AMERICA

'The Inauguration of Washington' as first President, on 30 April 1789 at the Old City Hall, New York; a Currier and Ives print of 1876

Debrett's PRESIDENTS OF THE UNITED STATES OF AMERICA

DAVID WILLIAMSON

Salem House Publishers
Topsfield, Massachusetts

First published in United States
by Salem House Publishers, 1989, 462 Boston Street, Topsfield, MA 01983

Designed by Vic Giolitto

Production by Nick Facer/Rob Kendrew

Picture research by Anne-Marie Ehrlich

Library of Congress Cataloging-in-Publication Data

Williamson, David.
Debrett's presidents of the United States of America.
Includes index.
1. Presidents—United States—Family. 2. Presidents—
United States—Genealogy. I. Title. II. Title:
Presidents of the United States of America.
E176.1.W7233 1989 973'.09'92 [B] 87–36934
ISBN 0–88162–366–0

First published in Great Britain 1989 by
Webb & Bower (Publishers) Limited, 9 Colleton Crescent, Exeter, Devon EX2 4BY
in association with Michael Joseph Limited, 27 Wright's Lane, London W8 5TZ

Typeset in Great Britain by J&L Composition Ltd, Filey, North Yorkshire

Colour reproduction by Peninsular Reproduction Service Limited, Exeter, Devon

Printed and bound in Great Britain by Purnell Book Production Limited, Paulton, Bristol

Contents

FOR ROBIN

Introduction

The year 1989 sees not only the inauguration of the forty-first President of the United States of America, but also the two-hundredth anniversary of the institution of that office.

When George Washington was inaugurated in New York City on 30 April 1789, nobody knew how the new system of administration by a chief executive elected for a limited period of years was going to work. We can now look back and say that on the whole it has worked remarkably well, even though the forty men (forty because Grover Cleveland served for two non-consecutive terms and therefore counts as both twenty-second and twenty-fourth President) who have filled the office for two centuries have been of different backgrounds, different creeds and different temperaments, some able, some not so able.

This book is an attempt to place the Presidents in the contexts of their times, to give a brief assessment of their characters, and to tell of the events leading up to their assumption of office. It does not set out to be a history of the United States and for that reason politics and events of national and world history only find mention in so far as they affected the individual lives of the Presidents.

In writing the book I have drawn on the two editions of Burke's *Presidential Families of the United States of America* (1975 and 1981), to which I was a major contributor. I have also found Tim Taylor's *The Book of Presidents* (New York, 1972) an invaluable source. In addition I have consulted a number of standard biographies of individual Presidents and digested innumerable newspaper and magazine articles.

I would like to thank all those who have contributed in some way, namely Edward Hanson, Charles Kidd, Richard Compton Miller, Simon Shackleton, Dr R Whitney Tucker, Michael Wood, and my two stalwart typists, Dianne Gorman and Pamela Milne.

David Williamson

George Washington 1789–1797

Born:	Wakefield, Pope's Creek, Westmoreland County, Virginia 11/22 February 1731/2, son of Capt Augustine Washington JP of Wakefield, Westmoreland County, Virginia, and his 2nd wife Mary Ball	Married:	New Kent County, Virginia, 6 January 1759, Martha (*b* New Kent County, Virginia, 21 June 1731; *d* Mount Vernon, Virginia, 22 May 1802; *bur* Mount Vernon), widow of Col Daniel Parke Custis and eldest dau of Col John Dandridge, of New Kent County, and Frances Jones
Elected (1st) President:	4 February 1789		
Inaugurated:	New York City 30 April 1789	Children:	None
Elected for 2nd term:	13 February 1793	Died:	Mount Vernon, Virginia, 14 December 1799
Inaugurated:	Philadelphia 4 March 1793	Buried:	Mount Vernon
Retired from presidency:	4 March 1797		

George Washington's portraits do not do him justice. The prim, thin-lipped, humourless expression with which he gazes out at the world, although to some extent indicative of his nature, was probably occasioned more by his ill-fitting false teeth than by any other cause. On the other hand, his wife Martha looks a motherly soul, but one who would certainly stand no nonsense.

Of all America's Presidents to date, George Washington possesses the most illustrious lineage. His male line ancestry can be traced back with certainty to William de Washington, who was granted the manor of Washington, near Sunderland in County Durham, by Hugh du Puiset, Bishop of Durham, in about 1180, in exchange for the manor of Hartburn in the parish of Stockton, which he had formerly held. Although documentary proof is lacking, William's father was in all probability Patric de Offerton, *alias* Patric fitz Dolfin, son of Dolfin fitz Uchtred, Lord of Raby, who had a grant of Staindrop from the Prior of Durham in 1131.

Dolfin's father Uchtred has been identified with an Uchtred (mentioned in 1116), who was son of Maldred, younger son of Maldred, the brother of King Duncan I of Scotland (Macbeth's victim). Duncan and Maldred were the sons of Crinan the Thane, Hereditary Lay Abbot of Dunkeld, who was of the kin of St Columba and lineally descended from Niall of the Nine Hostages, who reigned in Ireland in the first half of the fifth century AD. If this descent is correct, the Washingtons possess a male line pedigree, in common with the O'Neills and the Nevills, as old as any in Europe.

George Washington, of course, would have been quite unaware of all this and would probably have been unimpressed by it had he been aware. He knew that his family was one of respectable gentry before his great-grandfather Colonel John Washington emigrated to Virginia in 1656 and settled in Westmoreland County, where he acquired over 6,000 acres of land. He commanded the Virginian forces in the Indian War of 1675 and represented Westmoreland County in the House of Burgesses. John's son Lawrence also sat in the House of Burgesses and married a lady whose background was equally as aristocratic as his. Mildred Warner was the daughter of a Speaker of the Virginia House of Burgesses and through her mother, Mildred Reade, a descendant

A French engraving of George Washington during the War of Independence

of the Dymokes, Hereditary Champions of England, whose office it was to challenge any man to dispute the sovereign's right to the throne at English coronation banquets. It is one of the ironies of history that George Washington should descend from these staunch supporters of the English crown. Lawrence Washington's younger son Augustine received the estate of Epsewasson by transfer from his sister Mildred, to whom it had been bequeathed by their father, in 1726. Later renamed Mount Vernon, it was to become famous as George Washington's favourite residence, where he died and was buried.

Augustine Washington, having lost his first wife, Jane Butler, in 1729, married again in 1731 to Mary Ball, the daughter of a neighbouring landowner and their first child (but his fifth), George, was born at his house at Pope's Creek on the south bank of the Potomac River on 22 February 1732 (or 11 February 1731/2 by old-style reckoning then still in use in England and its colonies). The house where the birth took place, later named Wakefield, was to be destroyed by fire on Christmas Day 1779. A little over one hundred years later in 1882 its site was made over to the United States by the Washington heirs and the State of Virginia, and the Wakefield National Memorial Association painstakingly restored the house and grounds with the authorization of Congress. No records or paintings existed of the original house, so a typical Virginian plantation house of the period was erected and inaugurated as the George Washington Birthplace National Monument. It is now a great tourist attraction.

Almost nothing is known of George Washington's childhood and education. The well-known story of his cutting down his father's favourite cherry tree and confessing to so doing because he 'could not tell a lie' is almost certainly apocryphal. He was at any rate only eleven years old when his father died, at the early age of forty-eight or forty-nine in April 1743. Five years later, at the age of sixteen, George joined a surveying party to chart the western estate of Lord Fairfax beyond the Blue Ridge Mountains, and in the following year he received a surveyor's licence, the equivalent of a degree in engineering, from William and Mary College, and was appointed official surveyor of Culpeper County, Virginia. He practised as a surveyor for the next three years and acquired several thousand acres of land by purchase or inheritance by the time he was twenty-one. From September 1751 until January 1752 he accompanied his half-brother Lawrence on a voyage to Barbados. It was to be his only trip outside America and for a month in Barbados he was ill with smallpox.

In November 1752 Washington received his first military appointment as District Adjutant of Virginia, with the rank of Major, from Governor Robert Dinwiddie. In March 1754 he was commissioned Lieutenant-Colonel in the Virginia Regiment and his first taste of active service came two months later when he defeated a French scouting party. His next task was to build Fort Necessity at Great Meadows, Pennsylvania, but he was immediately obliged to surrender it to a superior combined force of French soldiers and Indians. In November 1754 Washington resigned his commission when the Virginia Regiment was divided into companies and he was only offered the reduced rank of Captain. The following May, however, he volunteered to join the staff of Major-General Edward Braddock, Commander of all British Forces in America, and was appointed his ADC. The army was ambushed by the French and Indians near Turtle Creek, Pennsylvania, in July. Washington narrowly escaped being wounded after having two horses shot under him and General Braddock was mortally wounded. In August Washington was appointed Colonel and Commander-in-Chief of the Virginia Regiment. He held this appointment until December 1758 when he resigned his commission following his election to the Virginia House of Burgesses.

On 6 January 1759 Washington married Mrs Martha Custis, a young widow of twenty-seven, his senior by about eight months. It was presumably a love match, but one cannot help feeling that George had decided that a wife was a necessary adjunct on his entry into politics and chose the most suitable person to hand. There were to be no children of the marriage, although Martha had had four children by her first husband. As both George and Martha were still in their twenties their childlessness leads one to suppose that he may have been sterile. He proved a kind stepfather to Martha's two surviving children, Jack and Patsy, and was later to be equally kind to Jack's orphaned children.

In the month following his marriage Washington took his seat in the House of Burgesses at Williamsburg. He was to remain a member, representing first Frederick County then Fairfax County, until 1774 when he was chosen as one of seven Virginia delegates to the First Continental Congress, which met at Philadelphia in September and October. In May 1775 Washington left Mount Vernon to attend the Second Continental Congress, little knowing that he was not to see his beloved home again for over six years. On 16 June he accepted a commission as commanding General of the Continental Army, becoming the first American General, and taking command of the Continental Army at Cambridge, Massachusetts, on 3 July. The flag of the United Colonies, thirteen alternating red and white stripes with the crosses of St George and St Andrew on a canton, was raised for the first time on 1 January 1776. The struggle for independence had begun and for the next seven years Washington, serving without a salary, led his countrymen to victory until the treaty of peace signed in Paris on 20 January 1783 ended the hostilities.

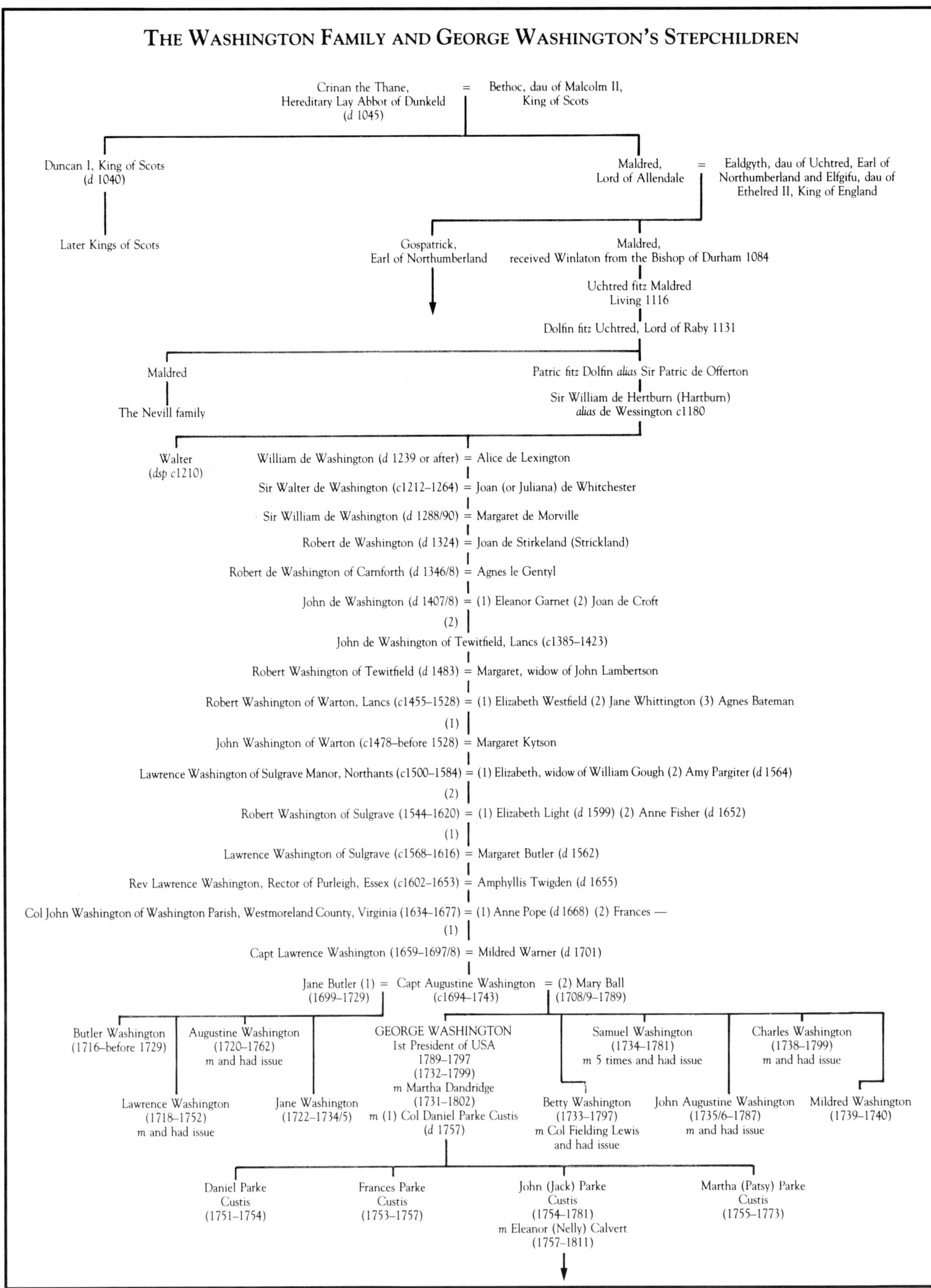
THE WASHINGTON FAMILY AND GEORGE WASHINGTON'S STEPCHILDREN
Crinan the Thane, Hereditary Lay Abbot of Dunkeld (d 1045) = Bethoc, dau of Malcolm II, King of Scots
Duncan I, King of Scots (d 1040)
Later Kings of Scots
Maldred, Lord of Allendale = Ealdgyth, dau of Uchtred, Earl of Northumberland and Elfgifu, dau of Ethelred II, King of England
Gospatrick, Earl of Northumberland
Maldred, received Winlaton from the Bishop of Durham 1084
Uchtred fitz Maldred Living 1116
Dolfin fitz Uchtred, Lord of Raby 1131
Maldred
The Nevill family
Patric fitz Dolfin alias Sir Patric de Offerton
Sir William de Hertburn (Hartburn) alias de Wessington c1180
Walter (dsp c1210)
William de Washington (d 1239 or after) = Alice de Lexington
Sir Walter de Washington (c1212–1264) = Joan (or Juliana) de Whitchester
Sir William de Washington (d 1288/90) = Margaret de Morville
Robert de Washington (d 1324) = Joan de Stirkeland (Strickland)
Robert de Washington of Carnforth (d 1346/8) = Agnes le Gentyl
John de Washington (d 1407/8) = (1) Eleanor Garnet (2) Joan de Croft
(2)
John de Washington of Tewitfield, Lancs (c1385–1423)
Robert Washington of Tewitfield (d 1483) = Margaret, widow of John Lambertson
Robert Washington of Warton, Lancs (c1455–1528) = (1) Elizabeth Westfield (2) Jane Whittington (3) Agnes Bateman
(1)
John Washington of Warton (c1478–before 1528) = Margaret Kytson
Lawrence Washington of Sulgrave Manor, Northants (c1500–1584) = (1) Elizabeth, widow of William Gough (2) Amy Pargiter (d 1564)
(2)
Robert Washington of Sulgrave (1544–1620) = (1) Elizabeth Light (d 1599) (2) Anne Fisher (d 1652)
(1)
Lawrence Washington of Sulgrave (c1568–1616) = Margaret Butler (d 1562)
Rev Lawrence Washington, Rector of Purleigh, Essex (c1602–1653) = Amphyllis Twigden (d 1655)
Col John Washington of Washington Parish, Westmoreland County, Virginia (1634–1677) = (1) Anne Pope (d 1668) (2) Frances —
(1)
Capt Lawrence Washington (1659–1697/8) = Mildred Warner (d 1701)
Jane Butler (1) (1699–1729) = Capt Augustine Washington (c1694–1743) = (2) Mary Ball (1708/9–1789)
Butler Washington (1716–before 1729)
Augustine Washington (1720–1762) m and had issue
Lawrence Washington (1718–1752) m and had issue
Jane Washington (1722–1734/5)
GEORGE WASHINGTON 1st President of USA 1789–1797 (1732–1799) m Martha Dandridge (1731–1802) m (1) Col Daniel Parke Custis (d 1757)
Samuel Washington (1734–1781) m 5 times and had issue
Charles Washington (1738–1799) m and had issue
Betty Washington (1733–1797) m Col Fielding Lewis and had issue
John Augustine Washington (1735/6–1787) m and had issue
Mildred Washington (1739–1740)
Daniel Parke Custis (1751–1754)
Frances Parke Custis (1753–1757)
John (Jack) Parke Custis (1754–1781) m Eleanor (Nelly) Calvert (1757–1811)
Martha (Patsy) Parke Custis (1755–1773)

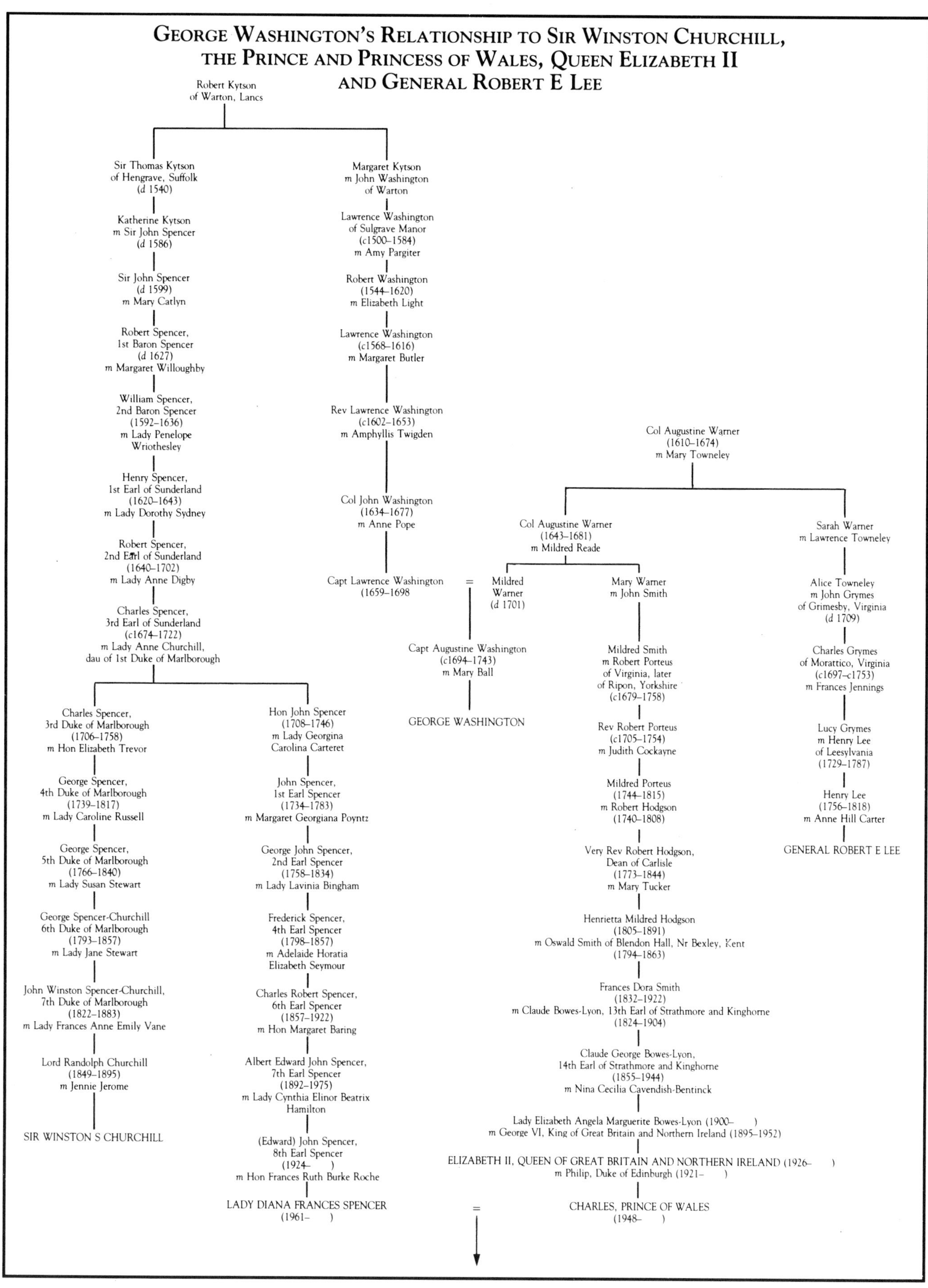
GEORGE WASHINGTON'S RELATIONSHIP TO SIR WINSTON CHURCHILL, THE PRINCE AND PRINCESS OF WALES, QUEEN ELIZABETH II AND GENERAL ROBERT E LEE
Robert Kytson of Warton, Lancs
Sir Thomas Kytson of Hengrave, Suffolk (d 1540)
Katherine Kytson m Sir John Spencer (d 1586)
Sir John Spencer (d 1599) m Mary Catlyn
Robert Spencer, 1st Baron Spencer (d 1627) m Margaret Willoughby
William Spencer, 2nd Baron Spencer (1592–1636) m Lady Penelope Wriothesley
Henry Spencer, 1st Earl of Sunderland (1620–1643) m Lady Dorothy Sydney
Robert Spencer, 2nd Earl of Sunderland (1640–1702) m Lady Anne Digby
Charles Spencer, 3rd Earl of Sunderland (c1674–1722) m Lady Anne Churchill, dau of 1st Duke of Marlborough
Charles Spencer, 3rd Duke of Marlborough (1706–1758) m Hon Elizabeth Trevor
George Spencer, 4th Duke of Marlborough (1739–1817) m Lady Caroline Russell
George Spencer, 5th Duke of Marlborough (1766–1840) m Lady Susan Stewart
George Spencer-Churchill 6th Duke of Marlborough (1793–1857) m Lady Jane Stewart
John Winston Spencer-Churchill, 7th Duke of Marlborough (1822–1883) m Lady Frances Anne Emily Vane
Lord Randolph Churchill (1849–1895) m Jennie Jerome
SIR WINSTON S CHURCHILL
Hon John Spencer (1708–1746) m Lady Georgina Carolina Carteret
John Spencer, 1st Earl Spencer (1734–1783) m Margaret Georgiana Poyntz
George John Spencer, 2nd Earl Spencer (1758–1834) m Lady Lavinia Bingham
Frederick Spencer, 4th Earl Spencer (1798–1857) m Adelaide Horatia Elizabeth Seymour
Charles Robert Spencer, 6th Earl Spencer (1857–1922) m Hon Margaret Baring
Albert Edward John Spencer, 7th Earl Spencer (1892–1975) m Lady Cynthia Elinor Beatrix Hamilton
(Edward) John Spencer, 8th Earl Spencer (1924–) m Hon Frances Ruth Burke Roche
LADY DIANA FRANCES SPENCER (1961–)
=
Margaret Kytson m John Washington of Warton
Lawrence Washington of Sulgrave Manor (c1500–1584) m Amy Pargiter
Robert Washington (1544–1620) m Elizabeth Light
Lawrence Washington (c1568–1616) m Margaret Butler
Rev Lawrence Washington (c1602–1653) m Amphyllis Twigden
Col John Washington (1634–1677) m Anne Pope
Capt Lawrence Washington (1659–1698 = Mildred Warner (d 1701)
Capt Augustine Washington (c1694–1743) m Mary Ball
GEORGE WASHINGTON
Col Augustine Warner (1610–1674) m Mary Towneley
Col Augustine Warner (1643–1681) m Mildred Reade
Mary Warner m John Smith
Mildred Smith m Robert Porteus of Virginia, later of Ripon, Yorkshire (c1679–1758)
Rev Robert Porteus (c1705–1754) m Judith Cockayne
Mildred Porteus (1744–1815) m Robert Hodgson (1740–1808)
Very Rev Robert Hodgson, Dean of Carlisle (1773–1844) m Mary Tucker
Henrietta Mildred Hodgson (1805–1891) m Oswald Smith of Blendon Hall, Nr Bexley, Kent (1794–1863)
Frances Dora Smith (1832–1922) m Claude Bowes-Lyon, 13th Earl of Strathmore and Kinghorne (1824–1904)
Claude George Bowes-Lyon, 14th Earl of Strathmore and Kinghorne (1855–1944) m Nina Cecilia Cavendish-Bentinck
Lady Elizabeth Angela Marguerite Bowes-Lyon (1900–) m George VI, King of Great Britain and Northern Ireland (1895–1952)
ELIZABETH II, QUEEN OF GREAT BRITAIN AND NORTHERN IRELAND (1926–) m Philip, Duke of Edinburgh (1921–)
CHARLES, PRINCE OF WALES (1948–)
Sarah Warner m Lawrence Towneley
Alice Towneley m John Grymes of Grimesby, Virginia (d 1709)
Charles Grymes of Morattico, Virginia (c1697–c1753) m Frances Jennings
Lucy Grymes m Henry Lee of Leesylvania (1729–1787)
Henry Lee (1756–1818) m Anne Hill Carter
GENERAL ROBERT E LEE

George Washington's Descent from King John and Nine Magna Carta Sureties

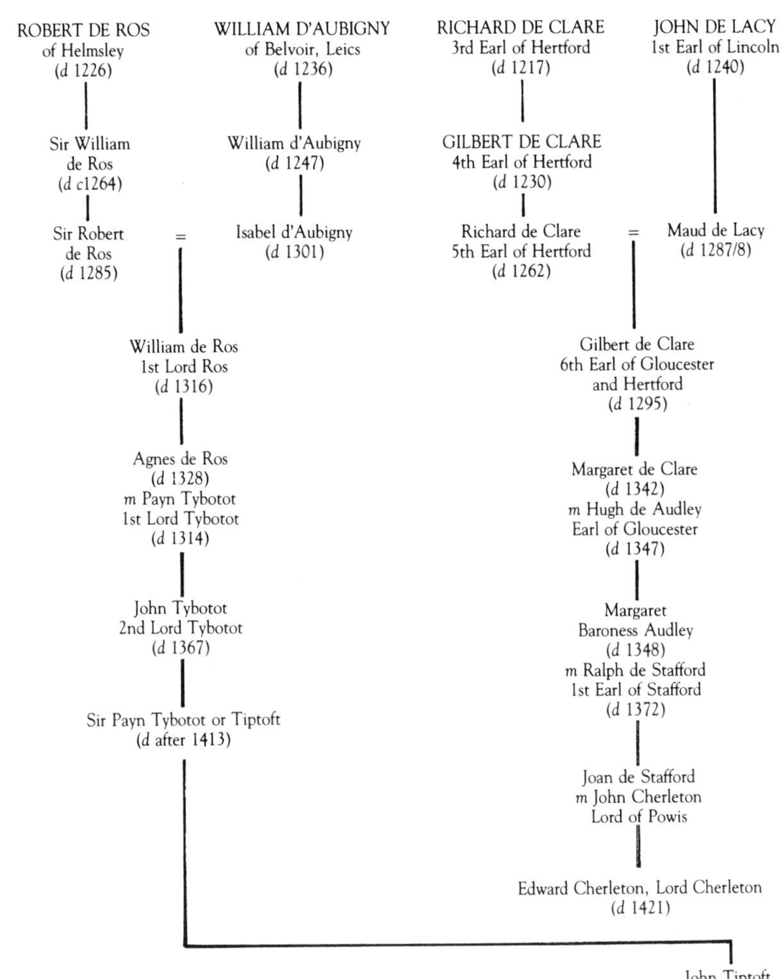
ROBERT DE ROS
of Helmsley
(d 1226)
WILLIAM D'AUBIGNY
of Belvoir, Leics
(d 1236)
RICHARD DE CLARE
3rd Earl of Hertford
(d 1217)
JOHN DE LACY
1st Earl of Lincoln
(d 1240)
Sir William
de Ros
(d c1264)
William d'Aubigny
(d 1247)
GILBERT DE CLARE
4th Earl of Hertford
(d 1230)
Sir Robert
de Ros
(d 1285)
=
Isabel d'Aubigny
(d 1301)
Richard de Clare
5th Earl of Hertford
(d 1262)
=
Maud de Lacy
(d 1287/8)
William de Ros
1st Lord Ros
(d 1316)
Gilbert de Clare
6th Earl of Gloucester
and Hertford
(d 1295)
Agnes de Ros
(d 1328)
m Payn Tybotot
1st Lord Tybotot
(d 1314)
Margaret de Clare
(d 1342)
m Hugh de Audley
Earl of Gloucester
(d 1347)
John Tybotot
2nd Lord Tybotot
(d 1367)
Margaret
Baroness Audley
(d 1348)
m Ralph de Stafford
1st Earl of Stafford
(d 1372)
Sir Payn Tybotot or Tiptoft
(d after 1413)
Joan de Stafford
m John Cherleton
Lord of Powis
Edward Cherleton, Lord Cherleton
(d 1421)
John Tiptoft
1st Lord Tiptoft
(d 1443)

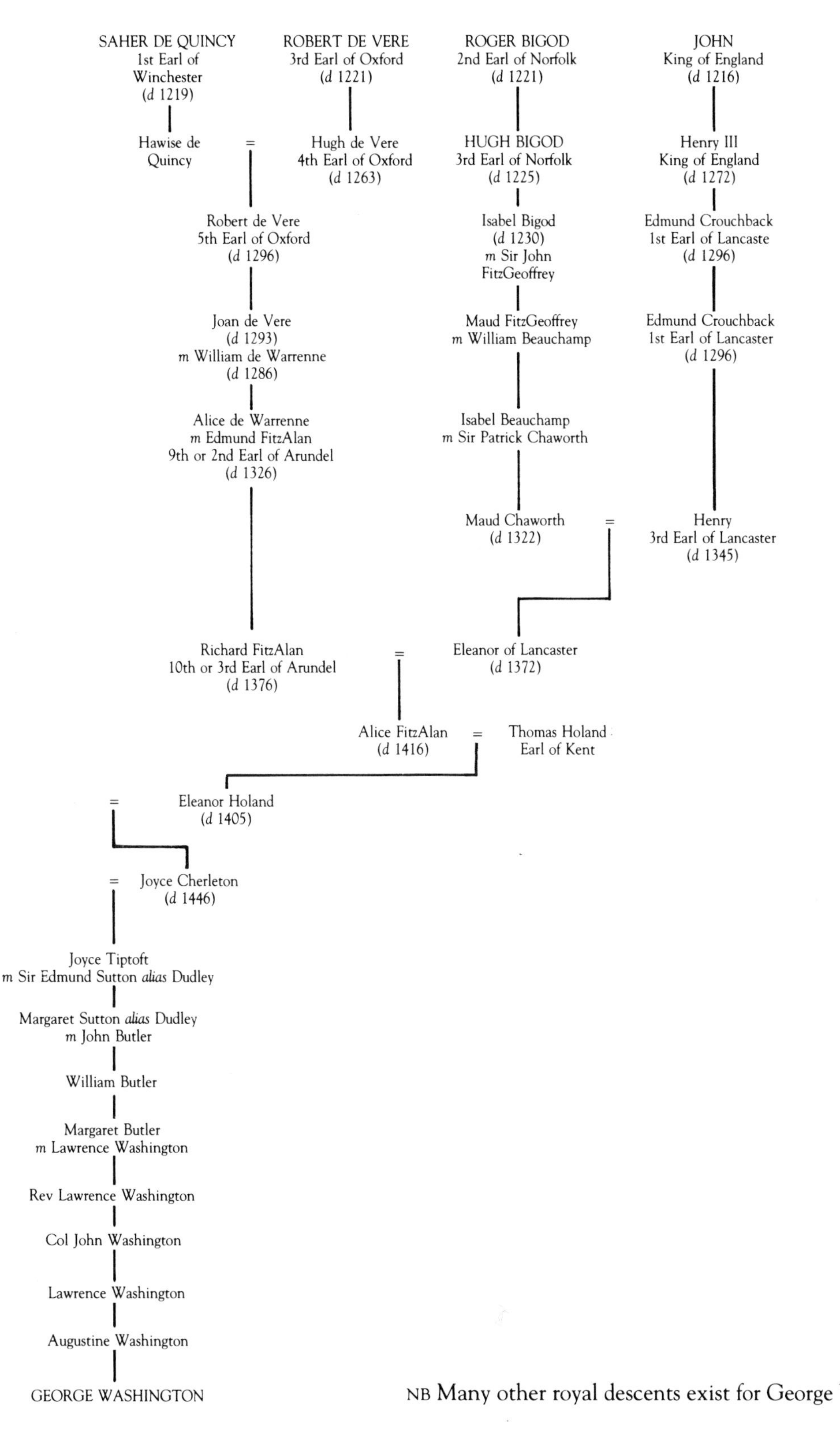
SAHER DE QUINCY
1st Earl of
Winchester
(*d* 1219)
ROBERT DE VERE
3rd Earl of Oxford
(*d* 1221)
ROGER BIGOD
2nd Earl of Norfolk
(*d* 1221)
JOHN
King of England
(*d* 1216)
Hawise de
Quincy
=
Hugh de Vere
4th Earl of Oxford
(*d* 1263)
HUGH BIGOD
3rd Earl of Norfolk
(*d* 1225)
Henry III
King of England
(*d* 1272)
Robert de Vere
5th Earl of Oxford
(*d* 1296)
Isabel Bigod
(*d* 1230)
m Sir John
FitzGeoffrey
Edmund Crouchback
1st Earl of Lancaste
(*d* 1296)
Joan de Vere
(*d* 1293)
m William de Warrenne
(*d* 1286)
Maud FitzGeoffrey
m William Beauchamp
Edmund Crouchback
1st Earl of Lancaster
(*d* 1296)
Alice de Warrenne
m Edmund FitzAlan
9th or 2nd Earl of Arundel
(*d* 1326)
Isabel Beauchamp
m Sir Patrick Chaworth
Maud Chaworth
(*d* 1322)
=
Henry
3rd Earl of Lancaster
(*d* 1345)
Richard FitzAlan
10th or 3rd Earl of Arundel
(*d* 1376)
=
Eleanor of Lancaster
(*d* 1372)
Alice FitzAlan
(*d* 1416)
=
Thomas Holland
Earl of Kent
=
Eleanor Holland
(*d* 1405)
=
Joyce Cherleton
(*d* 1446)
Joyce Tiptoft
m Sir Edmund Sutton *alias* Dudley
Margaret Sutton *alias* Dudley
m John Butler
William Butler
Margaret Butler
m Lawrence Washington
Rev Lawrence Washington
Col John Washington
Lawrence Washington
Augustine Washington
GEORGE WASHINGTON

NB Many other royal descents exist for George Washington

Washington spent the year making a round of triumphal visits, receiving honorary degrees, farewell addresses, and the congratulations of Congress. The army was disbanded in November and Washington took leave of his officers with the following words: 'With a heart full of love and gratitude I now take leave of you. I most devoutly wish that your latter days may be as prosperous and happy as your former ones have been glorious and honorable.' He resigned his commission as Commander-in-Chief at Annapolis, Maryland, on 23 December and the following day, Christmas Eve, returned to Mount Vernon to resume the life of a gentleman farmer.

Two years passed in tranquillity with Washington tending his plantations, attending the first general meeting of the Society of the Cincinnati in Philadelphia, receiving the gift of a jackass from King Carlos III of Spain, and granting lengthy interviews to his enthusiastic biographer, the Rev Mason Lock Weems ('Pastor Weems'), who was to publish the first edition of *The Life and Memorable Actions of George Washington* in 1800. It was to run into many editions and the famous cherry tree story first appeared in the fifth in 1806.

On 5 December 1786 Washington was appointed one of seven Virginia delegates to the proposed Convention of States. He was dubious about accepting, but eventually agreed and journeyed to Philadelphia to take part the following May. On the 25th he was unanimously elected President of the Federal Convention.

A portrait of Martha Washington in early life from an engraving in Sparks's *Life of Washington* after a painting by Woolaston

The Constitution of the United States was signed on 17 September 1787, Washington being one of the signatories, and the session of the Convention ended the same day. During the following months the states debated the Constitution and on 7 December Delaware was the first state to ratify it. The other states swiftly followed suit and on 21 June 1788 New Hampshire, the ninth state to do so, made the adoption of the Constitution decisive.

The Constitution having been adopted, the complicated machinery for the election of a President of the United States of America was put into operation for the first time. The chief executive hitherto had borne the style of President of the United States in Congress Assembled.

There were twelve candidates for the Presidency but it was practically a foregone conclusion that the hero of the War of Independence would emerge as the victor. In the event, when the ballot took place on 4 February 1789, Washington received sixty-nine of the electoral votes from the ten states which sent electors to New York. Of the remaining three states, North Carolina and Rhode Island had still to ratify the Constitution and New York itself had not yet got around to choosing presidential electors. The runner-up in the election was John Adams, of Massachusetts, with thirty-four votes, who duly became Vice-President. No other candidate received more than nine votes.

The new office of President was one which had to be approached cautiously and was to be subjected to a process of trial and error before settling into an accepted pattern. There were hardly any precedents to follow, the only other republic in the world with a similar presidential system being that of Switzerland, where the President held office for one year only. In America the presidential term was to last four years and the President was eligible for re-election for a second term. The office was seen as that of an elected monarch and there was some discussion as to whether the President should be styled 'Serene Highness' and his wife accorded the title of 'Lady'. Washington's personal dignity and that of his wife Martha added greatly to the prestige of the presidency during its early years and the receptions they held were sometimes referred to as 'the Republican Court'. 'In a comparatively short time,' wrote the historian Sir Denis Brogan, 'the office of President of the United States acquired the sacred character of the Roman consulate or the papal throne.' This situation could not have been brought about had not the early Presidents consistently been men of outstanding character and integrity, very different from some of the sad nonentities who have occupied the office from time to time since.

Mount Vernon, George Washington's house in Virginia; note the Washington coat-of-arms in the top left-hand corner of the print

Washington took the oath, administered by Robert R Livingston, Chancellor of the State of New York, on the balcony of the Senate Chamber of New York Federal Hall on Thursday 30 April 1789, and delivered his inaugural address from the floor of the Chamber immediately afterwards. Neither his wife nor his aged mother (who died the following August) was present at the ceremony.

Washington was a reluctant President and would have preferred to remain quietly on his plantations, but he was persuaded that it was his duty to take office and accordingly did so, even agreeing to serve a second term, although adamant that he would not stand for a third. Had he wished it, the presidency could have been his for life.

At the end of August 1790 the seat of government moved from New York to Philadelphia and on Washington's second inauguration day, 4 March 1793, he took the oath, administered by Associate Justice William Cushing, in the Senate Chamber of the Federal Hall in Philadelphia. His inaugural address on this occasion contained only 135 words and remains the shortest on record.

During his second term of office Washington had to cope with the difficulties arising from the repercussions of the French Revolution which divided the country. On 4 March 1797 he thankfully relinquished office and after attending the inauguration of his successor John Adams left Philadelphia and returned to Mount Vernon. In the following year President Adams appointed Washington Lieutenant-General and Commander-in-Chief and he paid his last visit to Philadelphia.

On 12 December 1799 Washington made his usual circuit of his farms on horseback in hail and snow. Later that day he complained of a sore throat, pneumonia developed, and two days later he died peacefully at Mount Vernon, aged sixty-seven. Martha Washington survived her husband over two years and died on 22 May 1802, aged seventy. George and Martha lie buried together at Mount Vernon.

John Adams 1797–1801

Born: Braintree (now Quincy), Massachusetts, 19/30 October 1735, eldest son of John Adams of Braintree, Massachusetts, and Susanna Boylston

Elected (1st) Vice-President: 4 February 1789

Inaugurated: New York City 21 April 1789

Re-elected Vice-President: 5 December 1792

Inaugurated: Philadelphia 4 March 1793

Elected (2nd) President: 7 December 1796

Inaugurated: Philadelphia 4 March 1797

Retired from presidency: 4 March 1801

Married: Weymouth, Massachusetts, 25 October 1764, Abigail (*b* Weymouth, Massachusetts, 11/22 November 1744; *d* Braintree (now Quincy), Massachusetts, 28 October 1818; *bur* Braintree), 2nd dau of Rev William Smith, Congregational Minister of Weymouth, and Elizabeth Quincy

Children
(1) Abigail, *b* Braintree 14 July 1765; *m* London, England, 12 June 1786, Col William Stephens Smith (*b* Long Island, New York, 8 November 1755; *d* Lebanon, New York, 10 June 1816); 3 sons, 1 dau; *d* Braintree 30 August 1813
(2) John Quincy (qv), later 6th President
(3) Susanna, *b* Boston 28 December 1768; *d* Boston 4 February 1770
(4) Charles, *b* Boston 29 May 1770; *m* 29 August 1795, Sarah (*b* 6 November 1769; *d* 8 August 1828), dau of John Smith and Margaret Stephens, and sister of William Stephens Smith (*see above*); 2 daus; *d* New York City 30 November 1800
(5) Thomas Boylston, Chief Justice of the Supreme Court of Massachusetts, *b* Penns Hill Farm, Braintree, 15 September 1772; *m* 1805, Ann Harrod (*b* 1774; *d* 1846); 4 sons, 3 daus; *d* 13 March 1832

Died: Quincy 4 July 1826

Buried: Quincy Congregational Church

A portrait of John Adams by Edgar Parker

John Adams sprang from a very different ancestral background from that of Washington. The Adams family belonged to the sturdy class of husbandmen, small tenant farmers, who with the slightly higher class of yeomen formed the solid backbone of rural England. They hailed from the village of Barton David in Somerset, where a John Adams is listed in the Muster Roll of 1539 as one of the billmen finding harness. His great-grandson Henry Adams emigrated to America in 1638 and settled at Braintree, Massachusetts, where he was buried on 8 October 1646. It is believed that his emigration was influenced by his wife's connection with Aquila and Thomas Purchase, who were among the 'Dorchester Adventurers' who sailed to New England in 1623. Henry Adams's ten children (nine sons and one daughter) all became persons of some consequence in Massachusetts, and it was his seventh son Joseph, farmer and maltster in Braintree, who was to become ancestor of the Adams Presidents and also of the Hon Samuel Adams, Governor of Massachusetts from 1794 to 1797, 'regarded as the chief moulder of public opinion in favour of revolution and separation'.

John Adams, the father of the first Adams President, was a cordwainer and farmer in Braintree (later renamed

Quincy), Massachusetts, and married Susanna, daughter of Peter Boylston, of Brookline, Massachusetts, in October 1734. John Adams, the future President, was the eldest of their three sons and was born at what is now 133 Franklin Street, Quincy, on 30 October (old style 19 October) 1735. After attending local schools and being privately tutored, the young John entered Harvard in November 1751 and graduated with a BA degree in July 1755. For the next three years he made his living as a schoolmaster in Worcester, Massachusetts, and also began studying law there under James Putnam. On 6 November 1758 he was admitted to the Massachusetts Bar in Boston. His father died in May 1761 and in the same year he was elected surveyor of highways for Braintree in spite of the fact that he had no surveying experience. It was one of the services to the community expected as a matter of course from all adult males.

On 25 October 1764, Adams married his third cousin Abigail Smith at Weymouth, Massachusetts, the officiating minister being her father the Rev William Smith, who was Congregational Minister of Weymouth. At nineteen, she was nine years his junior. There were five children of the marriage and Abigail was quite a character in her own right, being both intellectual and witty and a great asset to her husband.

In 1768 the Adamses moved to Boston, where he practised successfully at the Bar. In June 1774 John Adams was elected one of the five Massachusetts Delegates to the First Continental Congress and he attended its opening session at Philadelphia in September. It was Adams who proposed George Washington as Commander of the Continental Army in 1775 and in the same year he was himself elected Chief Justice of the Superior Court of Massachusetts.

In 1776 Adams was appointed a member of the five-man committee charged to draft the Declaration of Independence and the following day Chairman of the Board of War and Ordnance, in effect Secretary for War. On 2 August 1776 he was one of the signatories of the Declaration, which he had helped to draft.

The next year Adams embarked on the diplomatic phase of his career when Congress appointed him Commissioner to France. He sailed from Boston on 17 February 1778 and landed at Bordeaux on 29 March. In April he presented his credentials to the French Foreign Minister, the Comte de Vergennes, in Paris and in May was received by King Louis XVI at Versailles. In June 1779 he sailed for home, arriving in Boston in August, and was appointed a member of the committee to draft the Massachusetts State Constitution which was adopted in 1780. In November 1779 he returned to Europe and was appointed Minister Plenipotentiary to the United Provinces of the Netherlands. From August to October 1781 he was seriously ill with 'fever' and was in a coma for five days, but fortunately recovered and was instrumental in negotiating a loan of five million guilders and a treaty of amity and commerce with the Netherlands. In October 1782 he was ordered to Paris to commence negotiations for a peace treaty with Britain, and on 20 January 1783 Adams and Benjamin Franklin signed preliminary articles of peace and armistice with Great Britain at Versailles. The peace treaty was signed at Paris on 3 September and, having been appointed with Franklin and John Jay to negotiate a commercial treaty with Great Britain, Adams left for London in October.

Early in November he wrote to his wife asking her to join him with their eldest daughter. 'Come to Europe . . . as soon as possible,' he wrote, 'I cannot be happy nor tolerable without you.' It took a little while to organize and Mrs Adams and her daughter did not arrive in England until July 1784. Almost at once they were whisked off to France, where Adams had to confer with Franklin and Jefferson, but in February 1785 Congress appointed Adams the first US Minister Plenipotentiary to the Court of St James's and on being informed of the appointment in April the family returned to London in May. Adams presented his credentials to King George III on 1 June and his wife and daughter were presented at court and readily accepted into London society, which they greatly enjoyed. The younger Abigail was married in London on 12 June 1786 to William Stephens Smith, a young aide of her father's from New York, and their first son, John Adams's first grandchild, was also born in London the following April.

Adams's tour of duty in England came to an end in 1788. He sailed on 28 April and landed in Boston on 7 June to be greeted with the news that he had just been elected to the Continental Congress as the delegate from Massachusetts. The first presidential election was held in February 1789 and Adams emerged as America's first Vice-President, being inaugurated in New York on 21 April. He was elected for a second term and in 1796 won the presidency as Federalist candidate, gaining seventy-one of the electoral votes. His chief opponent, Thomas Jefferson, the Democratic-Republican candidate, gained sixty-eight votes and became Vice-President. To date this remains the only instance of the President and Vice-President representing different political parties.

As presiding officer of the Senate, Adams announced his own election and his inauguration took place in the Chamber of the House of Representatives at Philadelphia on Saturday 4 March 1797, the oath being administered by Chief Justice Oliver Ellsworth.

Adams was a small, insignificant-looking man and like many men of small stature inclined to be peppery on occasion and very much on his dignity. His policies as President were not always popular, but he weathered all storms with great resilience. He was, however, baulked of his hopes of a second term in office in the election of 1800. He had become completely estranged from

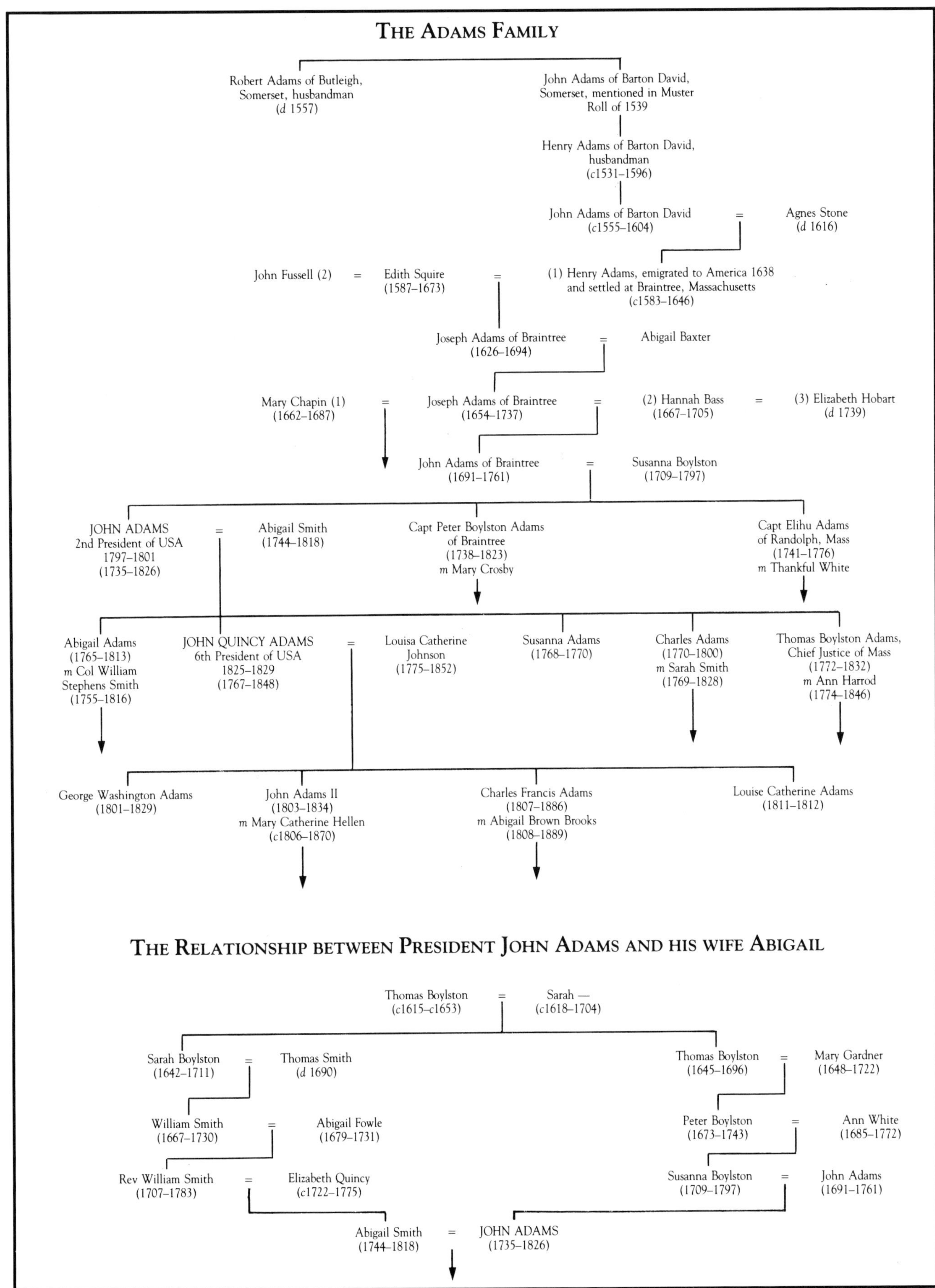
THE ADAMS FAMILY
Robert Adams of Butleigh, Somerset, husbandman (d 1557)
John Adams of Barton David, Somerset, mentioned in Muster Roll of 1539
Henry Adams of Barton David, husbandman (c1531–1596)
John Adams of Barton David (c1555–1604)
=
Agnes Stone (d 1616)
John Fussell (2)
=
Edith Squire (1587–1673)
=
(1) Henry Adams, emigrated to America 1638 and settled at Braintree, Massachusetts (c1583–1646)
Joseph Adams of Braintree (1626–1694)
=
Abigail Baxter
Mary Chapin (1) (1662–1687)
=
Joseph Adams of Braintree (1654–1737)
=
(2) Hannah Bass (1667–1705)
=
(3) Elizabeth Hobart (d 1739)
John Adams of Braintree (1691–1761)
=
Susanna Boylston (1709–1797)
JOHN ADAMS 2nd President of USA 1797–1801 (1735–1826)
=
Abigail Smith (1744–1818)
Capt Peter Boylston Adams of Braintree (1738–1823) m Mary Crosby
Capt Elihu Adams of Randolph, Mass (1741–1776) m Thankful White
Abigail Adams (1765–1813) m Col William Stephens Smith (1755–1816)
JOHN QUINCY ADAMS 6th President of USA 1825–1829 (1767–1848)
=
Louisa Catherine Johnson (1775–1852)
Susanna Adams (1768–1770)
Charles Adams (1770–1800) m Sarah Smith (1769–1828)
Thomas Boylston Adams, Chief Justice of Mass (1772–1832) m Ann Harrod (1774–1846)
George Washington Adams (1801–1829)
John Adams II (1803–1834) m Mary Catherine Hellen (c1806–1870)
Charles Francis Adams (1807–1886) m Abigail Brown Brooks (1808–1889)
Louise Catherine Adams (1811–1812)
THE RELATIONSHIP BETWEEN PRESIDENT JOHN ADAMS AND HIS WIFE ABIGAIL
Thomas Boylston (c1615–c1653)
=
Sarah — (c1618–1704)
Sarah Boylston (1642–1711)
=
Thomas Smith (d 1690)
Thomas Boylston (1645–1696)
=
Mary Gardner (1648–1722)
William Smith (1667–1730)
=
Abigail Fowle (1679–1731)
Peter Boylston (1673–1743)
=
Ann White (1685–1772)
Rev William Smith (1707–1783)
=
Elizabeth Quincy (c1722–1775)
Susanna Boylston (1709–1797)
=
John Adams (1691–1761)
Abigail Smith (1744–1818)
=
JOHN ADAMS (1735–1826)

Abigail, the intelligent wife of John Adams, at the age of twenty-two

Jefferson, whom he believed had slandered him, and declined to attend his inauguration, leaving Washington (the new federal capital where he had taken up residence in the White House a few months earlier) on the morning of 4 March and returning to his home in Quincy.

The remainder of Adams's life was spent in tending his farm and working on his autobiography. 'If I were to go over my life again,' he wrote to a friend, 'I would be a shoemaker rather than an American statesman.' At the end of 1811 he became reconciled with Thomas Jefferson through the mediation of Dr Benjamin Rush, a mutual friend. The last years of Adams's life were saddened by the deaths of his daughter Abigail Smith in August 1813 and that of his beloved wife on 28 October 1818. The tough old man lived on, surviving a bout of fever which confined him to his bed for two months at the age of eighty-five. He made his last public appearance in August 1821, when he reviewed two hundred West Point cadets from the porch of his house and after addressing them provided them with a cold buffet. In March 1825, Adams had the satisfaction of his son being inaugurated as President although he himself was unable to attend the ceremony. He celebrated his ninetieth birthday in October 1825 and died on Independence Day, 4 July 1826, a few hours after his old friend and sometime adversary had breathed his last at Monticello. Adams was buried with Abigail in a vault beneath Quincy Congregational Church.

THOMAS JEFFERSON 1801–1809

Born:	Shadwell, Goochland (now Albemarle) County, Virginia, 2/13 April 1743, eldest son of Col Peter Jefferson, of Shadwell, and Jane Randolph
Governor of Virginia:	1 June 1779 to 1 June 1781
(1st) Secretary of State:	22 March 1790 to 31 December 1793
Elected Vice-President:	8 February 1797
Inaugurated:	Philadelphia 4 March 1797
Elected (3rd) President:	17 February 1801
Inaugurated:	Senate Chamber of Capitol 4 March 1801
Elected for 2nd term:	13 February 1805
Inaugurated:	Senate Chamber of Capitol 4 March 1805
Retired from presidency:	4 March 1809
Married:	The Forest, Charles City County, Virginia, 1 January 1772, Martha (*b* Charles City County 19/30 October 1748; *d* Monticello, Virginia, 6 September 1782; *bur* Monticello), widow of Bathurst Skelton, and dau of John Wayles of The Forest, Charles City County, and his 1st wife Mary Eppes
Children:	(1) Martha (Patsy) Jefferson, *b* Monticello 27 September 1772; *m* Monticello 23 February 1790, Thomas Mann Randolph Jr of Edgehill, Albemarle County, Virginia, Governor of Virginia 1819–1822 (*b* Tuckahoe, Goochland County, Virginia, 17 May 1768; *d* Monticello 20 June 1828); 5 sons, 7 daus; *d* Edgehill 10 October 1836
	(2) Jane Randolph Jefferson, *b* Monticello 3 April 1774; *d* Monticello September 1775
	(3) A son (unnamed), *b* Monticello 28 May 1777; *d* Monticello 14 June 1777
	(4) Mary (Maria) Jefferson, *b* Monticello 1 August 1778; *m* Monticello 13 October 1797, John Wayles Eppes, Senator and Congressman (*b* City Point, Virginia, 7 April 1773; *d* Millbrook, Buckingham County, Virginia, 5 September 1823); 1 son, 1 dau (and one child of unknown sex); *d* Monticello 17 April 1804
	(5) Lucy Elizabeth Jefferson, *b* Monticello 3 November 1780; *d* Monticello 15 April 1781
	(6) Lucy Elizabeth Jefferson, *b* Monticello 8 May 1782; *d* Eppington *ca* 13 October 1784
Died:	Monticello 4 July 1826
Buried:	Monticello

Without a doubt, Thomas Jefferson remains the most brilliantly gifted man ever to grace the presidency. A polymath of the first order, he could turn his hand to all things and excel in them all.

The Jeffersons long believed themselves to be of Welsh origin, hailing from the Snowdon area and were so sure of this that Thomas's brother Randolph even named his property Snowden (*sic*). However, later researches have traced them to Suffolk, where Samuel Jeaffreson lived at Pettistree, near Woodbridge, at the end of the sixteenth century. His grandson, also Samuel, emigrated to the West Indies and acquired a plantation at St Kitts, where he died in 1649. This Samuel's grandson, Thomas, settled in Virginia and by 1677 was the owner of a plantation in Henrico County. He died in 1697, leaving an only son Captain Thomas Jefferson, of Osborne, Chesterfield County, who served as Justice of Chesterfield County Court and as High Sheriff of the County. Thomas's youngest son, Colonel Peter Jefferson, acquired a property known as Shadwell in Goochland (later renamed Albemarle) County, where he filled the same offices his father had done in Chesterfield County. His estate was named from his wife's birthplace, Shadwell, in the East End of London. She was Jane, the eldest daughter of Colonel Isham Randolph, a member of an important family with widespread connections throughout Virginia. Through the Isham family, to which Isham Randolph's mother belonged, he could trace descents from many knightly and aristocratic families in Northamptonshire, England.

Thomas Jefferson, the eldest son and third child of Peter and Jane, was born at Shadwell on 2 April (13 April new style) 1743 and was only fourteen years old when he inherited the estate on the death of his father in August 1757. He entered William and Mary College at Williamsburg in March 1760, but left two years later without taking a degree and entered the law office of George Wythe in Williamsburg. On 5 April 1767

A French engraving of Thomas Jefferson, made during his stay in Paris

Jefferson was admitted to the Virginia Bar, but before that he had taken over the management of his estate and been appointed a Justice of the Peace and a Vestryman for Goochland County, two offices which his father had held before him. In the same year in which he was called to the Bar he began planting at Monticello, near Charlottesville. On 11 May 1769 he was elected a member of the Virginia House of Burgesses for the first time and was to be re-elected every year until 1775.

The house at Shadwell was burnt down in February 1770 and in the following November Jefferson moved with his mother to Monticello, where the construction of an elegant mansion to his own design had begun the year before. On New Year's Day 1772 Jefferson married a young widow, Mrs Martha Skelton, whose father John Wayles, a native of Lancaster, England, had an extensive property known as The Forest in Charles City County, Virginia. There were to be six children of the marriage, of whom only two daughters survived infancy. In spite of that, Jefferson's progeny has been more prolific than that of any other President and the only one to have formed an association of descendants. Mrs Jefferson is a shadowy figure. There is no known authentic portrait of her and almost nothing can be gathered concerning her character. She died at the age of thirty-three in September 1782, four months after the birth of her youngest child, and was buried at Monticello. Jefferson did not marry again, but scurrilous rumours were circulated later alleging him to be the father of a 'slave family' by a mulatto slave, Sally Hemmings, who acted as nursemaid or companion to his orphaned daughters. The accusation is quite unsubstantiated and investigations have shown that the girl was almost certainly the half-sister of Mrs Jefferson, the daughter of her father John Wayles by one of his slaves, Betty, and that the five children she bore were probably fathered by Jefferson's nephew Peter Carr.

In 1775 Jefferson was elected a Delegate to the Second Continental Congress and the following year was appointed a member of the five-man committee charged to draft the Declaration of Independence, his fellow members being Benjamin Franklin, John Adams, Robert Livingston, and Roger Sherman. After the Declaration had been approved on 4 July, Jefferson became one of its signatories on 2 August 1776. A month later he resigned from the Continental Congress and was soon after re-elected to the Virginia House of Burgesses. At the same time Congress wished to appoint him a Commissioner to France with Benjamin Franklin and Silas Deane, but he declined and applied himself instead to work on a committee appointed to revise the laws of Virginia.

In January 1779 Jefferson was elected Governor of Virginia and he took office in June. He was instrumental in moving the state capital to Virginia, which he was forced to flee several times on the near approach of the

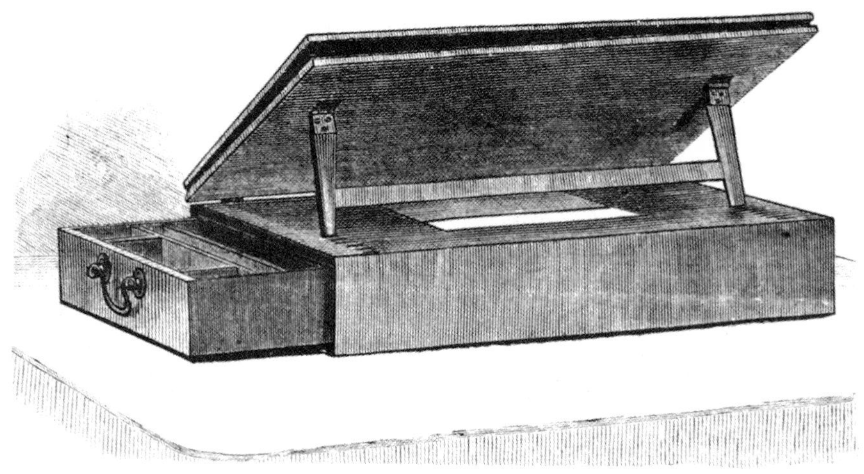

The desk on which Thomas Jefferson wrote out the Declaration of Independence

British forces. Re-elected Governor in 1780, Jefferson retired from office in 1781, declining to be nominated for a third year. In November 1782 he was appointed a peace commissioner to assist Franklin and Adams in their negotiations in Paris, but was unable to sail as his ship was icebound in Chesapeake Bay and on 1 April 1783 the appointment was withdrawn. Elected to Congress on 6 June 1783, Jefferson took his seat at Annapolis, Maryland, in November. He served as chairman of the currency committee and devised the decimal monetary system of dollars and cents which was adopted and has remained the United States currency ever since.

Jefferson became chairman of Congress on 12 March and two months later was again appointed a commissioner to France to negotiate commercial treaties with European powers. He sailed from Boston on 5 July and arrived in Paris on 6 August. The following March he was appointed Franklin's successor as Minister to France, presenting his credentials to the French court on 17 May. In March and April 1786 he visited England, where he was received at Windsor by King George III, and in the following years he made extensive tours of Southern France and Northern Italy and visited Amsterdam and Strasbourg.

In 1789, after declining an invitation to assist the French Constitutional Committee, Jefferson was granted six months' leave of absence to visit home and arrived in November to find a letter from Washington awaiting him. It informed him of his appointment as Secretary of State, a position which he at first felt inclined to refuse, but a second letter from Washington persuaded him to accept and he took office in March 1790, becoming the first US Secretary of State under the new Constitution. He held the position until 31 December 1793, having resigned on 31 July. His period in office had been marred by differences between him and Alexander Hamilton, Secretary of the Treasury, which all Washington's efforts had been unable to reconcile. Jefferson spent the next two years at Monticello, cultivating and improving his estate. He declined an appointment as special envoy to Spain and became a severe critic of Washington and the Federalists. When the presidential election of 1796 came up, Jefferson offered himself as the Democratic-Republican candidate and received sixty-eight of the electoral votes, becoming Vice-President to John Adams. In the next election Jefferson and Aaron Burr, of New York, were nominated as the Democratic-Republican candidates in opposition to John Adams and Charles Cotesworth Pinckney, the Federalists. When the electoral votes were tabulated by Congress, Jefferson and Burr tied for first place with seventy-three votes each and the House of Representatives had to ballot for President. It was not until the thirty-sixth ballot that Jefferson was elected and Burr became Vice-President. Jefferson was the first President to be inaugurated in Washington. He took the oath, administered by Chief Justice John Marshall, in the Senate Chamber of the Capitol on Wednesday 4 March 1801, and moved into the White House on 19 March.

Jefferson's first term in office was marked, among other things, by the admission of Ohio as the seventeenth state and the Louisiana purchase from France in 1803. In 1804 he was nominated for a second term and he and his running mate George Clinton received 162 of the 176 electoral votes. On 17 January 1806 Jefferson's grandson James Madison Randolph became the first child to be born in the White House.

Jefferson retired from office on 4 March 1809 and attended the inauguration of his successor James Madison the same day. Later in the month he returned to Monticello to resume his quiet life of a cultured country gentleman. In January 1815 Congress passed a bill authorizing the purchase for $23,950 of Jefferson's library, which was to form the nucleus of the Library of Congress. It consisted of nearly 6,500 volumes and was conveyed to Washington in ten waggon loads, carefully

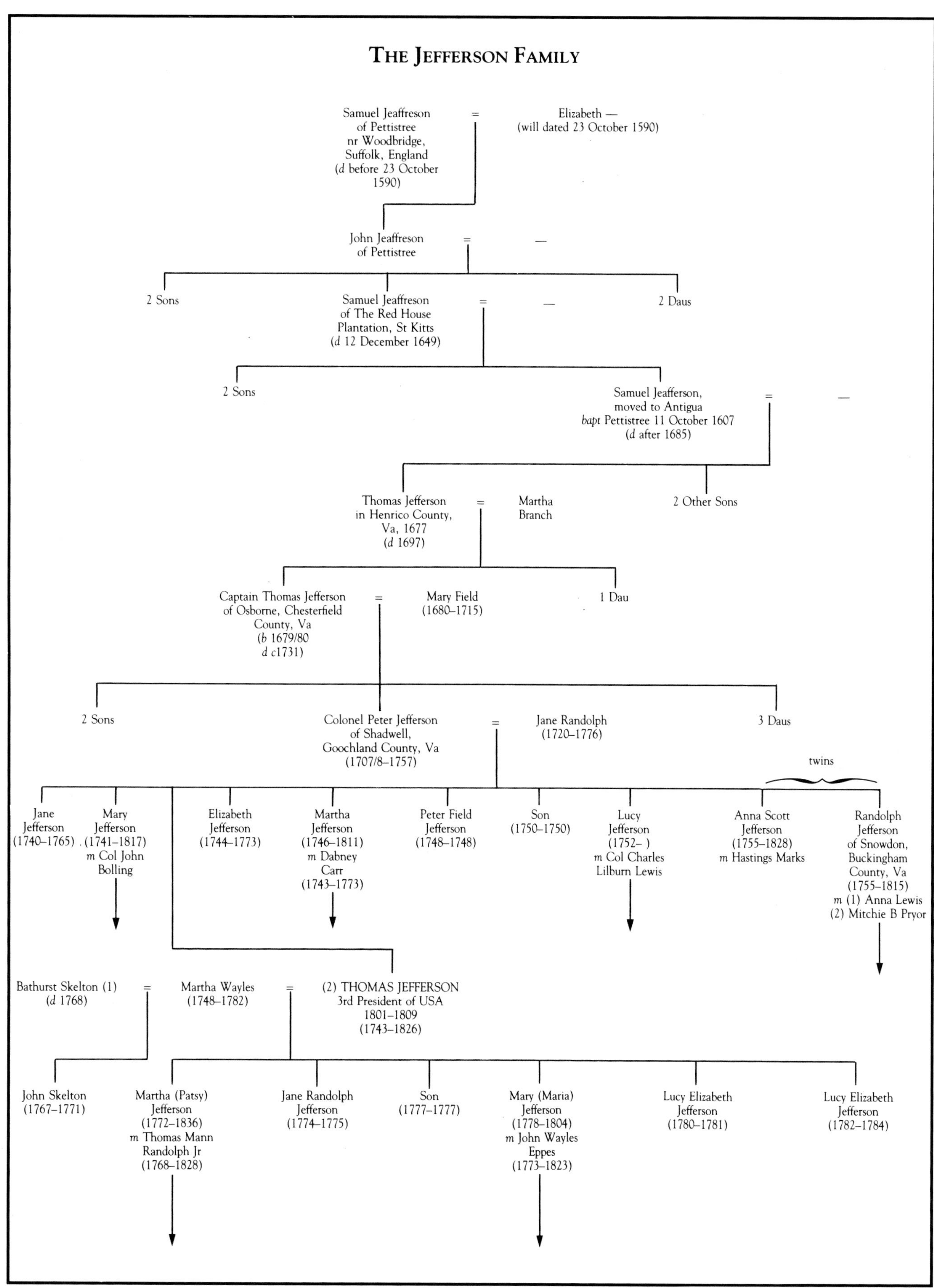
THE JEFFERSON FAMILY
Samuel Jeaffreson of Pettistree nr Woodbridge, Suffolk, England (d before 23 October 1590)
=
Elizabeth — (will dated 23 October 1590)
John Jeaffreson of Pettistree
=
—
2 Sons
Samuel Jeaffreson of The Red House Plantation, St Kitts (d 12 December 1649)
=
—
2 Daus
2 Sons
Samuel Jeafferson, moved to Antigua bapt Pettistree 11 October 1607 (d after 1685)
=
—
Thomas Jefferson in Henrico County, Va, 1677 (d 1697)
=
Martha Branch
2 Other Sons
Captain Thomas Jefferson of Osborne, Chesterfield County, Va (b 1679/80 d c1731)
=
Mary Field (1680–1715)
1 Dau
2 Sons
Colonel Peter Jefferson of Shadwell, Goochland County, Va (1707/8–1757)
=
Jane Randolph (1720–1776)
3 Daus
twins
Jane Jefferson (1740–1765)
Mary Jefferson (1741–1817) m Col John Bolling
Elizabeth Jefferson (1744–1773)
Martha Jefferson (1746–1811) m Dabney Carr (1743–1773)
Peter Field Jefferson (1748–1748)
Son (1750–1750)
Lucy Jefferson (1752–) m Col Charles Lilburn Lewis
Anna Scott Jefferson (1755–1828) m Hastings Marks
Randolph Jefferson of Snowdon, Buckingham County, Va (1755–1815) m (1) Anna Lewis (2) Mitchie B Pryor
Bathurst Skelton (1) (d 1768)
=
Martha Wayles (1748–1782)
=
(2) THOMAS JEFFERSON 3rd President of USA 1801–1809 (1743–1826)
John Skelton (1767–1771)
Martha (Patsy) Jefferson (1772–1836) m Thomas Mann Randolph Jr (1768–1828)
Jane Randolph Jefferson (1774–1775)
Son (1777–1777)
Mary (Maria) Jefferson (1778–1804) m John Wayles Eppes (1773–1823)
Lucy Elizabeth Jefferson (1780–1781)
Lucy Elizabeth Jefferson (1782–1784)

Monticello, Jefferson's Virginia mansion built to his own design; a photograph taken early this century

packed under Jefferson's supervision. He also provided a classified cataloguing system. When over seventy-five Jefferson designed and supervised the construction of the University of Virginia at Charlottesville in 1819. As the first Rector of the University he also laid down the curriculum and chose the faculty members.

Jefferson's hospitality and generosity to friends brought him continual financial embarrassment for many years, in spite of the sale of his library, and he was only saved from bankruptcy and losing his beloved Monticello when friends came to the rescue with a gift of $16,500. This occurred in the last year of his life. He was eighty-three years old when an attack of exhausting diarrhoea brought about his death on 4 July 1826, the same day, as we have already noted, as that of John Adams.

Jefferson's accomplishments and many talents were best summed up in an after-dinner speech delivered by President Kennedy to a company of Nobel Prize winners when he told them that they were 'the most extraordinary collection of talent, of human knowledge, that has ever been gathered together at the White House, with the possible exception of when Thomas Jefferson dined alone'.

JAMES MADISON 1809–1817

Born:	Port Conway, King George County, Virginia, 5/16 March 1750/1, eldest son of James Madison, of Orange County, Virginia, and Eleanor (Nelly) Rose Conway	Married:	Harewood, nr Charles Town, Jefferson County, Virginia, 15 September 1794, Dolley (*b* Guilford County, North Carolina, 20 May 1768; *d* Washington DC 12 July 1849; *bur* Congressional Cemetery, Washington, later transferred to Montpelier, Orange County, Virginia), widow of John Todd Jr and eldest dau of John Payne of Scotchtown, Hanover County, Virginia, and Mary Coles
Secretary of State:	2 May 1801 to 3 March 1809		
Elected (4th) President:	8 February 1809		
Inaugurated:	Chamber of House of Representatives 4 March 1809		
Elected for 2nd term:	10 February 1813	Children:	None
Inaugurated:	Chamber of House of Representatives 4 March 1813	Died:	Montpelier, Orange County, Virginia, 28 June 1836
Retired from presidency:	4 March 1817	Buried:	Montpelier

James Madison, America's fourth President, was a Virginian, as were two of his predecessors. His family was of English descent and his great-great-grandfather, John Madison, a ship's carpenter from Gloucester, was granted land in Virginia from 1653 onwards. His son, John, was Sheriff of King and Queen County, Virginia, in 1714, and was the father of Ambrose Madison who married Frances Taylor, great-aunt of the future (twelfth) President, Zachary Taylor (*qv*). James, the son of Ambrose and Frances, was a planter and farmer in Orange County, Virginia, where his estate was called Montpelier. He served as Lieutenant of Orange County and in September 1749 married Nelly Conway, who bore him twelve children.

James, the future President, was the eldest, and was born at Port Conway, King George County, Virginia, on 16 March 1751 (on 5 March 1750/1 by old style reckoning). His earliest education was received at a school conducted by Donald Robertson at Innes Plantation in King and Queen County, which he attended from 1762 to 1767. For the next two years he received tuition at home from the Rev Thomas Martin, and in September 1769 entered the College of New Jersey (later Princeton University). He graduated as Bachelor of Arts in September 1771, but remained in college until the following April studying Hebrew and ethics.

James Madison, from a portrait by John Vanderlyn

Madison then returned home to assist his father in running the estate and in December 1774 was elected a member of Orange County Committee of Safety, of which his father was chairman. In October 1775 he was commissioned Colonel of Orange County Militia and in April of the following year was elected Orange County Delegate to the Virginia Convention, where he served on the committee formed to draft the state constitution which was duly adopted in June. In October, Madison was elected a member of the first House of Delegates, the lower house of the Virginia State Assembly; but he failed to be re-elected the following April. Elected a member of the Governor's Council of State in November 1777, Madison took his seat therein in January 1778 and served under Governors Patrick Henry and Thomas Jefferson until 1779, at the end of which year he was elected a delegate to the Second Continental Congress, of which he became the youngest member at the age of twenty-eight. He served in the Continental Congress until 1783 and the following year was again elected to

The Executive Mansion after the fire of 1814, painted by Strickland

the Virginia House of Delegates, in which he served until 1786, when he was re-elected to the Continental Congress.

He took such a prominent part in the Constitutional Convention, where his long and carefully thought-out political theorizing came into full play, that he won universal admiration and was dubbed 'Father of the Constitution', of which he was one of the signers on 17 September 1787. His well-thought-out essays, published in the *Independent Journal* of New York in conjunction with those of Alexander Hamilton and John Jay, are regarded as model treatises on the art of government.

In March 1788 Madison was elected a member of the Virginia Convention to consider the ratification of the Constitution and he led the campaign in support of the ratification. As a result, Virginia was the tenth state to ratify, on 26 June, by a narrow margin of eighty-nine to seventy-nine. In October he was defeated in the election to the Senate, but in February 1789 was elected to the House of Representatives, in spite of the virulent opposition of Patrick Henry, and took his seat on 6 April.

A bachelor until the age of forty-three, Madison married Mrs Dorothea Payne Todd, a twenty-six-year-old widow, on 15 Sepember 1794. Known as Dolley, she was to be a great asset to her husband, being lively and outgoing, whereas he did not shine socially and was inclined to be shy and retiring. In 1801 Madison was appointed Secretary of State by Jefferson and in 1806 he published a pamphlet with the fulsome title *An Examination of the British Doctrine, which Subjects to Capture a Neutral Trade, Not Open in Time of Peace*, which ran into several editions.

On 23 January 1808 a congressional caucus of Democratic-Republicans nominated James Madison for President and George Clinton, of New York, for Vice-President. Their Federalist opponents were Charles Cotesworth Pinckney, of South Carolina, and Rufus King, of New York. When the electors cast their ballots on 7 December, Madison received 122 of the 176 votes from seventeen states, while Pinckney received 47 and Clinton 6 votes. In the vice-presidential election Clinton received 113 electoral votes and King 47. Madison resigned as Secretary of State on 3 March and took office as the fourth President on Saturday 4 March 1809, when he was inaugurated in the chamber of the House of Representatives in Washington, the oath being administered by Chief Justice John Marshall.

Madison's first term of office was largely taken up by trade disputes with Britain, the banning of British and French armed vessels from American waters, the admission of Louisiana as the eighteenth State and the declaration of war against Britain on 19 June 1812. Madison was re-nominated for the presidency in May 1812 with John Langdon, of New Hampshire, as running-mate, Vice-President Clinton having died on 20 April. However, Langdon declined the nomination and Elbridge Gerry, of Massachusetts (whose name was to originate a new word, 'gerrymandering', based on his unfair re-arranging of electoral districts to the advantage of his own party), one of the signers of the Declaration of Independence, was nominated in his place. When the electoral votes were cast Madison received 128 of the 217 and his opponent, De Witt Clinton, received 89. The inauguration took place on 4 March 1813, again in the House of Representatives with Chief Justice Marshall administering the oath.

The war with Britain worsened during Madison's second term and in August 1814 he and his cabinet were forced to flee to Virginia when the British sacked and burnt the Executive Mansion, Capitol and all government buildings with the exception of the Patent Office, in retaliation for the burning of York (now Toronto), Canada, by American forces in April 1813. The govern-

The Madison Family and its Connection with Zachary Taylor

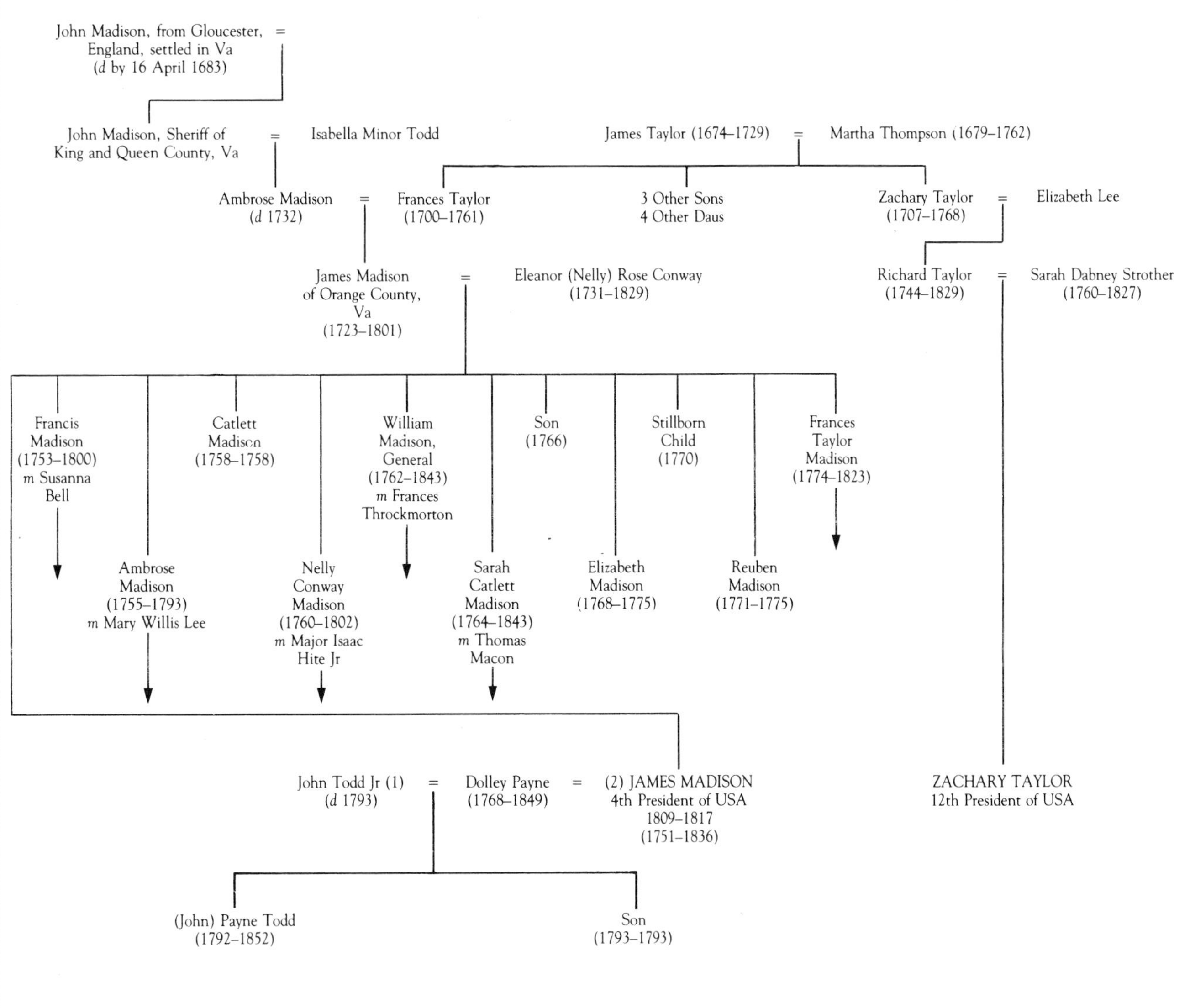

The vivacious Dolley Madison

ment was able to return to Washington at the end of August and while the Executive Mansion was being restored the President and Mrs Madison took up residence at Octagon House. Its sandstone exterior was painted white in the course of reconstruction, giving it the name of the White House, by which it popularly became known and which was made its official designation by President Theodore Roosevelt nearly one hundred years later.

Vice-President Gerry died in November 1814, leaving Madison again without a Vice-President. The war with Britain dragged on until a treaty of peace was finally concluded on 17 February 1815.

Madison retired from office on 4 March 1817 and, after attending the inauguration of his successor Monroe, retired to his Virginia estate at Montpelier, where he remained for the rest of his life, occasionally exchanging visits with Jefferson, whose Monticello estate was about thirty miles away. In 1821 Madison, now seventy, began work on his *Notes on the Federal Convention*, in which he was assisted by his wife. On 11 February 1829 his mother died at the age of ninety-eight and Madison himself died of general debility at Montpelier on 28 June 1836 at the age of eighty-five. His widow, the once lively Dolley who had led Washington society, sold his private papers to Congress in two lots in 1837 and 1848. She died at Washington on 12 July 1849, aged eighty-one, and after being first buried in the Congressional Cemetery, Washington, was removed to Montpelier to lie beside her husband. Madison was not a spectacular man, but a very sound one and as a Virginian landowner entertained many misgivings about the morality of owning slaves, although he had over one hundred.

JAMES MONROE 1817–1825

Born:	Monroe's Creek, Westmoreland County, Virginia, 28 April 1758, eldest son of Spence Monroe, of Westmoreland County, Virginia, and Elizabeth Jones	Married:	Trinity Episcopal Church, New York, 16 February 1786 Elizabeth (*b* New York City 30 June 1768; *d* Oak Hill, Loudoun County, Virginia, 23 September 1830; *bur* Oak Hill, transferred to Hollywood Cemetery, Richmond, Virginia 1903), eldest dau of Laurence Kortright of New York and Hannah Aspinwall
Senator from Virginia:	9 November 1790 to 27 May 1794	Children:	(1) Eliza Kortright, *b* Fredericksburg, Virginia, 5 December 1787; *m* 17 October 1808 Judge George Hay of Richmond, Virginia (*b* Williamsburg, Virginia, 15 December 1765; *d* Richmond, Virginia, 21 September 1830); 1 dau; *d* Paris 27 January 1840 (2) Son (James Spence?), *b* May 1799; *d* Richmond, Virginia, 28 September 1800 (3) Maria Hester, *b* Paris 1803; *m* White House, Washington DC, 9 March 1820 Samuel Laurence Gouverneur of New York, Postmaster of New York City 1828–36 (*b* 1799; *d* 1867); 2 sons, 1 dau; *d* Oak Hill, Loudoun County, Virginia, 1850
Minister Plenipotentiary to French Republic:	27 May 1794 to 30 December 1796		
Governor of Virginia:	6 December 1799 to 1802		
Diplomatic Appointments:	Envoy Extraordinary and Minister Plenipotentiary to France 11 January 1803 to 30 April 1807, Minister Plenipotentiary to Great Britain and Envoy Extraordinary to Spain 18 April 1803 to October 1807		
Governor of Virginia:	January to March 1811		
Secretary of State:	6 April 1811 to 30 September 1814 (*ad interim* until 28 February 1815), 28 February to 2 March 1815		
Elected (5th) President:	4 December 1816		
Inaugurated:	East Portico of Capitol 4 March 1817		
Elected for 2nd term:	6 December 1820	Died:	New York City 4 July 1831
Inaugurated:	Hall of Representatives 5 March 1821	Buried:	Marble Cemetery, New York City, transferred to Hollywood Cemetery, Richmond, Virginia, 1858
Retired from presidency:	4 March 1825		

James Monroe, the formulator of the Doctrine which bears his name, was the last president of the so-called 'Virginia Dynasty'. It has long been claimed that the Monroes are descended from the Monroes of Katewell, themselves an offshoot of the great Scottish baronial house of Munro of Foulis. Andrew Monroe, who settled as a tobacco planter in St Mary's County, Maryland, about 1641 was possibly, though by no means certainly, a son of David Monroe and grandson of George Monroe, 2nd of Katewell. If this conjectural descent is correct, the Monroes possess descents from Robert II, King of Scots, and Edward III, King of England.

Andrew Monroe was assessed in July 1642 for a tax of fifty pounds of tobacco to help sustain a war against the Susquehanna Indians. He was later involved in an insurrection against the Deputy Governor of Maryland and had his property confiscated, being forced to flee across the Potomac to Virginia. He is believed to have returned to Scotland in 1648 and fought under his kinsman General Sir George Monroe at the battle of Preston, at which he was taken prisoner. He managed to escape and return to Virginia where he received grants of land in Northumberland and Westmoreland Counties. His grandson, another Andrew, served as Sheriff of Westmoreland County in 1731 and was the father of Spence Monroe, who became a circuit judge and a signer of the Westmoreland County Virginia Resolutions which forbade the enforcement of the Stamp Act in the county. He married Elizabeth, daughter of James Jones, an architect of Welsh ancestry, and the future fifth President was their eldest son and second child.

James Monroe was born at Monroe's Creek in Westmoreland County on 28 April 1758. In June 1774 (the same year in which his father died) he entered William and Mary College. He left College in March 1776 to join the army as a Lieutenant and in September joined Washington's forces in New York City. He saw active service in the battles of Harlem Heights, White Plains, Trenton (in which he was wounded and later promoted Captain), Brandywine, Germantown (promoted Major thereafter) and Monmouth. In December 1778, Monroe resigned from the army and returned to

James Monroe in later life

Virginia, where he in 1779 began to study law at Williamsburg under Thomas Jefferson. In June 1780, Jefferson, then Governor of Virginia, appointed him Military Commissioner (with the rank of Lieutenant-Colonel) to visit the Southern army.

Monroe was elected delegate from King George County to the Virginia Assembly in 1782 and appointed to the Assembly's executive council. On 6 June the following year (1783) he was elected Delegate from Virginia to the Continental Congress, in which he served until 1786. Admitted to the Virginia Bar at Fredericksburg in October 1786, Monroe had acquired a wife earlier in the year when he married Elizabeth Kortright, the daughter of a New York merchant, at Trinity Episcopal Church, New York, on 16 February. In the following year he was re-elected to the Virginia Assembly and in 1788 appointed a member of the Virginia Convention to ratify the Federal Constitution. The same year saw his defeat by Madison in his attempt to enter the House of Representatives in the new Congress. Monroe returned to his law practice in 1789, but at the end of 1790 was elected Senator from Virginia in place of William Grayson, who had died.

In 1794 Washington appointed Monroe as Minister to France and he arrived in Paris in August. While in France he was instrumental in obtaining the release of Thomas Paine (the celebrated author of *Declaration of the Rights of Man*) from the Luxembourg Prison and took him into his household. Recalled to New York in 1796, Monroe arrived back in June 1797 and in December published a highly critical examination of Washington's foreign policy, *A View of the Conduct of the Executive in the Foreign Affairs of the United States*. In 1798 the Monroes moved to Ash Lawn, Charlottesville, Virginia, and on 5 December 1799 James was elected Governor of Virginia, a position which he held until 1802. In 1803 Monroe was appointed Envoy Extraordinary and Minister Plenipotentiary to France and Spain.

He arrived in Paris in April and was appointed Minister Plenipotentiary to Great Britain also. His wife and daughter accompanied him and a younger daughter was born in Paris after their arrival. The elder girl, Eliza, who was sixteen in the December following their arrival, enjoyed a great social success in Paris, where she was known as '*La Belle Americaine*' and became a close friend of Napoleon's stepdaughter Hortense, after whom she later named her only daughter. Monroe's tour of duty, in the course of which he (acting jointly with William Pinkney) signed a treaty of amity, commerce and navigation with Great Britain which Jefferson later refused to send to the Senate for ratification, ended in 1807 and he returned to the States in December. In the following year he was an unsuccessful presidential candidate and in 1810 was again elected a member of the Virginia Assembly. He served as Governor of Virginia from January to March 1811 and on 2 April that year was appointed Secretary of State by Madison, holding office until September 1814, when he was appointed Secretary of War but continued as Secretary of State *ad interim* until reappointed on 28 February 1815.

On 4 March 1816 Monroe was nominated for President by the Democratic-Republicans and on 4 December was elected President with 183 electoral votes, the Federalist candidate, Rufus King, receiving 34. Monroe was the first President to be inaugurated on the East Portico of the Capitol, where the oath was administered by Chief Justice John Marshall. As First Lady, Elizabeth Monroe, although an attractive woman, lacked Dolley Madison's sparkle and incurred a certain amount of criticism by expensively redecorating the White House and entertaining on a lavish scale. She was quite a frail creature, however, given to migraines and fits of depression.

Monroe, who dressed soberly and probably lacked a sense of humour, was little esteemed by his contemporaries. During his first presidential term he signed the Flag Act, establishing the 'stars and stripes' as the national flag and acquired Florida from Spain by a treaty signed in February 1819, while Illinois and Alabama most enlightened Citizens, and under which we have enjoyed unexampled felicity, this whole nation is devoted. We owe it therefore to candor, and to the amicable relations existing between the United States and those powers, to declare that we should consider any attempt on their part to extend their system to any portion of this Hemisphere, as dangerous to our peace and safety. With the existing Colonies or dependencies of any European power we have not interfered, and shall not interfere. But with the Governments who have declared their Independence, and maintained it, and whose Independence we have, on great consideration, and on just principles, acknowledged, we could not view any interposition for the purpose of oppressing them, or controuling in any other manner, their destiny, by any European power, in any other light, than as the manifestation of an unfriendly disposition towards the United States. In the war between those new Governments and Spain, we declared our neutrality at the time of their recognition, and to this we have

The Monroe Doctrine in James Monroe's handwriting, from the message to Congress, 2 December 1823

were both admitted as States. The States now numbered twenty-two, eleven slave and eleven free, and a bill to admit Missouri as a slave state threatened to upset the balance. As a compromise Maine was detached from Massachusetts to become the twenty-third State paired with Missouri which later became the twenty-fourth State and slavery was forbidden north of latitude 36° 30'. By another act signed in 1820 engaging in the slave trade was made a capital offence.

On 9 March 1820 the Monroes' younger daughter,

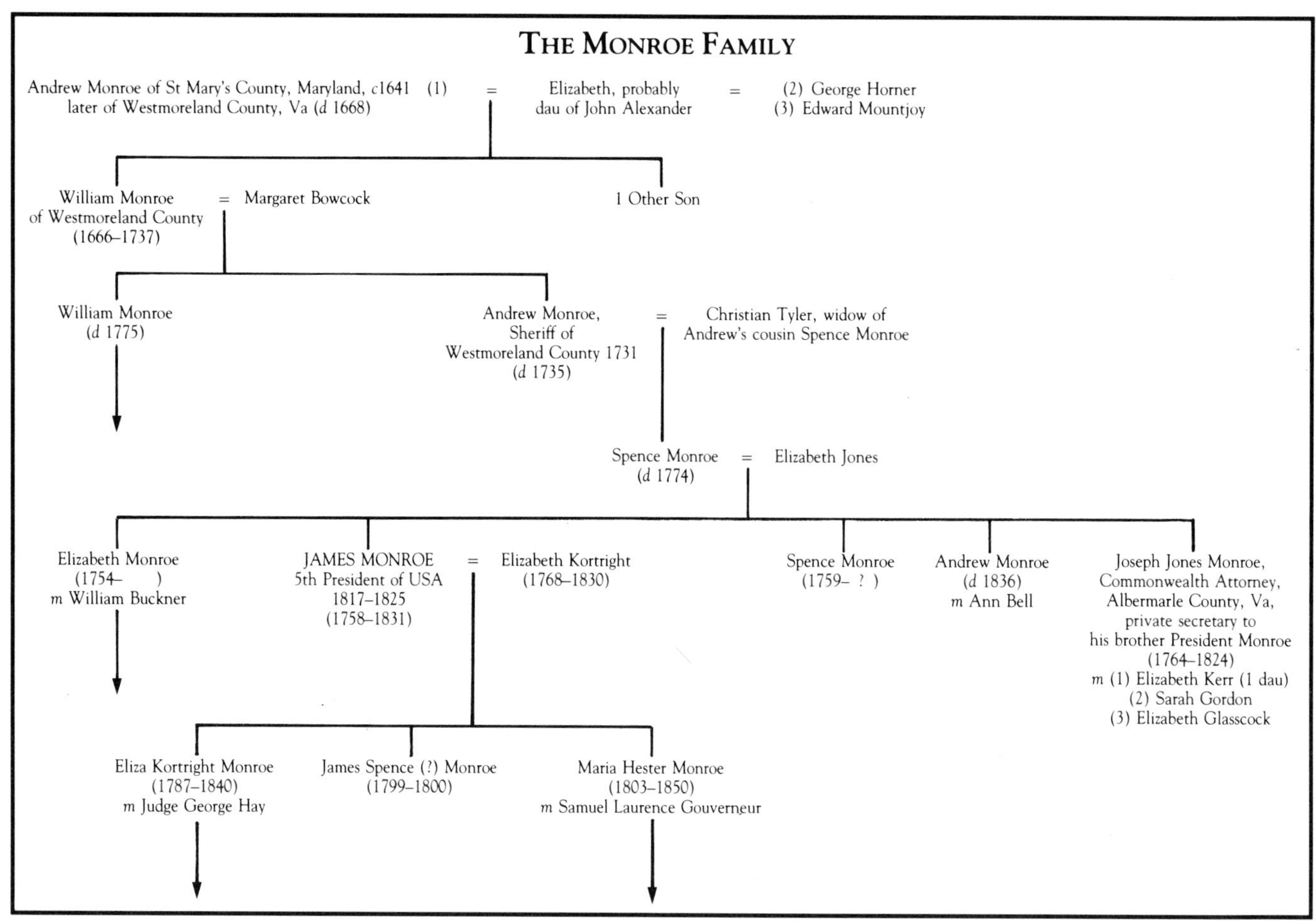

Maria Hester, became the first child of a President to be married at the White House. Her bridegroom was her first cousin, Samuel Laurence Gouverneur, who acted as private secretary to his father-in-law and served as Postmaster of New York City from 1828 to 1836.

Monroe was again nominated for the presidency in 1820, chiefly because he was the obvious candidate and the Federalists were in a state of collapse. He received 231 of the 232 electoral votes from the twenty-four states, the one vote not for him went to John Quincy Adams, the son of President John Adams. Monroe's second inauguration took place in the Hall of Representatives, because of inclement weather, on 5 March 1821 (the 4th being a Sunday). His second presidency saw the enunciation of the famous Monroe Doctrine (largely drafted by John Quincy Adams, Secretary of State) which, incorporated into the President's seventh State of the Union message to Congress in December 1823, opposed foreign colonization or intervention in the New World.

Monroe retired from the presidency on 4 March 1825 and after attending the inauguration of John Quincy Adams retired to Oak Hill, a mansion which had been designed for him by Jefferson in Loudoun County, Virginia, on land which he had inherited from his father-in-law Laurence Kortright in 1806. The estate took its name from the oak trees, one from each State of the Union, which Monroe planted personally. Like his predecessors Jefferson and Madison, Monroe found himself in dire financial straits. The President's salary had been fixed as $25,000 a year in 1789 and was not increased until 1873, when it was doubled. Former Presidents received no pension and on retirement Monroe petitioned Congress to reimburse him for expenses laid out in the public service. He eventually received $30,000. Mrs Monroe died in September 1830 and the following year Monroe sold Oak Hill and moved to New York City, where he made his home with his daughter and son-in-law. He did not live with them long and died of debility on Independence Day 4 July 1831, aged seventy-three. He was first buried in Marble Cemetery, New York City, but was reinterred at Hollywood Cemetery, Richmond, Virginia, in 1858. The body of Mrs Monroe, which had been buried at Oak Hill, was brought to lie beside him in 1903.

JOHN QUINCY ADAMS 1825–1829

Born: Braintree (now Quincy), Massachusetts, 11 July 1767, eldest son of John Adams (*qv*), (2nd) President of the United States of America

Diplomatic Appointments: Minister Resident to the Netherlands 1794–1801, Minister Plenipotentiary to Portugal 1796, Minister Plenipotentiary to Prussia 1797–1801

Senator from Massachusetts: 1803–1808

Diplomatic Appointments: Minister Plenipotentiary to Russia 1809–1815, Envoy Extraordinary and Minister Plenipotentiary to Great Britain 1815–1817

Secretary of State: 1817–1825

Elected (6th) President: 9 February 1825

Inaugurated: Hall of Representatives 4 March 1825

Retired from presidency: 4 March 1829

Member of House of Representatives: 1830–1848

Married: All Hallows, Barking-by-the-Tower, London, England, 26 July 1797, Louisa Catherine (*b* London 12 February 1775; *d* Washington DC 15 May 1852; *bur* Congressional Cemetery, Washington, transferred to Quincy), 2nd dau of Hon Joshua Johnson, of Baltimore, Maryland, American Consul-General in London, and Catherine Nuth

Children:
(1) George Washington, *b* Berlin 12 April 1801; *d* (drowned) Long Island Sound 30 April 1829
(2) John II, *b* Washington DC 4 July 1803; *m* White House 25 February 1828 Mary Catherine (*b* c1806; *d* 1870), dau of Walter Hellen and his 1st wife Nancy Johnson (sister of Mrs John Quincy Adams); 2 daus; *d* Washington DC 23 October 1834
(3) Charles Francis, member of Congress, US Minister to Great Britain 1861–1868; *b* Boston 18 August 1807; *m* Medford, Mass, 3 September 1829 Abigail Brown (*b* Medford, Mass., 25 April 1808; *d* 6 June 1889), yst dau of Peter Chardon Brooks and Ann Gorham; 5 sons 2 daus; *d* Boston 21 November 1886
(4) Louisa Catherine, *b* St Petersburg, Russia, 12 August 1811; *d* St Petersburg 15 September 1812

Died: Speaker's Room at the Capitol 23 February 1848

Buried: Quincy

John Quincy Adams is to date the only son of a President to have himself reached the presidency and, surviving as he did until 1848, he was the first President of whom a photographic likeness exists. He looks a gnome-like figure, peering at the camera, and the resemblance to his father is quite striking.

The eldest son of John Adams was born at Braintree, Massachusetts, on 11 July 1767, in a house adjacent to that in which his father had been born. As a child of eight he watched the battle of Bunker Hill with his mother, the redoubtable Abigail, from a vantage point on the top of Penn's Hill nearby. Three years later he journeyed to Paris with his father and entered a school at Passy. The next seven years were spent travelling to, from and about Europe with his parents and other members of his family. He received more schooling in Amsterdam and studied at Leyden University. A year was spent in St Petersburg with his father's secretary of legation, Francis Dana, who had been appointed Minister to Russia but was never officially received.

John Quincy Adams, the first President to be photographed; this daguerreotype was taken in 1847, the year before his death

The fifteen-year-old Adams was evidently extremely precocious and self-possessed for, on leaving St Petersburg in October 1782, he travelled alone through Finland, Sweden, Denmark and northern Germany to join his father at The Hague, where he arrived in April 1783. For the next two years the Adams family did the rounds of London, Paris and The Hague. They left Europe in May 1785 and arrived home to Braintree in July.

In March 1786 John Quincy Adams entered Harvard and after graduating in July 1787 began studying law under Theophilus Parsons in Newburyport, Massachusetts. He was admitted to the Boston Bar on 15 July 1790 and although he opened a law office he never built up a big practice, being far more interested in political affairs. He occupied himself in writing articles and letters of criticism for the Boston newspaper, *Columbian Centinel*, using the pseudonym of Publicola, and for the New York newspaper, *Minerva*, using the pseudonym Columbus. In 1794 President Washington appointed Adams Minister to the Netherlands and he sailed for Holland in September, arriving at The Hague in October. In 1796 he was further appointed Minister to Portugal but was asked to remain in Holland until a successor was appointed. In the meantime his father was elected President and in June John Quincy Adams left for London where his fiancée Louisa Catherine Johnson, the daughter of the American Consul-General in London, was waiting for him. On his arrival he learnt that his father had cancelled the Portuguese appointment and nominated him as Minister to Prussia instead. The marriage took place at All Hallows, Barking-by-the-Tower, on 26 July 1797 and in the autumn the newly married couple proceeded to Berlin, where he presented his credentials in November.

During his sojourn in Berlin, John Quincy perfected his German and made a translation of Christoph Martin Wieland's *Oberon*, which was never published as another translation by William Sotheby beat it to the post. In 1800 and 1801 Adams made a tour of Silesia and his *Letters from Silesia* were published in the Philadelphia *Portfolio* and later in book form in London. The Adamses' first child, George Washington Adams, was born in Berlin in April 1801 and in September their tour of duty ended and they returned to the States, where John Quincy resumed his law practice in Boston.

In 1802 he was elected a Federalist member of the Massachusetts State Senate, but was defeated in his attempt to win a seat in the House of Representatives. In the following year, however, he was appointed Senator from Massachusetts to fill an unexpired term until 1809. His appointment as Boylston Professor of Oratory and Rhetoric at Harvard came in 1806. In December 1807, Adams was the only Federalist Senator to support Jefferson's Embargo Act and the stand he took forced his resignation from the Senate on 8 June 1808, nine months earlier than the due date. He again resumed his law practice until President Madison appointed him Minister Plenipotentiary to Russia in 1809. He was to remain in Europe for the next eight years, in the course of which he was appointed and declined to serve as Associate Justice of the Supreme Court. In 1814 he was appointed one of the five US commissioners to negotiate peace with Great Britain and on the successful outcome of the negotiations the treaty of Ghent was signed on 24 December 1814. Adams then proceeded to Paris where he saw Napoleon's return from Elba and received news of his appointment as Envoy Extraordinary and Minister Plenipotentiary to Great Britain. He arrived in London in May and after concluding a new commercial treaty with Great Britian in July, found a residence for his family at Little Ealing, now a suburb, but then a pretty countrified area within easy reach of London. They remained there until Adams's appointment as Secretary of State by President Monroe recalled him to America in the summer of 1817. As Secretary he signed the Adams-Onis Treaty with Spain on 22 February 1819, whereby, among other things, Spain renounced all claim to West Florida and ceded East Florida to the United States.

Louisa, the President's wife, painted by Gilbert Stuart in 1818

In the presidential election of 1820 Adams received

the only electoral vote not cast for Monroe. In 1823 he played an important part in the formulation of the Monroe Doctrine and in February 1824 he was nominated for President by a faction of the Republican party. The Presidential Electors cast their ballots on 1 December 1824 and when the votes were tabulated by Congress it was found that no candidate (there were four) had received a clear majority. Accordingly the election was decided by the House of Representatives under the 12th Amendment to the Constitution on the basis of one vote per state and John Quincy Adams received thirteen, one more than the required majority, and was declared elected. He was inaugurated in the Hall of Representatives in the Capitol on Friday 4 March 1825, the oath being administered by Chief Justice John Marshall for the seventh time.

The presidency was a relatively quiet and uneventful one. On 25 February 1828 the President's second son, John Adams, became the first (and so far the only) son of a President to marry at the White House. His bride was his first cousin Mary Catherine Hellen.

Adams sought re-election in 1828 but was defeated by Andrew Jackson and retired from the presidency on 4 March 1829. The previous day he had moved to take up temporary residence on Meridian Hill in a suburb of Washington. He did not attend his successor's inauguration.

As former President, Adams had no intention of retiring from public life. A personal tragedy struck him on 30 April 1829 when his eldest son, George Washington Adams, was drowned in Long Island Sound after falling off a steamer bound for New York from Providence, Rhode Island. His body was later found on City Island off the Bronx. Whether his death was an accident (George was apparently drunk) or suicide was never established. In 1830 Adams was easily persuaded to run for Congress and on 1 November was elected as an Anti-Mason to the House of Representatives, where he took his seat the following year. He was to remain a member of the House for the rest of his life and was a vigorous campaigner for many causes. He could at times be virulent about his successor Andrew Jackson and objected strongly when Jackson received an honorary degree from Harvard, writing later, 'I would not be present to see my darling Harvard disgrace herself by conferring a Doctor's degree upon a barbarian and savage who could scarcely spell his own name'.

In 1833 Adams made a bid for the Governorship of Massachusetts but was defeated. He suffered another personal tragedy in October 1834 when his second son, John, who had acted as private secretary to his father, died leaving a widow and two little girls, the younger of whom, Fanny, was also to die before her grandfather in October 1839 in the same room and same bed in which she had been born. On 20 November 1846 Adams suffered a paralytic stroke in Boston and was incapacitated for several weeks. He partially recovered to celebrate his eightieth birthday and his golden wedding in July 1847, having returned to the House of Representatives in February. Early in the following year he collapsed with a second stroke in his seat in the House. He was carried to the Speaker's Room and made as comfortable as possible, dying peacefully two days later on 23 February 1848. His widow survived him a little over four years. John Quincy Adams was a dour man of little affability, but capable on occasion of great flights of eloquence ('Old Man Eloquence' was one of his nicknames). He was always convinced that his views on any subject were the right ones and never admitted that there could be two sides to an argument.

Adams's youngest and only surviving son, Charles Francis Adams, was a member of the House of Representatives (Congress) and also followed the family's diplomatic tradition as US Minister to England from 1861 to 1868. Several of his descendants have distinguished themselves as academics or as high-ranking officers in the US navy.

Note For the Adams family table, see page 18.

Andrew Jackson 1829–1837

Born:	Waxhaws, S Carolina, 15 March 1767, 3rd and posthumous son of Andrew Jackson, of Waxhaws, and Elizabeth Hutchinson	Elected for 2nd term:	5 December 1832
Member of House of Representatives:	1796–1797	Inaugurated:	Hall of Representatives 4 March 1833
Senator:	1797–1798	Retired from presidency:	4 March 1837
Judge of Tennessee Superior Court:	1798–1804	Married:	Natchez, Mississippi, August 1791, and Nashville, Tennessee, 17 January 1794, Rachel (*b* Pittsylvania County, Virginia, 15 June 1767; *d* The Hermitage, nr Nashville, Tennessee, 22 December 1828; *bur* The Hermitage Garden), formerly wife of Lewis Robards and (4th) dau of Col John Donelson, and Rachel Stockley
Major-General of US Volunteers:	1812	Children:	None
Brigadier-General and Major-General US army:	1814	Adopted son:	Andrew Jackson Jr (son of Severn Donelson, brother of Mrs Andrew Jackson, and Elizabeth Rucker), *b* nr Nashville 22 December 1809; legally adopted January 1810; *m* Philadelphia 24 November 1831 Sarah (*b* Philadelphia July 1805; *d* The Hermitage 23 August 1887), dau of Peter Yorke of Philadelphia; 4 sons, 1 dau; *d* 17 April 1865
Military Governor of Florida:	April–October 1821		
Senator:	1823–1825		
Elected (7th) President:	3 December 1828		
Inaugurated:	East Portico of Capitol 4 March 1829	Died:	Nashville, Tennessee, 8 June 1845
		Buried:	The Hermitage Garden

The first six Presidents were all men of solid upper- or middle-class background and some education; Andrew Jackson, the seventh President, was the first of the 'log-cabin' breed, with little or no formal education. His great-grandfather was Thomas Jackson, of Dundonald, Co Down, Ireland, whose son, Hugh Jackson, was a weaver and merchant at Carrickfergus, Co Antrim, and died about 1782. One of Hugh's four sons, Andrew Jackson, emigrated to South Carolina in 1765 and farmed in a small way at Waxhaws settlement there. He married Elizabeth Hutchinson before leaving Ireland, and died about 1 March 1767, leaving her a heavily pregnant widow with two small sons. Some two weeks later on 15 March 1767 she gave birth to another son, Andrew, who was probably born in the log cabin of her brother-in-law George McCamie (or McKemey) at Waxhaws.

The young Andrew received only a very rudimentary education and never attended college. At the age of thirteen he joined the Revolutionary army as a mounted orderly or messenger and received his baptism of fire at the battle of Hanging Rock the following month. In April 1781 he and his brother Robert were taken prisoner by the British. The high-spirited Andrew refused to clean a British officer's boots and received a sword slash on the head and hand for so doing. Both brothers then fell ill with smallpox and on 25 April on their mother's urgent plea were released. Robert died two days later. As their elder brother Hugh had been killed at the battle of Stone Ferry in June 1779, Andrew was now the only surviving child of his mother, who was ailing, and he returned to Waxhaws to live with her until her death from yellow fever in November 1781. Thereafter Jackson made his home with two uncles.

In March 1783 he received a small legacy of £300 to £400 from his paternal grandfather Hugh Jackson, but soon lost it all gambling and backing horses. In December 1784 Jackson began to study law in the offices of Spruce Macay in Salisbury, North Carolina, and continued his studies under Colonel John Stokes. He was admitted to the North Carolina Bar in November 1787 and began to practice law in Johnsonville, North Carolina, moving to Nashville (then in North Carolina, but now in Tennessee) in October 1788. A month later he was appointed Prosecuting Attorney for the western district of North Carolina.

In August 1791 Jackson married Mrs Rachel Donelson Robards at Natchez, Mississippi. Three months his junior, she had been married in 1785 to Lewis Robards. The marriage had not worked out and Rachel was under

Andrew Jackson after a painting by Ralph Earl

the impression that Robards had obtained a divorce in December 1790 and that she was free to remarry. In fact, however, he had not done so and did not do so until September 1793. As a result Jackson and Rachel went through a second marriage ceremony at Nashville on 17 January 1794. Great capital was to be made of all this by Jackson's political opponents in later years, branding him as an adulterer and his wife as a bigamist. There were no children and in 1810 the Jacksons legally adopted Rachel's month-old nephew, who became Andrew Jackson Jr.

In 1796 Jackson was appointed a delegate from Davidson County to the Knoxville Convention to draft a constitution for the State of Tennessee, and later (after statehood had been attained on 1 June) was elected unopposed as Tennessee's first member of the House of Representatives, in which he took his seat at Philadelphia on 5 December. At the end of his term the following March he declined to seek re-election, but was elected to the Senate in place of William Blount, who had been expelled, and took his seat on 20 November 1797. He resigned in April 1798 and in October was appointed Judge of the Tennessee Superior Court. In 1802 he was elected Major-General of militia. His rival for the appointment was John Sevier, ex-Governor of Tennessee. The two men had tied with seventeen votes each when the field officers of the Militia were polled and the casting vote in Jackson's favour was given by Archibald Roane, Sevier's successor as Governor.

Jackson and Sevier pursued a vendetta for over a year, Jackson accusing Sevier of being involved in a land swindle when he was again running for Governor. Sevier was able to talk his way out of it and was duly elected Governor. In a heated exchange on the courthouse steps at Knoxville he told Jackson, 'I know of no great service you have rendered the country, except take a trip to Natchez with another man's wife!' Jackson went for him with his cane and the two men had to be forcibly separated. Jackson at once challenged Sevier to a duel and when he refused to accept the challenge put an advertisement in the *Gazette* calling him 'a base coward and poltroon'. A hilariously farcical scene followed when the two men finally met at Southwest Point on 16 October 1803. Sevier arrived with several armed men. He and Jackson drew their pistols, had a heated exchange of words, then put up their arms. After more slanging Sevier drew his sword, thereby frightening his horse which 'ran away with the Governor's pistols'. Jackson again drew his pistol and Sevier hid behind a tree while his son drew on Jackson and Jackson's second drew on Sevier junior. At last the protagonists calmed down and Sevier left the scene.

Jackson resigned as Judge of the Superior Court in July 1804 and in August or September moved to The Hermitage, a property of 625 acres which he had purchased in 1795. The house, twelve miles east of Nashville, is now owned by the State of Tennessee and open to the public.

On 30 May 1806 Jackson again became involved in a duel. This time with Charles Dickinson, who had uttered disparaging remarks about Mrs Jackson. Dickinson fired first, wounding Jackson in the left breast.

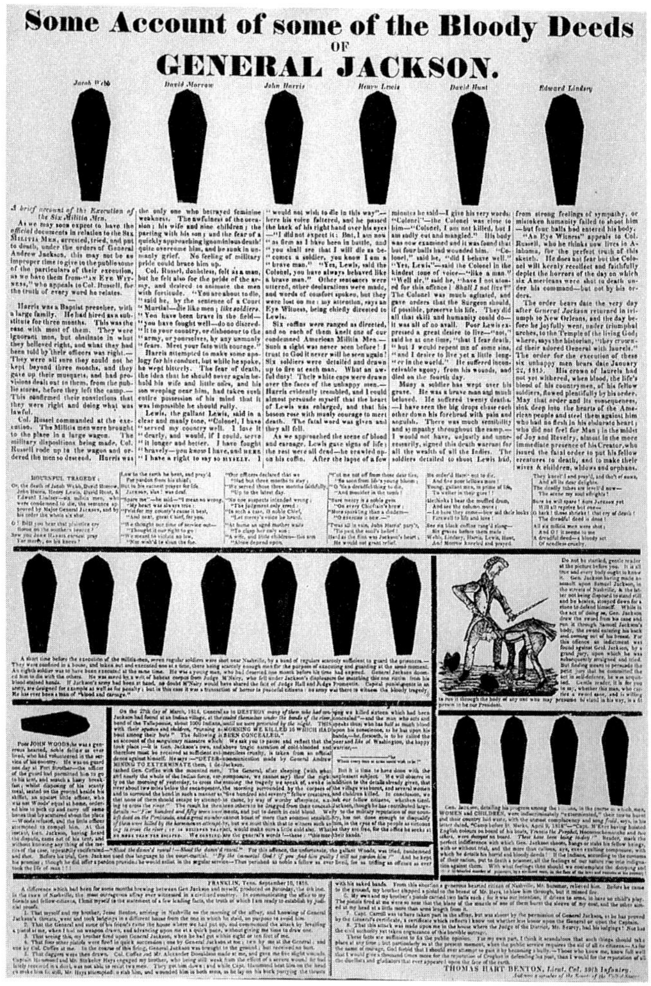

The notorious anti-Jackson 1828 'Coffin Handbill' which depicted Jackson as a ruthless bully who had killed his own Tennessee militiamen in cold blood

Jackson steadied himself and returned the fire, fatally wounding Dickinson, who died later that day. The bullet which wounded Jackson was too close to his heart to be removed and remained in his body for the rest of his life. Around this time Jackson became much involved with Aaron Burr and his schemes to conquer Texas, and in 1807 he was summoned as a witness in Burr's trial for treason at Richmond, but in the event was not called upon to give evidence. Burr was acquitted.

After the declaration of war on Great Britain in June 1812, Jackson offered the services of his 2,500 strong militia division and was appointed Major-General of US Volunteers by Governor William Blount of Tennessee. In January 1813 he led 2,000 volunteers to Natchez, where he was ordered to demobilize on his arrival by General James Wilkinson. He refused to do so, saying that he would return them to their own homes 'on my own means and responsibility'. It was during the 800 mile march back when one of the volunteers described him as being 'tough as hickory' that Jackson earned his famous nickname of 'Old Hickory'.

On 4 September 1813 the ever-quarrelsome Jackson went to the City Hotel, Nashville, with the intention of horsewhipping Thomas Hart Benton and was shot in the back by Benton's brother Jesse. His left shoulder was shattered and a ball was embedded in his left arm, but Jackson refused to submit to an amputation and recovered in due course.

Before the month was out he offered to Governor Blount the services of his volunteers to fight the Creek Indians who had massacred 250 people at Fort Mimms in Mississippi Territory (now Alabama). More than 300 Creeks were killed at Talladega on 9 November 1813, but the Tennessee Volunteers suffered a series of setbacks the following January in three successive encounters and sustained many casualties. The tide was turned in March when the Creeks and Cherokees were defeated at Horseshoe Bend (Tohopeka) with losses of 850 Indian braves. The victory brought Jackson national acclaim and he was rewarded with the rank of Brigadier-General in the US army, and almost immediately promoted to Major-General and given command of the Seventh Military District, comprising Tennessee, Louisiana and the Mississippi Territory. On 7 November with 3,000 men Jackson captured Pensacola from the British. He marched on to New Orleans, where he declared martial law and after several engagements won a decisive victory at the battle of New Orleans on 8 January 1815, in which the British forces of 5,300 were decimated by artillery and rifle fire in the course of half an hour. The British Commander, Major-General Sir Edward Pakenham, was among the 2,000 British killed or wounded, while the Americans, astoundingly, sustained little more than twenty casualties. By a strange irony of fate, the battle was fought after the treaty of Ghent ending the war had been signed, but the slow communications of the day rendered this fact unknown to the combatants.

In the course of the next four years Jackson was offered and declined the appointment as Secretary of War made by President Monroe, fought another successful Indian campaign (the First Seminole War), served as Military Governor of Florida from April to October 1821, refused the appointment as Minister Plenipotentiary to Mexico, and was again elected to the Senate in 1823. The Tennessee legislature nominated him for President in the 1824 presidential election, which resulted, as we have already seen, in no candidate receiving a clear majority and the House of Representatives electing John Quincy Adams.

In October 1825 Jackson resigned from the Senate after the Tennessee legislature had again nominated him for the presidency, saying that he considered it improper for him to continue in the Senate under the circumstances. The presidential electors cast their ballots on 3 December 1828, Jackson receiving 178 and Adams 83. Before the votes were tabulated by Congress, however,

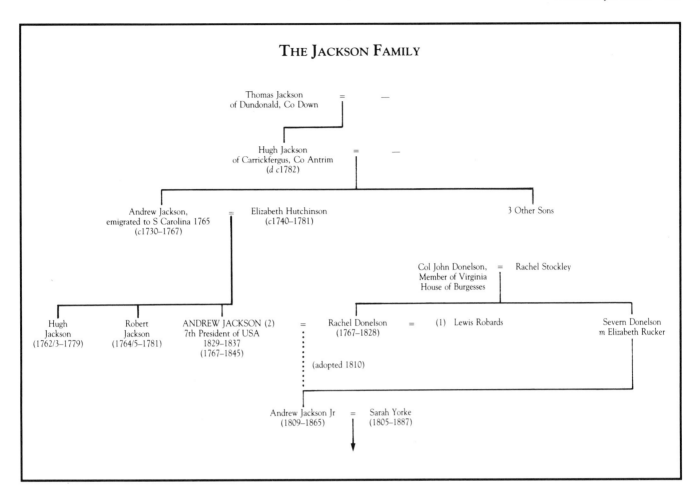

THE JACKSON FAMILY

Thomas Jackson of Dundonald, Co Down = —

Hugh Jackson of Carrickfergus, Co Antrim (d c1782) = —

- Andrew Jackson, emigrated to S Carolina 1765 (c1730–1767) = Elizabeth Hutchinson (c1740–1781)
  - Hugh Jackson (1762/3–1779)
  - Robert Jackson (1764/5–1781)
  - ANDREW JACKSON (2) 7th President of USA 1829–1837 (1767–1845) = Rachel Donelson (1767–1828) = (1) Lewis Robards
- 3 Other Sons

Col John Donelson, Member of Virginia House of Burgesses = Rachel Stockley

- Rachel Donelson (1767–1828)
- Severn Donelson m Elizabeth Rucker

Andrew Jackson Jr (1809–1865) (adopted 1810) = Sarah Yorke (1805–1887)

Mrs Jackson died at The Hermitage on 22 December 1828 and was buried in the garden there. It is difficult to gain much idea of her character and her few portraits do not flatter her, but Jackson was ever zealous in defence of her honour, as we know.

Andrew Jackson was inaugurated as seventh President on the East Portico of the Capitol on Wednesday 4 March 1829, Chief Justice John Marshall administering the oath of office for the eighth time. Jackson served two terms as President, being nominated for his second term at the first Democratic National Convention in May 1832 and gaining 219 of the 288 electoral votes. Chief Justice John Marshall officiated for the ninth and last time at Jackson's second inauguration which took place in the Hall of Representatives (the last inauguration to take place there) on 4 March 1833. Jackson's high-handed behaviour was to alienate many of his supporters during his eight years in office and he survived an assassination attempt in January 1835 when he was shot at on leaving the House of Representatives by Richard Lawrence, who was later committed to an asylum.

Jackson retired from office on 4 March 1837 and, after attending the inauguration of his protégé Van Buren, returned to The Hermitage, where he lived quietly for the rest of his life, emerging only to participate in the twenty-fifth anniversary celebrations of the battle of New Orleans, to campaign for the re-election of Van Buren, and actively to support the annexation of Texas. He died at the age of seventy-eight of consumption and dropsy on 8 June 1845 and was buried with Mrs Jackson in The Hermitage garden. The descendants of his adopted son continued to live at The Hermitage until well into this century.

A choleric yet likeable man, Jackson had an aristocratic appearance and bearing which belied his humble origin. In some portraits, in fact, he bears a remarkable resemblance to the first Duke of Wellington, also, it will be remembered, of Irish extraction.

MARTIN VAN BUREN 1837–1841

Born:	Kinderhook, Columbia County, New York, 5 December 1782, eldest son of Abraham Van Buren, of Kinderhook, and Maria Hoes
NY State Senator:	1813–1820
Attorney-General for State of New York:	1815–1819
Senator:	1821–1828
Governor of New York:	January to March 1829
Secretary of State:	1829–1831
Elected Vice-President:	6 November 1832
Inaugurated:	4 March 1833
Elected (8th) President:	8 November 1836
Inaugurated:	East Portico of Capitol 4 March 1837
Retired from presidency:	4 March 1841
Married:	Catskill, New York, 21 February 1807, Hannah (*b* Kinderhook, New York, 8 March 1783; *d* Albany, New York, 5 February 1819; *bur* Cemetery of Second Presbyterian Church, Albany, transferred to Kinderhook 1855), dau of John Dircksen Hoes (first cousin of Martin Van Buren) and Maria Quackenboss
Children:	(1) Abraham, *b* Kinderhook 27 November 1807; *m* November 1838, Angelica (*b* Sumpter District, S Carolina, 1816; *d* New York 29 December 1878), dau of Richard Singleton and — Coles; 3 sons, 1 dau; *d* New York 15 March 1873 (2) John, *b* Hudson, Columbia County, New York, 10 February 1810; *m* 22 June 1841 Elizabeth Vanderpoel (*b* 22 May 1810; *d* 19 November 1844); 1 dau; *d* at sea 13 October 1866 (3) Martin Jr, *b* Hudson 20 December 1812; *d unm* Paris, France, 19 March 1855 (4) A child, *b* and *d c* 1814 (5) Smith Thompson, *b* Hudson 16 January 1817; *m* (1) 18 June 1842 Ellen King (*b* 20 January 1813; *d* 3 October 1849), dau of William James of Albany, New York, and Catharine Barber; 1 son, 3 daus; *m* (2) 1 February 1855 Henrietta Eckford Irving (*b* Bournemouth, England, 13 April 1821), niece of Washington Irving, the author; 1 son, 2 daus; *d* 1876
Died:	Lindenwald, Kinderhook, 24 July 1862
Buried:	Kinderhook

Martin Van Buren has the double distinction of being the first President actually born a citizen of the United States and the first President of non-British descent. Apart from that he has little else for which to be remembered.

Cornelis Maessen, the first-known ancestor of the Van Burens, came to America from Buurmalsen, Gelderland (now the Netherlands), in 1631 and settled at Papsknee, near Greenbush, New York. He died in 1648, leaving four sons and one daughter. The descendants of one of his sons adopted the surname of Bloemendaal. Another son, Marten Cornelisz, lived at Albany, New York, and was Captain of a militia company in Colonel Pieter Schuyler's regiment. He married twice and died in 1703, leaving a son Pieter Martense, whose son, Martin, was the first to adopt or use the surname of Van Buren. One of Martin's sons, Abraham Van Buren, was a farmer and innkeeper at Kinderhook, Columbia County, New York. He married Maria, the widow of Johannes Van Alen, in 1776 and their eldest son, the future President, was born at Kinderhook on 5 December 1782.

Nothing is known of Martin Van Buren's childhood and early years until he began his law studies in the office of Francis Silvester in Kinderhook in 1796. He continued them under William Peter Van Ness, of New York City, and was admitted to the Bar there in November 1803. Shortly after that he returned to Kinderhook and began to practice. In February 1807 he married Hannah Hoes, his first cousin once removed. She died in 1819 before her husband rose to a position of prominence, so remains a shadowy figure. There were five children of the marriage, of whom one (sex unspecified) died in infancy.

Martin Van Buren served in the New York State Senate from 1813 to 1820 and held the office of State Attorney General from 1815 to 1819. In the three consecutive years 1817, 1818 and 1819 he lost his father, his mother and his wife and was left with four young sons to bring up.

Van Buren was elected to the US Senate in 1821 and re-elected in 1827, but resigned his seat on being elected

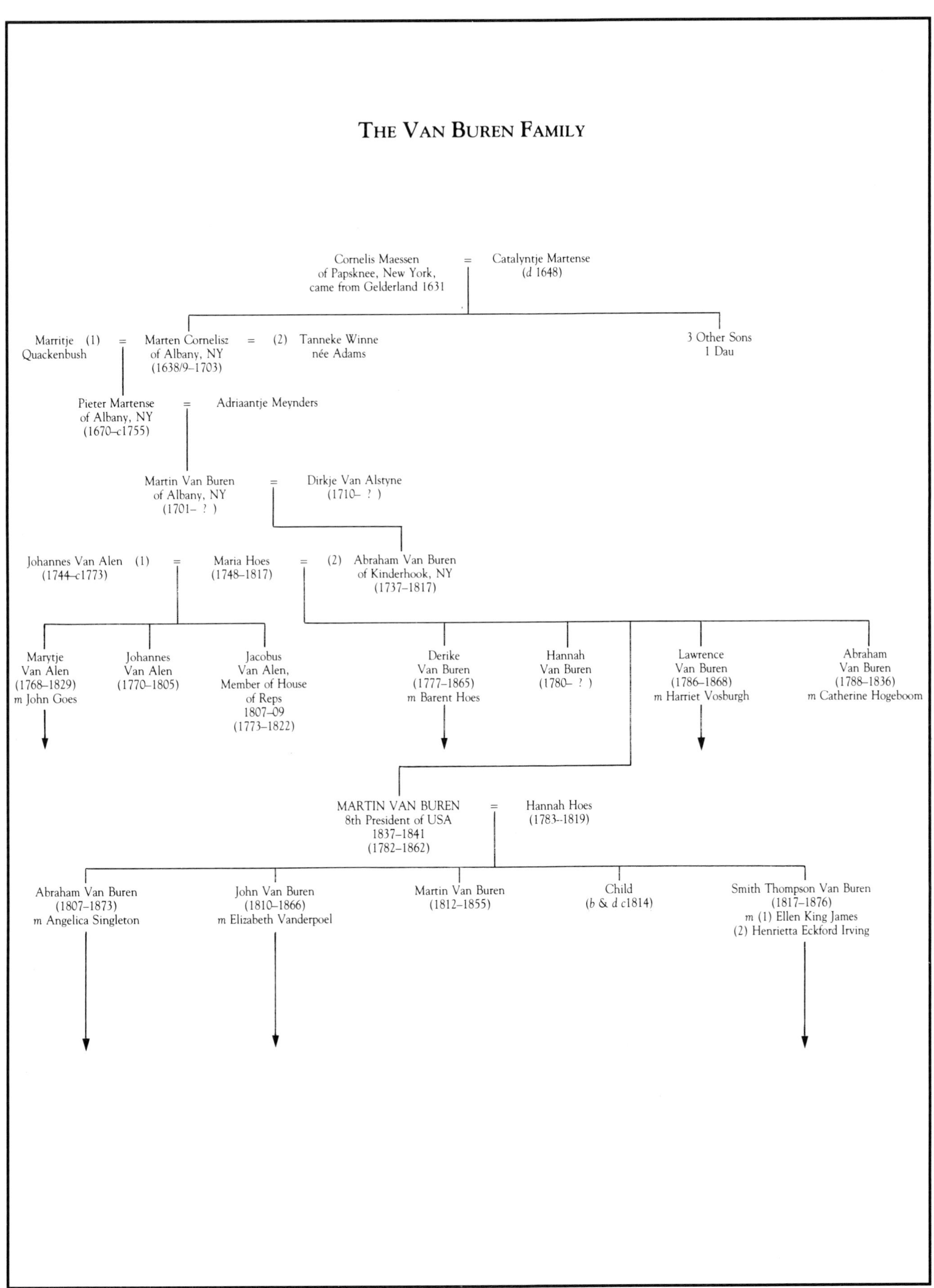
THE VAN BUREN FAMILY
Cornelis Maessen of Papsknee, New York, came from Gelderland 1631 = Catalyntje Martense (d 1648)
Marritje (1) Quackenbush = Marten Cornelisz of Albany, NY (1638/9–1703) = (2) Tanneke Winne née Adams
3 Other Sons 1 Dau
Pieter Martense of Albany, NY (1670–c1755) = Adriaantje Meynders
Martin Van Buren of Albany, NY (1701– ?) = Dirkje Van Alstyne (1710– ?)
Johannes Van Alen (1) (1744–c1773) = Maria Hoes (1748–1817) = (2) Abraham Van Buren of Kinderhook, NY (1737–1817)
Marytje Van Alen (1768–1829) m John Goes
Johannes Van Alen (1770–1805)
Jacobus Van Alen, Member of House of Reps 1807–09 (1773–1822)
Derike Van Buren (1777–1865) m Barent Hoes
Hannah Van Buren (1780– ?)
Lawrence Van Buren (1786–1868) m Harriet Vosburgh
Abraham Van Buren (1788–1836) m Catherine Hogeboom
MARTIN VAN BUREN 8th President of USA 1837–1841 (1782–1862) = Hannah Hoes (1783–1819)
Abraham Van Buren (1807–1873) m Angelica Singleton
John Van Buren (1810–1866) m Elizabeth Vanderpoel
Martin Van Buren (1812–1855)
Child (b & d c1814)
Smith Thompson Van Buren (1817–1876) m (1) Ellen King James (2) Henrietta Eckford Irving

Martin Van Buren, an unpopular President not least because of his seven outstanding predecessors

A campaign cartoon of 1840 depicting Van Buren with his Sub-treasury bill on his back, being led to the White House by Andrew Jackson for a second term (which did not come about)

Governor of New York in 1828. His term of office commenced on 1 January 1829, but on 6 March he was appointed Secretary of State by President Jackson, to whom he made himself indispensable, and accordingly resigned the governorship on 12 March, taking office as Secretary on 28 March. He remained Secretary of State until 1831, when he resigned on 11 April (effective from 23 May). On 25 June 1831 he was appointed Minister to Great Britain and sailed for England on 16 August. On arrival in September he was met by Washington Irving, Secretary of Legation, who was to become a lifelong friend. His journey to England had been a bit precipitate, however, for on 25 January 1832 the Senate rejected his nomination as Minister and he received news of this on 15 February. Nevertheless, he was received by King William IV at Windsor Castle on 5 March, and on leaving England he spent the months of April, May and June touring France, Germany and the Netherlands.

Van Buren arrived back in New York on 5 July 1832 to learn that he had been nominated for Vice-President. He was duly elected and inaugurated on 4 March 1833. On 20 May 1835 he was nominated for President by the Democratic Convention at Baltimore and in the ensuing election in 1836 Van Buren won 170 of the 294 electoral votes. He was inaugurated as eighth President on the East Portico of the Capitol on Saturday 4 March 1837, the oath of office being administered by Chief Justice Roger Brooke Taney.

The presidency got off to a bad start as a period of severe economic depression precipitated by a fall in cotton prices and the suspension of specie payments by

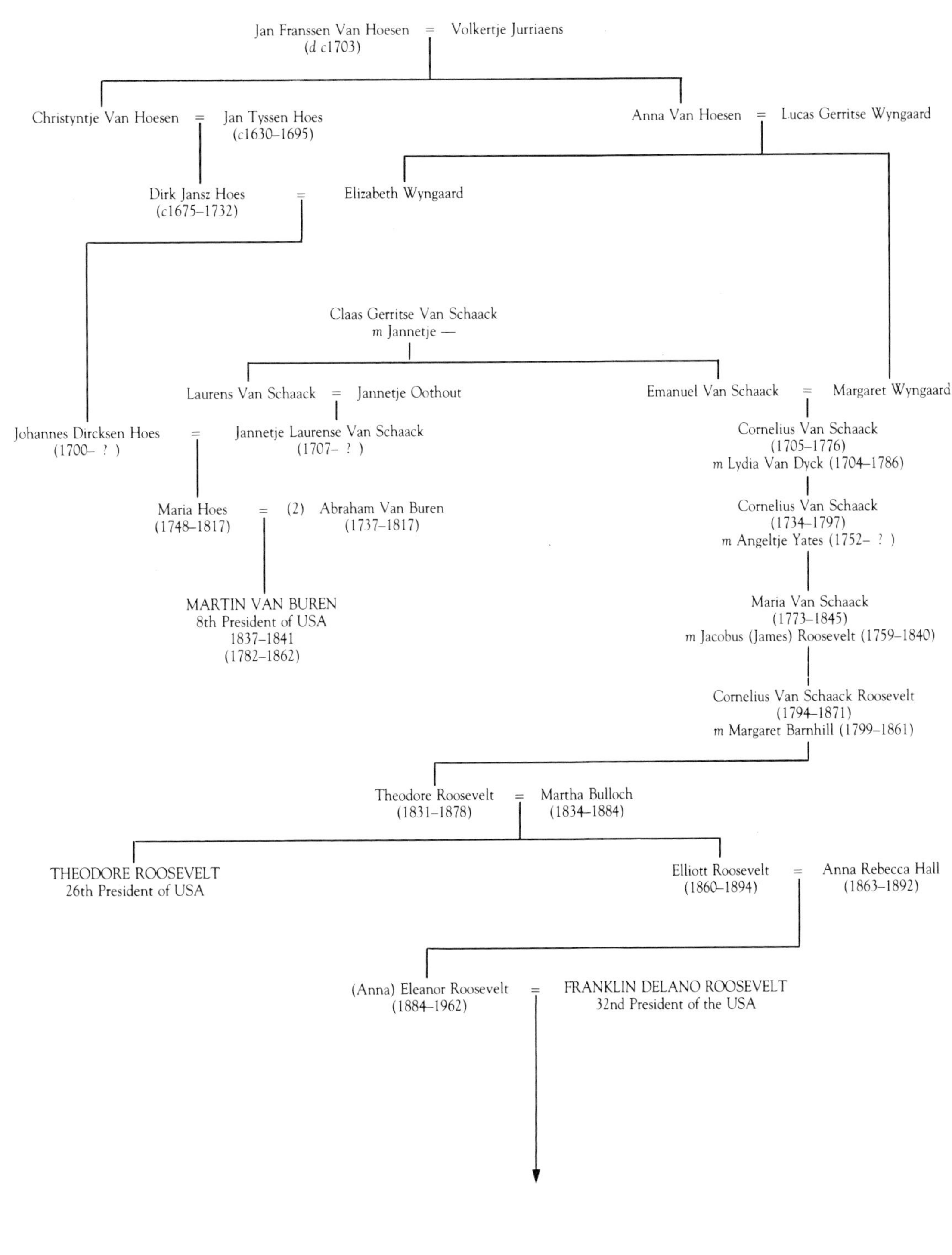
MARTIN VAN BUREN AND THE ROOSEVELTS
Jan Franssen Van Hoesen (d c1703) = Volkertje Jurriaens
Christyntje Van Hoesen = Jan Tyssen Hoes (c1630–1695)
Anna Van Hoesen = Lucas Gerritse Wyngaard
Dirk Jansz Hoes (c1675–1732) = Elizabeth Wyngaard
Claas Gerritse Van Schaack m Jannetje —
Laurens Van Schaack = Jannetje Oothout
Emanuel Van Schaack = Margaret Wyngaard
Johannes Dircksen Hoes (1700– ?) = Jannetje Laurense Van Schaack (1707– ?)
Cornelius Van Schaack (1705–1776) m Lydia Van Dyck (1704–1786)
Maria Hoes (1748–1817) = (2) Abraham Van Buren (1737–1817)
Cornelius Van Schaack (1734–1797) m Angeltje Yates (1752– ?)
MARTIN VAN BUREN
8th President of USA
1837–1841
(1782–1862)
Maria Van Schaack (1773–1845) m Jacobus (James) Roosevelt (1759–1840)
Cornelius Van Schaack Roosevelt (1794–1871) m Margaret Barnhill (1799–1861)
Theodore Roosevelt (1831–1878) = Martha Bulloch (1834–1884)
THEODORE ROOSEVELT
26th President of USA
Elliott Roosevelt (1860–1894) = Anna Rebecca Hall (1863–1892)
(Anna) Eleanor Roosevelt (1884–1962) = FRANKLIN DELANO ROOSEVELT
32nd President of the USA

banks throughout the country began in May and was to last for more than six years.

Martin Van Buren was a small man in every sense (his five foot six inches stature earned him the nickname of 'Little Matty') and his mediocrity was made more apparent in contrast with his seven outstanding predecessors in the presidency. As a professional politician he was mistrusted and considered sly, devious and unprincipled by his opponents. His attention to dress and appreciation of good food and wine earned him another nickname, that of 'King Matty', while his dapper second son was referred to as 'Prince John'.

It was hardly surprising that when he sought re-election in 1840, Van Buren lost to the Whig party candidate, William Henry Harrison. He attended Harrison's inauguration on 4 March 1841 and in May settled into Lindenwald, the mansion and 200 acre estate which he had bought near Kinderhook. His years of retirement were active ones. In 1842 he made a six-month trip along the Atlantic seaboard. In 1844 he again sought nomination as presidential candidate but was unsuccessful. He fared better in 1848, however, when he was nominated by the Barnburners (the anti-administration faction of the Democrats) and the Free Soil Party. In the ensuing election he received 291,263 popular votes but no electoral ones. Two years later in 1850 he renewed his allegiance to the Democrats and in 1852 supported Pierce's candidacy.

Van Buren made an extensive tour of Europe from 1853 to 1855, visiting England, France, Switzerland, Belgium, Holland and Italy and being received by Queen Victoria and Pope Pius IX. His third son, Martin, who accompanied him, died in Paris towards the end of the trip.

After his return home, Van Buren gave his support to Buchanan in 1856 and to Douglas in 1860. In the spring of 1862 his health began to fail and he went to New York City for consultation and treatment. On his return to Lindenwald he took to his bed and died of severe asthma spasms on 24 July 1862 at the age of seventy-nine. He was buried at Kinderhook. In 1852 he had begun work on *Inquiry into the Origin and Course of Political Parties in the United States*, which was edited by his surviving sons and published posthumously in 1867.

WILLIAM HENRY HARRISON March–April 1841

Born: Berkeley, Charles City County, Virginia, 9 February 1773, youngest son of Benjamin Harrison ('The Signer') of Berkeley and Elizabeth Bassett

Governor of Indiana Territory: 1801–1812

Brigadier-General US army: 1812

Major-General US army: 1813

Member of House of Representatives: 1816–1819

Ohio State Senator: 1819–1821

Presidential Elector for Ohio: 1820, 1824

Senator: 1825–1828

Minister to Colombia: 1828–1829

Elected (9th) President: November 1840

Inaugurated: East Portico of Capitol 4 March 1841

Married: North Bend, Ohio, 22 November 1795 Anna Tuthill (*b* Flatbrook, Sussex County, New Jersey, 25 July 1775; *d* North Bend, Ohio, 25 February 1864; *bur* Harrison Tomb), younger dau of Colonel John Cleves Symmes, sometime Chief Justice of New Jersey Supreme Court, and his first wife Anna Tuthill

Children:

(1) Elizabeth Bassett, *b* Fort Washington 29 September 1796; *m* 29 June 1814 her first cousin, Judge John Cleves Short (*b* 1792; *d* 1864), son of Peyton Short and Maria Symmes (sister of Mrs William Henry Harrison); 1 dau (*d* in infancy); *d* 27 September 1846

(2) John Cleves Symmes, *b* Fort Washington 28 October 1798; *m* 29 September 1819 Clarissa (*b* 24 February 1803; *d* 1 February 1837), dau of General Zebulon Montgomery Pike and Clarissa Brown; 3 sons, 3 daus; *d* 30 October 1830

(3) Lucy Singleton, *b* Richmond, Virginia, 5 September 1800; *m* 30 September 1819 David K Estes, Judge of the Superior Court of Ohio (*b* Morristown, New Jersey, 1786; *d* Cincinnati, Ohio, 1 April 1876); 3 sons, 1 dau; *d* Cincinnati, Ohio, 7 April 1826

(4) William Henry Jr, *b* Vincennes, Indiana, 3 September 1802; *m* 18 February 1824 Jane Findlay (*b* 1804; *d* 1846), dau of Archibald Irwin and Mary Ramsey; 2 sons; *d* North Bend, Ohio, 6 February 1838

(5) John Scott, member of the House of Representatives 1853–57; *b* Vincennes, Indiana, 4 October 1804; *m* (1) 1824 Lucretia Knapp Johnson (*b* Boone County, Kentucky, 16 September 1804; *d* 6 February 1830); 1 son, 2 daus; *m* (2) 12 August 1831 Elizabeth Ramsey (*b* Mercersburg, Pennsylvania, 18 July 1810; *d* North Bend, Ohio, 15 August 1850), dau of Archibald Irwin and Mary Ramsey; 7 sons (of whom the second, Benjamin Harrison (*qv*), became 23rd President), 3 daus; *d* Point Farm, nr North Bend, Ohio, 25 May 1878

(6) Benjamin MD, *b* Vincennes, Indiana, 5 May 1806; *m* (1) Louisa Smith Bonner; 1 son, *m* (2) Mary Raney; 2 sons; *d* 9 June 1840

(7) Mary Symmes, *b* Elletsville or Vincennes 22 (or 28) January 1809; *m* 5 March 1829 John Henry Fitzhugh Thornton MD (*b* 8 June 1798; *d* 6 December 1871), son of Captain Charles Thornton and Sarah Fitzhugh; 3 sons, 3 daus; *d* 16 November 1842

(8) Carter Bassett, *b* Vincennes 26 October 1811; *m* 16 June 1836 Mary Anne Sutherland (*b* 1814; *d* 1893); 1 dau; *d* 12 August 1839

(9) Anna Tuthill, *b* North Bend, Ohio, 28 October 1813; *m* 16 June 1836 her first cousin once removed, William Henry Harrison Taylor (*b* 1813; *d* 1894), eldest son of Thomas Taylor and Lucy Harrison Singleton (dau of Anthony Singleton and Lucy Harrison, sister of President William Henry Harrison); 3 sons, 9 daus; *d* 5 July 1865

(10) James Findlay, *b* North Bend, Ohio, 15 May 1814; *d* 6 April 1819

Died in office: The White House 4 April 1841

Buried: Harrison Tomb, opposite Congress Green Cemetery, North Bend, Ohio

William Henry Harrison from a portrait by E F Andrews

Until President Reagan was inaugurated in 1981, William Henry Harrison held the distinction of being the oldest man to be inaugurated for a first term. He still holds the records for the longest inaugural speech and the shortest presidency, the first being the primary cause leading to the second.

A Benjamin Harrison was in Virginia by 1633/4 when he signed a document as Clerk of the Council. His birthplace in England is unknown. He received grants of land on the James River and in 1642 was a member of the Virginia House of Burgesses. Benjamin's son, grandson, great-grandson, and great-great-grandson, all named Benjamin too, sat in the Virginia House of Burgesses and held important positions in the State giving valuable service to the community. The last in line was a signer of the Declaration of Independence on 4 July 1776, a member of Congress, Speaker of the House of Delegates, and from 1781 to 1784 Governor of Virginia. He married Elizabeth, daughter of the Rev William Bassett Jr of Eltham, New Kent County, Virginia, and the youngest of their seven children was William Henry, who was born at Berkeley on 9 February 1773.

At the age of thirteen William Henry entered Hampden-Sydney College, Virginia, where he stayed for about a year, going on to attend an academy in Southampton County, Virginia, for another two years. He spent a year studying medicine under Dr Benjamin Rush in Philadelphia, but gave it up on his father's death and entered the army, being commissioned Ensign in the 1st Infantry Regiment in 1791. The regiment was stationed at Fort Washington (now Cincinnati), Ohio, and in 1792 Harrison was promoted to Lieutenant and appointed Aide-de-camp to General Anthony Wayne. In December 1793 he took part in the expedition to build Fort Recovery on the Wabash River and was thanked in general orders, and in August 1794 took part in the battle of Fallen Timbers, in which Wayne's army defeated Little Turtle and his force of 800 Indians on the Maumee River, south of the present town of Toledo, Ohio.

Harrison was promoted Captain in May 1795 and in November married Anna Tuthill Symmes, the daughter of a former Chief Justice of the New Jersey Supreme Court who had moved to Ohio and settled at North Bend. The marriage was to produce ten children. Soon after his marriage Harrison assumed command of Fort Washington and remained there until 1 June 1798 when he resigned his commission preparatory to taking up at the end of the month his appointment, by President John Adams, as Secretary of Northwest Territory. In September 1799 he was elected territorial delegate to Congress by the territorial legislature which had been formed in February. This entitled him to present bills and take part in debates, but not to vote.

On 12 May 1800 President Adams appointed William Henry Harrison Governor of the new Indiana Territory and he took office at Vincennes, Indiana, in January 1801. He was reappointed by both Jefferson and Madison and retained the governorship until 1812, in the course of which he built a house in Vincennes (Grouseland, now open to the public and maintained by the Francis Vigo Chapter of the Daughters of the American Revolution), concluded several treaties with the Indians, served briefly as Governor of Louisiana Territory in 1804, and was a co-founder of Vincennes University Junior College.

In September 1809 the purchase of three million acres of land on the Wabash and White Rivers from several Indian tribes led to a dispute with Tecumseh, Chief of the Shawnees, who maintained that his tribe had not consented to the sale. A series of unsuccessful conferences with Tecumseh and his brother Elskwatawa (the Prophet) ensued and in September 1811, Harrison left Vincennes with a company of 900 men to take up a defensive military post on the junction of the Wabash and Tippecanoe Rivers. Fort Harrison, near the site of Terre Haute, Indiana, was completed on 28 October and on 6 November, Harrison and his force arrived at the Indian capital Prophetstown on Tippecanoe Creek. The famous battle of Tippecanoe, which was to give Harrison his nickname, 'Tippecanoe', was fought the next day.

—VOL. I. NO. 6.—

THE

AMERICAN ANTI-SLAVERY

ALMANAC,

FOR

1841.

BEING THE 65TH YEAR OF AMERICAN INDEPENDENCE.
CALCULATED FOR NEW YORK AND THE
MIDDLE STATES.

NEW YORK:
PUBLISHED BY S. W. BENEDICT.
NO. 131 NASSAU STREET.
1841.

The title page of *The American Anti-slavery Almanac* for 1841, the year of Harrison's presidency

The Indians attacked before dawn and after a day-long battle, in which the Americans suffered heavy losses, were finally repelled. Prophetstown was destroyed and Harrison returned in triumph to Fort Harrison to receive the congratulations of President Madison.

War against Great Britain was declared on 18 June 1812 and in August Harrison was commissioned as Major-General of the Kentucky militia and a week thereafter as Brigadier-General in the United States army. He was promoted Major-General in March 1813 and took part in the invasion of Canada that year, winning the decisive battle of the Thames, a little east of Thamesville, Ontario, in which his old antagonist Tecumseh, who had been commissioned as Brigadier-General by the British, was killed, allegedly by Richard Mentor Johnson, who was to be Vice-President under Martin Van Buren. Harrison received a gold medal for the victory somewhat belatedly in March 1818.

When the Secretary of War, John Armstrong, assigned Harrison to the Eighth Military Division, where he could expect no further active service, and then proceeded to issue direct orders to one of his subordinates, Harrison resigned from the army in May 1814.

In 1816 Harrison was elected to the House of Representatives and served until 1819, in which year he was elected a member of Ohio State Senate, serving until 1821. He served as Presidential Elector for Ohio in 1820 (when he voted for Monroe) and 1824 (when he voted for Henry Clay). In the latter year he was elected to the Senate and served from 1825 to 1828. On 19 May 1828 President John Quincy Adams appointed Harrison first United States Minister to Colombia and he sailed from New York City on 11 November. He landed at Maracaibo, Venezuela, on 22 December and proceeded overland to Bogota, where he arrived on 5 February 1829. He had been there just over a month when he was recalled by Andrew Jackson on 8 March. His departure was delayed for want of a ship, but he finally sailed for home on 9 January 1830 and on arrival retired to his farm at North Bend, Ohio, where he lived quietly for the next few years.

In 1835 Harrison was nominated for President in several states and was the unsuccessful Whig candidate in the presidential election of 1836. On 4 December

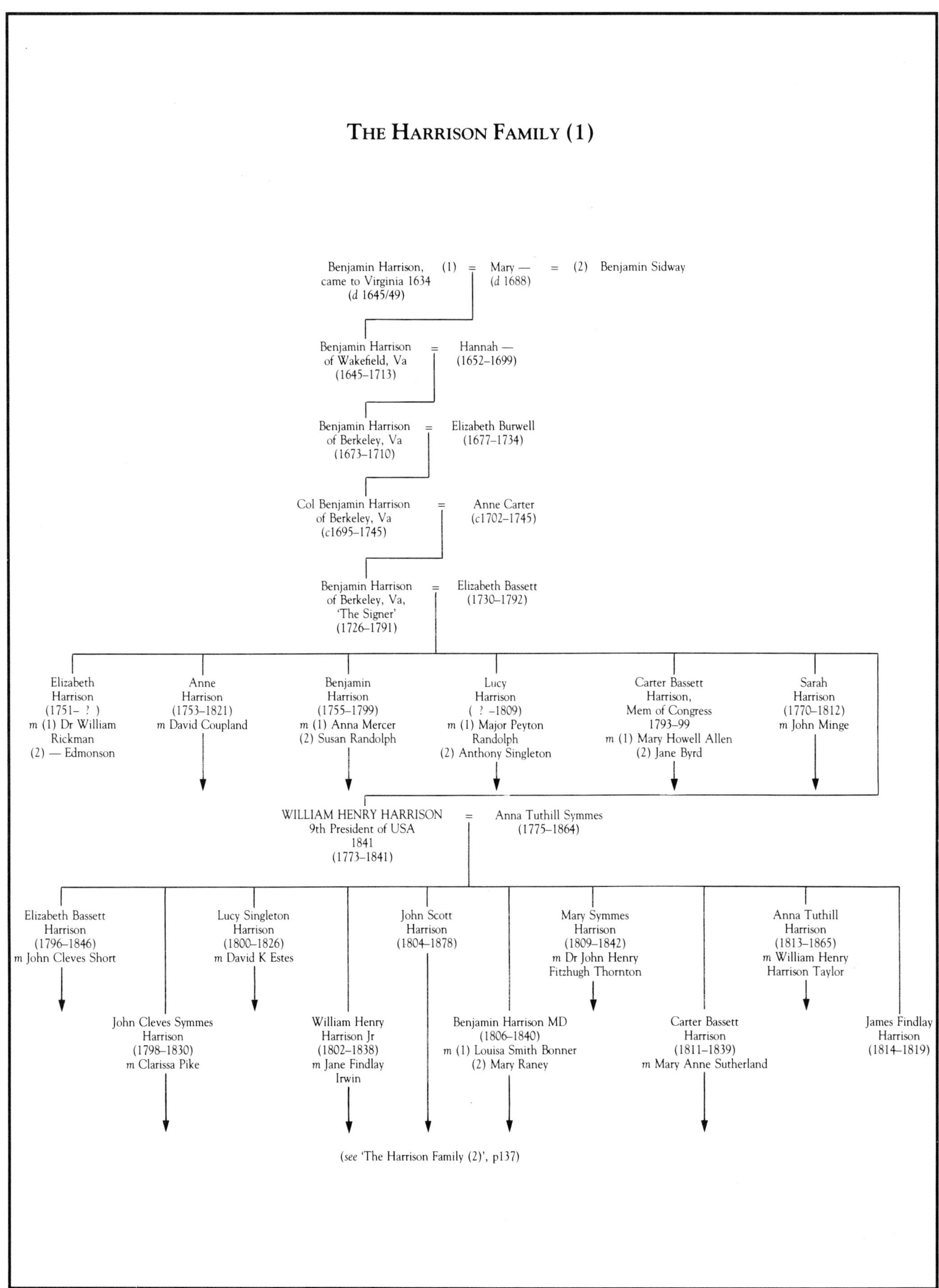
THE HARRISON FAMILY (1)
Benjamin Harrison, came to Virginia 1634 (d 1645/49) (1) = Mary — (d 1688) = (2) Benjamin Sidway
Benjamin Harrison of Wakefield, Va (1645–1713) = Hannah — (1652–1699)
Benjamin Harrison of Berkeley, Va (1673–1710) = Elizabeth Burwell (1677–1734)
Col Benjamin Harrison of Berkeley, Va (c1695–1745) = Anne Carter (c1702–1745)
Benjamin Harrison of Berkeley, Va, 'The Signer' (1726–1791) = Elizabeth Bassett (1730–1792)
Elizabeth Harrison (1751– ?) m (1) Dr William Rickman (2) — Edmonson
Anne Harrison (1753–1821) m David Coupland
Benjamin Harrison (1755–1799) m (1) Anna Mercer (2) Susan Randolph
Lucy Harrison (? –1809) m (1) Major Peyton Randolph (2) Anthony Singleton
Carter Bassett Harrison, Mem of Congress 1793–99 m (1) Mary Howell Allen (2) Jane Byrd
Sarah Harrison (1770–1812) m John Minge
WILLIAM HENRY HARRISON 9th President of USA 1841 (1773–1841) = Anna Tuthill Symmes (1775–1864)
Elizabeth Bassett Harrison (1796–1846) m John Cleves Short
John Cleves Symmes Harrison (1798–1830) m Clarissa Pike
Lucy Singleton Harrison (1800–1826) m David K Estes
William Henry Harrison Jr (1802–1838) m Jane Findlay Irwin
John Scott Harrison (1804–1878)
Benjamin Harrison MD (1806–1840) m (1) Louisa Smith Bonner (2) Mary Raney
Mary Symmes Harrison (1809–1842) m Dr John Henry Fitzhugh Thornton
Carter Bassett Harrison (1811–1839) m Mary Anne Sutherland
Anna Tuthill Harrison (1813–1865) m William Henry Harrison Taylor
James Findlay Harrison (1814–1819)
(see 'The Harrison Family (2)', p137)

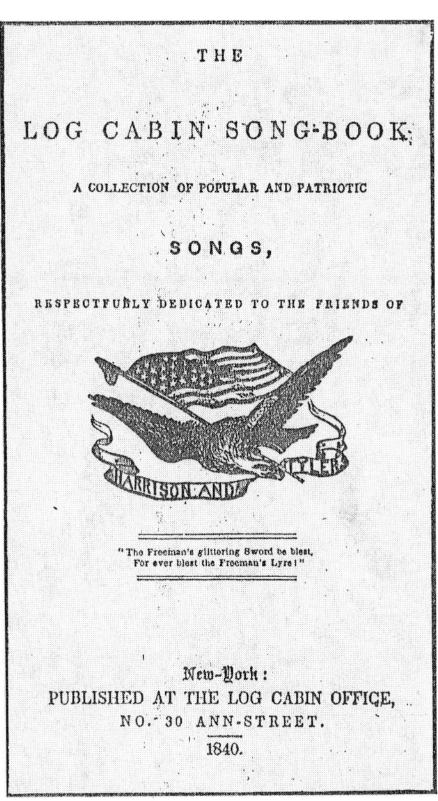

THE

LOG CABIN SONG-BOOK;

A COLLECTION OF POPULAR AND PATRIOTIC

SONGS,

RESPECTFULLY DEDICATED TO THE FRIENDS OF

HARRISON AND TYLER

"The Freeman's glittering Sword be blest,
For ever blest the Freeman's Lyre!"

New-York:
PUBLISHED AT THE LOG CABIN OFFICE,
NO. 30 ANN-STREET.
1840.

The *Log Cabin Song-book* from the William Henry Harrison presidential election campaign

1839 he was nominated for President by the Whig Party National Convention at Harrisburg, Pennsylvania, and in the election of 1840 received 234 of the 294 electoral votes.

William Henry Harrison's inauguration took place on Thursday 4 March 1841 on the East Portico of the Capitol, the oath being administered by Chief Justice Roger Brooke Taney. The President rode to the Capitol on horseback through a driving rainstorm, both hatless and coatless. His inaugural address, 8,441 words of platitudinous sentiment, took an hour and three-quarters to deliver. Later the President attended three inaugural balls. Next day he had a cold which developed into a severe chill, which forced him to take to his bed on 27 March; pneumonia developed and on 4 April, exactly one month after his inauguration, 'Old Tip' lay dead in the White House, the first President to die in office. He lay in state in the White House and was then taken to North Bend for burial in the Harrison Tomb opposite Congress Green Cemetery. His widow, who had been too unwell to come to Washington to attend his inauguration or be at his deathbed, survived him for nearly twenty-three years. She died at the age of eighty-eight in February 1864.

Harrison was a brave soldier and a decent, plain, honest man, unspectacular as a statesman but commanding respect for his integrity. Of his numerous descendants, one grandson, Benjamin, aged seven when his grandfather died, was also to become President of the United States.

JOHN TYLER 1841–1845

Born: Greenway, Charles City County, Virginia, 29 March 1790, 2nd son of John Tyler, of Greenway, sometime Governor of Virginia, and Mary Marot Armistead

Member of House of Representatives: 1816–1821

Governor of Virginia: 1825–1827

Senator: 1827–1836

Elected Vice-President: November 1840

Inaugurated: Washington 4 March 1841

Succeeded as (10th) President: 4 April 1841

Took oath of office: Indian Queen Hotel, Washington DC, 6 April 1841

Retired from presidency: 4 March 1845

Married: (1) Cedar Grove, New Kent County, Virginia, 29 March 1813 Letitia (*b* Cedar Grove 12 November 1790; *d* White House, Washington, 10 September 1842; *bur* Cedar Grove Plantation), 3rd dau of Robert Christian, of Cedar Grove, and Mary Brown

Children:

(1) Mary, *b* Charles City County, Virginia, 15 April 1815; *m* 14 December 1835 Henry Lightfoot Jones of Woodham, Virginia (*b* N Carolina 1813); 3 sons, 1 dau; *d* New Kent County, Virginia, 17 June 1848

(2) Robert, private secretary to his father, later Registrar of Confederate States Treasury and editor of *Montgomery Mail and Advertiser* (Alabama); *b* Charles City County, Virginia, 9 September 1816; *m* Bristol, Pennsylvania, 12 September 1839 (Elizabeth) Priscilla (*b* New York 14 June 1816; *d* Montgomery, Alabama, 29 December 1889), 2nd dau of Thomas Abthorpe Cooper, actor, and his 2nd wife Mary Fairlie; 3 sons, 6 daus; *d* Montgomery, Alabama, 3 December 1877

(3) John, Assistant Secretary of War to the Confederacy; *b* 27 April 1819; *m* 25 October 1838 Martha Rochelle (*b* 23 January 1820; *d* 11 January 1867); 1 son, 2 daus; *d* 1896

(4) Letitia, White House hostess for her father 1844; *b* 11 May 1821; *m* February 1839 James A Semple; no issue; *d* Baltimore 28 December 1907

(5) Elizabeth (Lizzie), *b* 11 July 1823; *m* White House, Washington, 31 January 1842, as his 1st wife, William Nevison Waller, of Williamsburg, Virginia, son of William Waller and Mary Berkely Griffin; 3 sons, 2 daus; *d* 1 June 1850

(6) Ann Contesse, *b* 5 April 1825; *d* in infancy

(7) Alice, *b* 23 March 1827; *m* Charles City County, Virginia, 11 July 1850 Rev Henry Mandeville Denison (*b* Wyoming, Pennsylvania, 1822; *d* 1858); 1 dau; *d* 8 June 1854

(8) Tazewell MD, Surgeon in Confederate States army, *b* 6 December 1830; *m* 1857 (div 1873) Nannie Brydges; 1 son, 1 dau; *d* California 8 January 1874

Married: (2) Church of Ascension, New York, 26 June 1844 Julia (*b* Gardiner's Island, New York, 4 May 1820; *d* Richmond, Virginia, 10 July 1889; *bur* Hollywood Cemetery, Virginia), dau of Senator David Gardiner and Juliana McLachlan

Children:

(1) (David) Gardiner, Congressman 1893–97, Judge of 14th Judicial Circuit of Virginia 1904; *b* East Hampton, New York, 12 July 1846; *m* Richmond, Virginia, 6 June 1894 Mary Morris (*b* Richmond 1 June 1865; *d* Sherwood Forest 30 August 1931), dau of James Alfred Jones and Mary Henry Lyon; 3 sons, 2 daus; *d* Sherwood Forest, Charles City County, Virginia, 1 September 1927

(2) John Alexander, *b* Sherwood Forest, Virginia, 7 April 1848; *m* East Hampton 5 August 1875 Sarah Griswold, dau of Samuel Buell Gardiner; 3 children; *d* Santa Fé 1 September 1883

(3) Julia Gardiner, *b* Sherwood Forest, Virginia, 25 December 1849; *m* New York 26 June 1869 William H Spencer; 1 dau; *d* 8 May 1871

(4) Lachlan MD, *b* Sherwood Forest, Virginia, 2 December 1851; *m* 1876

Georgia Powell; no issue; *d* 1902
(5) Lyon Gardiner LLD, President of William and Mary College 1888–1919, proprietor and editor of *William and Mary College Quarterly Historical Magazine*; *b* Sherwood Forest, Virginia, 24 August 1853; *m* (1) 14 November 1878 Annie Baker (*b* Charlottesville 8 April 1855; *d* Richmond 2 November 1921), dau of Lt-Col St George Tucker and Elizabeth Anderson Gilmer; 1 son, 2 daus; *m* (2) 12 September 1923 Sue (*b* Charles City County, Virginia, 5 May 1889; *d* 2 May 1953), dau of John Ruffin and Jane Cary Harrison; 3 sons; *d* 12 February 1935
(6) Robert FitzWalter, *b* Sherwood Forest, Virginia, 12 March 1856; *m* Fannie Glinn; no issue; *d* 1927
(7) Pearl, *b* Sherwood Forest, Virginia, 13 June 1860; *m* 1894 Major William Mumford Ellis (*b* 1846; *d* 1921); 4 sons, 4 daus; *d* 1947

Died: Richmond, Virginia, 18 January 1862
Buried: Hollywood Cemetery, Virginia

John Tyler, the first Vice-President to succeed to office through the death of a President, might have served as a prototype model for all the 'Southern gentlemen' who have appeared in fictitious multitudes both before and after the publication of *Gone with the Wind*. He was also a truly patriarchal figure, having fifteen children by his two wives. His youngest child, born when he was seventy, was not only forty-five years younger than her eldest halfsister, but also survived her father's birth by 157 years, which must surely constitute a record span for two generations.

Henry Tyler, who settled at Middle Plantation, near Williamsburg, Virginia, is believed to have emigrated from Shropshire, England, about the middle of the seventeenth century. He died in April 1672 and his son Henry served as Justice, Coroner and High Sheriff of York County, Virginia, married a lady of some standing in the colony and died in 1729. His son, John Tyler, was Justice of James City and the first of the family to attend William and Mary College. John's son, another John, was Marshal to the Vice-Admiralty Court of Virginia and married Anne, daughter of Dr Louis Contesse, a Huguenot who emigrated from France to Williamsburg about 1715. Their son, John Tyler, of Greenway, Charles City County, was sometime Speaker of the Virginia House of Burgesses, Judge of the Admiralty Court, Vice-President of Virginia Constitutional Convention, Judge of the General Court (1788–1808), Governor of Virginia (1808–1811) and Judge of the United States District Court of Virginia. He was the father of the future President. President Tyler's mother, Mary Marot Armistead, was the daughter of Robert Booth Armistead, whose ancestor, William Armistead, emigrated from England to Virginia in 1635.

John Tyler, the second son and sixth of his parents' eight children, was born at Greenway, Charles City County on 29 March 1790. His mother died when he was seven and after briefly attending William and Mary College in 1806 he studied law with his father until 1808, when the latter became Governor of Virginia, then under Edmund Randolph, who had been Secretary of State under Washington. Tyler was admitted to the Bar in 1809. At nineteen he was below the required age, but the examining judge neglected to ask how old he was.

A photograph of John Tyler by Brady

In 1811 Tyler was elected a member of the Virginia House of Delegates from Charles City County and was re-elected annually until 1815, when he was elected to the State Council. During this period he married his first wife Letitia Christian, the daughter of a neighbouring planter. She was destined to bear him eight children.

THE TYLER FAMILY

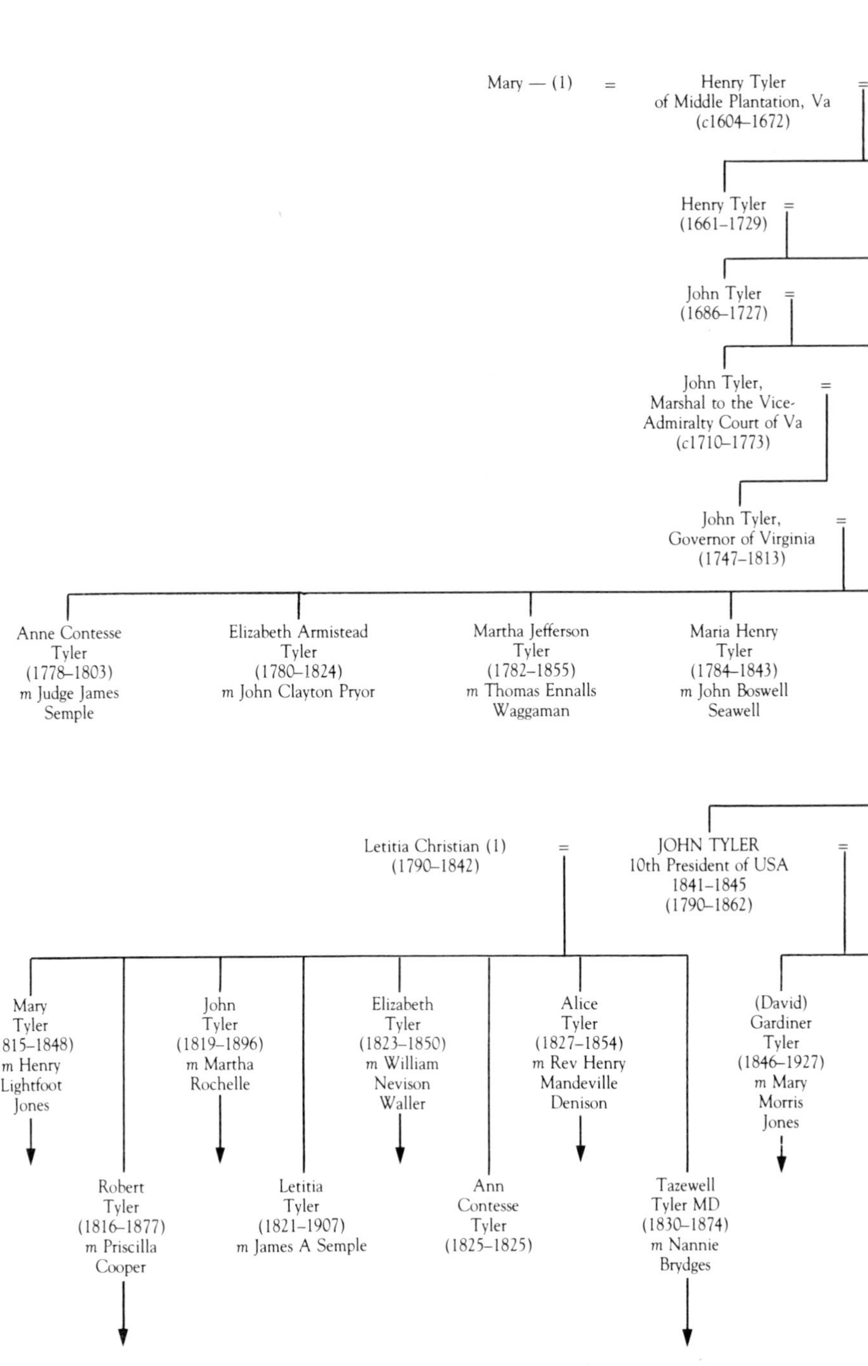

Mary — (1) = Henry Tyler of Middle Plantation, Va (c1604–1672) =
Henry Tyler (1661–1729) =
John Tyler (1686–1727) =
John Tyler, Marshal to the Vice-Admiralty Court of Va (c1710–1773) =
John Tyler, Governor of Virginia (1747–1813) =
Anne Contesse Tyler (1778–1803) m Judge James Semple
Elizabeth Armistead Tyler (1780–1824) m John Clayton Pryor
Martha Jefferson Tyler (1782–1855) m Thomas Ennalls Waggaman
Maria Henry Tyler (1784–1843) m John Boswell Seawell
Letitia Christian (1) (1790–1842) =
JOHN TYLER 10th President of USA 1841–1845 (1790–1862) =
Mary Tyler (1815–1848) m Henry Lightfoot Jones
Robert Tyler (1816–1877) m Priscilla Cooper
John Tyler (1819–1896) m Martha Rochelle
Letitia Tyler (1821–1907) m James A Semple
Elizabeth Tyler (1823–1850) m William Nevison Waller
Ann Contesse Tyler (1825–1825)
Alice Tyler (1827–1854) m Rev Henry Mandeville Denison
Tazewell Tyler MD (1830–1874) m Nannie Brydges
(David) Gardiner Tyler (1846–1927) m Mary Morris Jones

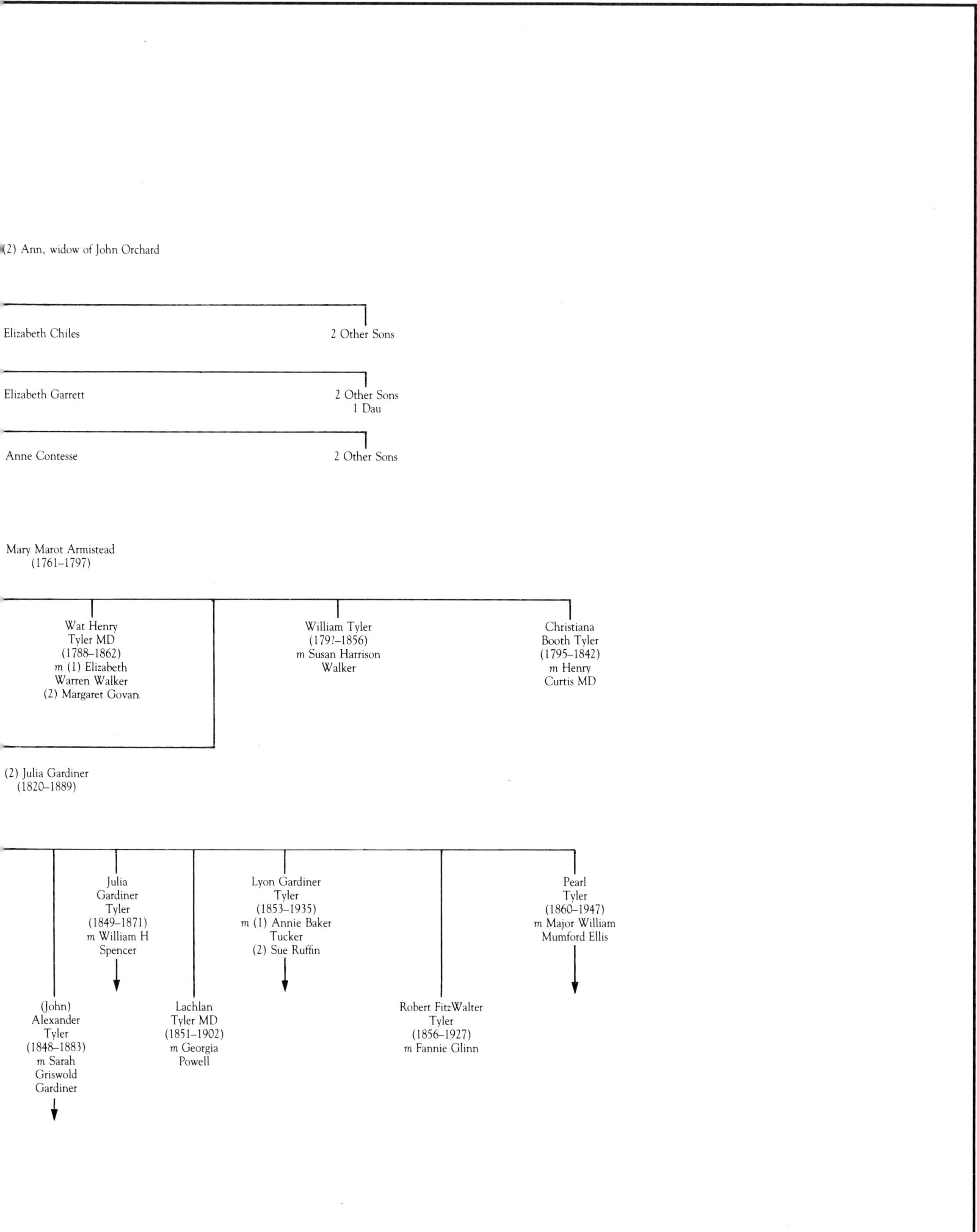
(2) Ann, widow of John Orchard
Elizabeth Chiles
2 Other Sons
Elizabeth Garrett
2 Other Sons
1 Dau
Anne Contesse
2 Other Sons
Mary Marot Armistead
(1761–1797)
Wat Henry
Tyler MD
(1788–1862)
m (1) Elizabeth
Warren Walker
(2) Margaret Govan
William Tyler
(179?–1856)
m Susan Harrison
Walker
Christiana
Booth Tyler
(1795–1842)
m Henry
Curtis MD
(2) Julia Gardiner
(1820–1889)
Julia
Gardiner
Tyler
(1849–1871)
m William H
Spencer
Lyon Gardiner
Tyler
(1853–1935)
m (1) Annie Baker
Tucker
(2) Sue Ruffin
Pearl
Tyler
(1860–1947)
m Major William
Mumford Ellis
(John)
Alexander
Tyler
(1848–1883)
m Sarah
Griswold
Gardiner
Lachlan
Tyler MD
(1851–1902)
m Georgia
Powell
Robert FitzWalter
Tyler
(1856–1927)
m Fannie Glinn

John Tyler's second wife, Julia Gardiner Tyler, striking a winsome pose in this portrait by Anelli

Tyler was elected to fill the unexpired term of John Clapton in the House of Representatives in November 1816 and was subsequently re-elected twice, serving in the 14th, 15th and 16th Congresses. He declined to seek re-election again in 1821 giving failing health as an excuse although he appears to have been perfectly hale and hearty (he was just coming up to thirty-one and was to live for over another forty years). Until 1823, Tyler retired into private life. He re-emerged when he was again elected to the Virginia House of Delegates in December of that year and served until 1825 when he was elected Governor of Virginia. As Governor he delivered an oration at the funeral of Thomas Jefferson in July 1826. He was unanimously re-elected Governor in December 1826, but resigned on 4 March 1827 after being elected Senator. He was re-elected to the Senate in 1833 and was the only Senator to vote against the Jackson bill to enforce the revenue laws by military force, if necessary.

In 1835 Tyler was nominated for Vice-President by the Whigs. He resigned from the Senate on 29 February 1836 after refusing the instructions of the Virginia legislature to vote for Thomas Hart Benton's resolution to expunge the vote of censure on President Jackson. On 1 November 1836, Tyler received forty-seven electoral votes as candidate for Vice-President. No candidate received a majority, the election being decided by the Senate in favour of Richard Mentor Johnson.

Tyler was again elected to the Virginia House of Delegates in 1838 and became Speaker of the House. In February 1839 he was again nominated for the Senate, but a deadlock situation developed after a number of indecisive ballots, and the election was postponed indefinitely. The Whig National Convention at Harrisburg nominated John Tyler for Vice-President on 4 December 1839 and the ensuing campaign was fought on the famous slogan 'Tippecanoe and Tyler Too'. Harrison and Tyler were duly elected President and Vice-President on 3 November 1840 and inaugurated on 4 March 1841. Harrison as we have seen, survived his elevation by exactly one month and a hitherto unprecedented situation arose. The Constitution provided that in the event of a president's 'Death, Resignation, or Inability to discharge the Powers and Duties of the said Office, the same shall devolve on the Vice-President'. John Quincy Adams interpreted this as meaning that the Vice-President merely became acting President, but Tyler received the backing of Secretary of State Daniel Webster and the members of the cabinet in his claim to be regarded as Tyler's successor in the presidency. The oath of office was administered by William Cranch, Chief Justice of the US Circuit Court of the District of Columbia, at the Indian Queen Hotel, Washington, on Tuesday 6 April 1841, two days after Harrison's death.

The first act Tyler signed as President was the grant of a pension of $25,000 dollars to Mrs Harrison, the first granted to a President's widow. His high-handed vetoing of a number of important bills soon alienated Tyler's Whig supporters so that he was formally expelled from the Whig party and earned himself the nickname of 'Old Veto'. There were demands for his resignation and threats of impeachment, but he tenaciously clung to office and weathered all storms.

Mrs Tyler died at the White House in September 1842, two months short of her fifty-second birthday. Tyler remained a widower for nearly two years and then made an equally happy second marriage to a lady thirty years his junior who was to bring him another seven children. In May 1844 Tyler was nominated for President by the Tyler Democrats at Baltimore, but he withdrew his candidature in August. After attending the inauguration of his successor President Polk on 4 March 1845, Tyler left Washington and travelled by coach to Richmond, Virginia, where he transferred to riverboat to complete the journey to Sherwood Forest, a 1,200 acre plantation which he had purchased during his presidency. The property is still in the possession of the family.

The rest of Tyler's life was spent at Sherwood Forest raising his second family. In 1859 he was appointed Chancellor of William and Mary College, an office which had been vacant since Washington's death. The war between the States was now approaching fast. On 4 February 1861, Tyler, now over seventy, was elected Chairman of the Peace Convention in Washington. At the end of the month he recommended the secession of Virginia from the Union and made a speech to that effect from the steps of the Exchange Hotel in Richmond. The following day he took his seat in the Virginia Convention on Policy and on 5 May was elected a member of the Provisional Congress of the Confederacy. Towards the end of the year he was elected to the permanent Congress of the Confederacy, but before he could take his seat he fell ill with a bilious fever and died at Richmond on 18 January 1862, aged seventy-one. He was buried at Hollywood Cemetery, Virginia, where his second wife joined him twenty-seven years later.

Tyler was ever affable and courteous, but his high-handed conduct as President cost him much sympathy and support, as we have seen. As the first President not actually elected to that office he probably felt a subconscious need to justify himself as more than a stopgap. He was the last Virginian to serve as President.

James Knox Polk 1845–1849

Born:	Mecklenburg County, North Carolina, 2 November 1795, eldest son of Samuel Polk and Jane Knox	Retired from presidency:	4 March 1849
Member of House of Representatives:	1825–1839	Married:	Murfreesboro, Rutherford County, Tennessee, 1 January 1824 Sarah (*b* near Murfreesboro 4 September 1803; *d* Nashville, Tennessee, 14 August 1891; *bur* Nashville), dau of Joel Childress, merchant and farmer, and Elizabeth Whitsitt
Speaker of the House:	1835–1839		
Governor of Tennessee:	1839–1841	Children:	None
Elected (11th) President:	12 November 1844	Died:	Nashville, Tennessee, 15 June 1849
Inaugurated:	East Portico of Capitol 4 March 1845	Buried:	Nashville

Certainly one of the dullest Presidents and now almost forgotten is James Knox Polk. His family, of Scottish origin, haled from Renfrewshire, and most probably descended from Sir John Pollok, who was killed at the battle of Lecherbie in 1593. His son, Robert, received a grant of lands in Coleraine, Co Derry, Ireland, and was the father of another Robert, a covenanter, who died about 1640. Robert Pollok, or Polke, who served as a Captain in Colonel Porter's regiment against King Charles and later emigrated to Maryland, was probably son of the last-named Robert. In 1687, he was granted land by Lord Baltimore which became known as Polke's Lott or Polke's Folly. His son William continued living in Maryland and was the father of another William who moved first to Pennsylvania and then to North Carolina, where he died about 1753. One of his sons, Colonel Ezekiel Polk, served in the Revolutionary War and later acquired land in Tennessee Territory, North Carolina. He died in 1824 leaving a son, Samuel, the father of the future President. Samuel's wife Jane was the daughter of Captain James Knox, of Iredell County, North Carolina, who also served in the Revolutionary War.

James Knox Polk, their eldest child, was born in Mecklenburg County, North Carolina on 2 November 1795. When he was eleven the family moved to Duck River Valley (now Maury County), Tennessee, and in January 1816 he entered the University of North Carolina, from which he graduated with first class honours in mathematics and classics in June 1818. He then studied in the law office of Felix Grundy at Nashville and was appointed Clerk of the Tennessee Senate in September 1819. In June 1820 he was admitted to the Tennessee Bar at Columbia, and in 1823 was elected a member of the State House of Representatives. On 1 January 1824, Polk married Sarah Childress, a grim-visaged lady who was to ban alcohol, dancing and card-playing from the White House during her tenure as First Lady. She probably disapproved of sex as well as there were no children of the marriage.

Polk was elected a member of the House of Representatives in 1825, taking his seat in December that year. He served until March 1839, being elected Speaker in 1835 and again in 1837. Having put himself forward as a candidate for the governorship of Tennessee in December 1838, Polk resigned from the House of

James Knox Polk from a portrait by G P A Healy

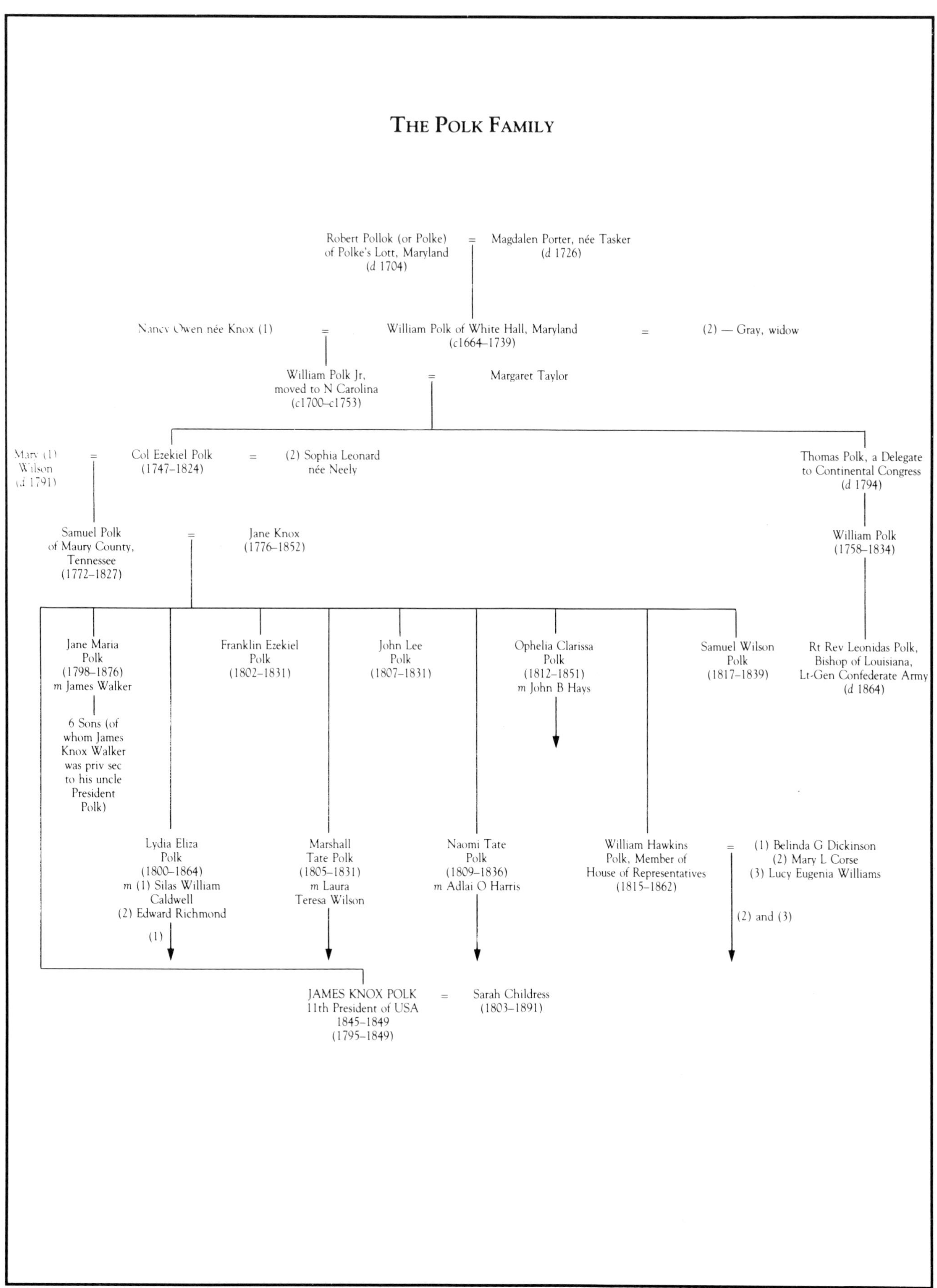
THE POLK FAMILY
Robert Pollok (or Polke) of Polke's Lott, Maryland (d 1704)
=
Magdalen Porter, née Tasker (d 1726)
Nancy Owen née Knox (1)
=
William Polk of White Hall, Maryland (c1664–1739)
=
(2) — Gray, widow
William Polk Jr, moved to N Carolina (c1700–c1753)
=
Margaret Taylor
Mary (1) Wilson (d 1791)
=
Col Ezekiel Polk (1747–1824)
=
(2) Sophia Leonard née Neely
Thomas Polk, a Delegate to Continental Congress (d 1794)
Samuel Polk of Maury County, Tennessee (1772–1827)
=
Jane Knox (1776–1852)
William Polk (1758–1834)
Jane Maria Polk (1798–1876) m James Walker
6 Sons (of whom James Knox Walker was priv sec to his uncle President Polk)
Franklin Ezekiel Polk (1802–1831)
John Lee Polk (1807–1831)
Ophelia Clarissa Polk (1812–1851) m John B Hays
Samuel Wilson Polk (1817–1839)
Rt Rev Leonidas Polk, Bishop of Louisiana, Lt-Gen Confederate Army (d 1864)
Lydia Eliza Polk (1800–1864) m (1) Silas William Caldwell (2) Edward Richmond
(1)
Marshall Tate Polk (1805–1831) m Laura Teresa Wilson
Naomi Tate Polk (1809–1836) m Adlai O Harris
William Hawkins Polk, Member of House of Representatives (1815–1862)
=
(1) Belinda G Dickinson (2) Mary L Corse (3) Lucy Eugenia Williams
(2) and (3)
JAMES KNOX POLK 11th President of USA 1845–1849 (1795–1849)
=
Sarah Childress (1803–1891)

An interesting photograph of Mrs James Knox Polk in her widow's weeds and accompanied by a lady described as her adopted daughter

Representatives to begin his campaign. He was duly elected on 1 August and inaugurated on 14 October 1839. The following year he was nominated for Vice-President by the Tennessee legislature but only received one electoral vote. He was unsuccessful, too, in seeking re-election as Governor in 1841 and 1843.

The Democratic National Convention, meeting at Baltimore, nominated Polk for President in May 1844. He had always been a strong partisan of Andrew Jackson – to such an extent that he was often referred to as 'Young Hickory' – and Jackson now gave his backing to the campaign. Election day fell on 12 November 1844 and Polk received 170 of the 275 electoral votes. He was inaugurated on the East Portico of the Capitol on Thursday 4 March 1845, the oath being administered by Chief Justice Roger Brooke Taney, officiating for the third time. Polk had announced that he intended to serve one term only and not seek re-election. He was what would now be termed a 'workaholic' and remained at his desk in the White House for ten or twelve hours at a stretch, working throughout the stifling humidity of Washington summers. He only spent six weeks away from Washington in the whole of his term of office. His wife complained that it was extremely difficult to get him to come out even for a drive.

Polk retired from office on 4 March 1849 and attended the inauguration of his successor, Zachary Taylor, the next day. On 4 May he left Washington to travel to his new home, Polk Place, a property in Nashville which he had bought from the executors of his old law teacher Senator Felix Grundy. His journey took him first down the Atlantic coast and across the Gulf of Mexico. He then boarded a Mississippi steamer to complete the journey. He was exhausted by numerous dinners, parades and other festivities held in his honour *en route* and became seriously ill with a severe attack of the chronic diarrhoea to which he had long been subject. A doctor, who was brought on board to attend him, diagnosed a mild case of cholera, but was probably wrong.

Polk rallied enough to visit his aged mother at her house in Columbia and then moved into his new residence in Nashville, where he at once began a scheme of reconstruction. His malady returned, however, and, weakened and dehydrated, he died on 15 June 1849, aged fifty-three. A week before his death he was baptized by a Methodist Minister. Mrs Polk survived until August 1891. No President, before or since, has survived his term of office by such a short period.

A second cousin of President Polk, the Right Reverend Leonidas Polk, Bishop of Louisiana, was to emulate the warrior bishops of the middle ages by becoming a Lieutenant-General in the Confederate army and being shot and killed while reconnoitring on Pine Mountain, Georgia, in June 1864.

ZACHARY TAYLOR 1849–1850

Born:	Montebello, Orange County, Virginia, 24 November 1784, 3rd son of Richard Taylor and Sarah Dabney Strother
Brevet Brigadier-General:	1823
Elected (12th) President:	7 November 1848
Inaugurated:	East Portico of Capitol 5 March 1849
Married:	Jefferson County, Kentucky, 21 June 1810 Margaret Mackall (*b* Calvert County, Maryland, 21 September 1788; *d* East Pascagoula, Mississippi, 14 August 1852; *bur* Zachary Taylor National Cemetery, Jefferson County, Kentucky), dau of Walter Smith and Ann Mackall
Children:	(1) Ann Margaret Mackall, *b* Jefferson County, Kentucky, 9 April 1811; *m* Fort Crawford, Prairie du Chien, Michigan Territory (now Wisconsin), 20 September 1829 Robert Crooke Wood MD, Acting Surgeon-General of the Union army during the Civil War (*b* Rhode Island 23 September 1801; *d* 28 March 1869); 2 sons, 2 daus; *d* Freiburg, Germany, 2 December 1875 (2) Sarah Knox, *b* Vincennes, Indiana, 6 March 1814; *m* Louisville, Kentucky, 17 June 1835 as his first wife Jefferson Finis Davis, later President of the Confederate States of America (*b* Fairview, Kentucky, 3 June 1808; *d* New Orleans 6 December 1889), son of Samuel Emory Davis and Jane Cook; no children; *d* Locust Grove, Louisiana, 15 September 1835 (3) Octavia Pannill Taylor, *b* Jefferson County, Kentucky, 16 August 1816; *d* Bayou Sara, Louisiana, 8 July 1820 (4) Margaret Smith Taylor, *b* Jefferson County, Kentucky, 27 July 1819; *d* Bayou Sara, Louisiana, 22 October 1820 (5) Mary Elizabeth Taylor, *b* Jefferson County, Kentucky, 20 April 1824; *m* (1) 5 December 1848 Lt-Col William Smith Bliss, Adjutant-General to his father-in-law, President Taylor (*b* 17 August 1815; *d* 4 August 1853), son of Capt John Bliss, US army, and Olive Hall Simonds; no children; *m* (2) 11 February 1858 as his 2nd wife Philip Pendleton Dandridge, son of Adam Stephen Dandridge and Sarah Pendleton; no children; *d* Winchester, Virginia 25 July 1909 (6) Richard Taylor, Lt-Gen in the Confederate army; *b* near Louisville 27 January 1826; *m* 10 February 1851 Louise Marie Myrthé (*b* Hermitage Plantation, St James Parish, Louisiana, 18—; *d* 1875), dau of Michel Doradon Bringier and Aglaé du Bourg de St Colombe; 2 sons, 3 daus; *d* New York 12 April 1879
Died in office:	The White House 9 July 1850
Buried:	Zachary Taylor National Cemetery, Jefferson County, Kentucky

Zachary Taylor is remembered for his deeds as a soldier, which rendered him a national hero, rather than for being the twelfth President, an office which he held for one year and 126 days only.

Zachary Taylor's great-great-grandfather, James Taylor, is believed to have emigrated from Carlisle, England, about 1635 and settled in Tidewater County (later Caroline County), Virginia, acquiring large estates on the Mattaponi river. He died in 1698 and his son, Colonel James Taylor, served as a member of the Virginia House of Burgesses and Surveyor-General of the Colony. He was the great-grandfather of two Presidents, James Madison (*qv*) and Zachary Taylor. Colonel James Taylor's second son, Zachary, was the father of Richard Taylor, who fought in the Revolutionary War and was later a collector of internal revenues at Louisville, Kentucky. The future President was his third son and was born in the proverbial log cabin at Montebello, Orange County, Virginia, on 24 November 1784. Before he was a year old the family moved to Beargrass Creek, near Louisville, Kentucky.

Very little is known of Zachary Taylor's early life before he was commissioned as 1st Lieutenant in the Seventh Infantry Regiment of the United States army on 3 May 1808 in his twenty-fourth year. Two years later he married Margaret Mackall Smith, daughter of Walter Smith, a rich planter who had served in the Revolutionary War, and a descendant of Richard Smith, sometime Attorney-General of Maryland. In November 1810, Taylor was promoted to Captain and the following July was given the task of reorganizing the garrison at Fort Knox, Vincennes, Indian Territory, which had become demoralized after a personal feud had led to the shooting of an officer by the commandant.

Taylor served in the War of 1812 and repulsed an Indian attack on Fort Harrison, above Vincennes, in

The Taylor Family

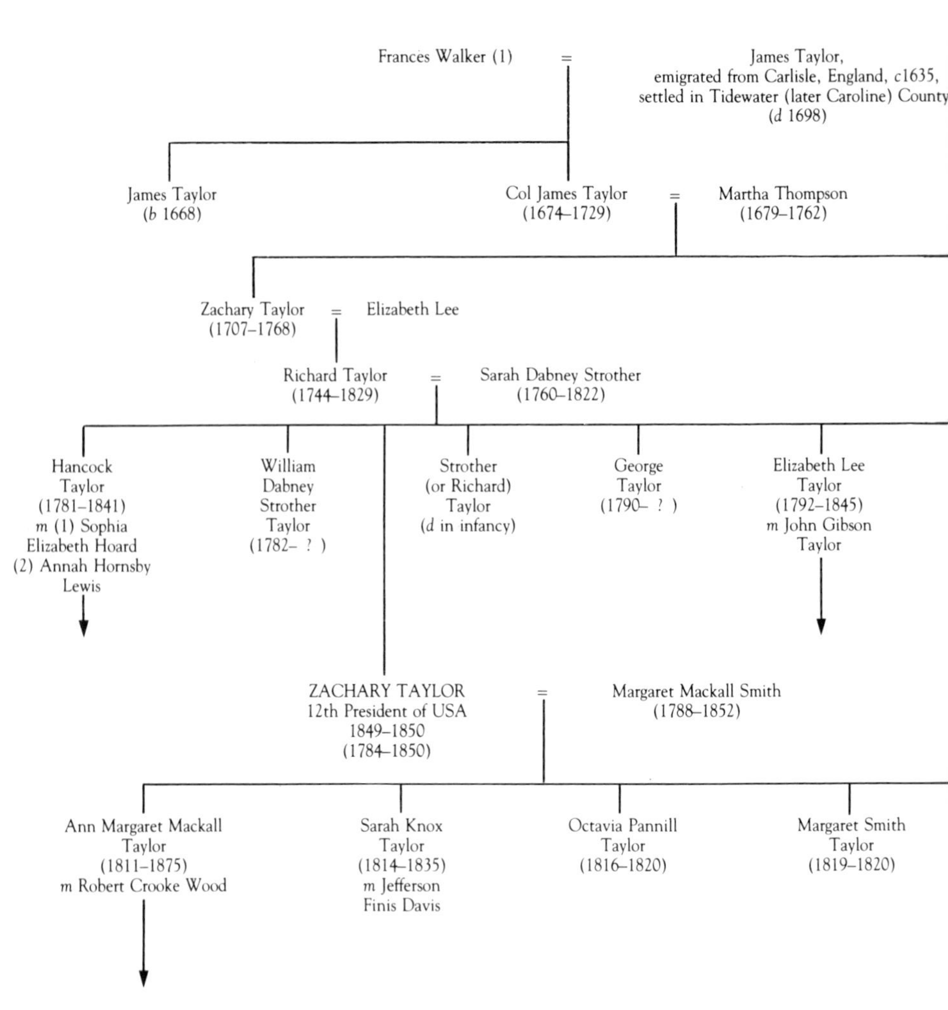

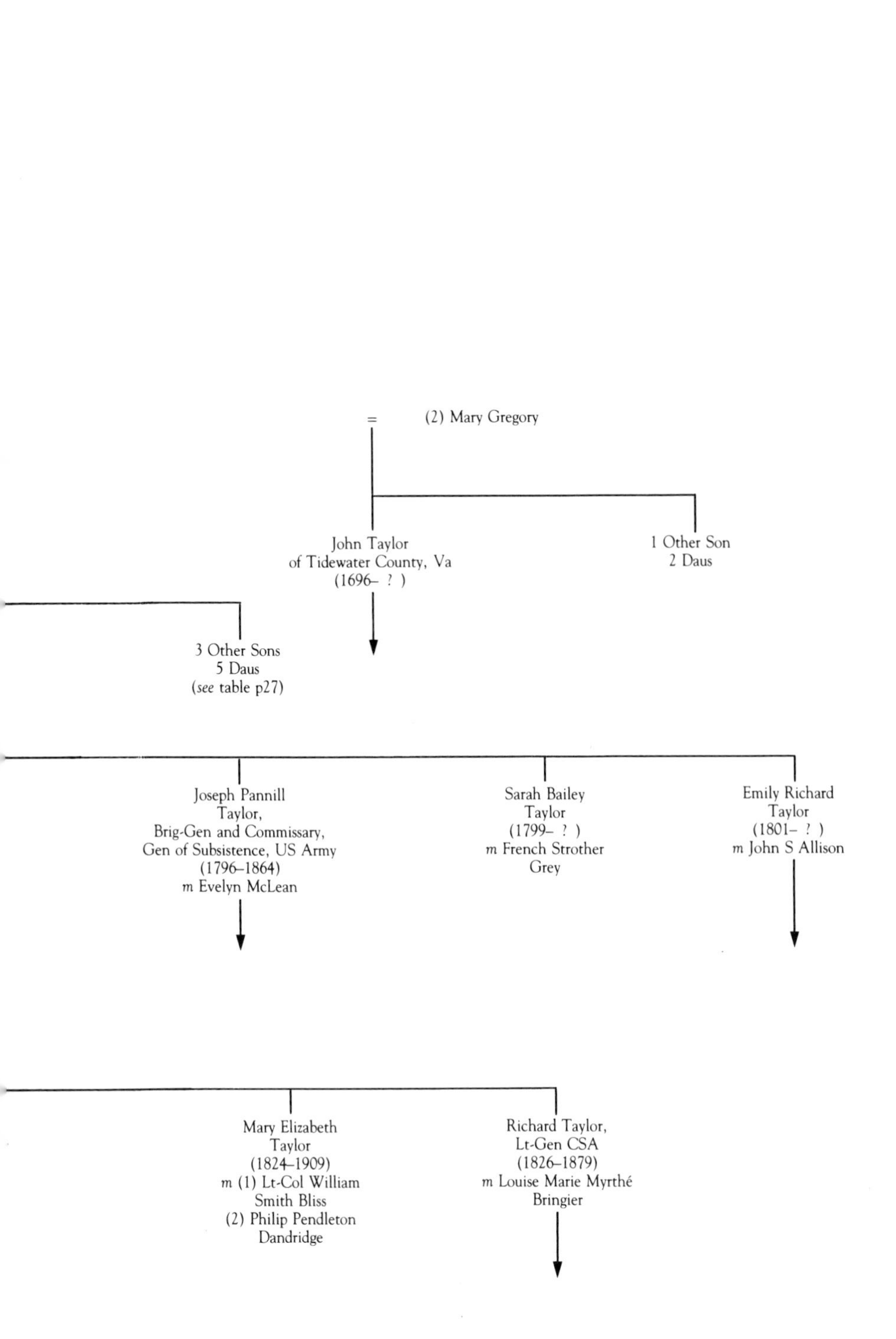
= (2) Mary Gregory
John Taylor
of Tidewater County, Va
(1696– ?)
1 Other Son
2 Daus
3 Other Sons
5 Daus
(*see* table p27)
Joseph Pannill
Taylor,
Brig-Gen and Commissary,
Gen of Subsistence, US Army
(1796–1864)
m Evelyn McLean
Sarah Bailey
Taylor
(1799– ?)
m French Strother
Grey
Emily Richard
Taylor
(1801– ?)
m John S Allison
Mary Elizabeth
Taylor
(1824–1909)
m (1) Lt-Col William
Smith Bliss
(2) Philip Pendleton
Dandridge
Richard Taylor,
Lt-Gen CSA
(1826–1879)
m Louise Marie Myrthé
Bringier

Zachary Taylor as a general, during the Mexican War

September 1812, being promoted to Brevet Major in recognition a month later, the first brevet rank ever awarded by the United States army. Between 1812 and 1815 he took part in a series of frontier campaigns against the British and the Indians, from Indiana to Missouri. In January 1815 he was notified of his promotion to Major as from 5 May 1814, but on the army being reduced to 10,000 men by an act of Congress on 3 March 1815, when Taylor was reduced to Captain, he resigned his commission and returned to Kentucky. He was recommissioned as Major on 17 May 1816 and stationed at Fort Howard, then under construction at Green Bay, Michigan Territory (now Wisconsin). He remained there until the late summer of 1818 when he returned to Louisville to supervise the recruiting service for the next year. He was promoted Lieutenant-Colonel in April 1819.

In February 1829, before joining his regiment in Mississippi, Taylor settled his family at Bayou Sara, Louisiana. It proved an unhealthy spot as several members of the family were stricken with swamp fever in the ensuing summer and Taylor's two youngest daughters died. In the course of the next few years, Taylor held various commands, purchased a 300-acre plantation in Feliciana Parish, Louisiana, and 137 acres in Wilkinson County, Mississippi. He was promoted Colonel in April 1832, a month before the outbreak of the Black Hawk War in which he served under General Henry Atkinson, until after the decisive battle of the Bad Axe (3 August), when he assumed command of Fort Crawford and received Chief Black Hawk as a prisoner. Taylor remained in command there until November 1836. In June 1835 he and his wife opposed the marriage of their second daughter, Sarah Knox Taylor, to Jefferson Finis Davis, who had served on Taylor's staff as a Lieutenant. The marriage took place but did not last long as Sarah died of malaria less than three months later. Jefferson Davis was later to become President of the Confederacy.

In November 1836, Taylor assumed command of Jefferson Barracks, Missouri, but he was recalled to Fort Crawford for a month from May to June 1837 because of Indian scares, which came to nothing. In November 1837 the Second Seminole War brought about his transfer to Florida and on Christmas Day he defeated the Seminoles near Lake Okeechobee, a deed for which he was promoted Brevet Brigadier-General. On 15 May 1838, Taylor was appointed Commanding Officer of all Florida Forces, a command which he held until May 1839, when he resigned and made a tour of the eastern United States until November. In 1841 he assumed command of the second department of the western division of the army at Fort Smith, Arkansas.

Taylor had purchased a further 163 acres in Louisiana in 1838 and in December 1841 he sold all his Mississippi and Louisiana holdings, using the sum realized to purchase Cypress Grove plantation in Jefferson County, Louisiana, the following April. In June 1844, Taylor assumed command of the first department of the western division of the army at Fort Jesup, Louisiana. War with Mexico becoming imminent, in July 1845 Taylor was ordered by President Polk to occupy a point 'on or near the Rio Grande' from which to defend Texas. The following January he was ordered to cross the Rio Grande at his own discretion having regard to the weather and the locality. He led his 3,000 men out of Corpus Christi on 8 March and on two successive days (8 and 9 May) defeated the Mexicans in pitched battles at Palo Alto and Resaca de la Palma.

War was officially declared on 13 May 1846 and a month later Taylor was promoted Major-General (having been promoted Brevet Major-General immediately after the two battles). The battle of Monterey was fought from 21 to 24 September 1846, ending with the surrender of the Mexican General Pedro de Ampudia on condition that he and his forces might be permitted to retreat with their arms and not be pursued for a period of eight weeks. Taylor's acquiescence to this request, vitually a two-month armistice, was severely criticized in Washington and in November Polk ordered General Winfield Scott to proceed to Mexico and Taylor to turn over four-fifths of his men and material of war to Scott.

Scott was ordered to push on to Vera Cruz and Mexico City, while Taylor with his remaining force was to stay on the defensive. Taylor defended his position regarding the armistice in a letter to General Edmund P Gaines which was published in the New York *Morning Express* on 22 January 1847.

On 23 February 1847, Taylor ignored his orders to stay on the defensive and took up a position at Buena Vista where he was attacked by 20,000 Mexicans led by General Antonio Lopez de Santa Anna. Taylor had only 5,000 men, but the superiority of his artillery won the battle and the Mexicans broke ranks and fled after suffering heavy casualties. Taylor became a national hero overnight and after relinquishing his command of the United States forces in northern Mexico in December 1847 received a tumultuous welcome when he arrived in New Orleans.

The Whig National Convention at Philadelphia nominated Taylor for President in June 1848 and in the election he received 163 of the 290 electoral votes, his main rival, Lewis Cass of Michigan, receiving 127 and Martin Van Buren none. General Zachary Taylor was inaugurated as twelfth President on Monday 5 March 1849, with Chief Justice Roger Brooke Taney administering the oath for the fourth time. Taylor's nickname of 'Old Rough and Ready' aptly describes him. He was a small, bandy-legged man and, even in his soldiering days, preferred wearing civilian clothes topped by a battered straw hat. On 4 July 1850 he attended a celebration ceremony in Washington and, feeling overcome by the heat, injudiciously partook of some cold meat, iced water and milk, which brought on a severe attack of gastro-enteritis, leading in turn to a coronary thrombosis from which he died five days later on 9 July 1850, aged sixty-five. He was the second President to die in office.

Millard Fillmore 1850–1853

Born:	Locke (now Summerhill), Cayuga County, New York, 7 January 1800, eldest son of Nathaniel Fillmore and his 1st wife Phoebe Millard
Member of House of Representatives:	1833–1842
Comptroller of New York State:	1848–1849
Elected Vice-President:	7 November 1848
Inaugurated:	5 March 1849
Succeeded as (13th) President:	9 July 1850
Took oath:	Hall of Representatives 10 July 1850
Retired from the presidency:	4 March 1853
Married:	(1) Moravia, New York, 5 February 1826 Abigail (*b* Stillwater, Saratoga County, New York, 17 March 1798; *d* Willard Hotel, Washington DC, 30 March 1853; *bur* Forest Lawn Cemetery, Buffalo), yr dau of Rev Lemuel Powers, Baptist Minister, and Abigail Newland
Children:	(1) Millard Powers, *b* East Aurora, New York, 23 April 1828; *d* Buffalo 15 November 1889 (2) Mary Abigail, *b* Buffalo 27 March 1832; *d* Aurora, New York 26 July 1854
Married:	(2) Albany, New York, 10 February 1858 Caroline (*b* Morristown, New Jersey, 21 October 1813; *d* Buffalo 11 August 1881; *bur* Forest Lawn Cemetery, Buffalo), widow of Ezekiel C McIntosh of Albany, New York, and dau of Charles Carmichael and Temperance Blackley
Died:	Buffalo 8 March 1874
Buried:	Forest Lawn Cemetery, Buffalo

Millard Fillmore, the second Vice-President to succeed to the presidency through the death of the incumbent, was a nonentity who today ranks among the forgotten Presidents.

Precisely when the Fillmore family arrived in the American colonies from England has not been established. The future President's great-great-grandfather, John Fillmore, of Ipswich, Massachusetts, was a mariner and died at sea on his homeward passage from Martinique in about 1711. His elder son, also John, was a sea captain and later settled in Norwich, Connecticut, where he published a work with the lengthy title *A Narrative of John Fillmore on Board the Noted Pirate Vessel Commanded by Captain John Phillips*. He married three times and had a large family, dying at Norwich on 22 February 1777. John's eldest son by his second wife, Nathaniel Fillmore, settled at Bennington, Vermont and served in the Revolutionary War. His second son, also named Nathaniel, farmed at sundry places in New York State and was a civil magistrate. His first wife, Phoebe, was the daughter of Dr Abiathar Millard, of Bennington, Vermont, and Millard, the eldest of their six sons, was born in a log cabin at Locks (now Summrhill) in Cayuga County, New York, on 7 January 1800.

Fillmore's early education was rudimentary and at the age of fourteen he was apprenticed to a wool carder and cloth dresser. After completing the first term of his apprenticeship he walked a hundred miles home to spend Christmas with his family. In 1818 he spent a year

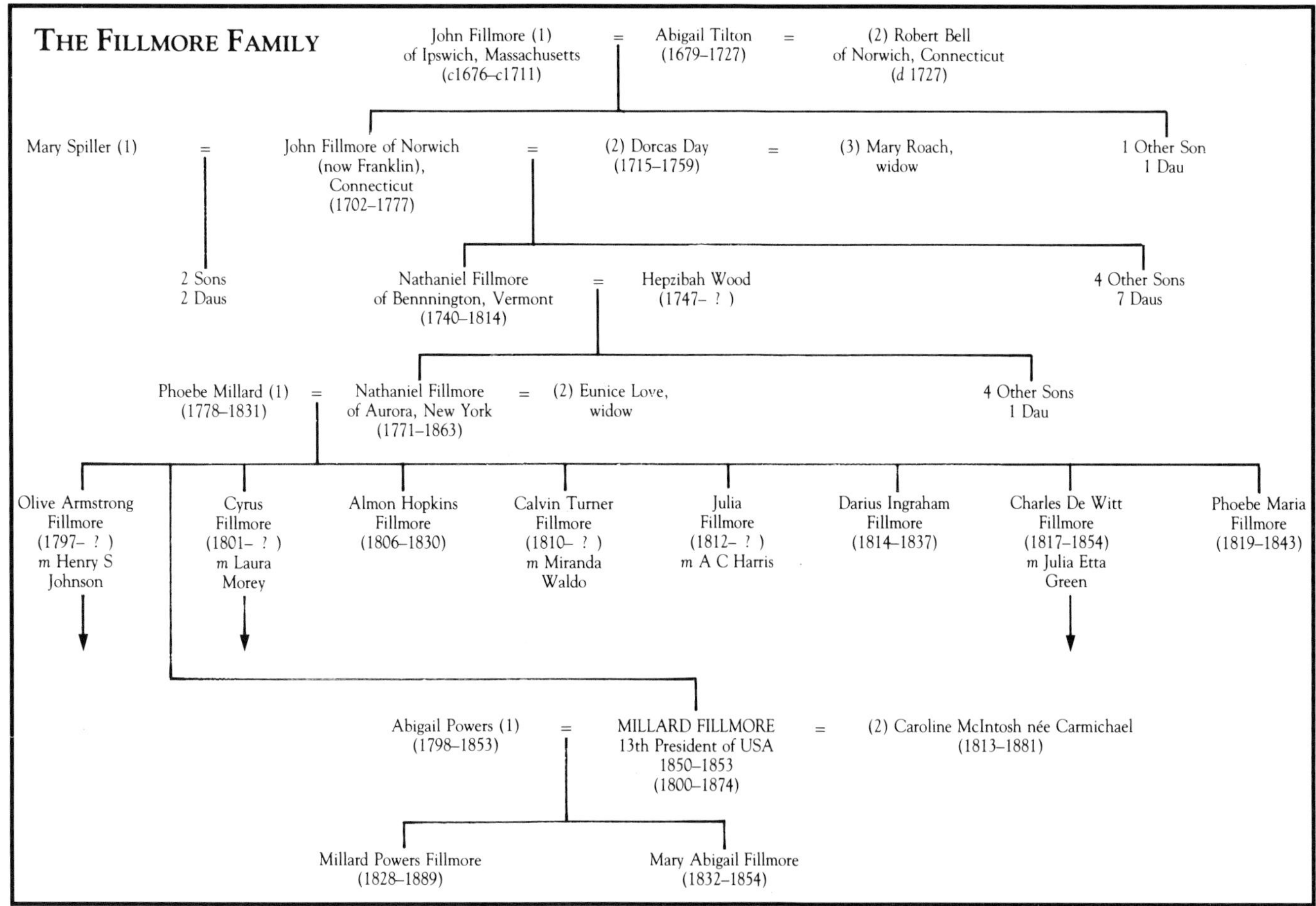

as a schoolmaster at Scott, New York, and in 1819 began to study law at Montville and Moravia, New York. The Fillmore family moved to Aurora (later East Aurora), Erie County, New York, in 1821 and the following year Millard read law in Buffalo, New York. He was admitted to the New York Bar in 1823 and began to practise law in Aurora. On 5 February 1826 he was married at Moravia, New York, to Abigail, the younger daughter of the Rev Lemuel Powers, a Baptist Minister, and in the following year was admitted as an attorney of New York Supreme Court. In 1828 he was elected as an Anti-Mason to represent Erie County in the New York State Assembly and served for three consecutive one-year terms. During this period he moved to Buffalo and drafted a bill to abolish imprisonment for debt which was passed in 1831.

Fillmore was elected a member of the House of Representatives in 1832, taking his seat on 2 December 1833. He joined the Whig party in 1834 and the following year retired from active politics and resumed his law practice. He was re-elected to the House of Representatives in 1836, 1838 and 1840 and served as chairman of the ways and means committee from 1841 to 1843. Fillmore was unsuccessful in seeking nomination for the vice-presidency at the Whig National Convention at Baltimore in 1844, but was later nominated for the governorship of New York, in which he was defeated by Silas Wright. Having been elected Comptroller of New York State in 1847 (taking office 1 January 1848), he won the nomination for Vice-President at the Whig National Convention at Philadelphia in 1848 and was duly elected on 7 November, being inaugurated on 5 March 1849.

The sudden death of Zachary Taylor in July 1850 brought Millard Fillmore to the presidency and he took the oath, administered by William Cranch, Chief Justice of the United States Circuit Court of the District of Columbia.

Fillmore looked like a respectable gentleman's outfitter, bland and affable. An entirely colourless personality, he neither aroused great fervour nor incurred any strong feeling against him. The only memorable events during his term of office were the admission of California as the thirty-first State, the passing of the Fugitive Slave Act (known as the Compromise of 1850), the abolition of the slave trade in the District of Columbia, and the appointment of the Mormon leader Brigham Young as Governor of Utah Territory.

OPPOSITE Millard Fillmore in a daguerreotype taken between 1850 and 1855 by J H White Curst

In 1852 Fillmore was unsuccessful in seeking renomination for the presidency. He retired from office on 4 March 1853, attending the inauguration of his successor Franklin Pierce the same day. The sickly Mrs Fillmore, who had allowed her daughter to act as White House hostess on her behalf but had nevertheless been instrumental in founding the White House library, having been horrified to find no books in the place when her husband first took office, caught cold at Pierce's inauguration and died at the Willard Hotel, Washington, on 30 March 1853. Fillmore returned to his home in Buffalo and in the spring of 1854 spent nearly three months touring the southern states and later, accompanied by his son, the midwest. His only daughter, Mary Abigail, died in July 1854. The summer of 1855 saw Fillmore embarking on an extensive visit to Europe, where he was received by Pope Pius IX. While in Rome he learnt that he had been nominated for President by the American (Know Nothing) National Convention at Philadelphia. He wrote a letter of acceptance from Paris and returned to New York City in June 1856. His nomination was endorsed by the Whig National Convention at Baltimore and in the ensuing election he received eight electoral votes, all from Maryland.

On 10 February 1858, Fillmore married again. His bride, Mrs Caroline Carmichael McIntosh, was a childless widow of suitable age. The extended honeymoon was spent in Europe, where the winter of 1858/59 was spent mostly in Paris and Madrid. The rest of Fillmore's life was passed in Buffalo, where he lived quietly making occasional public appearances and no utterances of any great import. He died of general debility on 8 March 1874, aged seventy-four. His widow survived until August 1881, and his only son, Millard Powers Fillmore, who never married, until November 1889.

FRANKLIN PIERCE 1853–1857

Born:	Hillsborough (now Hillsboro), New Hampshire, 23 November 1804, 4th son of General Benjamin Pierce and his 2nd wife Anna Kendrick
Member of House of Representatives:	1833–1836
Senator:	1837–1842
Elected (14th) President:	2 November 1852
Inaugurated:	East Portico of Capitol 4 March 1853
Retired from presidency:	4 March 1857
Married:	Amherst, New Hampshire, 19 November 1834 Jane Means (*b* Hampton, New Hampshire, 12 March 1806; *d* Andover, Massachusetts, 2 December 1863; *bur* Concord, New Hampshire), dau of Rev Jesse Appleton and Elizabeth Means
Children:	(1) Franklin, *b* Hillsborough, New Hampshire, 2 February 1836; *d* 5 February 1836 (2) Frank Robert, *b* Concord, New Hampshire, 27 August 1839; *d* Concord 14 November 1843 (3) Benjamin, *b* Concord, New Hampshire, 13 April 1841; *k* in a railway accident near Andover, Massachusetts, 6 January 1853
Died:	Concord, New Hampshire, 8 October 1869
Buried:	Concord, New Hampshire

It is generally conceded that Franklin Pierce was the most inept of the Presidents who preceded the Civil War, if not the most inept to date (he certainly has some close contenders). In view of the fact that in modern parlance he 'had everything going for him', this can be regarded as something of a tragedy.

The founder of the family in America was Thomas Pierce, who emigrated from England to Charlestown, Massachusetts, in 1633/4. His descendants played little part in local or state affairs until General Benjamin Pierce, the father of the future President. The General served in the Revolutionary War, was a member of New Hampshire legislature from 1789 to 1801, Governor of New Hampshire from 1827 to 1830, and Vice-President of the Massachusetts Society of the Cincinnati. He married twice. His first wife, Elizabeth Andrews, died in childbirth in 1788, leaving one daughter. In February 1790 he married Anna, daughter of Benjamin Kendrick, and they had five sons and another three daughters. Franklin Pierce, the fourth son, was born in a log cabin (the fourth President to be so) at Hillsborough (now shortened to Hillsboro), New Hampshire, on 23 November 1804.

Pierce received his early education at Hancock Academy and Francestown Academy and in October 1820 entered Bowdoin College, Brunswick, Maine, from which he graduated in 1824 with an AB degree. For the next two years he studied law and was admitted to the New Hampshire Bar in September 1827. He began his law practice in an office built for him by his father, who also stood half the cost of his law library. In 1829 Pierce was elected to represent Hillsborough in the State legislature, where he took his seat in June, having been appointed a Justice of the Peace for Hillsborough in

Franklin Pierce, a likeable but superficial man

May. He was re-elected to the State legislature three times and on the last two occasions was also elected Speaker of the House.

Pierce was elected to the House of Representatives in 1833 and took his seat on 2 December. On 19 November 1834 he married Miss Jane Means Appleton, whose father, the Rev Jesse Appleton, a Congregational Minister, was President of Pierce's old Alma Mater, Bowdoin College. She had some interesting family connections, one second cousin being married to the poet Longfellow and another to Jerome Napoleon Bonaparte. Mrs Pierce was a sickly, nerve-prone woman, and her condition was

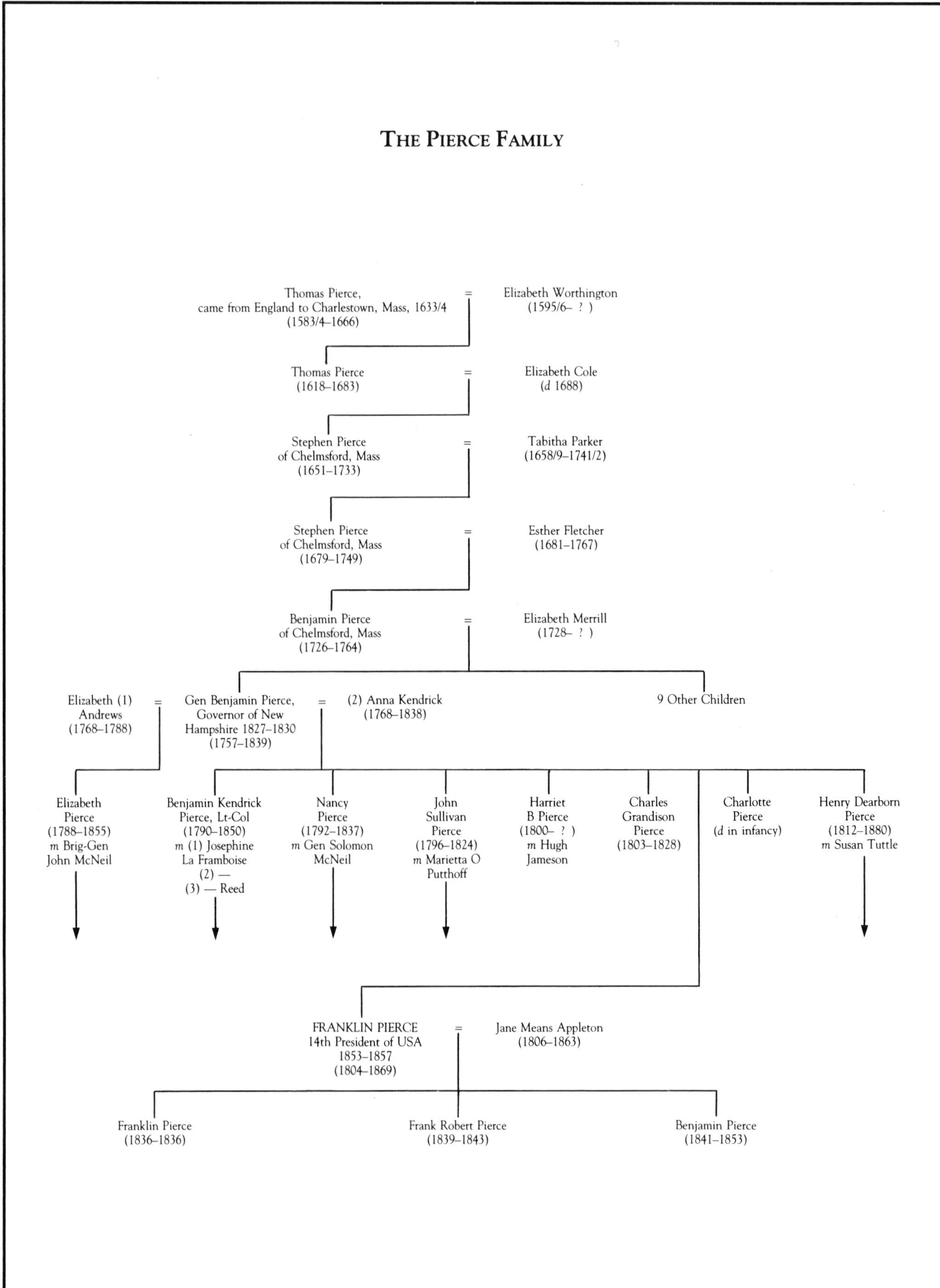
THE PIERCE FAMILY
Thomas Pierce, came from England to Charlestown, Mass, 1633/4 (1583/4–1666) = Elizabeth Worthington (1595/6– ?)
Thomas Pierce (1618–1683) = Elizabeth Cole (d 1688)
Stephen Pierce of Chelmsford, Mass (1651–1733) = Tabitha Parker (1658/9–1741/2)
Stephen Pierce of Chelmsford, Mass (1679–1749) = Esther Fletcher (1681–1767)
Benjamin Pierce of Chelmsford, Mass (1726–1764) = Elizabeth Merrill (1728– ?)
Elizabeth (1) Andrews (1768–1788) = Gen Benjamin Pierce, Governor of New Hampshire 1827–1830 (1757–1839) = (2) Anna Kendrick (1768–1838)
9 Other Children
Elizabeth Pierce (1788–1855) m Brig-Gen John McNeil
Benjamin Kendrick Pierce, Lt-Col (1790–1850) m (1) Josephine La Framboise (2) — (3) — Reed
Nancy Pierce (1792–1837) m Gen Solomon McNeil
John Sullivan Pierce (1796–1824) m Marietta O Putthoff
Harriet B Pierce (1800– ?) m Hugh Jameson
Charles Grandison Pierce (1803–1828)
Charlotte Pierce (d in infancy)
Henry Dearborn Pierce (1812–1880) m Susan Tuttle
FRANKLIN PIERCE 14th President of USA 1853–1857 (1804–1869) = Jane Means Appleton (1806–1863)
Franklin Pierce (1836–1836)
Frank Robert Pierce (1839–1843)
Benjamin Pierce (1841–1853)

Mrs Franklin Pierce, who never ceased to grieve over the deaths of her three sons and wore perpetual mourning, had some surprising family connections, as can be seen by reference to the genealogical tables

worsened by her tragic maternity record. Her first son died after three days; the second died of typhus at the age of four; and the third and last, Bennie, was killed when the train in which he and his parents (who escaped without injury) were travelling was derailed near Andover, Massachusetts, in January 1853, just two months before his father was due to be inaugurated. Mrs Pierce never recovered from the blow and was unable to take her place as First Lady throughout her husband's tenure of office, her aunt Mrs Abby Kent Means deputizing for her.

Pierce was re-elected to the House of Representatives in 1835 and in 1836 was elected to the Senate, taking his seat on 4 March 1837, when he was the youngest member. In August 1838 the Pierces moved to Concord, New Hampshire. Pierce resigned from the Senate in February 1842 and resumed his law practice in Concord. President Polk appointed him US District Attorney for New Hampshire in 1844 and the following year Pierce declined appointment to the Senate and the Democratic nomination for Governor of New Hampshire.

A new phase of Pierce's career began in May 1846, when, enthused by the declaration of war against Mexico, he enlisted as a private soldier with the Concord Volunteers. He declined the offer of a cabinet post in September that year and in February 1847 was commissioned as Colonel of Infantry in the US army, being advanced to Brigadier-General a month later. In May he sailed for Mexico from Newport, Rhode Island, with three companies of the Ninth Regiment under his command, and landed at Veracruz on 27 June. It took him nearly a month to find mules to transport him and his men to join General Scott, which they eventually did on 6 August. The advance on Mexico City began four days later and Pierce saw active service in the battles of Contreras and Churubusco. He served on the armistice commission at the end of August but missed the battle of Chapultepec and the capture of Mexico City as he was in the throes of a bad attack of dysentery, known locally as 'Montezuma's revenge'. He entered Mexico City on 14 September and remained there until 9 December, when he left for home, sailing from Veracruz on 28 December. On his return to Concord, Pierce received a hero's welcome and was presented with a ceremonial sword by the State legislature in January 1848. He resumed his law practice and later in the year again declined the Democratic nomination for Governor. In 1850 he was elected President of the State Constitutional Convention and supported the Compromise of 1850.

On 4 June 1852 the Democratic National Convention at Baltimore nominated Pierce for President and

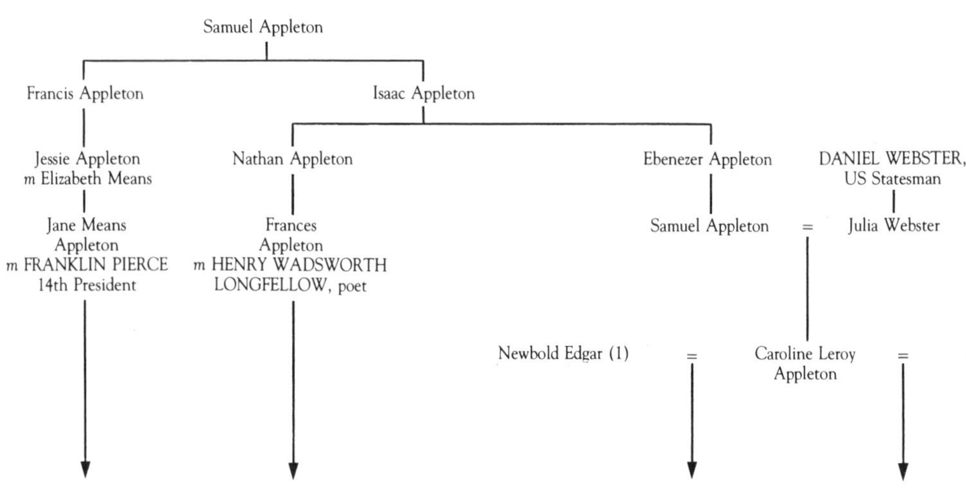

when the election took place he gained 254 of the 296 electoral votes. His inauguration as 14th President took place on Friday 4 March 1853, the oath again being administered by Chief Justice Roger Brooke Taney, acting in that capacity for the fifth time. Pierce chose to affirm rather than to swear and impressed the assembled company by delivering his address without any reference to notes or a prepared script, unlike all his predecessors.

Although good-looking, well-educated and likeable, Pierce was extremely superficial and appears to have held no very strong opinions on any subject. Throughout his presidency he was the object of a virulent denigrating campaign conducted by the Whigs with such success that his erstwhile popularity fell away from him. His well-meaning attempts to maintain a balance between the northern and southern (slave-owning) States came to naught. He exercised his right to veto nine times, only to have five overridden by Congress.

Pierce retired from the presidency a sadly disillusioned man and after attending the inauguration of his successor spent two months as a guest of his former Secretary of State, William Learned Marcy. He and Mrs Pierce spent the summer of 1857 travelling through New England and the winter in Madeira. An eighteen-month tour of Europe followed, in the course of which the Pierces visited Portugal, Spain, France, Switzerland, Italy,

A portrait of Franklin Pierce

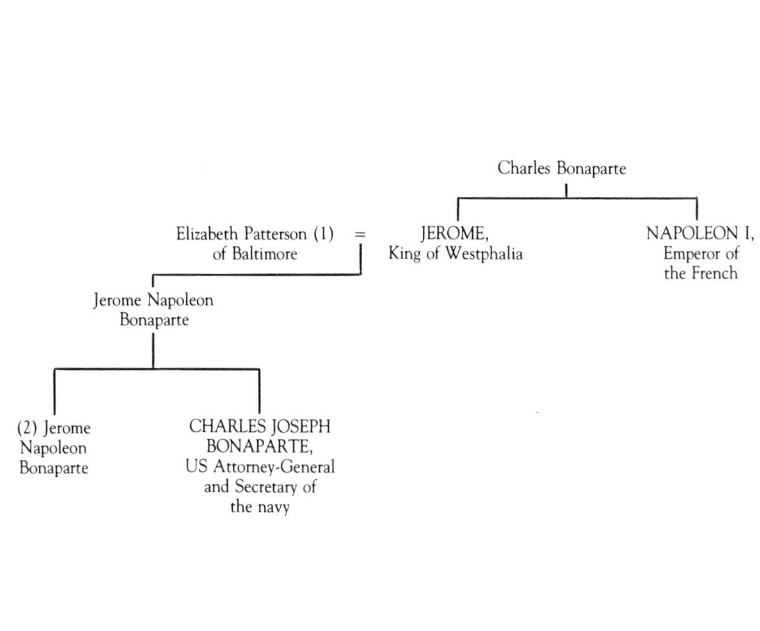

Austria, Germany, Belgium and England. The winter of 1860–61 was spent in Nassau, Bahamas. On 16 April 1861, Pierce suggested a meeting of the five living former Presidents in an attempt to avert the Civil War, but nothing came of his idea.

Pierce was opposed to Lincoln's war policies, which added to his general unpopularity, although he urged the people to support the government against the Confederacy.

Mrs Pierce died in December 1863, still mourning the loss of her son Bennie. After her death Pierce became an alcoholic for a time but managed to overcome it and in 1865 joined the Episcopal Church. He suffered a severe illness in 1868, but recovered and made his last public appearance and speech at the annual meeting of the Society of the Cincinnati in Baltimore later that year. He fell ill again in 1869 and his malady appears to have been a recurrence of 'Montezuma's revenge', with which he had been afflicted in Mexico over twenty years before. He died at his house in Concord on 8 October 1869 at the age of sixty-four.

JAMES BUCHANAN 1857–1861

Born:	Stony Batter, near Mercersburg, Pennsylvania, 23 April 1791, eldest son of James Buchanan and Elizabeth Speer	Minister to Great Britain:	1853–1856
Member of House of Representatives:	1821–1831	Elected (15th) President:	4 November 1856
Minister to Russia:	1831–1833	Inaugurated:	East Portico of Capitol 4 March 1857
Senator:	1834–1845	Retired from presidency:	4 March 1861
Secretary of State:	1845–1848	Died:	Wheatland, Lancaster, Pennsylvania, 1 June 1868
		Buried:	Lancaster, Pennsylvania

James Buchanan, to date America's only bachelor President, was unfortunate in being the last President of what might be termed the *ancien régime*, before the Civil War completely swept away the old order and the proud boast set out so magniloquently in the Declaration of Independence 'that all men are created equal' became a reality at last.

Although James Buchanan's ancestry cannot be proved with any certainty beyond his grandfather, it has been claimed that he descended from Sir Walter Buchanan of that Ilk, living in 1398, whose second wife, Isobel, was a great-granddaughter of Robert II, King of Scots. Sir Walter's descendants by his unknown first wife emigrated to Ireland in the seventeenth century and in the eighteenth century persons of the name are found at Ramelton in County Donegal. John Buchanan of Ramelton married Jane Russell and had a son, James, born about 1761, who went to Pennsylvania in 1783, where he carried on the occupations of merchant and farmer. In April 1788 he married Elizabeth, daughter of James Speer, and had eleven children, of whom the future President was the eldest son and second child.

James Buchanan, the fifth President to be born in a log cabin, first saw the light of day at Stony Batter, near Mercersburg, Pennsylvania, on 23 April 1791. His birthplace was to have an adventurous history. In 1850 it was moved (either on rollers or log by log) to Fayette Street, Mercersburg, where it became a weaver's shop. A group of businessmen bought it in 1925 and moved it again to Chambersburg, where it became first a gift shop and then headquarters of the local Democratic party. Finally, in 1953 it was returned to Mercersburg through the beneficence of Dr Charles S Tippetts and installed on the parking circle of Mercersburg Academy, where it is open to public view by appointment.

The Buchanans moved to Mercersburg when James was five years old and he attended local schools and Old Stone Academy there before entering Dickinson College, Carlisle, Pennsylvania, in September 1807. In 1808 he was expelled for disorderly conduct, but after Dr John King, the Minister of Mercersburg Presbyterian Church and president of the college's board of trustees, interceded on his behalf, he was reinstated on undertaking to behave himself in future. He graduated in September 1809 with a Bachelor of Arts degree and in December began reading law under James Hopkins, of Lancaster, Pennsylvania. He was admitted to the Pennsylvania Bar in November 1812 and the following March was appointed Assistant Prosecutor of Lebanon

A photograph of James Buchanan

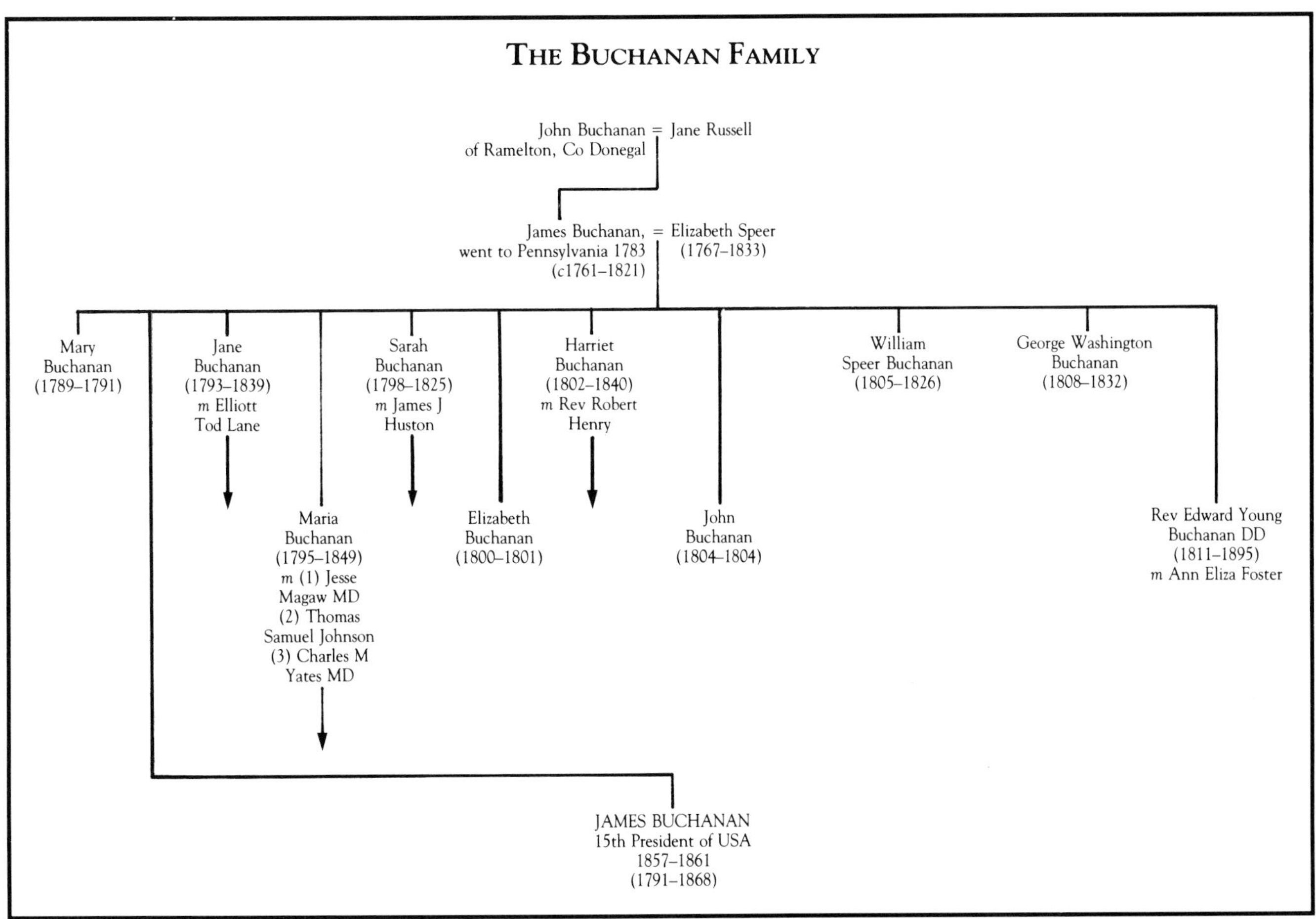

County, Pennsylvania. In October 1814 Buchanan was elected to the State assembly, in which he served two terms.

In the summer of 1819 Buchanan became engaged to Ann Caroline Coleman, but early in December she abruptly broke the engagement, presumably after a quarrel, and went to visit her sister Margaret in Philadelphia, where she died suddenly on 9 December. Buchanan wrote to her father, Robert Coleman, a millionaire, asking permission to attend her funeral as a mourner, but his letter was returned unopened, furthering the suspicion that the unfortunate girl had committed suicide for a love which she had found unrequited. There was never any suggestion of another romance in Buchanan's life, which remained free from involvement in sexual scandal of any sort, so it seems reasonable to conclude that he was cold and undersexed by nature.

Buchanan was nominated by the Federalists for the House of Representatives in August 1820 and was duly elected in October, taking his seat on 3 December 1821. He was re-elected four times. In 1831 Jackson appointed him Minister to Russia and he sailed for Europe in April 1832, arriving at St Petersburg in June. After successfully concluding a treaty of commerce with Russia in December 1832, Buchanan started for home in August 1833, visiting Paris and London *en route* and arriving back in the States in November.

On 6 December 1834, Buchanan was elected Senator by the Pennsylvania legislature. He was twice re-elected and remained in the Senate until appointed Secretary of State by President Polk in 1845. He negotiated the Oregon Treaty with Great Britain in 1846 and in 1848 made his first unsuccessful attempt to obtain the Democratic nomination for President. He was unsuccessful again in 1852 and in April 1853 was appointed Minister to Great Britain by President Pierce, arriving in London in August. In October 1854, Buchanan conferred at Ostend, Belgium, with the US Ministers to France and Spain and together they framed the Ostend Manifesto recommending the purchase or annexation of Cuba, a recommendation which was rejected by Pierce but served to increase Buchanan's standing with the southern Democrats, who had long been clamouring for the annexation as providing additional slave territory. Buchanan returned home in April 1856 and in June was nominated for President at the Democratic National Convention in Cincinnati. At the election he gained 174 of the 296 electoral votes, his opponents John Charles Fremont and ex-President Millard Fillmore gaining 114 and 8 respectively.

Buchanan was inaugurated as fifteenth President on Wednesday 4 March 1857, the oath being administered by Chief Justice Roger Brooke Taney, officiating for the sixth time. Since Buchanan was a bachelor, the duties of White House hostess were undertaken by his charming niece, Harriet Rebecca Lane, who later founded the Choir School of Washington Cathedral, and the Harriet Lane Home for Invalid Children in Baltimore, married a banker and died in 1906. Throughout his presidency Buchanan strove hard to maintain the balance between north and south without favouring either side. As a northerner his sympathies were probably really with the abolitionists, but he realized that slavery was guaranteed by the constitution and that a compromise was necessary.

Buchanan did not seek re-election for a second term, having stated in his inaugural speech that in his opinion Presidents should restrict themselves to one term only. He retired from office on 4 March 1861 and after attending the inauguration of Lincoln returned to Wheatland, the house in Lancaster, Pennsylvania, which he had purchased in 1848 for $6,750 and which is now maintained as a National Historic Landmark open to the public. He spent his retirement quietly, gathering notes for an autobiography which never materialized. His only book, *Mr Buchanan's Administration on the Eve of the Rebellion* was published in New York in 1866.

Buchanan died at his home of rheumatic gout on 1 June 1868, aged seventy-seven.

ABRAHAM LINCOLN 1861–1865

Born:	Sinking Spring Farm, near Hodgenville, Hardin County (now Larue County), Kentucky, 12 February 1809, son of Thomas Lincoln and Nancy Hanks
Member of House of Representatives:	1847–1849
Elected (16th) President:	6 November 1860
Inaugurated:	East Portico of Capitol 4 March 1861
Elected for 2nd term:	8 November 1864
Inaugurated:	East Portico of Capitol 4 March 1865
Married:	Springfield, Illinois, 4 November 1842 Mary Ann (*b* Lexington, Kentucky, 13 December 1818; *d* Springfield, Illinois, 16 July 1882; *bur* Springfield), dau of Robert Smith Todd and Ann Eliza Parker
Children:	(1) Robert Todd, Secretary of War under Presidents Garfield and Arthur 1881–85; Minister to Great Britain 1889–92, *b* Springfield, Illinois, 1 August 1843; *m* 24 September 1868 Mary Eunice (*b* 25 September 1846; *d* 31 March 1937), dau of Senator James Harlan of Iowa, sometime Secretary of the Interior, and Ann Eliza Peck; 1 son; 2 daus; *d* Manchester, Vermont, 25 July 1926 (2) Edward Baker, *b* Springfield, Illinois, 10 March 1846; *d* Springfield 1 February 1850 (3) William Wallace, *b* Springfield, Illinois, 21 December 1850; *d* the White House, Washington DC, 20 February 1862 (4) Thomas (Tad), *b* Springfield, Illinois, 4 April 1853; *d* Chicago 15 July 1871
Died:	William Petersen House, Washington DC, 15 April 1865 (having been shot by an assassin at Ford's Theater, Washington, the previous night)
Buried:	Springfield, Illinois

Most of Lincoln's biographers to date have done such a hagiographical job that it is only recently that some picture of the true man is emerging. Certainly an unbiased person, judging him from his appearance in the innumerable photographs, portraits and statues which exist, would hardly feel inspired by the dour, almost satanic countenance which stares out without a glimmer of humanity or compassion discernible in the features. The mephistophelean appearance is often enhanced by the tall, stovepipe hat, in the lining of which, we are told, Lincoln kept a writing pad and pencil with which to make notes and jot down odd thoughts as they came to him, his pockets, where one would naturally expect to find these things, being crammed full of his wife's spare pairs of gloves, which her fetish for absolute spotlessness obliged her to change several times daily.

The dour-looking Abraham Lincoln

The Lincolns came from Norfolk, England, where a Sir Thomas Lincoln occurs as a benefactor of the church in Norwich in 1298. Abraham Lincoln's line can be traced back to Robert Lincoln of Hingham, Norfolk, who died in 1543, and was the great-great-grandfather of Samuel Lincoln, a mariner, who went to Salem, Massachusetts, in 1635 and later settled in Hingham (named after his birthplace), where he became a proprietor in 1649. Fifth in descent from Samuel was Thomas Lincoln, a farmer and carpenter, who was born in Virginia and spent most of his adult years in Kentucky, Indiana, and finally Illinois. He married first,

ABOVE The log cabin of Sinking Spring Farm at Big South Fork, Nolin's Creek, near Hodgenville, where Lincoln was born

RIGHT Mary Todd Lincoln

in June 1806, Nancy Hanks, whose parentage has long been the subject of controversy, but who is now believed to have been the daughter of one Thomas Hanks and his wife Mary Berry. Thomas and Nancy had three children, of whom Abraham was the second. He was born at Sinking Spring Farm, near Hodgenville in Hardin County (now Larue County), Kentucky, on 12 February 1809. His birthplace, the traditional log cabin, was later enclosed in a marble memorial building and has become a National Historic Site open to the public.

In the spring of 1811 the family moved to Knob Creek, Kentucky, where Lincoln received some elementary schooling, and in December 1816 they moved to Spencer County, Indiana, where Mrs Lincoln died in October 1818. In December 1819 Thomas Lincoln married again. His new wife was a widow with three children of similar age to the Lincoln children. She proved herself a kind stepmother and the ten-year-old Abraham soon became very fond of her. It was through her encouragement that he attended classes held by itinerant schoolmasters and gained a smattering of formal education.

Throughout 1826, Lincoln worked on James Taylor's ferry crossing the Anderson River, for a wage of thirty-seven cents a day. In 1828 he built his own boat and took a cargo of produce to New Orleans, where he sold the produce and the boat and returned home in style by steamboat. The Lincolns moved to Illinois in March 1830 and settled first near Decatur on the Sangamon River. A year later they moved to Coles County, Illinois, but Abraham decided to stay behind and made another trip to New Orleans with his stepbrother John Johnston and cousin John Hanks. In September 1831 he moved to New Salem, where he found employment as a clerk in a general store at a wage of $15 a month plus a room.

In the ensuing winter, Lincoln decided to run for the State legislature. In April, however, he volunteered for military service on the outbreak of the Black Hawk War and served until he was mustered out in July. He was defeated as a candidate for the State legislature in August and, after buying a half-interest in a general store which did not prosper, was appointed Postmaster of New Salem in May 1833, a position which he retained until 1836. He was successful in his next bid to enter the State legislature in 1834 and in the same year began to study law. Lincoln was re-elected to the State legislature in 1836 and also licensed to practice law that year. In 1837 he moved from New Salem to Springfield, which became the capital of Illinois in July 1839.

He was re-elected to the State legislature again in 1838 and 1840 and in the latter year became engaged to Mary Ann Todd, the daughter of a banker. They planned to marry on New Year's Day 1841, but the engagement was broken off before that date, and Lincoln was ill for three weeks, supposedly from depression caused by the broken engagement. Eventually the couple came together again and married on 4 November 1842. Mary was plump, pretty and pretentious and the couple were to have a stormy married life thanks to their incompatibilities.

Lincoln was nominated for the House of Representatives at the Whig State Convention in Petersburg, Illinois, in May 1846 and was duly elected, taking his seat in December 1847. He retired from the House in

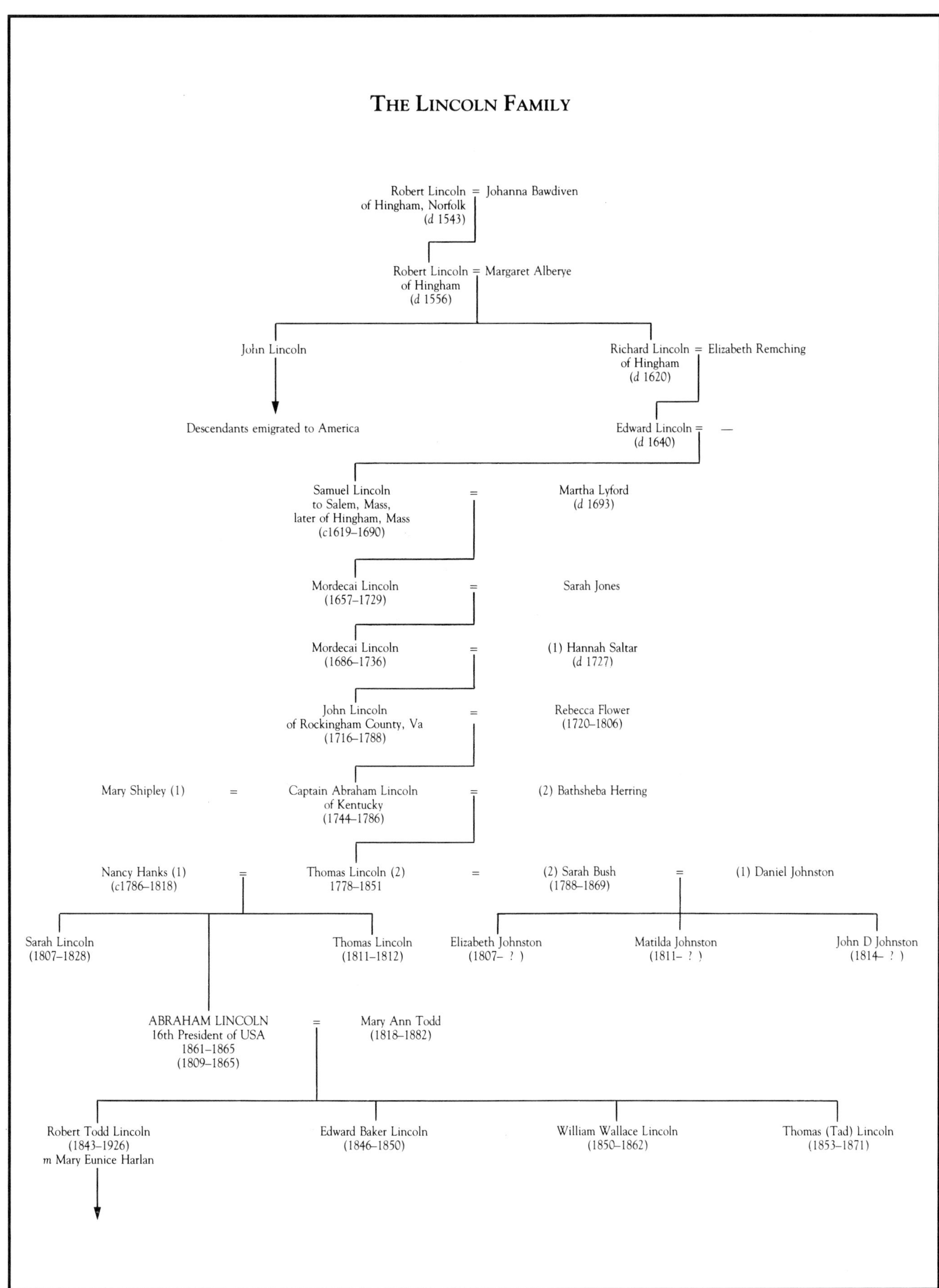
THE LINCOLN FAMILY
Robert Lincoln = Johanna Bawdiven
of Hingham, Norfolk
(d 1543)
Robert Lincoln = Margaret Alberye
of Hingham
(d 1556)
John Lincoln
Descendants emigrated to America
Richard Lincoln = Elizabeth Remching
of Hingham
(d 1620)
Edward Lincoln = —
(d 1640)
Samuel Lincoln
to Salem, Mass,
later of Hingham, Mass
(c1619–1690)
=
Martha Lyford
(d 1693)
Mordecai Lincoln
(1657–1729)
=
Sarah Jones
Mordecai Lincoln
(1686–1736)
=
(1) Hannah Saltar
(d 1727)
John Lincoln
of Rockingham County, Va
(1716–1788)
=
Rebecca Flower
(1720–1806)
Mary Shipley (1)
=
Captain Abraham Lincoln
of Kentucky
(1744–1786)
=
(2) Bathsheba Herring
Nancy Hanks (1)
(c1786–1818)
=
Thomas Lincoln (2)
1778–1851
=
(2) Sarah Bush
(1788–1869)
=
(1) Daniel Johnston
Sarah Lincoln
(1807–1828)
Thomas Lincoln
(1811–1812)
Elizabeth Johnston
(1807– ?)
Matilda Johnston
(1811– ?)
John D Johnston
(1814– ?)
ABRAHAM LINCOLN
16th President of USA
1861–1865
(1809–1865)
=
Mary Ann Todd
(1818–1882)
Robert Todd Lincoln
(1843–1926)
m Mary Eunice Harlan
Edward Baker Lincoln
(1846–1850)
William Wallace Lincoln
(1850–1862)
Thomas (Tad) Lincoln
(1853–1871)

Abraham Lincoln 'The Railsplitter', a portrait by an anonymous artist c1858

1849 and resumed his law practice in Springfield until 1854, when he re-entered politics and was again elected to the State legislature. He was defeated as a candidate for the Senate in February 1855 and resumed law practice until 1856, when he sought and failed to obtain nomination for Vice-President.

In June 1858 Lincoln was unamimously nominated for the Senate by the Republican State Convention at Springfield, but defeated in the election the following year. He then made a tour of the Midwest and New England and in May 1860 was nominated for President by the Republican National Convention at Chicago. He was one of four candidates and, although he did not receive a clear majority of the popular vote, he gained 180 of the 303 electoral votes and was duly elected. Lincoln was inaugurated on the East Portico of the Capitol on Monday 4 March 1861, the oath being administered by Chief Justice Roger B Taney, officiating for the seventh and last time.

Lincoln was regarded with suspicion by many and his ungainliness, habit of cracking bad jokes, and general lack of polish were much criticized by the press throughout his term of office, as were his wife's extravagances of dress. His sympathies during the Civil War were even considered as pro-southern and several members of Mrs Lincoln's family were known to have sided with the Confederacy. His attitude towards the freed slaves was also ambiguous and he is on record as saying that the best solution would be to return the blacks to Africa. He was really a man of very little ability pushed to the forefront by the momentous happenings which had finally come to a head in his tenure of office. When he delivered his famous Gettysburg address it was criticized for its brevity. Today it merely seems trite.

In spite of the apparent lack of enthusiasm for him as a person, Lincoln was re-elected in 1864 with 212 of the 234 electoral votes (reduced in number because of the secession of the southern States) and fifty-five per cent of the popular vote. He was inaugurated in the customary manner, the oath being administered by Chief Justice Salmon Portland Chase, who was Lincoln's distant kinsman although probably neither was aware of this fact.

On the evening of Good Friday, 14 April 1865 (a singularly inappropriate day, one would have thought, for such a performance), Lincoln and his wife went to Ford's Theater in Washington to see *Our American Cousin*, a comedy by Tom Taylor. While the policeman on duty at the door of the presidential box had absented himself to indulge his thirst, John Wilkes Booth, a slightly deranged out-of-work actor with pro-slavery sentiments, entered the back of the box and shot the President in the head. He then leapt to the stage, breaking a leg in the process, and made his escape in the ensuing pandemonium. A doctor from the audience rushed to attend the President, who was unconscious and, after cleaning the wound, pronounced that in his opinion recovery was impossible. Lincoln was carried to a small house opposite the theatre, where he died at 7.22am the following morning.

Booth, who had been part of a conspiracy, managed to hide out with David E Herold, one of his fellow conspirators, for ten days, but was finally caught up with while sleeping in a barn in Virginia. Herold surrendered to the soldiers, but Booth declared he would never be taken alive. The soldiers fired the barn, a shot was heard, and the dying Booth was dragged out. He had probably shot himself, although a Sergeant Corbett was to claim the credit for the fatal shot. Four other conspirators, including Herold and one woman, were hanged on 7 July 1865.

Lincoln was buried at Springfield, Illinois. His death was the beginning of the Lincoln cult which has survived to this day and bears strange parallels to the Kennedy cult.

Mrs Lincoln survived until 1882, completely bereft of her reason for many years, the result it has been claimed of having been infected with syphilis by her husband in the early days of their marriage.

ANDREW JOHNSON 1865–1869

Born: Casso's Inn, Fayetteville Street, Raleigh, North Carolina, 29 December 1808, yr son of Jacob Johnson and Mary (Polly) McDonough

Member of House of Representatives: 1843–1853

Governor of Tennessee: 1853–1857

Senator: 1857–1862

Military Governor of Tennessee: 1862–1864

Elected Vice-President: 8 November 1864

Inaugurated: Washington 4 March 1865

Succeeded as (17th) President and took oath: 15 April 1865

Retired from presidency: 4 March 1869

Senator: 1875

Married: Warrensburg (?), Greene County, Tennessee, 17 May 1827 Eliza (*b* Greeneville, Tennessee, 4 October 1810; *d* Carter County, Tennessee, 15 January 1876; *bur* Andrew Johnson Cemetery, Greeneville), dau of John McCardle (McCardell, McCartle or McArdle) and Sara(h) Phillips

Children:
(1) Martha, White House hostess for her father 1865–69; *b* Greeneville, Tennessee, 25 October 1828; *m* Greeneville 13 December 1855 David Trotter Patterson, Judge of Tennessee Circuit Court and US Senator (*b* Cedar Creek, Tennessee, 28 February 1818; *d* Afton, Tennessee, 3 November 1891), son of Andrew Patterson and Susanna Trotter; 1 son, 1 dau; *d* Greeneville 10 July 1901
(2) Charles, *b* Greeneville 19 February 1830; *d* (accidentally *k*) Nashville, Tennessee, 4 April 1863
(3) Mary, *b* Greeneville 8 May 1832; *m* (1) Greeneville 27 April 1852 Col Daniel Stover (*b* Carter County, Tennessee, 14 November 1826; *ka* Nashville 18 December 1864), son of William Stover and Sarah Murray Drake; 1 son, 2 daus; *m* (2) 20 April 1869 (div 1876), William Ramsay Brown; no children; *d* Bluff City, Tennessee, 19 April 1883
(4) Robert, Col 1st Tennessee Cavalry; *b* Greeneville 22 February 1834; *d* Greeneville 22 April 1869
(5) Andrew (Frank) Jr, newspaper publisher; *b* Greeneville 5 August 1852; *m* Rutland, Hot Springs, North Carolina, 25 November 1875 Kate May (Bessie), dau of James H Rumbough and Caroline Powell; no children; *d* Elizabethton, Tennessee, 12 March 1879

Died: Carter's Station, Tennessee, 31 July 1875

Buried: Andrew Johnson Cemetery, Greeneville, Tennessee

Andrew Johnson must surely be the ugliest man yet to have held the presidential office; photographs disclose his scowling, unrefined features, his coarse hair and his barber's rash. He was, however, a courageous man, which he needed to be as successor of the almost deified Lincoln.

Andrew Johnson's origins were the humblest of any President. Even the name of his paternal grandfather is unknown. His father, Jacob Johnson, was born on the 5 or 15 April 1778, in Northumberland, England, according to some accounts. If he was born in England it is not known how or when he emigrated to the United States. There have been attempts to prove that he was a son of William Johnson Sr of North Carolina, or of Andrew Johnson of Augusta County, Virginia, but the commonness of the surname and the paucity of evidence make it highly improbable that the riddle will ever be solved. Jacob Johnson followed the occupations of ostler, janitor and constable in Raleigh, North Carolina. On 9 September 1801 he obtained a licence to marry Mary (known as Polly) McDonough, who had been born on 17 July 1782 or 1783, and was the daughter of Andrew McDonough, of Beaufort, Tyrrell and Wake Counties, North Carolina, and Bledsoe County, Tennessee, who had fought in the Revolutionary War.

Jacob and Polly Johnson had three children, of whom Andrew was the youngest. He was born at Casso's Inn, Raleigh, on 29 December 1808 and was barely four years old when his father died, on 4 January 1812. A year or two later his mother married again to one Turner Daugherty, of Raleigh, who took on the upbringing of his two stepsons (the little girl had died). In 1822 Johnson was apprenticed to James J Selby, a local tailor. He had received no schooling whatsoever; his fellow apprentices taught him the alphabet and by borrowing books he painfully taught himself to read. He must have

Andrew Johnson, who succeeded to the presidency on Lincoln's assassination

found his apprenticeship irksome, however, for in 1824 he ran away (his employer offering $10 reward for his return) and set up as a journeyman tailor in Laurens, South Carolina, for two years. He then returned to Raleigh and a few months later moved his mother and stepfather to Greeneville, Tennessee, where he set up shop as a tailor.

On 17 May 1827, at the age of eighteen, Johnson married the sixteen-year-old Eliza McCardle (the name is also spelt McCardell, McArdle and McCartle), whose father, John, was a shoemaker in Warrensburg, Tennessee, and later became an innkeeper. She was to teach him how to write in addition to his acquired reading skills. Johnson was one of those people determined to 'get on' and in 1829 was elected Alderman of Greeneville before completing his twenty-first year. He was re-elected in 1829 and 1830, in which year he was elected Mayor, an office which he filled until 1833. Meanwhile he bought a tailor's shop and house (now part of the Andrew Johnson National Historic Site).

In 1835 Johnson was elected representative for Greene and Washington Counties to the Tennessee State legislature after nominating himself. He was defeated for re-election in 1837 because of his opposition to internal improvements, but was elected again in 1839. In 1840 he campaigned for Van Buren, gaining a reputation for his oratory, and in 1841 he was elected to the State Senate as representative for Greene and Hawkins Counties. Johnson was elected to the House of Representatives in 1843, taking his seat on 4 December. He was to be re-elected four times and in 1853 was elected Governor of Tennessee, being re-elected in 1855. Two years later he was elected to the Senate, taking his seat on 7 December 1857.

In December 1860 and again in March 1861, Johnson made impassioned speeches against secession in the Senate and when Tennessee seceded from the Union on 8 June 1861 he fled across the State line and became the only southerner in the Senate, of which he remained a member until his resignation in March 1862, when he returned to Nashville following his appointment by Lincoln as Military Governor of Tennessee and his commissioning as Brigadier-General of US Volunteers. He organized a provisional government for the State and raised twenty-five regiments for the Union army as well as completing the construction of the railroad from Nashville to the Tennessee River. The good record Johnson built up as Military Governor induced Lincoln to adopt him as his running-mate in the presidential election of 1864.

When the two had been duly elected and inauguration day was approaching, Johnson requested to be allowed to take the oath in Nashville, but Lincoln insisted he should return to Washington. He arrived hot and tired from the journey and hastily drank three brandies before entering the Senate chamber. Consequently his acceptance speech was slurred and he exhibited other signs of intoxication which led Lincoln to send an investigator to Nashville to enquire about Johnson's drinking habits and, although the result was negative, his public lapse put a powerful weapon into the hands of his political opponents.

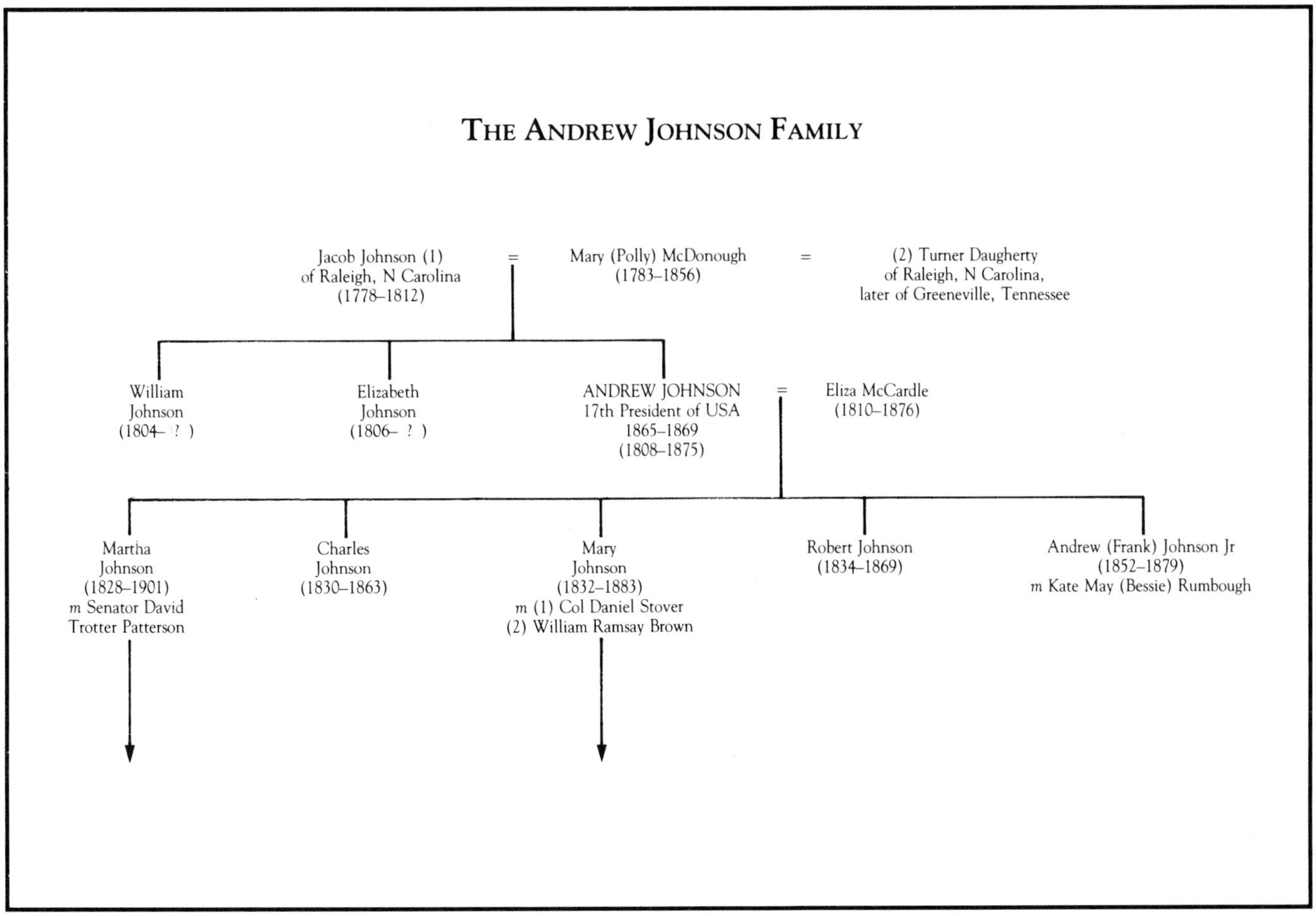

THE ANDREW JOHNSON FAMILY
Jacob Johnson (1) of Raleigh, N Carolina (1778–1812)
=
Mary (Polly) McDonough (1783–1856)
=
(2) Turner Daugherty of Raleigh, N Carolina, later of Greeneville, Tennessee
William Johnson (1804– ?)
Elizabeth Johnson (1806– ?)
ANDREW JOHNSON 17th President of USA 1865–1869 (1808–1875)
=
Eliza McCardle (1810–1876)
Martha Johnson (1828–1901) m Senator David Trotter Patterson
Charles Johnson (1830–1863)
Mary Johnson (1832–1883) m (1) Col Daniel Stover (2) William Ramsay Brown
Robert Johnson (1834–1869)
Andrew (Frank) Johnson Jr (1852–1879) m Kate May (Bessie) Rumbough

Johnson was in Washington when Lincoln was assassinated and he became the third Vice-President to succeed to the presidential office through death. He took the oath of office, administered by Chief Justice Salmon Portland Chase, in his suite at the Kirkwood House Hotel on Saturday 15 April 1865.

The period of reconstruction of the Union after the Civil War would have been a difficult one for any administration, but Johnson had the advantage of having presided successfully over the re-unification of Tennessee. In attempting to apply the same methods, however, he was soon at loggerheads with Congress and a move for his impeachment was begun, coming to a head in February 1868 when the House voted 126 to 47 to impeach. A court of impeachment was set up the following month and Johnson was called upon to defend the charges of 'high crimes and misdemeanours' committed during his tenure of office. His trial began on 30 March and, after Johnson had been acquitted on three of the eleven articles of impeachment because the Senate vote

One of the tickets issued for the impeachment trial of President Andrew Johnson

To be taken up at
MAIN ENTRANCE
U.S. SENATE
U.S. SENATE
Impeachment of the President
ADMIT THE BEARER
MARCH 13. 1868
Sergeant-at-Arms.
Philp & Solomons. Wash. D.C.

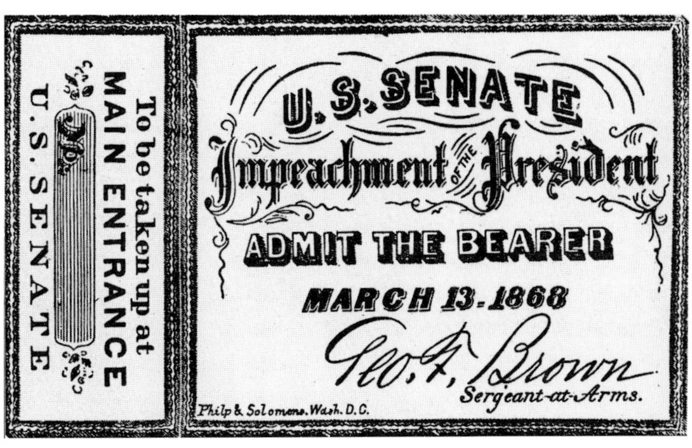

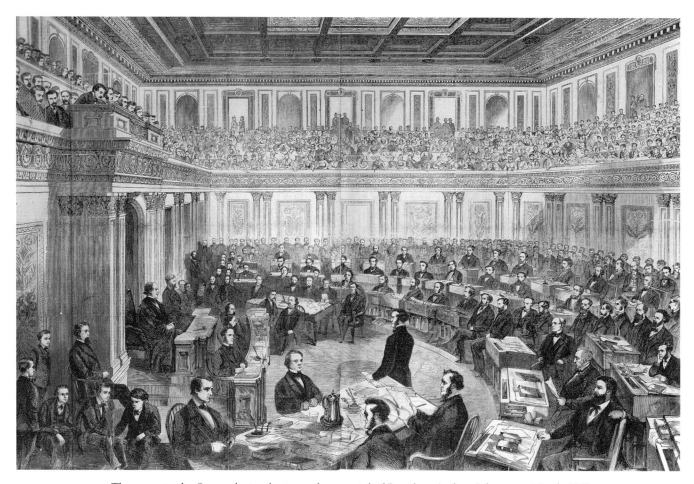

The scene in the Senate during the impeachment trial of President Andrew Johnson in March 1868

failed to attain the required majority (two-thirds) for a conviction, the proceedings were adjourned *sine die* and he completed his term of office on 4 March 1869.

Because of Grant's hostility towards him Johnson did not attend Grant's inauguration and in April returned to his home in Greeneville where he received a great welcome, passing under a banner reading 'Welcome Home, Andrew Johnson, Patriot', where eight years earlier he had been vilified as 'Andrew Johnson, Traitor', when he fled for his life after Tennessee had joined the Confederacy.

In 1871, Johnson made an unsuccessful bid for election to the Senate and in 1872 for election to the House of Representatives. He tried for the Senate again in 1875 and this time was successful, taking his seat on 5 March, being the only former President to do so. The old animosities were now forgotten and he was received in the Senate chamber with applause and with flowers garlanding his seat. It was to be his swansong. At the end of the session he returned to Greeneville and in July joined his wife at their daughter's house in Carter Station, Tennessee. Shortly after his arrival he suffered a stroke and died on 31 July 1875, aged sixty-six.

Ulysses S Grant 1869–1877

Born: Point Pleasant, Clermont County, Ohio, 27 April 1822, eldest son of Jesse Root Grant and Hannah Simpson

Brigadier-General: 1861

Major-General of Volunteers: 1862

Major-General US army: 1863

Lt-General US army: 1864

Secretary of War: 1867–1868

Elected (18th) President: 3 November 1868

Inaugurated: East Portico of Capitol 4 March 1869

Elected for 2nd term: 5 November 1872

Inaugurated: East Portico of Capitol 4 March 1873

Retired from presidency: 4 March 1877

General (retired list) US army: 1885

Married: St Louis, Missouri, 22 August 1848 Julia Boggs (*b* White Haven, St Louis, Missouri, 16 February 1826; *d* Washington DC 14 December 1902; *bur* Grant's Tomb), eldest dau of Col Frederick Dent and Ellen Bray Wrenshall

Children:

(1) Frederick Dent, Major-General US army, US Minister of Austria-Hungary 1889–93, Police Commissioner of New York City 1894–98, *b* St Louis, Missouri, 30 May 1850; *m* Chicago, Illinois, 20 October 1874 Ida Marie (*b* Louisville, Kentucky, 4 June 1854; *d* Washington DC 1930), dau of Henry Hamilton Honoré and Elizabeth Carr; 1 son, 1 dau; *d* New York 11 April 1912

(2) Ulysses S Jr, *b* Bethel, Claremont County, Ohio, 22 July 1852; *m* (1) New York 1 November 1880 (Fannie) Josephine (*b* Adrian, Michigan, 16 January 1857; *d* San Diego, California, 10 November 1909), dau of Senator Jerome Bunty Chaffee and Miriam Barnard Comstock; 2 sons, 3 daus; *m* (2) 1913 Mrs America Will née Workman (*b* Santa Barbara, California, 1881; *d* San Diego 29 October 1942); no children; *d* San Diego 26 September 1929

(3) Ellen (Nellie) Wrenshall, *b* Wish-ton-wish 4 July 1855; *m* (1) the White House, Washington, 21 May 1874 Algernon Charles Frederick Sartoris JP (*b* London, England, 1 August 1851; *d* Capri, Italy, 3 February 1893), son of Edward John Sartoris JP and Adelaide Kemble; 2 sons, 2 daus; *m* (2) 4 July 1912 Frank Hatch Jones, first Assistant Postmaster-General under President Cleveland; no children; *d* Chicago 30 August 1922

(4) Jesse Root Grant, *b* Hardscrabble 6 February 1858; *m* (1) San Francisco 30 September 1880 (div) Elizabeth (*b* Minneapolis, Minnesota, 10 January 1858; *d* San Diego 28 February 1945), dau of William Smith Chapman and Sarah Armstrong; 1 son, 1 dau; *m* (2) 26 August 1918 Lillian (*b* near Warwick, Maryland, 1864; *d* New York 1 July 1924), widow of John Anthony Wilkins and dau of Capt Owen Burns, US navy, and Martha Ann Armstrong; no children; *d* Los Altos, California, 8 June 1934

Died: Mount McGregor, New York, 23 July 1885

Buried: Grant's Tomb, Riverside Park, New York

Ulysses S Grant was living proof that a good General does not always make a good President and on his death the New York *Tribune* wisely commented that 'the greatest mistake of his life was the acceptance of the presidency'.

The first Grant forebear to reach America was Matthew Grant, who sailed from Plymouth, England, on board the *Mary and John* and landed at Nantasket on 30 May 1630. He eventually settled in Windsor, Connecticut, where he served as town clerk for twenty-five years. His descendants prospered and Captain Noah Grant (the younger) served in the Revolutionary army. He married twice and his eldest son by his second wife, Rachel Kelley, was Jesse Root Grant, who became the prosperous owner of a tannery at Georgetown, Brown County, Ohio. He married Hannah Simpson, a native of Montgomery County, Pennsylvania, and the eldest of their six children was the future President. Hiram

General Ulysses S Grant

Ulysses Grant, as he was originally named, was born at Point Pleasant, Clermont County, Ohio, on 27 April 1822 in a weatherboard cabin, which, in the customary manner for presidential birthplaces, was later to be restored and opened to the public by the Ohio Historical Society.

The family moved to Georgetown, Ohio, in 1823 and as he grew older the young Grant attended the village school and worked at home on the farm, where he showed a particular aptitude for dealing with horses, driving wagons at the age of eight and ploughing at the age of eleven. He received his later schooling at Maysville Seminary, Kentucky, and the Presbyterian Academy at Ripley, Ohio, and in March 1839 was appointed to the US Military Academy at West Point on his father's application. It was at this period of his life that his name became changed to Ulysses S Grant when the Congressman who sponsored his application completed the form wrongly. The initial 'S' was never expanded by Grant or anyone else, but presumably it stood for his mother's maiden name Simpson.

Grant made a leisurely journey to West Point, for which he felt no great enthusiasm, as he later confessed in his memoirs. He travelled by river boat and railroad, stopping off for several days in Philadelphia and New York *en route* and arriving at West Point at the end of May. Grant was not happy at West Point and although he excelled in horsemanship and established a high-jump record which was not broken for twenty-five years, his academic record was poor and when he graduated twenty-first out of a class of thirty-nine in July 1843, his request to be assigned to a cavalry regiment was denied and he was commissioned Brevet 2nd Lieutenant in the 4th Infantry. He first saw active service in the Mexican War, participating in the battles of Palo Alto, Resaca de La Palma, Cerro Gordo, Churubusco, Molino del Rey, and Chapultepec (for which he was mentioned in despatches) and entered Mexico City on 14 September 1847, being promoted substantive 1st Lieutenant a few days later. After the war had been brought to an end by the treaty of Guadalupe Hidalgo on 30 May 1848, the regiment left Mexico and was sent to Pascagoula, Mississippi.

On 22 August 1848 Grant was married at St Louis, Missouri, to Julia Boggs Dent, whose brother had been his room-mate at West Point and whose father was a judge and planter in Missouri. The marriage, which produced four children, remained a happy one throughout. Grant served in various postings until 1854, when he resigned from the army after his commanding officer had found him drunk in a public place and demanded his trial or resignation. Grant's drinking was a direct result of the long separation from his wife and growing family and his depression over the fact that he could not afford to pay for them to join him. After his resignation he returned to St Louis and spent the next four years in an unsuccessful attempt at farming before entering the real estate business in partnership with his wife's cousin Harry Boggs. He gave that up in 1860 and moved to Galena, Illinois, where he was employed in his father's hardware and leather goods store at a salary of $800. After the attack on Fort Sumter in April 1861, Grant rejoined the army as a volunteer at Springfield, Illinois, and in June was promoted to Colonel commanding the 21st Illinois Regiment and given command of the south-east district of Missouri. In August he was promoted Brigadier-General (antedated to May) and in November he attacked and captured the Confederate camp at Belmont, Missouri, with 175 prisoners and two guns, but was forced back by a counter-attack in which his horse was shot from under him. The losses on both sides amounted to over 11,000 men.

Throughout 1862 Grant engaged in a series of successful battles against the Confederates, including the defeat of Generals Johnston and Beauregard at Shiloh in April. In 1863 he crossed the Mississippi, captured Vicksburg, was appointed Commander-in-chief in the western area of operations, and defeated General Bragg at the battle of Chattanooga (24–25 November).

In March 1864 Grant was summoned to Washington by President Lincoln and put in command of all the

A photograph of Grant by Brady

Mrs Ulysses S Grant with her two younger children, Nellie and Jesse

Union's land forces, becoming the first officer in the US army to attain the rank of full General since Washington. It seemed as though nothing could stay his arms and he continued to advance from victory to victory until he received Lee's surrender at Appomattox Court House on 9 April 1865. When Grant's men began firing their guns into the air to celebrate the victory he told them: 'The war is over, the rebels are again our countrymen, and the best sign of rejoicing will be to abstain from all demonstrations in the field.' After reporting to Washington, Grant set out on a tour of the northern states and Canada. He returned home to Galena in August and the grateful citizens presented him and his wife with a house on Bouthillier Street (now open to the public as The Grant Home State Memorial).

On 12 August 1867, Grant was appointed Secretary of War *ad interim* by President Andrew Johnson and on 21 May 1868 he was unanimously nominated for President at the Republican National Convention in Chicago. In the ensuing election he received 214 electoral votes as opposed to 80 for Horatio Seymour, the Democratic candidate. Grant was inaugurated as eighteenth President on the East Portico of the Capitol on Thursday 4 March 1869, the oath being administered by Chief Justice Salmon Portland Chase.

Grant enjoyed great personal standing as a war hero, but he was no statesman and no great judge of people, making some very bad appointments, including a Secretary of War who was impeached for accepting a bribe. However, he was re-nominated and elected for a second term, gaining 286 electoral votes as opposed to 66 for Horace Greeley, the Democratic and Liberal-Republican candidate. His second inauguration day took place on 4 March 1873, when the oath was administered by Chief Justice Salmon P Chase on the East Portico of the Capitol. In September there was a financial panic following the failure of Jay Cooke and Company, a major New York banking house, and beginning a depression which was to last until 1878. The celebrations of the centennial year of 1876 were marred by the impeachment of William W Belknap, Secretary of War, on charges of financial manipulation (of which he was acquitted by the Senate) and by other bribery scandals involving members of the cabinet. Charges were also made against Grant's private secretary, Orville Babcock. Grant retired from office on 4 March 1877 and spent the years from 1877 to 1879 in a world tour with his wife and youngest son Jesse. He was well received wherever he went and met many crowned heads, including Pope Leo XIII. The story of his trip, *Around the World With*

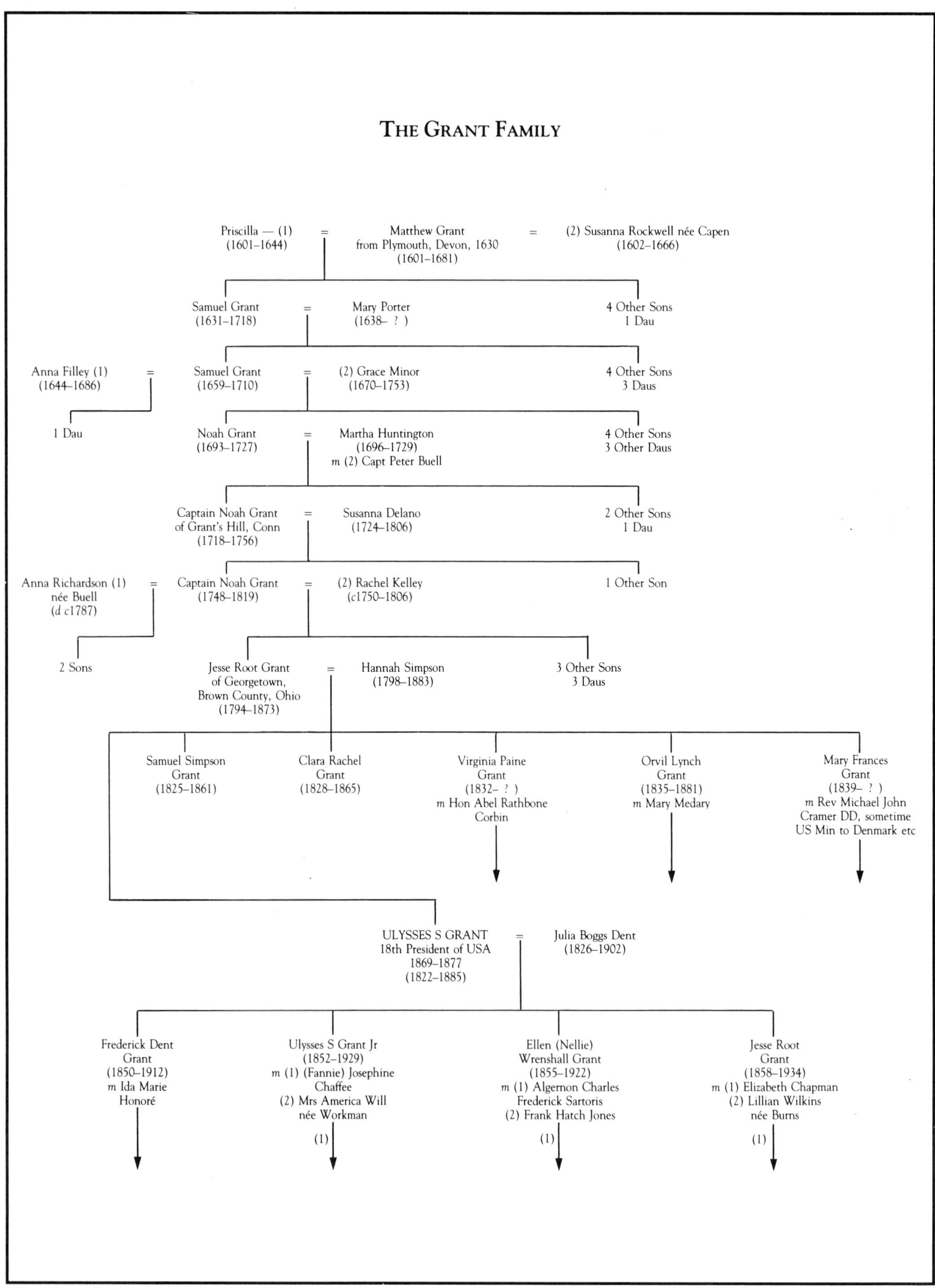
THE GRANT FAMILY
Priscilla — (1) (1601–1644)
=
Matthew Grant from Plymouth, Devon, 1630 (1601–1681)
=
(2) Susanna Rockwell née Capen (1602–1666)
Samuel Grant (1631–1718)
=
Mary Porter (1638– ?)
4 Other Sons 1 Dau
Anna Filley (1) (1644–1686)
=
Samuel Grant (1659–1710)
=
(2) Grace Minor (1670–1753)
4 Other Sons 3 Daus
1 Dau
Noah Grant (1693–1727)
=
Martha Huntington (1696–1729) m (2) Capt Peter Buell
4 Other Sons 3 Other Daus
Captain Noah Grant of Grant's Hill, Conn (1718–1756)
=
Susanna Delano (1724–1806)
2 Other Sons 1 Dau
Anna Richardson (1) née Buell (d c1787)
=
Captain Noah Grant (1748–1819)
=
(2) Rachel Kelley (c1750–1806)
1 Other Son
2 Sons
Jesse Root Grant of Georgetown, Brown County, Ohio (1794–1873)
=
Hannah Simpson (1798–1883)
3 Other Sons 3 Daus
Samuel Simpson Grant (1825–1861)
Clara Rachel Grant (1828–1865)
Virginia Paine Grant (1832– ?) m Hon Abel Rathbone Corbin
Orvil Lynch Grant (1835–1881) m Mary Medary
Mary Frances Grant (1839– ?) m Rev Michael John Cramer DD, sometime US Min to Denmark etc
ULYSSES S GRANT 18th President of USA 1869–1877 (1822–1885)
=
Julia Boggs Dent (1826–1902)
Frederick Dent Grant (1850–1912) m Ida Marie Honoré
Ulysses S Grant Jr (1852–1929) m (1) (Fannie) Josephine Chaffee (2) Mrs America Will née Workman
(1)
Ellen (Nellie) Wrenshall Grant (1855–1922) m (1) Algernon Charles Frederick Sartoris (2) Frank Hatch Jones
(1)
Jesse Root Grant (1858–1934) m (1) Elizabeth Chapman (2) Lillian Wilkins née Burns
(1)

General Grant, by John Russell Young, became a best-seller when it was published in 1879.

In 1880 Grant sought nomination for a third term as President (the first to do so), but was defeated at the Republican National Convention in Chicago. The following year he moved from Galena to New York City. In 1884 Grant lost a considerable amount of money in unsuccessful business ventures and decided to try and recoup his losses by writing his memoirs. At the same time he fell ill and cancer at the root of the tongue was diagnosed. In March 1885 he was nominated as General on the retired list with full pay ($13,500 a year) by President Arthur. He spent his last months struggling to complete his memoirs. On 26 June 1885 he moved to Mount McGregor, near Saratoga, New York. He completed his memoirs on 19 July and died four days later on 23 July 1885, aged sixty-three. He was buried in the magnificent mausoleum, Grant's Tomb, which has become one of the sights of New York. His memoirs, *Personal Memoirs of U.S. Grant*, were published posthumously and sold more than 300,000 copies, from which Mrs Grant received royalties in excess of $440,000 to keep her in comfort and luxury for the remaining seventeen years of her life.

Rutherford Birchard Hayes 1877–1881

Born: Delaware, Ohio, 4 October 1822, yst (and posthumous) son of Rutherford Hayes and Sophia Birchard

Member of House of Representatives: 1865–1867

Governor of Ohio: 1868–1872 and 1876–1877

Elected (19th) President: 7 November 1876 (officially declared 2 March 1877)

Took oath: (privately) The White House 3 March 1877

Inaugurated: East Portico of Capitol 5 March 1877

Retired from presidency: 4 March 1881

Married: Cincinnati, Ohio, 30 December 1852, Lucy Ware (*b* Chillicothe, Ohio, 28 August 1831; *d* Fremont, Ohio, 25 June 1889; *bur* Oakwood Cemetery, Fremont, later transferred to Spiegel Grove), only dau of Dr James Webb and Maria Cook

Children:

(1) Sardis Birchard (later Birchard Austin), *b* Cincinnati 4 November 1853; *m* 30 December 1886 Mary Nancy (*b* Erie County, Ohio, 15 May 1859; *d* Toledo, Ohio, 22 June 1924), dau of Nathan Gould Sherman and Elizabeth Otis; 5 sons; *d* Toledo, Ohio, 24 January 1926

(2) James Webb (later called Webb Cook), Lt-Col US Volunteers, received Congressional Medal of Honor for services in the Philippines, joint founder with the State of Ohio of Hayes Memorial Library and Museum; *b* Cincinnati 20 March 1856; *m* 30 September 1912; Mrs Mary Otis Brinkerhoff (*b* Fremont, Ohio, 11 April 1856; *d* Phoenix, Arizona, 3 March 1935), dau of Anson H Miller and Nancy Otis; no children; *d* Marion, Ohio, 26 July 1935

(3) Rutherford Platt, *b* Cincinnati 24 June 1858; *m* 24 October 1894 Lucy Hayes (*b* Columbus, Ohio, 14 September 1868; *d* Clearwater, Florida, 4 December 1939), dau of William Augustus Platt and Sarah Follet; 3 sons; *d* Tampa, Florida, 31 July 1927

(4) Joseph Thompson, *b* Cincinnati 21 December 1861; *d* near Charleston, West Virginia, 24 June 1863

(5) George Crook, *b* Chillicothe, Ohio, 29 September 1864; *d* Chillicothe 24 May 1866

(6) Frances (Fanny), *b* Cincinnati 2 September 1867; *m* 1 September 1897 (div), Capt Harry Eaton Smith US navy (*b* Fremont, Ohio, 28 December 1869; *d* 1931); 1 son (who assumed the surname of Hayes); *d* Lewiston, Maine, 18 March 1950 (having resumed her maiden name)

(7) Scott Russell, *b* Columbus, Ohio, 8 February 1871; *m* September 1912 Maude Anderson (*b* 7 July 1873; *d* San Francisco 19 November 1966); no children; *d* Croton-on-Hudson, New York, 6 May 1923

(8) Manning Force, *b* Fremont, Ohio, 1 August 1873; *d* Fremont 28 August 1874

Died: Fremont, Ohio, 17 January 1893

Buried: Oakwood Cemetery, Fremont, later transferred to Spiegel Grove

Rutherford Birchard Hayes, third in the long line of mediocre Presidents who followed the Civil War, was well summed up by Henry Adams, grandson of President John Quincy Adams, who described him as 'a third rate nonentity, whose only commendation is that he was obnoxious to no one'.

George Hayes, who settled at Windsor, Connecticut, in 1680, is very improbably claimed to have been a native of Scotland. His great-great-grandson, Rutherford Hayes, was a farmer and storekeeper in Delaware, Ohio. He married Sophia Birchard of Wilmington, Vermont, on 13 September 1813 and two sons and two daughters were born to them. By 1822 the elder boy and girl had both died and Sophia was again pregnant, when Rutherford himself died of fever on 20 July, aged thirty-five. Seventy-seven days later, on 4 October 1822, Sophia gave birth to another son, Rutherford Birchard Hayes, the future President. In 1825 he became her only surviving son when his brother Lorenzo died at the age of ten.

From the age of six Rutherford attended school in Delaware and later Norwalk Academy, Ohio. In 1837 he entered Isaac Webb's School at Middletown, Connecticut, from which he went on to Kenyon College, Gambier, Ohio, where he graduated with a BA degree in 1842. He began to study law with a local law

Rutherford Birchard Hayes

firm the same year and in August 1843 entered Harvard Law School. In 1845 he was admitted to the Ohio Bar, graduated from Harvard with an LLB degree and was upped to MA by Kenyon College. The following year he began law practice in partnership with Ralph P Buckland in Lower Sandusky (now Fremont), Ohio. A throat ailment compelled him to spend the winter of 1848–9 in Texas and in 1850 he moved to Cincinnati and resumed the practice of law.

On 30 December 1852, Hayes married Lucy Ware Webb, the twenty-one-year-old daughter of a local doctor. Until 1856 she had to share his affections with his sister Fanny, to whom he was inordinately attached to an almost unhealthy degree in spite of the fact that Fanny had a husband and children. When Fanny died in childbirth Hayes told Lucy: 'You are sister Fanny to me now.' Lucy was a sensible, well-educated woman of pleasant appearance, but a lifelong total abstainer who, as First Lady, would not allow alcohol to be served at the White House, thereby earning herself the nickname of 'Lemonade Lucy'.

On the outbreak of the Civil War, Hayes, who had been appointed City Solicitor by Cincinnati City Council in 1858, was commissioned as Major in the 23rd Ohio Volunteer Infantry Regiment on 27 June 1861 and promoted to Lieutenant-Colonel the following October. He served throughout the war, seeing active service at the battles of South Mountain (in which he was wounded in the left arm by a musket ball), Winchester, and Cedar Creek among others. He was successively promoted Colonel, Brevet Brigadier-General and Brevet Major-General before resigning from the army in June 1865.

Hayes had joined the Republican party in 1855 and was elected to the House of Representatives in October 1864, taking his seat on 4 December 1865. He was re-elected in 1866 and in 1867 was nominated for Governor of Ohio at the Republican State Convention in June and elected in October, taking office in January 1868. He was re-elected in 1869 but declined to seek re-election for a third term in 1871. In 1872 he was nominated for the House of Representatives but failed to gain a seat. In 1874 his maternal uncle, Sardis Birchard, who had been his guardian, died and left Hayes his house and twenty-five acres of ground at Spiegel Grove, Fremont. The following year he was again nominated for Governor of Ohio and duly elected, taking office in 1876. In June that year the Republican National Convention in Cincinnati nominated Hayes for President but in the ensuing election neither he, nor Samuel Jones Tilden,

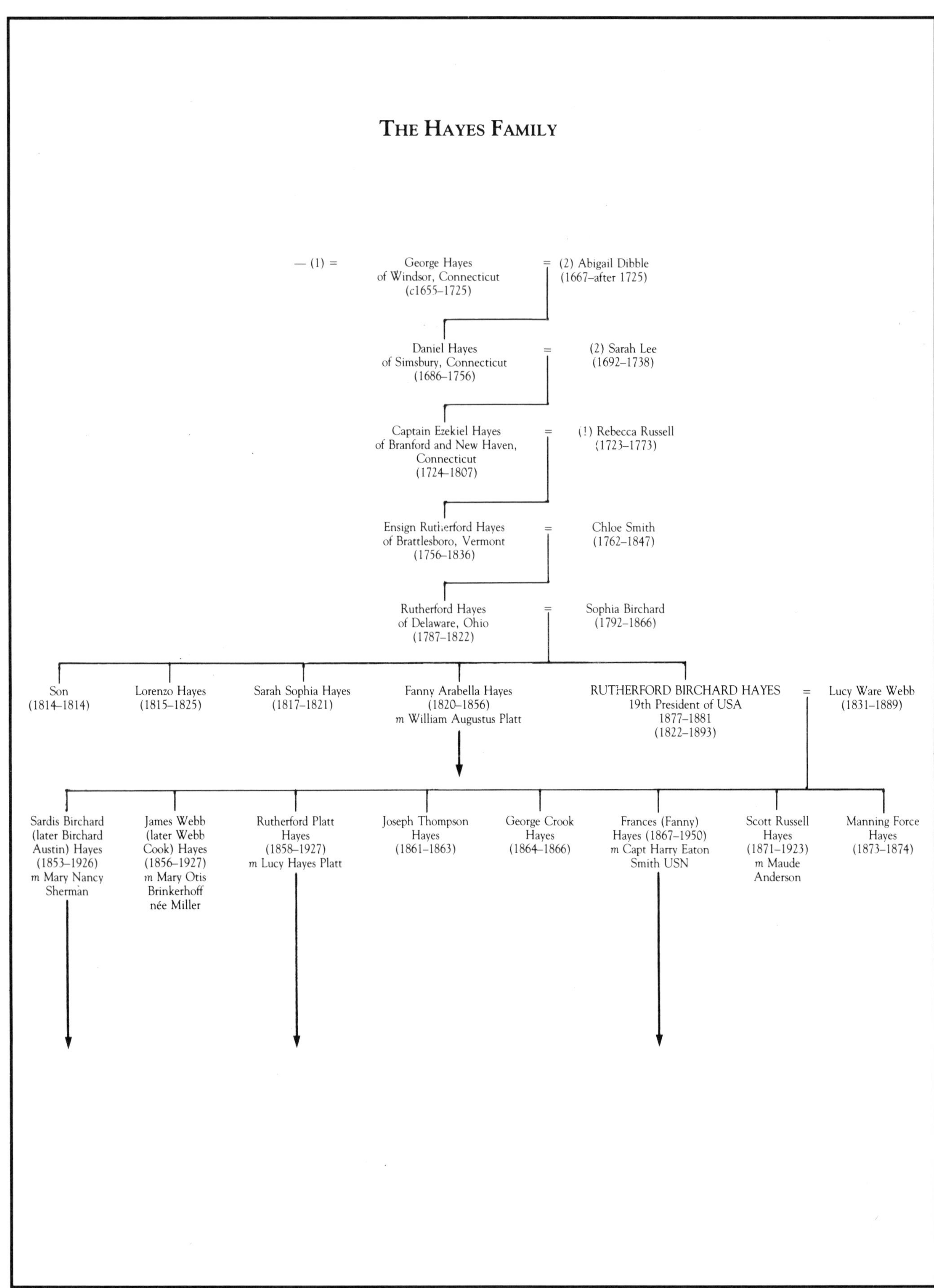
THE HAYES FAMILY
— (1) =
George Hayes
of Windsor, Connecticut
(c1655–1725)
= (2) Abigail Dibble
(1667–after 1725)
Daniel Hayes
of Simsbury, Connecticut
(1686–1756)
=
(2) Sarah Lee
(1692–1738)
Captain Ezekiel Hayes
of Branford and New Haven,
Connecticut
(1724–1807)
=
(1) Rebecca Russell
(1723–1773)
Ensign Rutherford Hayes
of Brattlesboro, Vermont
(1756–1836)
=
Chloe Smith
(1762–1847)
Rutherford Hayes
of Delaware, Ohio
(1787–1822)
=
Sophia Birchard
(1792–1866)
Son
(1814–1814)
Lorenzo Hayes
(1815–1825)
Sarah Sophia Hayes
(1817–1821)
Fanny Arabella Hayes
(1820–1856)
m William Augustus Platt
RUTHERFORD BIRCHARD HAYES
19th President of USA
1877–1881
(1822–1893)
=
Lucy Ware Webb
(1831–1889)
Sardis Birchard
(later Birchard
Austin) Hayes
(1853–1926)
m Mary Nancy
Sherman
James Webb
(later Webb
Cook) Hayes
(1856–1927)
m Mary Otis
Brinkerhoff
née Miller
Rutherford Platt
Hayes
(1858–1927)
m Lucy Hayes Platt
Joseph Thompson
Hayes
(1861–1863)
George Crook
Hayes
(1864–1866)
Frances (Fanny)
Hayes (1867–1950)
m Capt Harry Eaton
Smith USN
Scott Russell
Hayes
(1871–1923)
m Maude
Anderson
Manning Force
Hayes
(1873–1874)

Mrs Hayes with her children Scott and Fanny and a friend, taken by New York photographer Pach

the Democratic candidate, gained the 185 electoral votes necessary for election. The matter had to be submitted to an electoral commission, which met in the Hall of the House of Representatives and finally settled in favour of Hayes, who was duly inaugurated on Monday 5 March 1877 after having taken the oath privately at the White House on Saturday 3 March.

Hayes was a small, unimpressive man with a straggling, wiry beard and deep-set eyes. He was not without flashes of humour as, for instance, when referring to his large family of seven sons and only one daughter he described his wife and himself as being 'in the boy business'.

Hayes decided from the outset that he would not seek re-election for a second term and by the time he retired from the presidency in 1881 he had gained a certain amount of respect. Hayes and his wife returned to their home in Fremont where he busied himself with his interests in education (particularly of blacks in the south), prison reform and the welfare of Civil War veterans. He served as President of the National Prison Association from 1883 to his death.

Mrs Hayes's death in June 1889 was a great blow to her husband. On 14 January 1893 he suffered a heart attack on the train in which he was returning to Fremont from a business trip. He died three days later on 17 January, aged seventy, and was buried beside Lucy in the grounds of Spiegel Grove.

James Abram Garfield March–September 1881

Born:	Orange, Ohio, 19 November 1831, yst son of Abraham (Abram) Garfield and Eliza Ballou
Member of House of Representatives:	1863–1880
Elected (20th) President:	2 November 1880
Inaugurated:	East Portico of Capitol 4 March 1881
Married:	Hiram, Portage County, Ohio, 11 November 1858, Lucretia (*b* Garretsville, Portage County, Ohio, 19 April 1832; *d* South Pasedena, California, 4 March 1918; *bur* Garfield Memorial, Lake View Cemetery, Cleveland, Ohio), dau of Zebulon Rudolph and Arabella Mason
Children:	(1) Eliza Arabella, *b* Hiram, Ohio, 3 July 1860; *d* Hiram 3 December 1863 (2) Harry Augustus, *b* Hiram, Ohio, 11 October 1863; *m* Cleveland, Ohio, 14 June 1888 Belle Hartford (*b* Cleveland, Ohio, 7 July 1864; *d* 27 June 1944), dau of James Mason; 3 sons, 1 dau; *d* Williamstown, Massachusetts, 12 December 1942 (3) James Rudolf, Secretary of the Interior 1907–9; *b* Hiram, Ohio, 17 October 1865; *m* 30 December 1890 Helen Newell (*b* Cleveland, Ohio, 12 February 1866; *d* 26 August 1930), dau of John Hills and Judith Poole; 4 sons; *d* Cleveland, Ohio, 24 March 1950 (4) Mary, *b* Washington DC 16 January 1867; *m* Mentor, Ohio, 14 June 1888 Joseph Stanley Brown (*b* Washington DC 19 August 1858; *d* Pasadena, California, 2 November 1941), son of John Leopold Brown and Elizabeth Frances Marr; 1 son, 2 daus; *d* Pasadena, California, 30 December 1947 (5) Irvin McDowell, *b* Hiram, Ohio, 3 August 1870; *m* Boston, Massachusetts, 16 October 1906 Susan (*b* Boston 9 March 1878; *d* ?) dau of Nathaniel Henry Emmons and Eleanor Gassett Bacon; 1 son, 2 daus; *d* Boston 19 July 1951 (6) Abram, *b* 21 November 1872; *m* (1) Cleveland, Ohio, 14 October 1897, Sarah Granger (*b* Cleveland 10 January 1873; *d* Cleveland 3 February 1945), dau of Edward Porter Williams and Mary Louise Mason; 1 son, 1 dau; *m* (2) Shaker Heights, Ohio, 12 April 1947 Helen Grannis Matthews (*b* 1902); no issue; *d* Cleveland, Ohio, 16 October 1958 (7) Edward Garfield, *b* Hiram, Ohio, 25 December 1874; *d* Washington DC 25 October 1876
Died:	Francklyn Cottage, Elberon, New Jersey, 19 September 1881 (from injuries received when he was shot at Baltimore and Potomac Railroad Station, Washington DC, 2 July 1881)
Buried:	Cleveland, Ohio

James Abram Garfield, the last of the 'log cabin' Presidents was born at Orange, Ohio, on 19 November 1831. A replica of the cabin in which he was born is to be seen today in the grounds of Lawnfield, the property at Mentor, Ohio, which Garfield bought in 1876.

The English place of origin of Edward Garfield, the first of the family in America, is not known. There were Garfields in Warwickshire and Northamptonshire in the sixteenth century and a Ralph Garfield of Kilsby, Northamptonshire, was a substantial London merchant and the owner of two ships, *The Falcon* and *The Rose*. It has been surmised that Edward was a kinsman and emigrated on one of them. Edward was one of the first settlers of Watertown, Massachusetts, where he received grants of land in 1636 and 1637. He appears to have married three times and died at the great age of ninety-seven or thereabouts in June 1672. His youngest son Benjamin served as town clerk of Watertown, married twice, and was the father of Thomas Garfield, of Lincoln, Massachusetts. Thomas's grandson, Solomon Garfield, fought in the Revolutionary War and later settled in Worcester, New York, where he died as the result of a fall in 1807. His grandson Abraham (called Abram) Garfield was a farmer and a canal construction supervisor, whose work took him to Orange, Ohio. In 1820 he married Eliza, daughter of James Ballou, of Richmond, New Hampshire, a farmer of French Huguenot descent. The future President was the youngest of their five children.

Garfield was less than two years old in May 1833 when his father died and his mother had a hard struggle to bring up her four surviving children, who had to work as farm hands and attend school when they could during the winter months. In 1848 and 1849 Garfield worked

James Abram Garfield, President for only six and a half months

on the Ohio canal boats and during the following two years attended Geauga Seminary in Chester, Ohio, working as a carpenter during the vacations. He joined the Disciples of Christ Church in 1850 and in 1851 entered Hiram Eclectic Institute (now Hiram College), Ohio, where he remained for three years, paying his way by teaching in the English department and giving instruction in ancient languages.

In September 1854 he entered Williams College, Williamstown, Massachusetts, from which he graduated top of his class with a BA degree in 1856. He went back to teach Latin and Greek at Hiram Eclectic Institute for a year and was President of the Institute from 1857 to 1860. On 11 November 1858 Garfield married Lucretia Rudolph, the daughter of a local farmer and carpenter. The following year he was elected to represent Portage and Summit counties in the state Senate. Having studied law intermittently since 1858, he was admitted to the Ohio Bar in 1860.

After the outbreak of the Civil War, Garfield was commissioned as Lieutenant-Colonel of the 42nd Regiment of Ohio Volunteers. In November 1861 he was promoted to Colonel and a month later given command of the 18th Brigade of the army of Ohio. He participated in the battles of Middle Creek (promoted to Brigadier-General) Shiloh and Chickamauga (promoted to Major-General) before receiving his commission in December 1863 to take his seat in the House of Representatives, to which he had been elected in September 1862.

He proved himself a useful member of Congress, serving on several committees. On 13 January 1880 Garfield was elected to the Senate by the Ohio legislature for the term beginning 4 March 1881, but as he was subsequently elected President he never actually took his seat as a Senator. He was nominated for President by the Republican National Convention at Chicago on 8 June 1880 and in the election received 214 of the 369 electoral votes. Garfield was inaugurated on the East Portico of the Capitol on Friday 4 March 1881, the oath being administered by Chief Justice Morrison Remick Waite. His seventy-nine-year-old mother was the first mother of a President to attend her son's inauguration.

What Garfield's presidency would have brought forth can only be a matter of speculation. On 2 July 1881 he was walking to the train by which he was to proceed to Williamstown, Massachusetts, to deliver an address at his old college, when he was shot in the back at Baltimore and Potomac Railroad Station in Washington. His assailant was one Charles Jules Guiteau, a deranged

The Garfield Family

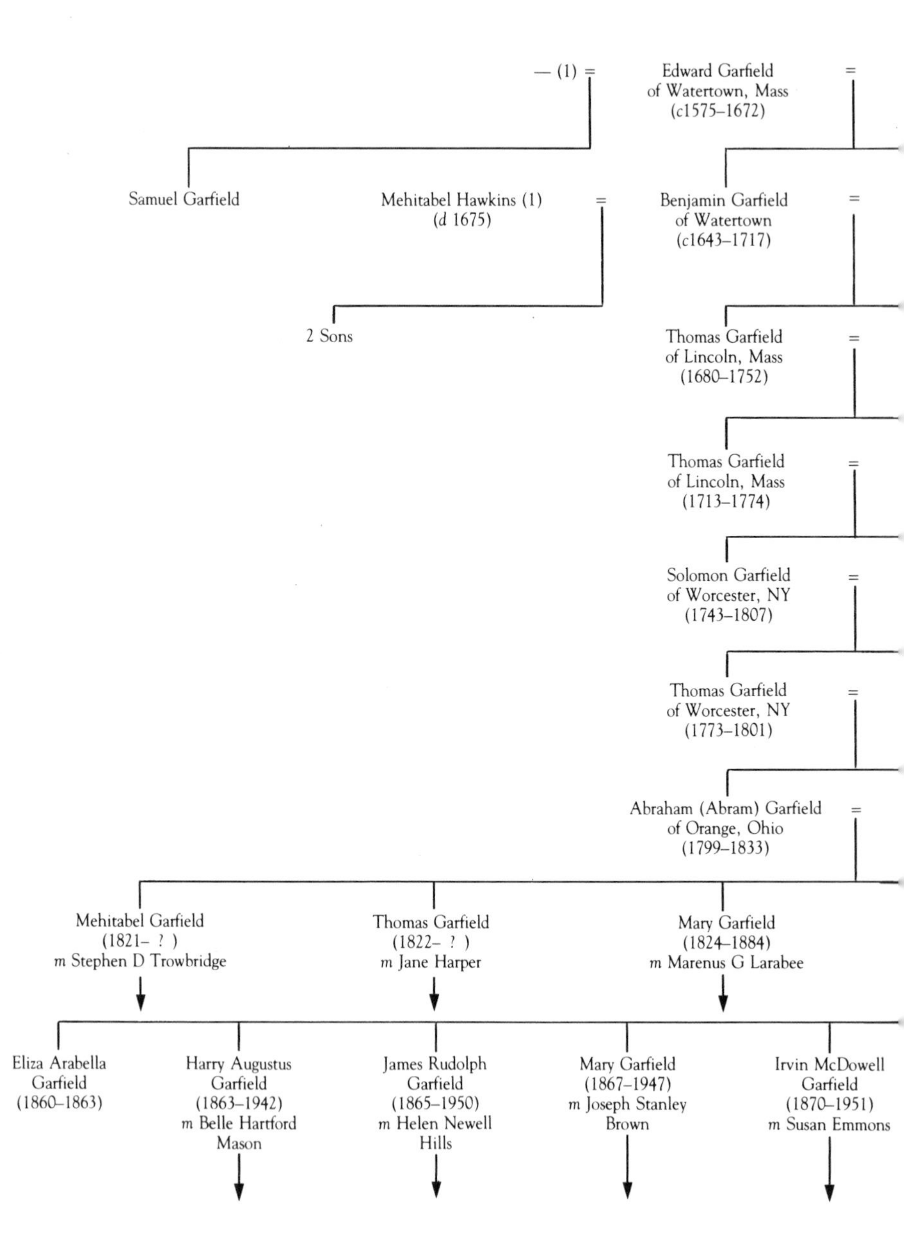
— (1) =
Edward Garfield
of Watertown, Mass
(c1575–1672)
=
Samuel Garfield
Mehitabel Hawkins (1)
(d 1675)
=
Benjamin Garfield
of Watertown
(c1643–1717)
=
2 Sons
Thomas Garfield
of Lincoln, Mass
(1680–1752)
=
Thomas Garfield
of Lincoln, Mass
(1713–1774)
=
Solomon Garfield
of Worcester, NY
(1743–1807)
=
Thomas Garfield
of Worcester, NY
(1773–1801)
=
Abraham (Abram) Garfield
of Orange, Ohio
(1799–1833)
=
Mehitabel Garfield
(1821– ?)
m Stephen D Trowbridge
Thomas Garfield
(1822– ?)
m Jane Harper
Mary Garfield
(1824–1884)
m Marenus G Larabee
Eliza Arabella
Garfield
(1860–1863)
Harry Augustus
Garfield
(1863–1942)
m Belle Hartford
Mason
James Rudolph
Garfield
(1865–1950)
m Helen Newell
Hills
Mary Garfield
(1867–1947)
m Joseph Stanley
Brown
Irvin McDowell
Garfield
(1870–1951)
m Susan Emmons

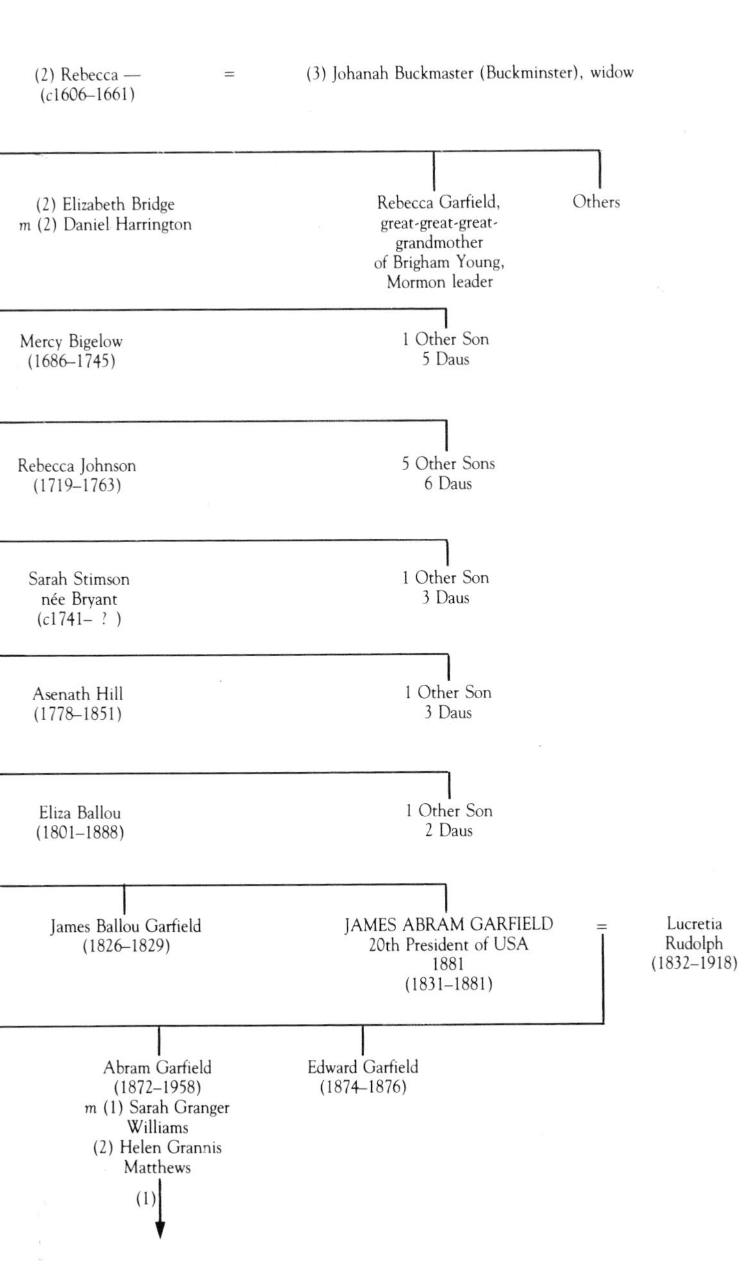
(2) Rebecca —
(c1606–1661)
=
(3) Johanah Buckmaster (Buckminster), widow
(2) Elizabeth Bridge
m (2) Daniel Harrington
Rebecca Garfield,
great-great-great-
grandmother
of Brigham Young,
Mormon leader
Others
Mercy Bigelow
(1686–1745)
1 Other Son
5 Daus
Rebecca Johnson
(1719–1763)
5 Other Sons
6 Daus
Sarah Stimson
née Bryant
(c1741– ?)
1 Other Son
3 Daus
Asenath Hill
(1778–1851)
1 Other Son
3 Daus
Eliza Ballou
(1801–1888)
1 Other Son
2 Daus
James Ballou Garfield
(1826–1829)
JAMES ABRAM GARFIELD
20th President of USA
1881
(1831–1881)
=
Lucretia
Rudolph
(1832–1918)
Abram Garfield
(1872–1958)
m (1) Sarah Granger
Williams
(2) Helen Grannis
Matthews
(1)
Edward Garfield
(1874–1876)

The scene at the Baltimore and Potomac Railroad Station as the President is shot in the back and his assailant is apprehended

lawyer whose motive remained obscure.

The President's injury did not at first seem serious, the bullet having lodged in a muscle. He was taken to the White House, where he became the victim of his doctors, who probed for the bullet with unsterilized instruments but were unable to extract it. Two months later Garfield asked to be taken by special train to Francklyn Cottage, Elberon, New Jersey, where he hoped the sea air would help his recovery. He appeared to rally for a time, but by 15 September it became apparent that blood-poisoning had set in and he died at 10.35pm on 19 September 1881, aged forty-nine. His body was taken to Cleveland, Ohio, for burial. Mrs Garfield survived her husband for nearly thirty-six years, dying on 14 March 1918. Charles Guiteau paid for his crime on the gallows.

Portraits of the Presidents of the United States of America

In Chronological Order

George Washington (1789–1797), the first US President, in the uniform of a Colonel of the Virginia militia; a painting by Charles Willson Peale

John Adams (1797–1801);
a painting by Edgar Parker

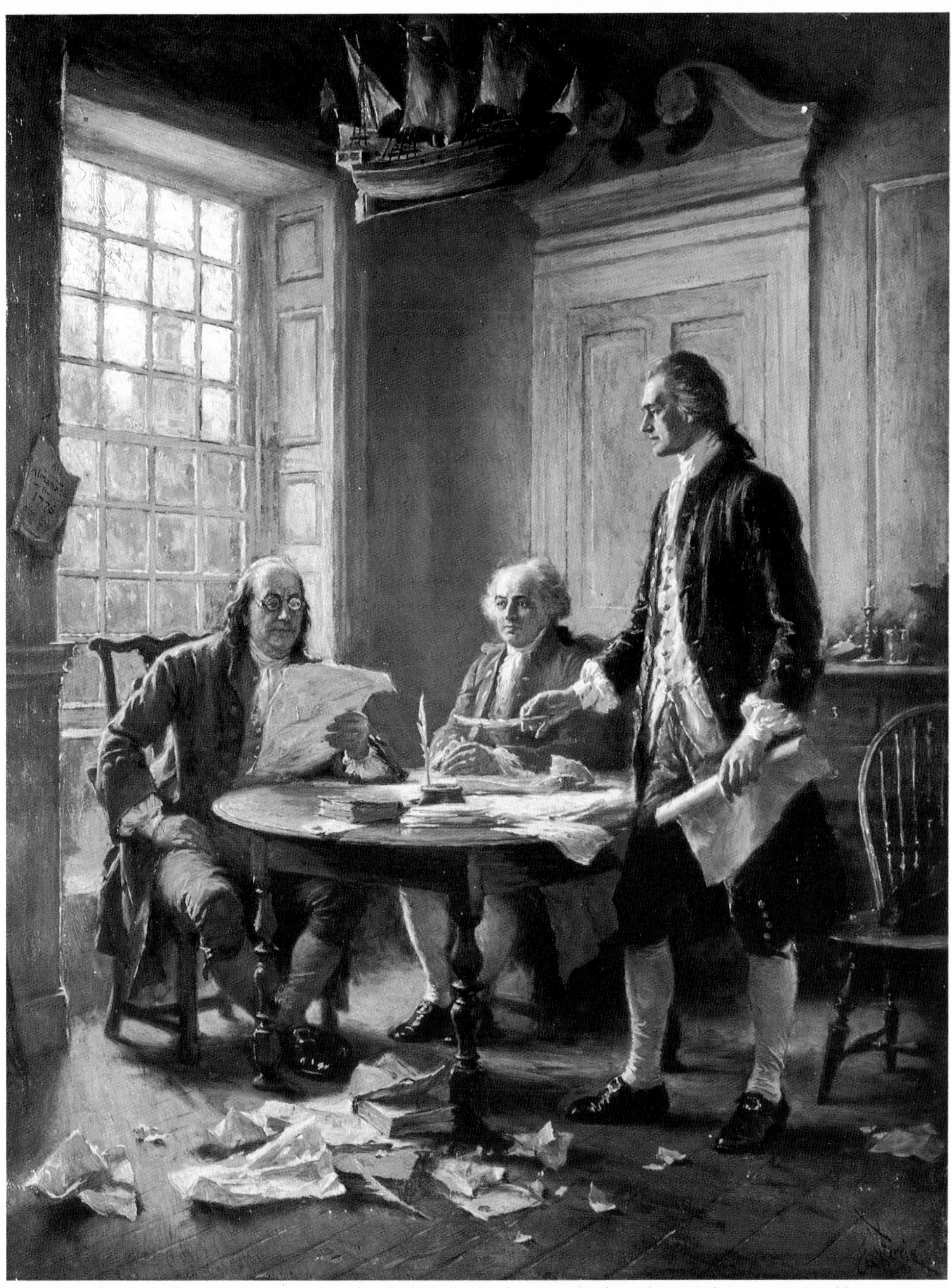

Thomas Jefferson (1801–1809), right, drafting the Declaration of Independence with Benjamin Franklin, left, and John Adams; a painting by J L G Ferris

ABOVE **James Madison (1809–1817)**; a painting by John Vanderlyn

BELOW **James Monroe (1817–1825)**, as a young man

ABOVE **John Quincy Adams (1825–1829)**; a painting by G P A Healy

BELOW **Andrew Jackson (1829–1837)**, shown on horseback wearing his military uniform, with the Tennessee army in the background

Martin Van Buren (1837–1841)

William Henry Harrison (March–April 1841); a painting by E F Andrews

John Tyler (1841–1845); a painting by G P A Healy

James Knox Polk (1845–1849); a painting by G P A Healy

ABOVE **Zachary Taylor (1849–1850)**, on the white horse in the foreground, at the battle of Buena Vista in 1847; a painting by Samual Chamberlain

Millard Fillmore (1850–1853); a painting by G P A Healy

Franklin Pierce (1853–1857);
a painting by G P A Healy

James Buchanan (1857–1861); a painting by William M Chase

Abraham Lincoln (1861–1865), in 1864

ABOVE **Andrew Johnson (1865–1869)**

BELOW **Ulysses S Grant (1869–1877)**

Rutherford Birchard Hayes (1877–1881); a photographic portrait by M Adolphe of Paris

James Abram Garfield (March–September 1881)

Chester Alan Arthur (1881–1885); a caricature satirizing his taste for finery

LICAN CLUB
According to your cloth you 've cut your coat,
O Dude of all the White House residents;
We trust that it will help you with the vote,
When next we go to nominating Presidents.

BELOW **Grover Cleveland (1885–1889 and 1893–1897)**, in a cartoon by Gillam for *Judge* called 'The Administration Typewriter'; it shows Cleveland struggling over the programme for his second term in office and exclaiming 'Blame the thing – I can't make it work!'

Benjamin Harrison (1889–1893),
sinking under the hat of his grandfather William Henry

William McKinley (1897–1901); a painting by Charles Ayer Whipple

Theodore Roosevelt (1901–1909), campaigning

William Howard Taft (1909–1913)

(Thomas) Woodrow Wilson (1913–1921), standing, at the Paris Peace Conference in 1919

Warren Gamaliel Harding (1921–1923); a painting by E Hodgson Smart

(John) Calvin Coolidge (1923–1929) and Greta Garbo, two people not famed for their loquacity, in an 'Impossible Interview'; a *Vanity Fair* cartoon of 1932

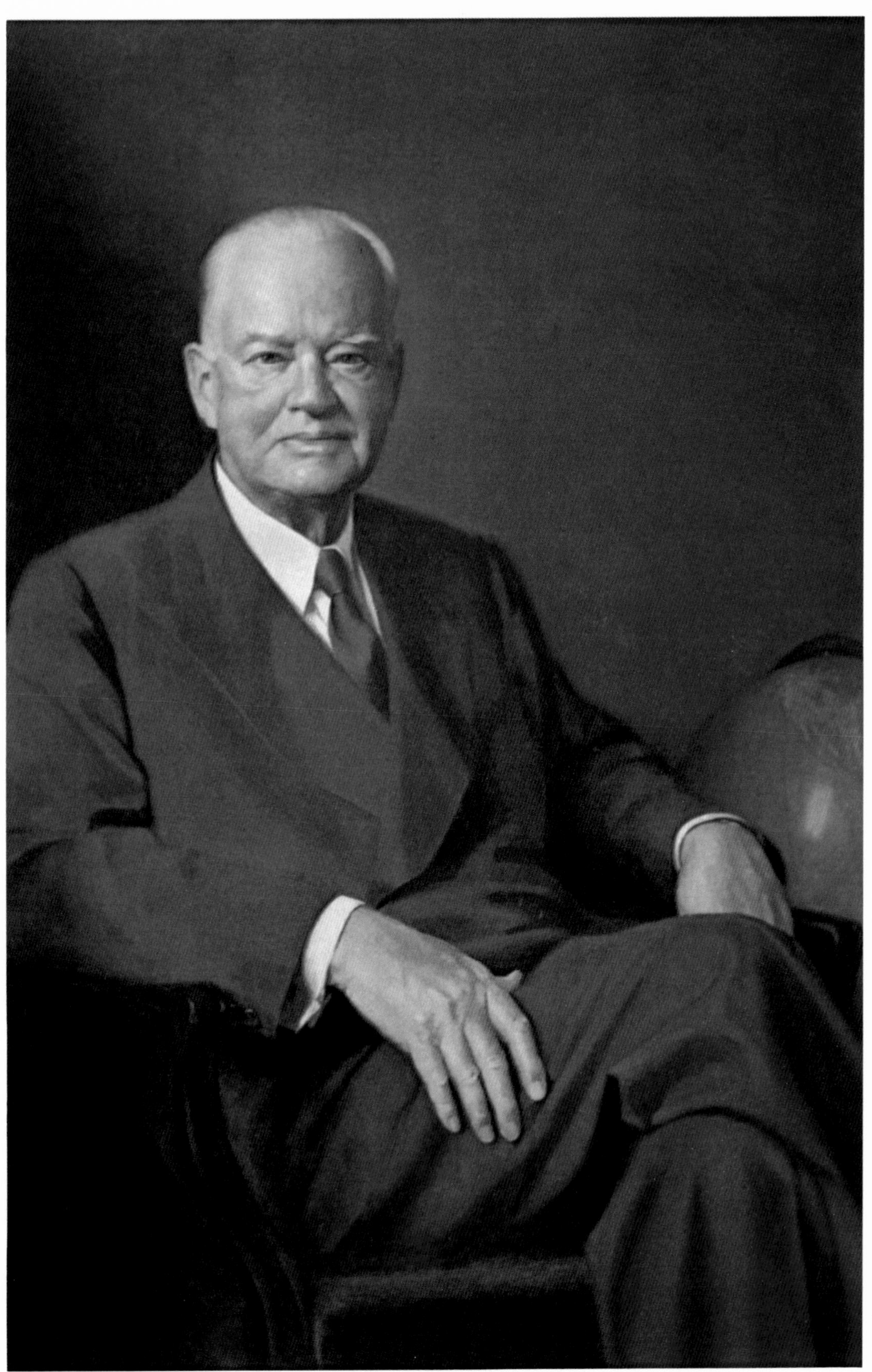

Herbert Clark Hoover (1929–1933); a painting by Elmer W Greene

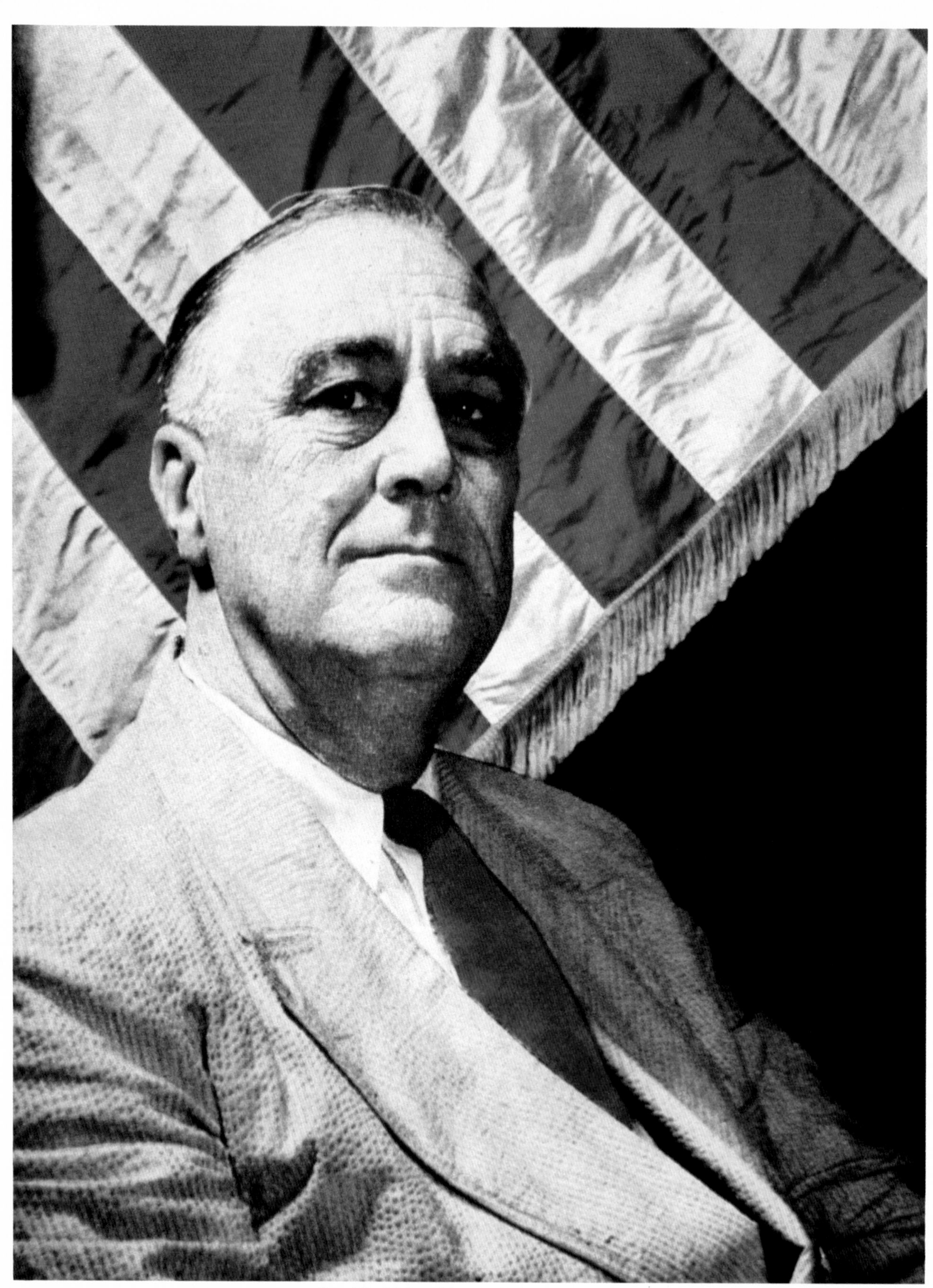

Franklin Delano Roosevelt (1933–1945)

Harry S Truman (1945–1953); a campaign button

Dwight David Eisenhower (1953–1961),
in his US army General uniform

John Fitzgerald Kennedy (1961–1963)

Lyndon Baines Johnson (1963–1969)

Richard Milhous Nixon (1969–1974)

Gerald Rudolph Ford (1974–1977)

James Earl Carter (1977–1981)

Ronald Wilson Reagan (1981–1989)

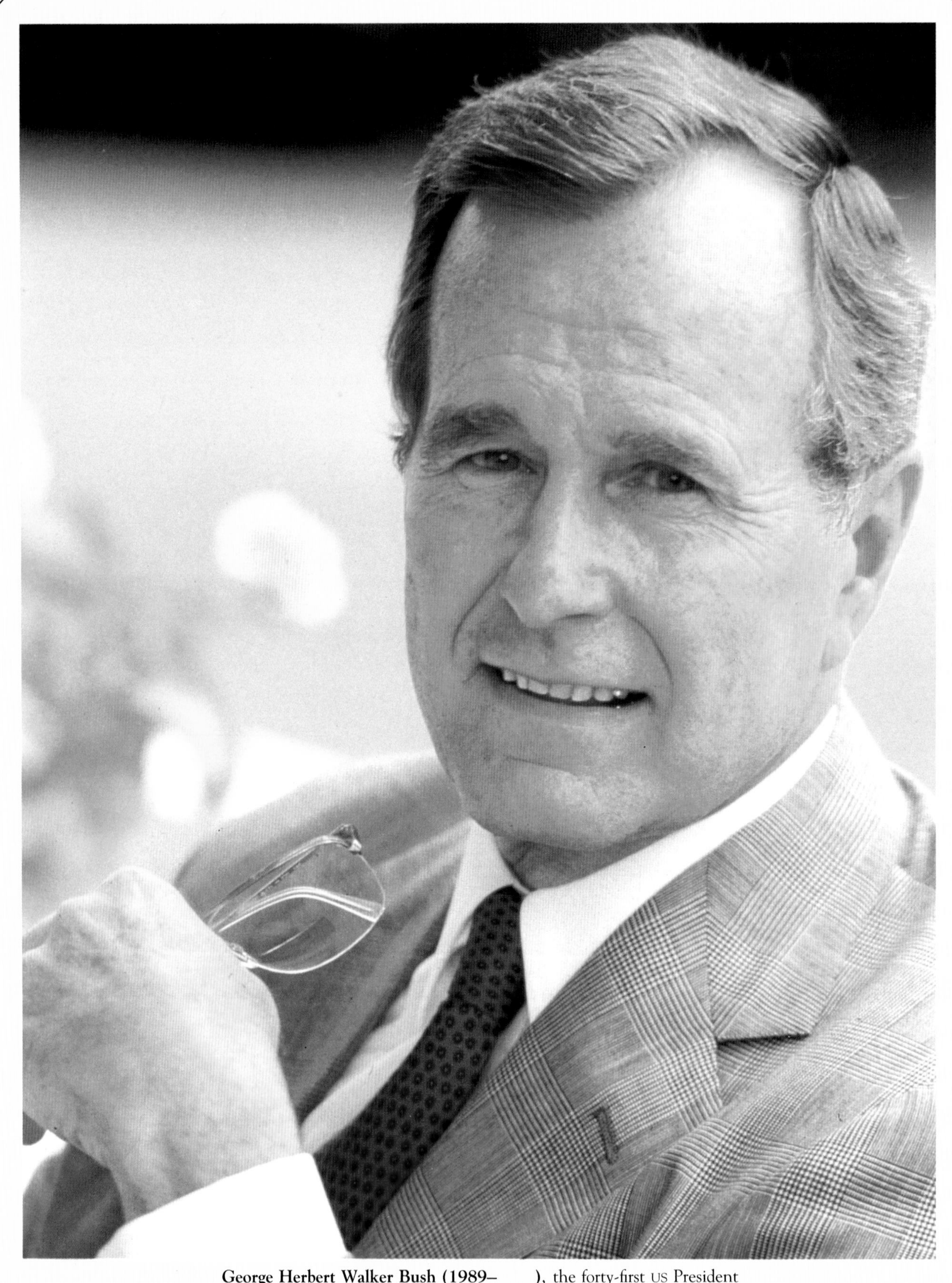

George Herbert Walker Bush (1989–   ), the forty-first US President

Chester Alan Arthur 1881–1885

Born:	Fairfield, Vermont (or possibly Canada), 5 October 1829 (not 1830 as formerly believed), eldest son of Rev William Arthur and Malvina Stone	Children:	(1) William Lewis Herndon, *b* New York 10 December 1860; *d* Englewood, New Jersey, 7 July 1863
Collector of Port of New York:	1871–1878		(2) Chester Alan Jr, *b* New York 25 July 1864; *m* (1) 8 May 1900 (div 1929) Mrs Myra Townsend Andrews (*b* New York 1 January 1870; *d* 11 September 1935), dau of Joel Adams Fithian and Fannie Barrett Conolly; 1 son, 1 dau; *m* (2) 3 November 1934 Mrs Rowena Graves (*b* 8 November 1894), dau of Richard Edward Dashwood; no children; *d* Colorado Springs 18 July 1937
Elected Vice-President:	2 November 1880		(3) Ellen (Nell) Herndon, *b* New York 21 November 1871; *m* 1907 Charles Pinkerton (*b* West Chester, Pennsylvania, 2 July 1871; *d* Mount Kisco, New York, 31 January 1974, aged 102); no children; *d* Mount Kisco, New York, 6 September 1915
Inaugurated:	4 March 1881	Died:	New York City, 18 November 1886
Succeeded as (21st) President:	19 September 1881	Buried:	Albany, New York
Took oath:	(privately) 20 September and (publicly) 22 September 1881		
Retired from presidency:	4 March 1885		
Married:	Calvary Church, New York, 25 October 1859 Ellen Lewis (*b* Culpeper, Virginia, 30 August 1837; *d* New York 12 January 1880; *bur* Rural Cemetery, Albany, New York), only child of Commodore William Lewis Herndon and Frances Elizabeth Hansbrough		

Chester Alan Arthur, Chester A Arthur, or 'Chet', as he was known to his intimates, is the least memorable of the 'accidental' Presidents – those who succeeded to the office through the deaths of their predecessors. In appearance he was a burly and prosperous-looking man and might well have been taken for a successful business-man or perhaps an entrepreneur. Certainly few would have guessed that he was the son of a Baptist minister (although he himself was an Episcopalian).

Arthur's great-grandfather, Gavin Arthur, lived at a house known as The Draen (ie 'The Place of Thorns'), near Ballymena in Co Antrim, Ireland. Gavin's son Alan also lived there and was the father of William Arthur, who went to America in 1815 at the age of nineteen and became a Baptist minister there. He was an antiquary of some note and published *The Derivation of Family Names* among other works. In 1821 he married Malvina Stone, a native of Berkshire, Vermont, whose father, George Washington Stone, was fourth in descent from Hugh Stone, of Andover, Massachusetts. William and Malvina had nine children, of whom the future President was the fifth and eldest son. Although his birthplace was always given as Fairfield, Vermont, it is highly likely that he was actually born in Canada where his parents resided for a time. If so, he is the only President not born on American soil and therefore, strictly speaking, ineligible to hold the office, but both parents were US citizens and his right was never

Chester Alan Arthur who succeeded to the presidency on the death by bullet of James Abram Garfield

A drawing by W R Leigh of the inaugural oath being administered to Arthur by Judge Brady at Arthur's house on Lexington Avenue

challenged. It has only been established fairly recently, too, that the year of his birth was 1829 and not 1830 as it had always been given.

Little is known of Arthur's childhood and early years until he entered Union College, Schenectady, New York, in September 1845. He graduated BA in July 1848 and went to teach at North Pownal, Vermont, while studying law intermittently. He must have been highly regarded in his work as he was appointed Principal of North Pownal Academy in 1849. Two years later he received his MA degree from Union College, and in 1853 he joined the law firm of Culver and Parker in New York City as a clerk. In May 1854, Arthur was admitted to the New York Bar and the firm became Culver, Parker, and Arthur. Two years later he formed a new law firm with Henry D Gardiner.

On 25 October 1859 Arthur married the twenty-two-year-old Ellen Lewis Herndon, whose father, Commodore William Lewis Herndon, had won fame as the explorer of the Amazon. An extremely attractive young woman, Ellen bore Arthur three children and died in January 1880 at the early age of forty-two. Arthur did not remarry and his sister Mrs John McElroy acted as his hostess at the White House.

During the Civil War, Arthur served in administrative capacities, first as State Engineer-in-Chief (with the rank of Brigadier-General) on Governor Edwin D Morgan's staff, then successively as Assistant Quartermaster-General, Inspector-General and finally as Quartermaster-General. He resigned this last commission on 31 December 1863 and resumed his law practice in New York. From 1869 to 1870 he was counsel to New York City Tax Commission. In 1871 Arthur was appointed Collector of the Port of New York by President Grant and after confirmation by the Senate commissioned for four years. He was re-appointed for another four years in 1875. Following the Jay Commission charges criticizing his management of the Custom House, Arthur's resignation was requested by the Secretary of the Treasury, but Arthur refused to resign and made a reply refuting the charges. In July 1878 President Hayes suspended him as Collector and he resumed his law practice.

The Republican National Convention at Chicago nominated Arthur for Vice-President on 8 June 1880. He formally accepted the nomination a month later and was elected on 2 November 1880, taking the oath in the Senate Chamber on 4 March 1881. Garfield's death from his bullet wound on 19 September brought about

The Arthur Family

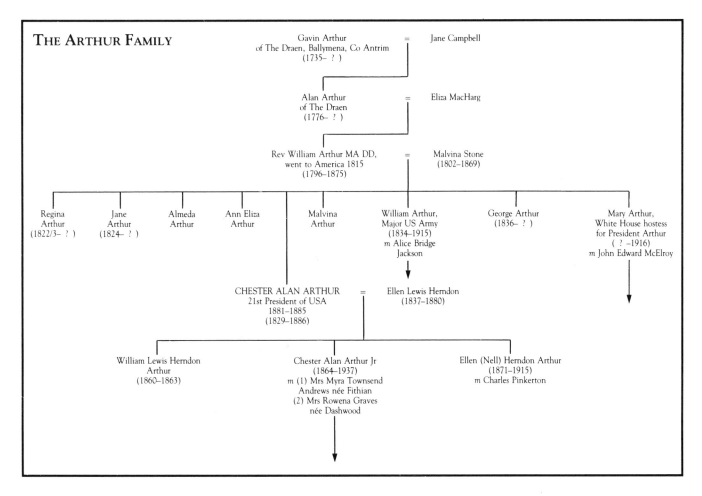

Gavin Arthur of The Draen, Ballymena, Co Antrim (1735– ?) = Jane Campbell

Alan Arthur of The Draen (1776– ?) = Eliza MacHarg

Rev William Arthur MA DD, went to America 1815 (1796–1875) = Malvina Stone (1802–1869)

- Regina Arthur (1822/3– ?)
- Jane Arthur (1824– ?)
- Almeda Arthur
- Ann Eliza Arthur
- CHESTER ALAN ARTHUR, 21st President of USA 1881–1885 (1829–1886) = Ellen Lewis Herndon (1837–1880)
  - William Lewis Herndon Arthur (1860–1863)
  - Chester Alan Arthur Jr (1864–1937) *m* (1) Mrs Myra Townsend Andrews née Fithian (2) Mrs Rowena Graves née Dashwood ↓
  - Ellen (Nell) Herndon Arthur (1871–1915) *m* Charles Pinkerton
- Malvina Arthur
- William Arthur, Major US Army (1834–1915) *m* Alice Bridge Jackson ↓
- George Arthur (1836– ?)
- Mary Arthur, White House hostess for President Arthur (? –1916) *m* John Edward McElroy ↓

Arthur's accession to the presidency. He took the oath of office in his own house, 123 Lexington Avenue, New York, in the afternoon of Tuesday 20 September 1881 and again two days later in a private ceremony in the Vice-President's room at the Capitol.

Arthur's tenure of the presidency was good if not spectacular, and he applied himself to a number of necessary reforms in the Civil Service. He also refurnished the White House and had the first elevator installed. His failure to gain nomination for re-election in 1884 was a disappointment to him, but one he accepted gracefully. He retired from office on 4 March 1885, attended the inauguration of Cleveland, and then quietly resumed his law practice. In February 1886 it was found that he was suffering from Bright's disease and he was forced to retire. Treatment brought relief for a few months, but on 16 November 1886 he suffered a cerebral haemorrhage and died two days later. He was buried at Albany, New York.

President Arthur's descendants became extinct on the death of his grandson Chester Alan Arthur III in April 1972.

(Stephen) Grover Cleveland 1885–1889 and 1893–1897

Born:	Caldwell, New Jersey, 18 March 1837, 3rd son of Rev Richard Falley Cleveland and Anne Neal
Governor of New York:	1883–1885
Elected (22nd) President:	4 November 1884
Inaugurated:	East Portico of Capitol 4 March 1885
Retired from presidency:	4 March 1889
Elected (24th) President:	9 January 1893
Inaugurated:	East Portico of Capitol 4 March 1893
Retired from presidency:	4 March 1897
Married:	The White House, Washington DC, 2 June 1886 Frances (*b* Buffalo, New York, 21 July 1864; *m*(2) 10 February 1913 Thomas Jex Preston Jr, Professor of Archaeology at Princeton; *d* Baltimore, Maryland, 29 October 1947; *bur* Princeton), dau of Oscar Folsom and Emma Cornelia Harmon
Children:	(1) Ruth, *b* New York City 3 October 1891; *d* Princeton, New Jersey, 7 January 1904 (2) Esther, *b* the White House 9 September 1893; *m* Westminster Abbey. London, England, 14 March 1918 Capt William Sidney Bence Bosanquet DSO, Coldstream Guards (*b* 1893; *d* Redcar, Yorkshire, England 5 March 1966), yst son of Sir Frederick Albert Bosanquet KC and his 2nd wife Philippa Frances Bence-Jones; 2 daus; *d* New Hampshire 25 June 1980 (3) Marion, *b* Buzzards Bay, Massachusetts, 7 July 1895; *m* (1) 28 November 1917 (div) William Stanley Dell (*b* 1894); 1 dau; *m* (2) 25 July 1926 John Harlan Amen (*b* Exeter, New Hampshire, 15 September 1898; *d* New York 10 March 1960), son of Harlan Page Amen and Mary Rawson; 1 son; *d* — (4) Richard Folsom, *b* Princeton, New Jersey, 28 October 1897; *m* (1) 20 June 1923 (div 1940) Ellen Douglas (*b* 1897; *d* 17 February 1954), dau of Bishop Gailor; 1 son, 2 daus; *m* (2) 12 June 1943 Jessie Maxwell (*b* Baltimore 1 March 1919), dau of George C Black and Jessie Maxwell; 1 son, 2 daus; *d* Baltimore 10 January 1974 (5) Francis Grover, *b* Buzzard Bay, Massachusetts, 18 July 1903; *m* 20 June 1925 Alice (*b* 24 March 1904), dau of Rev Charles Erdman; 1 dau
Died:	Princeton, New Jersey, 24 June 1908
Buried:	Princeton

Grover Cleveland holds the unique distinction of having served for two non-consecutive presidential terms. He is therefore reckoned as both the twenty-second and the twenty-fourth President. Naturally, this has caused a lot of confusion and many people find it hard to understand how President Reagan, for example, although officially reckoned as the fortieth President is only the thirty-ninth man to have held the presidential office.

The brothers Moses and Aaron Cleveland emi-rated from Ipswich, Suffolk, England, to Plymouth, Massachusetts, in 1635. Moses died in 1702 and his son, grandson, great-grandson and great-great-grandson were all called Aaron. The last of them was grandfather of the Rev Richard Falley Cleveland, a Presbyterian minister, who in 1829 married Anne Neal of Baltimore and in due time became the father of nine children, of whom Stephen Grover Cleveland, the future President, was the third son and was born in the Manse of the First Presbyterian Church at Coldwell, New Jersey, on 18 March 1837.

By the time Grover was sixteen his father's ministry had led to three moves for the family and it was soon after the last, to Holland Patent, New York, that the Rev Richard Falley Cleveland died, on 1 October 1853 at the age of forty-nine, leaving his widow and all their children surviving, quite a remarkable feat in those days.

Cleveland did not attend college or university, but in 1853 went to work for a year as a clerk and assistant teacher with the New York Institute for the Blind in New York City. He then joined his uncle, Lewis F Allen, as assistant editor of the *American Shorthorn Handbook*, of which Allen was the founder and editor. He worked on several editions while simultaneously studying law and was admitted to the New York Bar in Buffalo in 1859, when he became managing clerk for Rogers, Bowen and Rogers. He was appointed Assistant District Attorney of Erie County in 1863 but was unsuccessful as Democratic candidate for District Attorney in 1865. Shortly thereafter he formed a law firm with Isaac K Vanderpoel and when Vanderpoel resigned in 1869 the firm became Lanning, Cleveland and Folsom. Cleveland served as Sheriff of Erie County from 1871 to

Grover Cleveland and his family

1874, when he returned to law practice. It was in 1874 that Cleveland became involved with a local widow, Mrs Maria Halpin (née Crofts), who on 14 September 1874 gave birth to a son, of whom she claimed Cleveland was the father. Rather strangely she named the boy Oscar Folsom Cleveland after Cleveland's law partner and future father-in-law. Cleveland admitted paternity and arranged for the child to be admitted to an orphanage and later adopted. When he grew up he became a doctor.

In 1881 Cleveland was elected Mayor of Buffalo and took office on 1 January 1882. In September the Democratic State Convention at Syracuse, New York, nominated him for Governor of New York and he was duly elected and took office on 1 January 1883. In July the Democratic National Convention at Chicago nominated him for President and in the election Cleveland received 219 of the 401 electoral votes, his Republican opponent James Gillespie Blaine receiving 182.

Cleveland had made a clean breast of his affair with the widow and his honesty in so doing stood him in good stead with the electors. He appointed a strong cabinet and by use of the veto took a firm hand in attempting to curb the then current trend of abuse of political patronage. He vetoed a total of 414 bills during his first term, more than twice the number vetoed by all his predecessors put together, and 282 of them were pension bills which he judged to be on behalf of undeserving veterans. Only two of these vetoes were overridden.

On 2 June 1886 the forty-nine-year-old bachelor Cleveland was married at the White House to Frances Folsom, the twenty-one-year-old daughter of his law partner. The marriage was blessed with five children. Four and a half years after Cleveland's death his widow married again to a Professor of Archaeology at Princeton University. She died in October 1947.

Cleveland was re-nominated for President in 1888, but lost the election to Harrison. 'We are coming back just four years from today,' Mrs Cleveland is reputed to have told the White House staff as they left on 4 March 1889. Cleveland returned to his law practice and bided his time. In June 1892 the Democratic National Con-

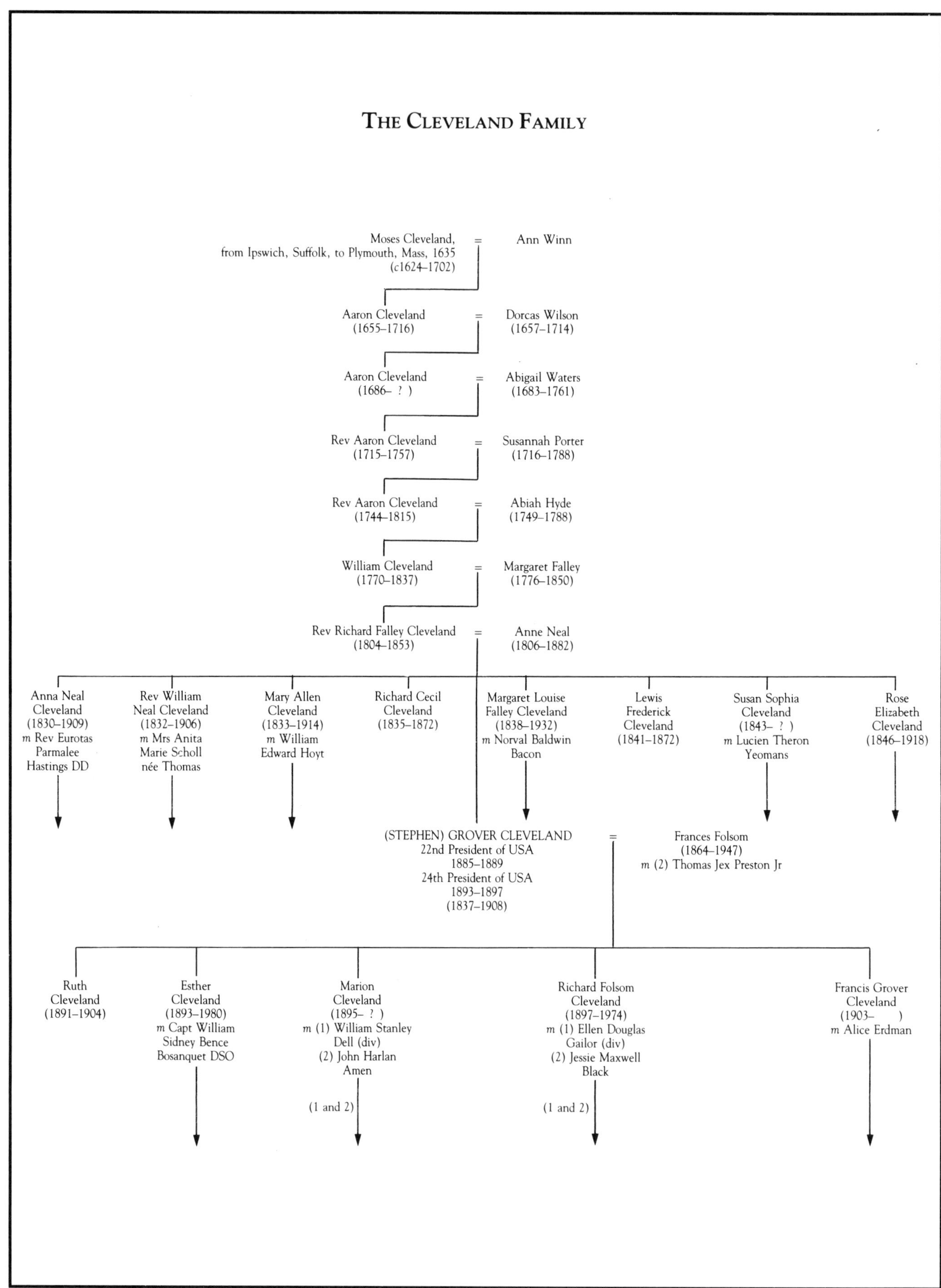
THE CLEVELAND FAMILY
Moses Cleveland, from Ipswich, Suffolk, to Plymouth, Mass, 1635 (c1624–1702)
=
Ann Winn
Aaron Cleveland (1655–1716)
=
Dorcas Wilson (1657–1714)
Aaron Cleveland (1686– ?)
=
Abigail Waters (1683–1761)
Rev Aaron Cleveland (1715–1757)
=
Susannah Porter (1716–1788)
Rev Aaron Cleveland (1744–1815)
=
Abiah Hyde (1749–1788)
William Cleveland (1770–1837)
=
Margaret Falley (1776–1850)
Rev Richard Falley Cleveland (1804–1853)
=
Anne Neal (1806–1882)
Anna Neal Cleveland (1830–1909) m Rev Eurotas Parmalee Hastings DD
Rev William Neal Cleveland (1832–1906) m Mrs Anita Marie Scholl née Thomas
Mary Allen Cleveland (1833–1914) m William Edward Hoyt
Richard Cecil Cleveland (1835–1872)
Margaret Louise Falley Cleveland (1838–1932) m Norval Baldwin Bacon
Lewis Frederick Cleveland (1841–1872)
Susan Sophia Cleveland (1843– ?) m Lucien Theron Yeomans
Rose Elizabeth Cleveland (1846–1918)
(STEPHEN) GROVER CLEVELAND 22nd President of USA 1885–1889 24th President of USA 1893–1897 (1837–1908)
=
Frances Folsom (1864–1947) m (2) Thomas Jex Preston Jr
Ruth Cleveland (1891–1904)
Esther Cleveland (1893–1980) m Capt William Sidney Bence Bosanquet DSO
Marion Cleveland (1895– ?) m (1) William Stanley Dell (div) (2) John Harlan Amen
(1 and 2)
Richard Folsom Cleveland (1897–1974) m (1) Ellen Douglas Gailor (div) (2) Jessie Maxwell Black
(1 and 2)
Francis Grover Cleveland (1903–) m Alice Erdman

Frances Folsom Cleveland, the President's wife

vention at Chicago nominated him for President on the first ballot and in the election he won back the presidency from Harrison. The twenty-second President had become the twenty-fourth. Cleveland's second inauguration took place on Saturday 4 March 1893, the oath being administered by Chief Justice Melville Weston Fuller on the East Portico of the Capitol.

Within a few months of his inauguration Cleveland became gravely ill and cancer of the jaw was diagnosed. The matter was not made public and on 1 July 1893 the President was operated on in the utmost secrecy on board the yacht *Oneida*, anchored in Long Island Sound. Most of his upper left jaw, part of his palate and two contiguous teeth were removed. A second operation on 17 July removed further malignant tissue and Cleveland was fitted with an artificial jawbone, one of the earliest instances of prosthetic surgery. The cancer was completely eradicated and it was given out officially that the President had had two teeth extracted. The full details were not published until 1917, although an account appeared in the Philadelphia *Press* in August 1893, only to be promptly denied by presidential aides.

Cleveland's recovery was rapid and he was soon back in the swing of things looking as robust as he had ever done. The depression of 1893 served to lose Cleveland much of his new-found popularity and by the time he retired from office on 4 March 1897 he was surrounded by ridicule and hate on all sides.

After attending McKinley's inauguration, Cleveland went on a short shooting and fishing trip in Virginia and then joined his wife and family in the new house they had bought at Princeton and named Westland. His retirement years were spent as a lecturer and member of the board of trustees of Princeton University and in reorganizing the Equitable Life Assurance Society of US in New York City, which led to his election as President of the Association of Presidents of Life Insurance Companies at a salary of $25,000 a year. Cleveland died of a heart attack at Princeton on 24 June 1908 at the age of seventy-one.

Benjamin Harrison 1889–1893

Born:	North Bend, Ohio, 20 August 1833, yst son of John Scott Harrison (5th son of President William Henry Harrison *qv*) and his 2nd wife Elizabeth Ramsey Irwin
Senator:	1881–1887
Elected (23rd) President:	4 November 1888
Inaugurated:	East Portico of Capitol 4 March 1889
Retired from presidency:	4 March 1893
Married:	(1) Oxford, Ohio, 20 October 1853 Caroline Lavinia (*b* Oxford, Ohio, 1 October 1832; *d* the White House 25 October 1892; *bur* Crown Hill Cemetery Indianapolis, Indiana), 3rd dau of Rev Dr John Witherspoon Scott and Mary Potts Neal
Children:	(1) Russell Benjamin, *b* Oxford, Ohio, 12 August 1854; *m* Omaha, Nebraska, 9 January 1884, Mary Angeline (*b* 16 November 1861; *d* Washington DC 28 November 1944), dau of Senator Alvin Saunders; 1 son, 1 dau; *d* Indianapolis 13 December 1936
	(2) Mary Scott, *b* Indianapolis 3 April 1858; *m* Indianapolis 5 November 1884 (James) Robert McKee (*b* Madison, Indiana, 9 December 1857; *d* Greenwich, Connecticut, 21 October 1942), son of Robert S McKee; 1 son, 1 dau; *d* Greenwich, Connecticut, 28 October 1930
	(3) A daughter, *d* at birth 13 June 1861
Married:	(2) St Thomas's Protestant Episcopal Church, New York, 6 April 1896 Mary Scott (*b* Honesdale, Pennsylvania, 30 April 1858; *d* New York 5 January 1948; *bur* Crown Hill Cemetery, Indianapolis), widow of Walter Erskine Dimmick and dau of Russell Farnham Lord and Elizabeth Mayhew Scott (sister of the first Mrs Benjamin Harrison)
Children:	(1) Elizabeth, *b* Indianapolis 21 February 1897; *m* New York 6 April 1921 James Blaine Walker Jr (*b* Helena, Montana, 20 January 1889; *d* New York City 15 January 1878), son of James Blaine Walker and Mary Gertrude Scannell; 1 son, 1 dau; *d* New York City 25 December 1955
Died:	Indianapolis, Indiana, 13 March 1901
Buried:	Crown Hill Cemetery, Indianapolis

Benjamin Harrison is the only grandson of a President also to become President and the fact that he was the grandson of the hero of Tippecanoe and the great-grandson of 'the Signer' went a long way in his favour when it came to running for office. He was born at North Bend, Ohio, on 20 August 1833, his father John Scott Harrison being the fifth son of William Henry Harrison.

Benjamin was his father's third son and the second by his second wife Elizabeth Ramsey Irwin. He grew up in an atmosphere of solid, well-to-do comfort, attending local schools and being privately tutored at home before entering Farmer's College, near Cincinnati, in 1848. His mother died in August 1850, a month before he entered Miami University in Oxford, Ohio, from which he graduated fourth in his class with a BA degree in June 1852. He followed the familiar pattern of then reading law but before being admitted to the Ohio Bar in 1854 married Caroline Lavinia Scott, the daughter of the Rev Dr John Witherspoon Scott, a Presbyterian minister and also Professor of Mathematics and Natural Sciences at Miami University. It was an entirely suitable marriage and produced one son and one daughter. A second daughter died at birth in 1861.

Harrison practised law in Indianapolis, joined the Republican party, was elected City Attorney in 1857,

Benjamin Harrison in a cartoon called 'The Raven': the raven is croaking 'Nevermore' to Harrison's efforts for another term

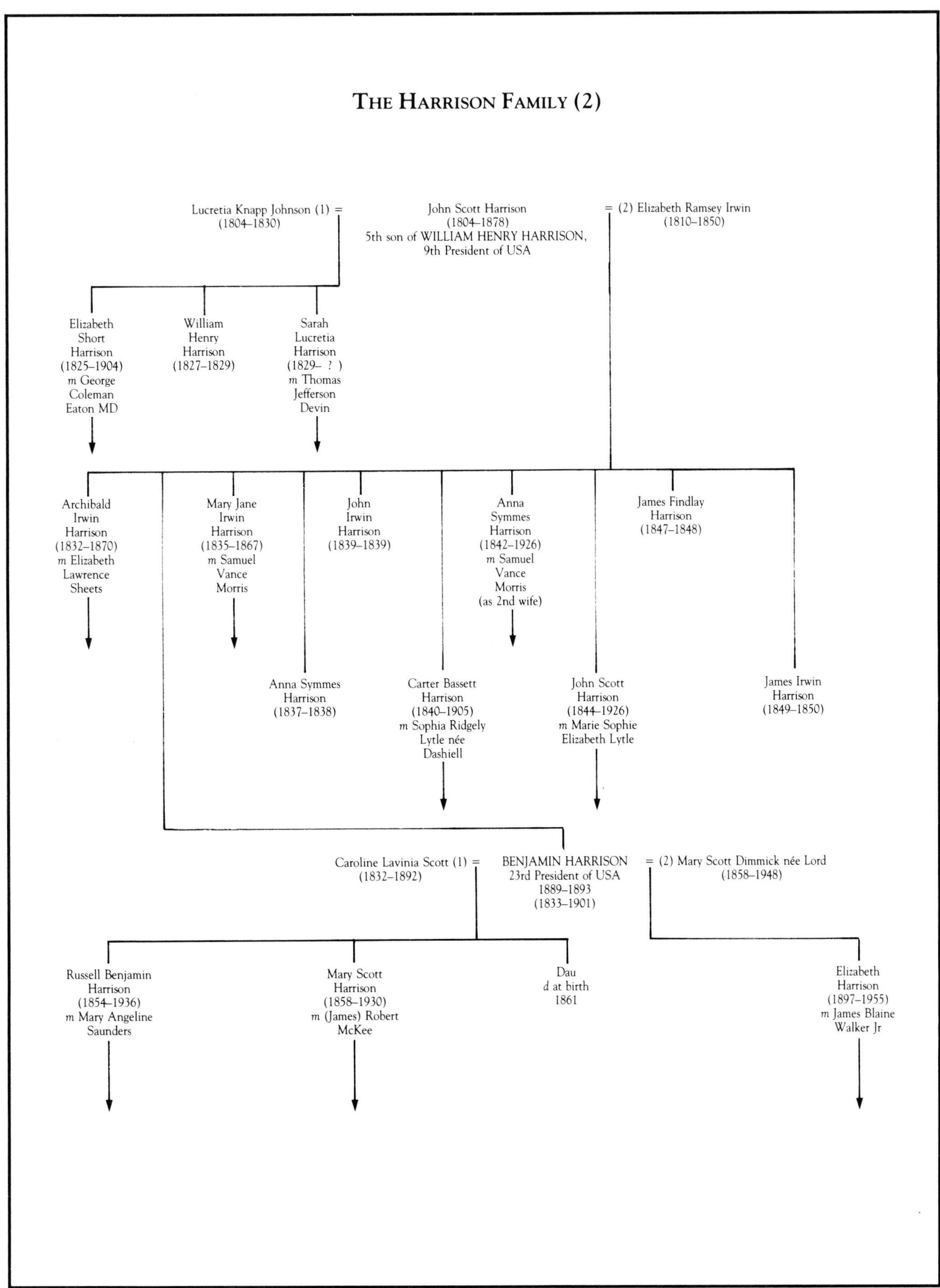
THE HARRISON FAMILY (2)
Lucretia Knapp Johnson (1) = (1804–1830)
John Scott Harrison (1804–1878) 5th son of WILLIAM HENRY HARRISON, 9th President of USA
= (2) Elizabeth Ramsey Irwin (1810–1850)
Elizabeth Short Harrison (1825–1904) m George Coleman Eaton MD
William Henry Harrison (1827–1829)
Sarah Lucretia Harrison (1829– ?) m Thomas Jefferson Devin
Archibald Irwin Harrison (1832–1870) m Elizabeth Lawrence Sheets
Mary Jane Irwin Harrison (1835–1867) m Samuel Vance Morris
John Irwin Harrison (1839–1839)
Anna Symmes Harrison (1842–1926) m Samuel Vance Morris (as 2nd wife)
James Findlay Harrison (1847–1848)
Anna Symmes Harrison (1837–1838)
Carter Bassett Harrison (1840–1905) m Sophia Ridgely Lytle née Dashiell
John Scott Harrison (1844–1926) m Marie Sophie Elizabeth Lytle
James Irwin Harrison (1849–1850)
Caroline Lavinia Scott (1) = (1832–1892)
BENJAMIN HARRISON 23rd President of USA 1889–1893 (1833–1901)
= (2) Mary Scott Dimmick née Lord (1858–1948)
Russell Benjamin Harrison (1854–1936) m Mary Angeline Saunders
Mary Scott Harrison (1858–1930) m (James) Robert McKee
Dau d at birth 1861
Elizabeth Harrison (1897–1955) m James Blaine Walker Jr

The first Mrs Benjamin Harrison

and Reporter of Indiana Supreme Court in 1860. In 1862 he joined the Union army, was swiftly promoted to Colonel and saw active service in Kentucky and Tennessee in 1862 and 1863. In December 1864 he took part in the battle of Nashville and in January 1865 was breveted Brigadier-General of Volunteers. A few days later he was struck down with scarlet fever in New York and lay seriously ill for several weeks. He returned to his duties at the end of February and was again posted south, where he witnessed General Johnston's surrender to General Sherman at Durham's Station, North Carolina, on 26 April. He received his commission as Brigadier-General in May and a month later was discharged from the army and returned to Indianapolis to resume his law practice.

After two unsuccessful bids for the governorship of Indianapolis, Harrison was elected to the Senate in 1881, but was defeated for re-election in 1887. Early the following year he opened his presidential campaign in Detroit, Michigan. He was nominated for President at the Republican National Convention in Chicago in June 1888 and in the ensuing election gained 233 electoral votes as opposed to Cleveland's 168. He was inaugurated on Monday 4 March 1889 on the East Portico of the Capitol with Chief Justice Melville W Fuller administering the oath.

Harrison was inclined to be stiff and formal in manner and has been described as being 'as cold as an iceberg'. He found the presidency onerous and often referred to the White House as 'my jail'. Mrs Harrison, who had accepted the position of first President-General of the Daughters of the American Revolution in 1890, began to ail in 1892 and took to her room. Her widowed niece, Mrs Mary Scott Dimmick, came to the White House to act as her secretary, take over the official hostessing, and help look after her. Mrs Harrison finally died on 25 October 1892.

Harrison was not keen to seek re-election in 1895 and was probably relieved when he lost to Cleveland and was able to return to his law practice in Indianapolis, which he built up into one of the best in the country. In April 1896 he was married in New York to Mrs Dimmick. His son and daughter by his first wife both strongly disapproved of their father's marriage to their own first cousin and refused to attend the ceremony. The following February the new Mrs Harrison gave birth to a daughter, her first and only child and Harrison became a father again at the age of sixty-three. He lived another four years, dying of pneumonia on 13 March 1901 at the age of sixty-seven and was buried in Crown Hill Cemetery, Indianapolis, where both his wives also lie. The second Mrs Harrison survived until January 1948.

WILLIAM McKINLEY 1897–1901

Born:	Niles, Ohio, 29 January 1843, 3rd son of William McKinley and Nancy Campbell Allison	Married:	First Presbyterian Church, Canton, Ohio, 25 January 1871 Ida (*b* Canton, Ohio, 8 June 1847; *d* Canton, Ohio, 26 May 1907; *bur* Canton, Ohio), elder dau of James Asbury Saxton and Kate Dewalt
Member of House of Representatives:	1877–1890	Children:	(1) Katherine (Katie), *b* Canton, Ohio, 25 December 1871; *d* Canton, Ohio, 25 June 1876 (2) Ida, *b* Canton, Ohio, 1 April, *d* 22 August 1873
Governor of Ohio:	1892–1896		
Elected (25th) President:	3 November 1896		
Inaugurated:	East Portico of Capitol 4 March 1897		
Elected for 2nd term:	6 November 1900	Died in office:	Buffalo, New York, 14 September 1901 (of wounds received when he was shot by an anarchist 6 September)
Inaugurated:	East Portico of Capitol 4 March 1901	Buried:	Canton, Ohio

William McKinley is probably the saddest President, not just because he was assassinated but because of his touching devotion to his invalid wife, forever grieving the loss of their two children, and his dying in the knowledge that she would have to suffer his loss as well with no one to sustain her.

David McKinley emigrated from Ulster with his wife and family in 1743 and settled in York County, Pennsylvania, where he set up as a weaver. His grandson, another David, fought in the Revolutionary War and was the grandfather of William McKinley, of Niles, Ohio, who managed a blast furnace foundry. He married Nancy Campbell Allison and had nine children, of whom the seventh was William McKinley, the future President, born at Niles on 29 January 1843.

William received his early schooling in Niles and when the family moved to Poland, Ohio, in 1852 he entered the Union Seminary there, going on to Allegheny College, Meadville, Pennsylvania, in 1859. He left there after a year because of ill health and returned to Poland where he worked as a schoolteacher and then as a Post Office clerk until enlisting as a private in the Ohio

President McKinley photographed fifteen minutes before he was assassinated on 6 September 1901

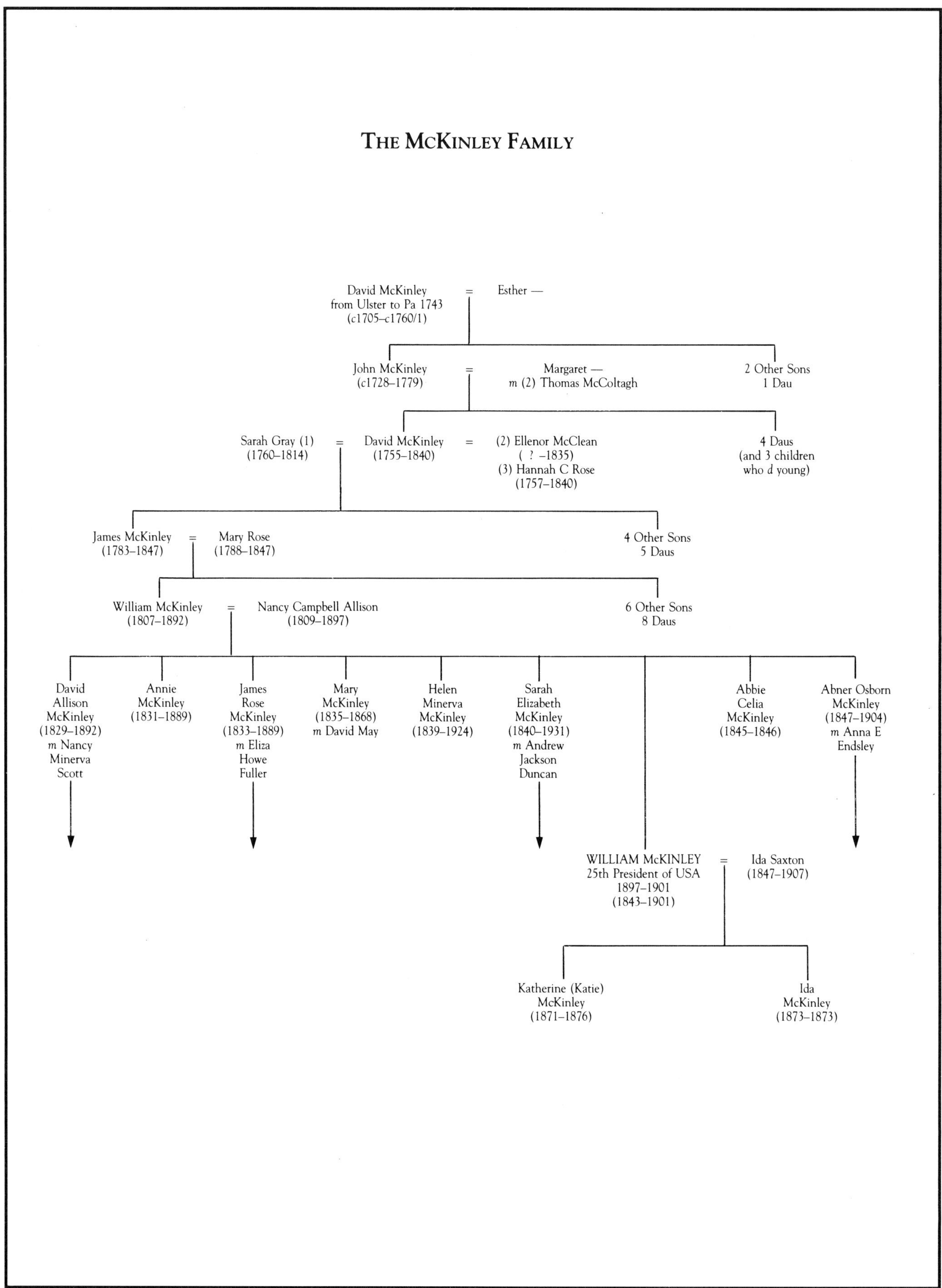
THE McKINLEY FAMILY
David McKinley from Ulster to Pa 1743 (c1705–c1760/1) = Esther —
John McKinley (c1728–1779) = Margaret — m (2) Thomas McColtagh
2 Other Sons 1 Dau
Sarah Gray (1) (1760–1814) = David McKinley (1755–1840) = (2) Ellenor McClean (? –1835) (3) Hannah C Rose (1757–1840)
4 Daus (and 3 children who d young)
James McKinley (1783–1847) = Mary Rose (1788–1847)
4 Other Sons 5 Daus
William McKinley (1807–1892) = Nancy Campbell Allison (1809–1897)
6 Other Sons 8 Daus
David Allison McKinley (1829–1892) m Nancy Minerva Scott
Annie McKinley (1831–1889)
James Rose McKinley (1833–1889) m Eliza Howe Fuller
Mary McKinley (1835–1868) m David May
Helen Minerva McKinley (1839–1924)
Sarah Elizabeth McKinley (1840–1931) m Andrew Jackson Duncan
Abbie Celia McKinley (1845–1846)
Abner Osborn McKinley (1847–1904) m Anna E Endsley
WILLIAM McKINLEY 25th President of USA 1897–1901 (1843–1901) = Ida Saxton (1847–1907)
Katherine (Katie) McKinley (1871–1876)
Ida McKinley (1873–1873)

President William and Mrs Ida McKinley

Infantry in June 1861. He was the last President to serve in the Civil War and saw active service at the battles of Antietam, Winchester, Opequon, Cedar Creek, and Fishers Hill among others. He reached the rank of Brevet Major before he was mustered out of the army in July 1865. On returning to civilian life McKinley began to study law and attended a law school at Albany, New York, in 1866. He was admitted to the Ohio Bar in 1867 and began to practise in Canton, Ohio. He was elected Prosecuting Attorney for Stark County, Ohio, in 1869, but failed to be re-elected in 1871.

On 25 January 1871 McKinley was married at the First Presbyterian Church in Canton to Ida Saxton, the daughter of a local banker. She was inclined to be frail and delicate and the loss of her two daughters in early childhood as well as that of her mother caused her to lapse into chronic invalidism, suffering from phlebitis and epilepsy.

McKinley was elected to the House of Representatives in 1876 and took his seat on 4 March 1877. He chaired several committees and two Republican State Conventions before he was defeated for re-election in 1890. In 1891 he was elected Governor of Ohio and served two terms, retiring in January 1896. The Republican National Convention in St Louis, Missouri, nominated McKinley for President in June 1896 and he received 271 of the 447 electoral votes in the ensuing election. He was inaugurated on the East Portico of the Capitol on Thursday 4 March 1897, Chief Justice Melville W Fuller administering the oath for the third time.

McKinley's presidency was concerned with tariff schedules and a crisis over Cuba, leading to war with Spain in 1898. In the election of 1900 McKinley was re-elected with a larger vote of 292 and his second inauguration day took place on 4 March 1901. Mrs McKinley, an ever-growing source of anxiety to her husband, suffered an epileptic seizure during the inaugural ball. On 6 September 1901 McKinley attended a reception in the Temple of Music at the Pan-American Exposition in Buffalo, New York. He was shaking hands with visitors when he was approached by Leon .F Czolgosz, an anarchist, who shot him twice in the chest and stomach with a revolver concealed in a handkerchief draped round his hand to resemble a bandage. The President received emergency treatment at a nearby hospital and was then taken to the home of his host, John G Milburn, where he appeared to be making a recovery until 14 September 1901, when he died at 2.15am. His last days were concerned with how the news might be broken to his wife and his last words were: 'Good-bye, all. Good-bye. It is God's way. His will be done.' After lying in state in the Capitol Rotunda, McKinley was taken to Canton for burial. Mrs McKinley joined him there six years later.

THEODORE ROOSEVELT 1901–1909

Born: 33 (later re-numbered 28) East Twentieth Street, New York, 27 October 1858, elder son of Theodore Roosevelt and Martha Bulloch

Governor of New York: 1899–1900

Elected Vice-President: 6 November 1900

Inaugurated: Washington 4 March 1901

Succeeded as (26th) President: 14 September 1901

Took oath: Buffalo 14 September 1901

Elected for 2nd term: 8 November 1904

Inaugurated: East Portico of Capitol 4 March 1905

Retired from presidency: 4 March 1909

Married: (1) First Parish Church (Unitarian), Brookline, Massachusetts, 27 October 1880 Alice Hathaway (*b* Chestnut Hill, Boston, Massachusetts, 29 July 1861; *d* 6 West 57th Street, New York, 14 February 1884; *bur* Greenwood Cemetery, Brookline), 2nd dau of George Cabot Lee and Caroline Watts Haskell

Children: (1) Alice Lee, *b* 6 West 57th Street, New York, 12 February 1884; *m* the White House, Washington DC, 15 February 1906 Hon Nicholas Longworth, Speaker of House of Representatives 1925–31 (*b* Cincinnati, Ohio, 5 November 1869; *d* Aiken, South Carolina, 9 April 1931) elder son of Nicholas Longworth, Justice of the Supreme Court of Ohio, and Susan Walker; 1 dau; *d* Washington DC 20 February 1980

Married: (2) St George's Church, Hanover Square, London, England, 2 December 1886 Edith Kermit (*b* Norwich, Connecticut, 6 August 1861; *d* Sagamore Hill, Oyster Bay, Long Island, New York, 30 September 1948; *bur* Youngs Memorial Cemetery, Oyster Bay), dau of Charles Carow and Gertrude Elizabeth Tyler

Children: (1) Theodore Jr, DSC, DSM, Asstnt Sec of the Navy 1921–24, Gov of Puerto Rico 1929–32, Gov-Gen of the Philippines 1932–33, *b* Oyster Bay, Long Island, 13 September 1887; *m* New York 29 June 1910 Eleanor Butler (*b* New York 1889; *d* Oyster Bay 29 May 1960), dau of Henry Addison Alexander and Grace Green; 3 sons, 1 dau; *d* Normandy, France, 12 July 1944

(2) Kermit, *b* Oyster Bay 10 October 1889; *m* Madrid, Spain, 10 June 1914 Belle Wyatt (*b* Baltimore, Maryland, 1 July 1892; *d* Manhattan, New York, 30 March 1968) dau of Joseph Edward Willard and Belle Layton Wyatt; 3 sons, 1 dau; *d* Alaska 4 June 1943

(3) Ethel Carow, *b* 13 August 1891; *m* Oyster Bay 4 April 1913 Richard Derby MD (*b* New York 7 April 1881; *d* Brattleboro, Vermont, 21 July 1963) eldest son of Dr Richard Henry Derby and Sarah Coleman Alden; 1 son, 3 daus; *d* Oyster Bay 3 December 1977

(4) Archibald Bulloch, *b* Washington DC 9 April 1894; *m* Boston, Massachusetts, 14 April 1917 Grace Stackpole (*d* Cold Spring Harbor, New York, June 1971), only dau of Thomas St John Lockwood and Emmeline Dabney Stackpole; 2 sons, 2 daus; *d* Palm Springs, Florida, October 1979

(5) Quentin, *b* Washington DC 19 November 1897; *ka* Cambrai, France, 14 July 1918

Died: Sagamore Hill, Oyster Bay, Long Island, New York, 6 January 1919

Buried: Youngs Memorial Cemetery, Oyster Bay

Theodore Roosevelt was without doubt possessed with a greater zest for life than any of his predecessors or successors. His *bonhomie* and spirit of adventure made him appear like an overgrown schoolboy and one English diplomat once said in a kindly fashion: 'You must always remember that the President is about six.' He bore a certain resemblance to a teddy bear, the stuffed toy named after him, which has become the most popular of all its kind world wide.

The Roosevelts trace their descent from Claes Maertenszen Van Rosenvelt who emigrated from Holland to the New Netherlands (as New York State was then named) some time before 1648. His son Nicholas was Alderman of New Amsterdam (now New York City)

President Theodore Roosevelt and his family – a photograph taken in 1903; left to right, Quentin, the President, Ted, Archie, Alice, Kermit, Edith, Ethel

from 1698 to 1701 and died in 1742, leaving several children, of whom the second son, Johannes, was ancestor of Theodore Roosevelt, and the third, Jacobus, ancestor of Franklin Delano Roosevelt, the thirty-second President. Johannes and his descendants became prosperous New York businessmen and allied themselves by marriage with other New York families of Dutch descent, thereby creating several close links with the Van Burens (*see* table on page 43). Cornelius Van Schaack Roosevelt, a great-grandson of Johannes, married Margaret Barnhill in 1821 and their sixth and youngest son, Theodore Roosevelt, a merchant and glass importer who served as Collector of the Port of New York, married Martha Bulloch, whose father, Major James Stephens Bulloch, was fifteenth in descent from Robert III, King of Scots. They had two sons and two daughters. Theodore Roosevelt was the elder son and was born in his parents' house on East Twentieth Street, New York, on 27 October 1858. He was a sickly, asthmatic child and his parents took him to Europe for a year from 1869 to 1870 in a vain attempt to improve his health, which only began to mend when he started an exercise regime after their return. They made another trip abroad, visiting Europe, Egypt and the Holy Land, from 1872 to 1873. It was those trips which probably fostered the young Roosevelt's spirit of adventure and love of travel so manifest later in life.

In 1876, Roosevelt entered Harvard after studying for three years at home under a tutor. He graduated with an AB degree in June 1880, spent the summer on camping and shooting trips, and on 27 October married Alice Hathaway Lee, the daughter of a Boston banker. From 1880 to 1882 he studied law at Columbia Law School. In 1881 he took his wife on a tour of Europe and

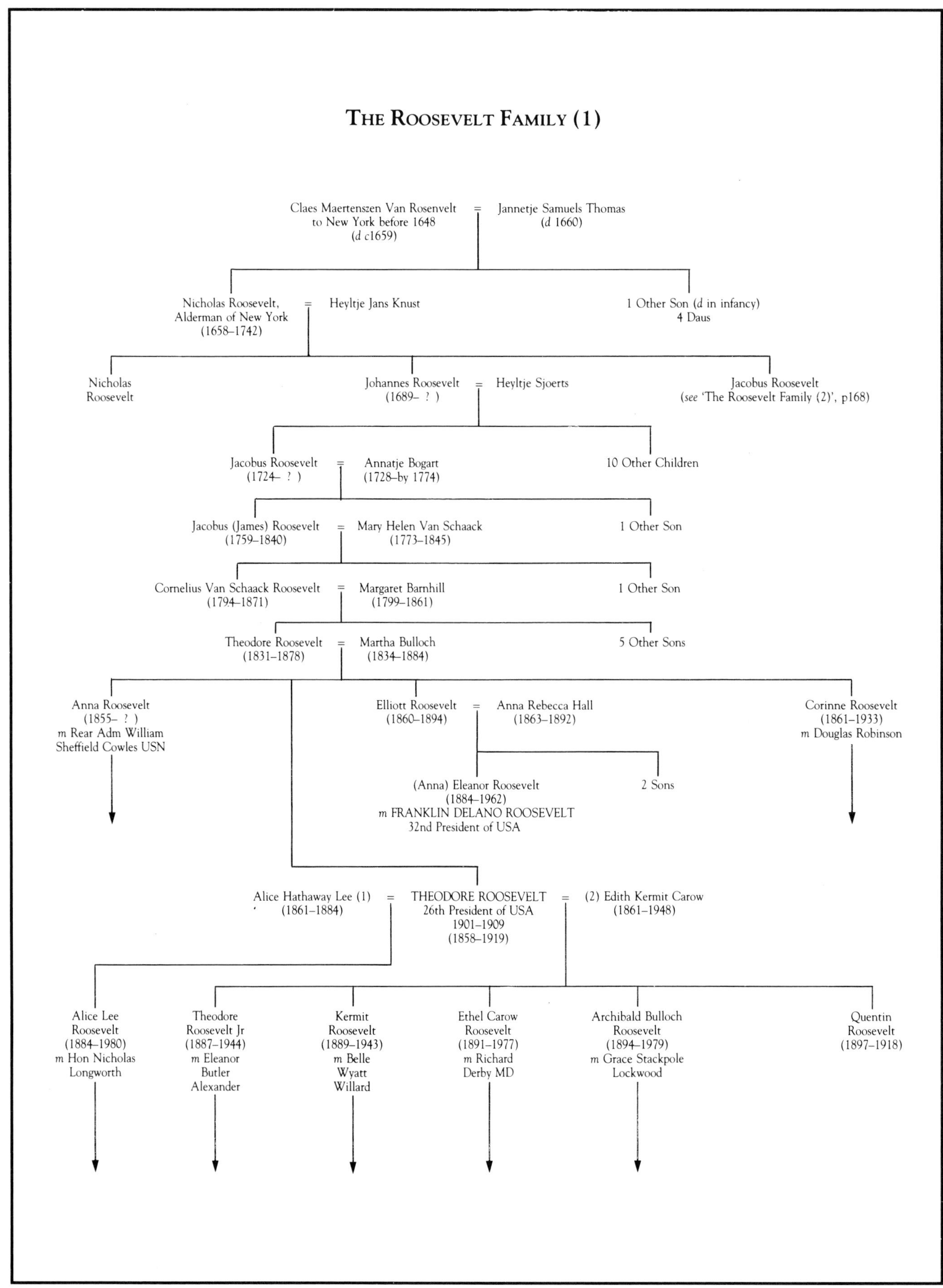
THE ROOSEVELT FAMILY (1)
Claes Maertenszen Van Rosenvelt to New York before 1648 (d c1659) = Jannetje Samuels Thomas (d 1660)
Nicholas Roosevelt, Alderman of New York (1658–1742) = Heyltje Jans Knust
1 Other Son (d in infancy) 4 Daus
Nicholas Roosevelt
Johannes Roosevelt (1689– ?) = Heyltje Sjoerts
Jacobus Roosevelt (see 'The Roosevelt Family (2)', p168)
Jacobus Roosevelt (1724– ?) = Annatje Bogart (1728–by 1774)
10 Other Children
Jacobus (James) Roosevelt (1759–1840) = Mary Helen Van Schaack (1773–1845)
1 Other Son
Cornelius Van Schaack Roosevelt (1794–1871) = Margaret Barnhill (1799–1861)
1 Other Son
Theodore Roosevelt (1831–1878) = Martha Bulloch (1834–1884)
5 Other Sons
Anna Roosevelt (1855– ?) m Rear Adm William Sheffield Cowles USN
Elliott Roosevelt (1860–1894) = Anna Rebecca Hall (1863–1892)
Corinne Roosevelt (1861–1933) m Douglas Robinson
(Anna) Eleanor Roosevelt (1884–1962) m FRANKLIN DELANO ROOSEVELT 32nd President of USA
2 Sons
Alice Hathaway Lee (1) (1861–1884) = THEODORE ROOSEVELT 26th President of USA 1901–1909 (1858–1919) = (2) Edith Kermit Carow (1861–1948)
Alice Lee Roosevelt (1884–1980) m Hon Nicholas Longworth
Theodore Roosevelt Jr (1887–1944) m Eleanor Butler Alexander
Kermit Roosevelt (1889–1943) m Belle Wyatt Willard
Ethel Carow Roosevelt (1891–1977) m Richard Derby MD
Archibald Bulloch Roosevelt (1894–1979) m Grace Stackpole Lockwood
Quentin Roosevelt (1897–1918)

Theodore Roosevelt and the origin of the 'Teddy Bear'; this cartoon of 1902 by Clifford K Berryman depicts the President refusing to shoot a bear cub during a hunting trip

in November was elected a member of New York State Assembly, in which he served until 1885. On 14 February 1884, he was devastated by the deaths of his mother from typhoid fever (his father had died in 1878) and his wife two days after giving birth to a daughter. In an attempt to overcome his grief he went on a long ranching trip to Dakota, where he remained on and off until October 1886. While there he arranged the building of a house, Sagamore Hill, Oyster Bay, Long Island, which was to become his principal residence.

A month after his return from Dakota, Roosevelt was defeated as Republican candidate for the mayoralty of New York City. He departed for Europe and at London on 2 December 1886 married his second wife Edith Kermit Carow, whose family was of Huguenot descent. They remained happily married for the rest of his life and had five children. Roosevelt was already a prolific author of historical and biographical works as well as books on ranching and hunting and was to continue writing and publishing books for the rest of his life.

From 1889 to 1894 Roosevelt served as US Civil Service Commissioner. In 1895 he was elected President of New York City Police Board, and in 1897 President McKinley appointed him Assistant Secretary of the Navy. He resigned this post in May 1898 to take part in the Spanish-American war, raising a cavalry regiment (Roosevelt's Rough Riders), of which he became Colonel and leading his men in typical dashing style in several small skirmishes in Cuba until the end of hostilities.

In November 1898 Roosevelt was elected Governor of New York, taking office in January 1899 and serving until 1900. At the Republican National Convention in Philadelphia in June 1900 he was nominated for Vice-President and was elected to serve with McKinley, taking the oath on 4 March 1901. President McKinley's assassination in September brought Roosevelt to the presidency. He took the oath of office, administered by Judge John R Hazel of the US District Court, in the house of Ansley Wilcox at Buffalo on Saturday 14 September 1901. At forty-two he was the youngest ever incumbent of the presidency.

Given his interests, it was hardly surprising that Roosevelt ('that damned cowboy', as one of his political opponents called him) gave much attention during the first year of his presidency to the setting up of Forest Reserves all over the States. His friendly, open manner and transparent honesty soon won him great popularity and in 1904 he was re-elected President by 336 votes as opposed to 140 for Alton B Parker, the Democratic candidate. His second inauguration took place in traditional style on the East Portico of the Capitol on 4 March 1905, the oath being administered by Chief Justice Melville W Fuller. In 1905 Roosevelt offered his services as mediator to end the Russo-Japanese war and in 1906 was instrumental in bringing about the Algeciras Conference, to determine matters between France and Germany regarding policy in Morocco. As a result he was awarded the Nobel Peace Prize.

Roosevelt retired from office on 4 March 1909 and

after attending the inauguration of President Taft went on a big game expedition to East Africa, accompanied by his nineteen-year-old son Kermit. His wife and daughter Ethel joined them at Khartoum in March 1910 and they then made a trip to Europe, being received with singular marks of honour by royalty and heads of state. On 20 May 1910 Roosevelt was the official US representative at the funeral of King Edward VII of Great Britain. On his return to New York on 18 June 1910 he was accorded a welcoming parade on Fifth Avenue which remained unsurpassed until Charles Lindbergh returned after his solo flight of the Atlantic in 1927.

In 1912 Roosevelt made another bid for the presidency but was defeated by Wilson. In the course of the campaign he was shot and slightly wounded by a fanatic in Milwaukee, Wisconsin, but in typical fashion refused to be deterred by his injury and went on to speak for nearly an hour.

Roosevelt's last years were spent exploring in South America and writing. The last year of his life was saddened by the death of his youngest son Quentin, killed in action in France. Roosevelt became ill in November 1918 and spent some weeks in Roosevelt Hospital, New York City. He returned to Sagamore Hill on Christmas Day and died there of a coronary embolism on 6 January 1919, aged sixty. Mrs Roosevelt survived until 1948.

William Howard Taft 1909–1913

Born:	2038 Auburn Avenue, Cincinnati, Ohio, 15 September 1857, son of Alphonso Taft and his 2nd wife Louisa Maria Torrey
Solicitor-General:	1890–1892
Circuit Judge:	1892–1896
Governor-General of Philippine Islands:	1901–1903
Secretary of War:	1904–1908
Elected (27th) President:	3 November 1908
Inaugurated:	Senate Chamber 4 March 1909
Retired from presidency:	4 March 1913
Chief Justice of the United States:	1921–1930
Married:	Cincinnati, Ohio, 19 June 1886 Helen (Nellie) (*b* Cincinnati, Ohio, 2 June 1861; *d* Washington DC, 22 May 1943; *bur* Arlington National Cemetery), 3rd dau of Judge John Williamson Herron and Harriet Anne Collins
Children:	(1) Robert Alphonso, Senator from Ohio 1939–53, *b* Cincinnati 8 September 1889; *m* Washington DC 17 October 1914 Martha Wheaton (*b* Winona, Minnesota, 17 December 1891; *d* Cincinnati 2 October 1958), dau of Lloyd Wheaton-Bowers, Solicitor-General, and Louise Bennett Wilson; 4 sons; *d* New York City 31 July 1953 (2) Helen Herron, Dean of Bryn Mawr College 1917–1941, *b* Cincinnati 1 August 1891; *m* 15 July 1920 Professor Frederick Johnson Manning (*b* East Braintree, Massachusetts, 1894; *d* Nevis, British West Indies, 15 December 1966); 2 daus; *d* — (3) Charles Phelps II, *b* Cincinnati 20 September 1897; *m* Waterbury, Connecticut, 6 October 1917 Eleanor Kellogg (*b* Waterbury 9 October 1891; *d* Cincinnati 28 August 1961), 2nd dau of Irving Hall Chase and Elizabeth Hosmer Kellogg; 2 sons, 5 daus; *d* —
Died:	Washington DC 8 March 1930
Buried:	Arlington National Cemetery, Arlington, Virginia

William Howard Taft was the largest man to hold the presidency, being six feet tall and with a weight fluctuating between 300 and 332 pounds ($21\frac{1}{2}$ to $23\frac{3}{4}$ stones). It was an alarming sight to see his vast, walrus-like bulk clambering into a carriage while footmen and aides clung desperately to the other side to prevent it from tipping over with his weight.

The Taft family in America can be traced back to Robert Taft, or Taffe, who emigrated from England in about 1678 and settled at Braintree, Massachusetts, moving thence to become an original settler of Mendon, when it was set off from Braintree. His great-great-grandson, Peter Rawson Taft, settled in Cincinnati, Ohio, in 1841 and became Judge of the Supreme Court there. His son, Alphonso Taft, also became a Judge of the Supreme Court and was an unsuccessful Republican candidate for nomination as Governor of Ohio in 1857 and 1879. He served as Secretary of War and Attorney-General under President Grant and as Minister to Austria-Hungary and to Russia under President Arthur. Alphonso married twice, his second wife being his distant cousin, Louisa Maria Torrey, also a descendant of Robert Taft the immigrant. William Howard Taft, their second son, was born at Cincinnati on 15 September 1857.

President Taft, looking like a man whose utterances carry a lot of weight, or was he just full of hot air?

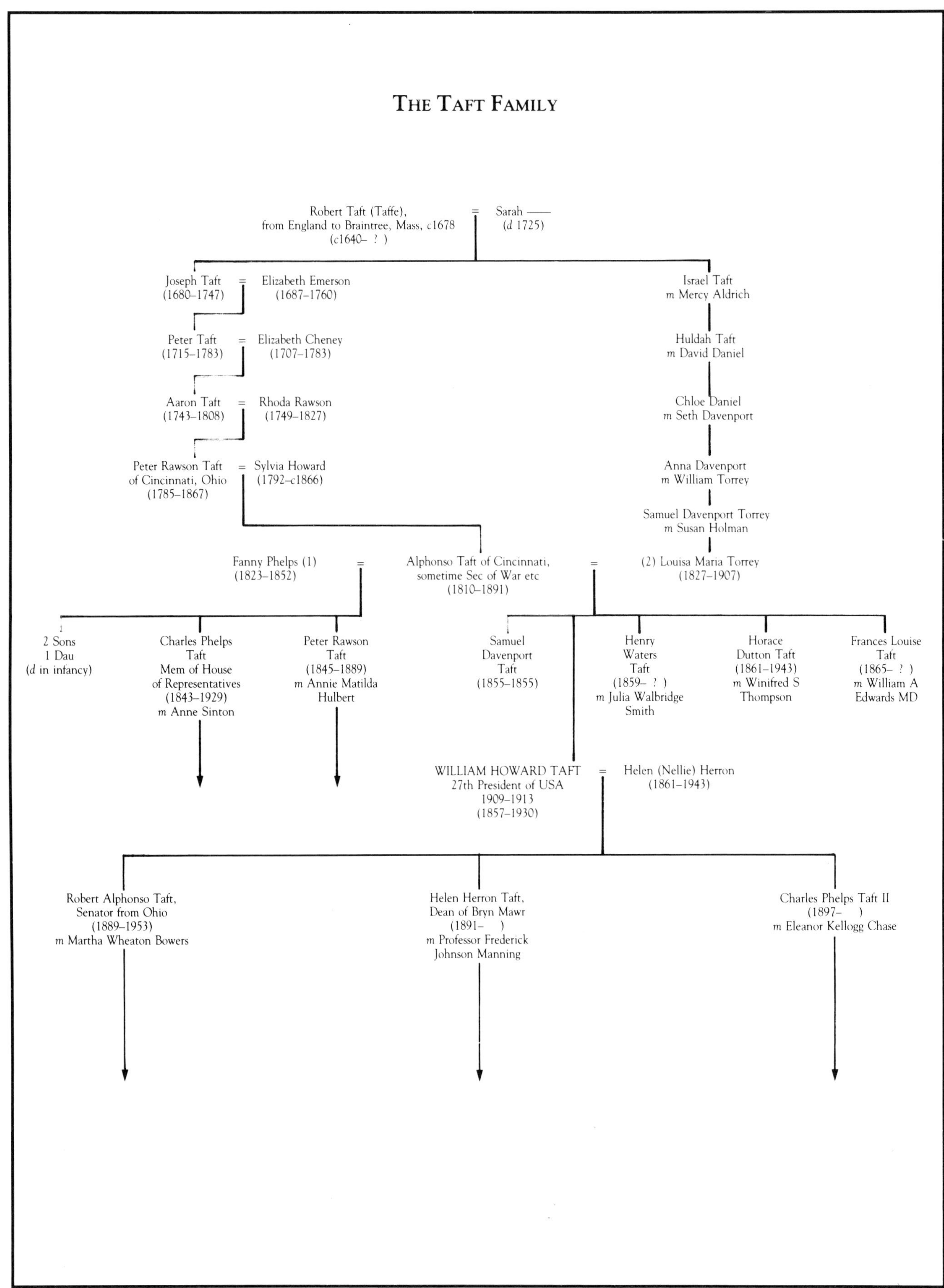
THE TAFT FAMILY
Robert Taft (Taffe), from England to Braintree, Mass, c1678 (c1640– ?)
= Sarah —— (d 1725)
Joseph Taft (1680–1747)
= Elizabeth Emerson (1687–1760)
Israel Taft m Mercy Aldrich
Peter Taft (1715–1783)
= Elizabeth Cheney (1707–1783)
Huldah Taft m David Daniel
Aaron Taft (1743–1808)
= Rhoda Rawson (1749–1827)
Chloe Daniel m Seth Davenport
Peter Rawson Taft of Cincinnati, Ohio (1785–1867)
= Sylvia Howard (1792–c1866)
Anna Davenport m William Torrey
Samuel Davenport Torrey m Susan Holman
Fanny Phelps (1) (1823–1852)
=
Alphonso Taft of Cincinnati, sometime Sec of War etc (1810–1891)
=
(2) Louisa Maria Torrey (1827–1907)
2 Sons 1 Dau (d in infancy)
Charles Phelps Taft Mem of House of Representatives (1843–1929) m Anne Sinton
Peter Rawson Taft (1845–1889) m Annie Matilda Hulbert
Samuel Davenport Taft (1855–1855)
Henry Waters Taft (1859– ?) m Julia Walbridge Smith
Horace Dutton Taft (1861–1943) m Winifred S Thompson
Frances Louise Taft (1865– ?) m William A Edwards MD
WILLIAM HOWARD TAFT 27th President of USA 1909–1913 (1857–1930)
= Helen (Nellie) Herron (1861–1943)
Robert Alphonso Taft, Senator from Ohio (1889–1953) m Martha Wheaton Bowers
Helen Herron Taft, Dean of Bryn Mawr (1891–) m Professor Frederick Johnson Manning
Charles Phelps Taft II (1897–) m Eleanor Kellogg Chase

ABOVE Outgoing President Taft gladly dumps the problem of the 'Mexican situation' to his successor Wilson in 1913

LEFT The ambitious and attractive Mrs Taft who did everything in her power to forward her husband's career

Taft was educated at Woodward High School, Cincinnati, and then went on to Yale, from whence he graduated BA in June 1878. He then entered Cincinnati Law School, gained an LLB degree, and was admitted to the Ohio Bar in May 1880. The following January he was appointed Assistant Prosecutor of Hamilton County and in March 1882 Collector of Internal Revenue by President Arthur, a position he held until January 1883. From 1883 to 1884 Taft practised law in Cincinnati with his father's old partner, Harlan Page Lloyd. In 1885 he was appointed Assistant County Solicitor of Hamilton County.

On 19 June 1886, Taft married Helen Herron, whose father was also a judge. She was ambitious and combined with his family in pushing on the already corpulent and slothful Taft to higher things.

In March 1887 he was appointed Judge of the Cincinnati Superior Court; in February 1890 he was appointed Solicitor-General of the United States by President Benjamin Harrison; and in March 1892 a US Circuit Judge, succeeding as Senior US Circuit Judge of the Sixth Circuit in March 1893.

From 1896 to 1900 Taft was Professor of Law and Real Property and Dean of Cincinnati Law School. He relinquished this post when President McKinley appointed him Chairman of the Commission set up to establish civil government in the Philippines in February 1900. The following year he was appointed first Governor-General of the Philippines, a position which he held until 1903, when he returned to Washington to take up the office of Secretary of War under President Theodore Roosevelt in February 1904.

On 18 June 1908 Taft was nominated for President at the Republican National Convention in Chicago. He resigned as Secretary of War on 30 June and in the election won the presidency with 321 of the 483 electoral votes.

Taft was inaugurated on Thursday 4 March 1909, the oath being administered by Chief Justice Melville W Fuller, officiating for the sixth and last time. The ceremony took place in the Senate chamber as a blizzard made it impossible to hold it on the East Portico as had become customary. Taft's inaugural address was the second longest ever made, beaten only by that of William Henry Harrison. After the ceremony Mrs Taft drove back to the White House with her husband, establishing another precedent, as no first lady had done so before.

Taft was renominated for President in 1912, but the Republicans had lost much ground to the Democrats and the vote was also split by the Progressive party, to which Theodore Roosevelt had gone over, so that in the election Taft only received eighty electoral votes. He retired from office on 4 March 1913 and attended the inauguration of Wilson, to whom he made a very gracious little speech: 'I wish you a successful administration and the carrying out of all your aims; we will all be behind you.' After a golfing holiday in Georgia, Taft took up the position of Kent Professor of Law at Yale, while his wife settled down to write her memoirs (*Recollection of Full Years*, published in 1914).

The best was yet to be; in 1921 Taft was appointed Chief Justice of the United States by President Harding. It was the fulfilment of his life's ambition and in his own estimation far more desirable than the presidency. In his capacity as Chief Justice he administered the oath to two of his presidential successors, Coolidge and Hoover.

Taft resigned as Chief Justice for health reasons on 3 February 1930 and died in Washington a little over a month later on 8 March at the age of seventy-two. He was buried in Arlington National Cemetery, where Mrs Taft joined him in May 1943.

(THOMAS) WOODROW WILSON 1913–1921

Born: Presbyterian Manse, North Coalter Street, Staunton, Virginia, 28 December 1856, elder son of Rev Joseph Ruggles Wilson DD and Janet (Jessie) Woodrow

Governor of New Jersey: 1911–1913

Elected (28th) President: 5 November 1912

Inaugurated: East Portico of Capitol 4 March 1913

Elected for 2nd term: 7 November 1916

Inaugurated: East Portico of Capitol 5 March 1917

Retired from Presidency: 4 March 1921

Married: (1) Savannah, Georgia, 24 June 1885 Ellen Louise (*b* Savannah 15 May 1860; *d* the White House 6 August 1914; *bur* Myrtle Hill Cemetery, Rome, Georgia), eldest dau of Rev Samuel Edward Axson and Margaret Jane Hoyt

Children: (1) Margaret Woodrow, *b* Gainesville, Georgia, 16 April 1886; *d* Pondicherry, India, 12 February 1944

(2) Jessie Woodrow, *b* Gainesville, Georgia, 28 August 1887; *m* the White House 25 November 1913 Francis Bowes Sayre, Professor of Law, Harvard Law School, sometime Assistant Secretary of State and High Commissioner to the Philippines (*b* South Bethlehem, Pennsylvania, 30 April 1885; *d* Washington DC 29 March 1972), 2nd son of Robert Heysham Sayre and Martha Finley Nevin; 2 sons, 1 dau; *d* Cambridge, Massachusetts, 15 January 1933

(3) Eleanor Randolph, *b* Middletown, Connecticut, 5 October 1889; *m* the White House 7 May 1914 (div 25 July 1935) Senator William Gibbs McAdoo, Secretary of the Treasury 1913–18, Senator from California 1933–39 (*b* near Marietta, Georgia, 31 October 1863; *d* 1 February 1941), son of Judge William Gibbs McAdoo and Mary Faith Floyd; 2 daus; *d* Montecito, California, 5 April 1967

Married: (2) Washington DC 18 December 1915 Edith (*b* Wytheville, Virginia, 15 October 1872; *d* Washington DC 28 December 1961; *bur* Washington), widow of Norman Galt (whom she *m* 30 April 1896, and who *d* 28 January 1908), and only dau of Judge William Holcombe Bolling and Sally White

Died: Washington DC 3 February 1924

Buried: Washington Cathedral

Woodrow Wilson, the only true academic to become President, has long been regarded as a controversial character, admired on the one hand for his austerity and strict Presbyterian morality, despised and sneered at on the other for his intellectual superiority, his lack of humour and his high-handed behaviour at the Paris Peace Conference.

Wilson's grandfather, James Wilson, was born in Scotland in 1786 or 1787 and emigrated to America in 1807. He married a girl from Philadelphia and they had no less than seven sons, two of whom distinguished themselves in the Union army during the Civil War. Another son was the Rev Joseph Ruggles Wilson, who entered the Presbyterian ministry. He married Janet (always called Jessie) Woodrow, who was born in Carlisle, England, whence her father, the Rev Thomas Woodrow, another Presbyterian minister, had emigrated to the States with his family in 1836. The couple had two daughters and then two sons, of whom Thomas Woodrow was the elder. He was born in the Presbyterian Manse at 24 North Coalter Street, Staunton, Virginia, on 28 December 1856. The house is now open to the public, as is almost inevitable for presidential birthplaces, under the auspices of the Woodrow Wilson Birthplace Foundation.

Wilson, who soon discarded his first name of Thomas, spent his early life in an intellectual family atmosphere moving from place to place as his father's ministerial appointments took them. In 1873 Wilson entered Davidson College in North Carolina, but a bout of ill health forced him to leave after a few months and return home to his family. In September 1875, his health restored, he entered the College of New Jersey (now Princeton University), where he had a brilliant academic career and graduated as a BA in June 1879. In September 1879 he entered the University of Virginia Law School, but another bout of ill health forced him to leave in 1880. He continued to study law at home and was admitted to the Bar of Georgia at Atlanta in August 1882. He practised law for a year and then enrolled as a postgraduate student at Johns Hopkins University, Baltimore.

The year 1885 saw the publication of Wilson's first book *Congressional Government; A Study in American Politics*, and his marriage in June to Ellen Louise Axson, the bride's grandfather, the Rev Isaac Stockton Keith

Woodrow Wilson and his second wife Edith

Axson, and Wilson's father being the officiating ministers. The marriage was a happy one and produced three daughters. Wilson's book served as the thesis for the PhD degree, which he received from Johns Hopkins University in 1886.

Meanwhile he had taken the position of Associate Professor of history at Bryn Mawr College, Pennsylvania, where he remained until 1888, when he was appointed Professor of History at the Wesleyan University, Middletown, Connecticut. In 1890 he was appointed Professor of Jurisprudence and Political Economy in the College of New Jersey, which became Princeton University in 1896.

During his time at Princeton he published a number of books, including a biography of George Washington (1893) and a five-volume *History of the American People* (1902). In June 1902 he was unanimously elected President of Princeton by the trustees and took office in October.

Wilson's entry into politics was first mooted in 1906 when he was mentioned as a potential presidential candidate by the editor of *Harper's Weekly*. The following year he toyed with the idea of standing for the Senate, and finally in 1910 he agreed to run for Governor of New Jersey and was nominated by the Democratic State Convention at Trenton in September 1910. On 20 October he resigned as President of Princeton and on 8 November was elected Governor, being inaugurated on 17 January 1911. On 2 July 1912 the Democratic National Convention at Baltimore nominated Wilson for President and when the presidential electors cast their ballots he received 435 of the 531 electoral votes.

Wilson was inaugurated on the East Portico of the Capitol on Tuesday 4 March 1913, the oath of office being administered by Chief Justice Edward Douglas White.

The new President was a self-willed man, intent on getting his own way. He was, in spite of all appearances, no dry-as-dust scholar. His books were readable and his

A Democratic campaign truck in New York City

oratory inspiring. Moreover, he was quite a ladies' man. He courted his first wife with ardour and on her death at the White House after nearly thirty years of marriage, courted his second wife, a forty-three-year-old widow, with a like ardour.

At the outbreak of the First World War in Europe in August 1914, America was intent on maintaining its neutrality, although as time went on it became more and more obvious that the country was bound to be involved. The sinking of the *Lusitania* in May 1915 outraged public opinion and provoked three strong protest notes to Germany and in April 1916, following further submarine warfare involving American citizens, an ultimatum threatening to sever diplomatic relations with Germany unless it 'immediately declare its purpose to abandon its present methods of submarine warfare against passengers and freight-carrying vessels' brought an apology from the Kaiser's government. Wilson was renominated for President in 1916 and re-elected with 277 of the 531 electoral votes, the other 254 going to his Republican opponent Charles Evans Hughes. As 4 March 1917 fell on a Sunday, Wilson took the oath privately in the President's Room of the Capitol and publicly the next day on the East Portico with Chief Justice Edward Douglas White again officiating.

The German aggression against shipping had continued unabated and on 6 April 1917 Wilson signed the declaration of war resolution passed by the Senate and in the House, and a proclamation of war against Germany was issued. Wilson threw all his energies into aiding the war effort and after the signing of the Armistice on 11 November 1918 departed to attend the Peace Conference in Paris.

Wilson dominated the Peace Conference and energetically espoused the cause of the new League of Nations. One of the few people to stand up to him was the redoubtable Queen Marie of Roumania, who won favourable terms and an increase in territory for her country in spite of Wilson's dislike of monarchical forms of government (one of the first acts of his presidency had been to recognize the Chinese Republic).

Wilson finally returned to America in July 1919. It was a time of unrest and strikes. Early in September the President departed on a speaking tour in support of the League of Nations. On 26 September he was taken ill in Pueblo, Colorado, with a nervous breakdown and forced to cancel the rest of the tour. On 2 October he suffered a stroke which partially incapacitated him. Mrs Wilson nursed him well and guarded him jealously, so much so that it was said that many of his purported decisions were

THE WILSON FAMILY

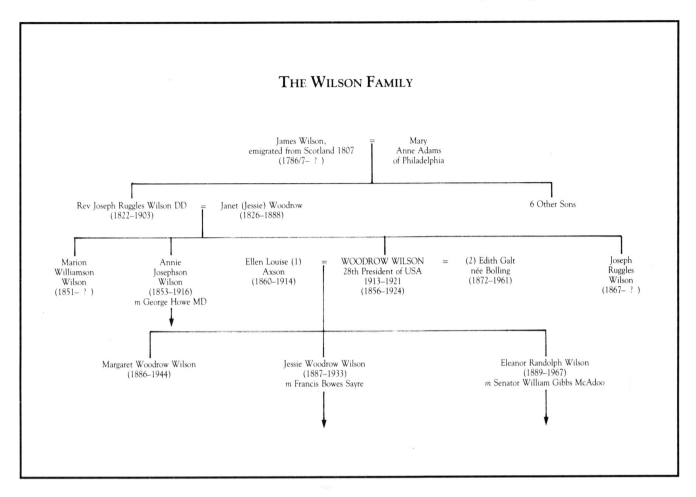

James Wilson, emigrated from Scotland 1807 (1786/7– ?) = Mary Anne Adams of Philadelphia

- Rev Joseph Ruggles Wilson DD (1822–1903) = Janet (Jessie) Woodrow (1826–1888)
  - Marion Williamson Wilson (1851– ?)
  - Annie Josephson Wilson (1853–1916) m George Howe MD ↓
  - Ellen Louise (1) Axson (1860–1914) = WOODROW WILSON 28th President of USA 1913–1921 (1856–1924) = (2) Edith Galt née Bolling (1872–1961)
    - Margaret Woodrow Wilson (1886–1944)
    - Jessie Woodrow Wilson (1887–1933) m Francis Bowes Sayre ↓
    - Eleanor Randolph Wilson (1889–1967) m Senator William Gibbs McAdoo ↓
  - Joseph Ruggles Wilson (1867– ?)
- 6 Other Sons

really hers and she, not he, was the effective President throughout his last year in office.

In December 1920 Wilson was awarded the Nobel Peace Prize which was accepted on his behalf by the US Minister in Christiania (now Oslo), Norway.

Wilson retired from the presidency on 4 March 1921. He rode to the Capitol with his successor President Harding, but left before the inauguration ceremony and drove with his wife to the new house they had bought, 2340 South Street, NW Washington DC. In failing health, he lived quietly for his remaining years, accepting the Polish Order of the White Eagle in 1922 (the only foreign order he ever accepted) and emerging to attend the funeral of President Harding in August 1923. His last public speech was made to an Armistice Day crowd gathered outside his house in November 1923. On his sixty-seventh birthday, 28 December 1923, friends subscribed to present him with a custom-built Rolls Royce in black with orange trimming, the Princeton colours.

Wilson fell ill with digestive trouble in January 1924 and it precipitated another stroke from which he died at his home on 3 February. He was buried in Washington Cathedral, of which his grandson Francis Bowes Sayre was later to become Dean. Mrs Wilson survived until December 1961.

Warren Gamaliel Harding 1921–1923

Born:	Corsica (later renamed Blooming Grove), Ohio, 2 November 1865, eldest son of Dr George Tryon Harding and his 1st wife Phoebe Elizabeth Dickerson	Married:	Marion, Ohio, 8 July 1891 Florence Mabel (*b* Marion, Ohio, 15 August 1860; *d* Marion, Ohio, 21 November 1924; *bur* Marion), formerly wife of Henry (Pete) De Wolfe (whom she *m* March 1880 and div May 1886; he *d* 1894), and only dau of Amos H Kling and his 1st wife Louisa M Bouton
Lieutenant-Governor of Ohio:	1904–1906		
Senator from Ohio:	1915–1920	Children:	none
Elected (29th) President:	2 November 1920	Died in office:	Palace Hotel, San Francisco, 2 August 1923
Inaugurated:	East Portico of Capitol 4 March 1921	Buried:	Marion, Ohio

It is generally agreed that Warren G Harding was one of the most inept and probably one of the most corrupt Presidents to have held office. The presidency was in a sense thrust upon him by his ambitious wife and a group of Republican party hacks. Harding, at best an amicable and easygoing fool, was heard to say sometime after his election: 'I knew this job would be too much for me.' They were the truest words he ever spoke.

Political opponents were keen to spread the rumour that the Hardings had negro blood, but this is quite unfounded. The family can be traced back to Stephen Harding, a blacksmith in Providence, Rhode Island, who was admitted Freeman there in 1669 and died in 1698. His grandson, another Stephen, was a tanner and currier in Providence and later shipbuilder and sea captain. He moved to New London County, Connecticut, where he bought a farm with his brother Israel and died in 1750. His son, Abraham Harding, moved to Orange County, New York, and served in the Continental army in the Revolutionary War. The next two generations moved to Pennsylvania and thence to Ohio.

George Tryon Harding, the eldest of seventeen children of Amos Harding, settled in Corsica (now Blooming Grove), Ohio, in 1820, and his grandson and namesake, Dr George Tryon Harding, was the father of the future President. Dr Harding married three times, but only had children by his first marriage, of whom Warren Gamaliel Harding, born at Blooming Grove on 2 November 1865, was the eldest. He was named after the Rev Warren Gamaliel Bancroft, of Wisconsin, a Methodist minister who had married his mother's sister, Malvina Dickerson.

In 1873 the family moved to Caledonia, Ohio, where Warren attended the local school and learned the printing trade in the office of the *Caledonia Argus*, which his father had purchased in 1875. In 1880 he entered Ohio Central College (now no longer in existence) at Iberia, Ohio. He became a horn-player in the school band and editor of the school yearbook. While he was in college the family moved to Marion, Ohio, and he joined them there after graduating with a BSc degree in 1882. After a very short period teaching, he began to work for the Marion *Mirror* in 1883 and a year later purchased the Marion *Star* with two partners for $300. In 1886 he was able to buy them both out and was able also to make the paper pay by developing it as a Republican journal. In November 1886 he was appointed a member of the Republican County Committee.

In July 1891 the good-looking, twenty-five-year-old Harding married a thirty-year-old divorcee of forbidding appearance and manner. Mrs Florence Mabel Kling De Wolfe, whom Warren was to nickname 'Duchess', had, her grim exterior notwithstanding, managed to get herself pregnant at the age of nineteen and forced marriage upon one Henry (Pete) De Wolfe six months before the birth of her only child in September 1880. Six years later she divorced him and returned to her parents' home in Marion, where Warren met her. He obviously realized that she was a 'catch' and she that he was someone she could make into whatever image she desired. The marriage was one of convenience on both sides without romance and with no question of there being any further children.

Harding fell ill soon after his marriage and 'Duchess' took over the running of the *Star*, which she did with great energy and success. 'I went down there intending to help out for a few days', she said, 'and remained fourteen years.' The affable, lazy Harding was quite content to leave matters in his wife's hands and lead a pleasant social life with his friends, playing in the town band, golfing, enjoying a drink and taking a hand at poker. He served two terms in the Ohio State Senate and was elected to serve as Lieutenant-Governor of Ohio

Warren G Harding and his wife Florence: 'Duchess' adjusts 'Wurren's' tie for the camera

from 1904 to 1906. In November 1910 he was defeated as Republican candidate for Governor, but four years later was elected to the Senate. A 'Harding for President' campaign began in February 1919. At this time Harding was conducting an affair with Nan Britton, a twenty-two-year-old doctor's daughter from Claridon, Ohio. On 22 October 1919 she gave birth to a daughter, Elizabeth Ann Christian, also known as Emma Eloise Britton. This was kept secret at the time, and when Harding's candidacy for President was being considered by the Republican National Convention at Chicago in June 1920, he assured them that there was nothing in his past which could embarrass the party in any way. He was also involved with a married woman in Marion. If Mrs Harding knew about these matters, she turned a blind eye. She could hardly have felt any pangs of jealousy but might have been alarmed by the possibility that 'Wurren's' behaviour might jeopardize the future she had planned for him. Harding's nomination, then, was duly made and in the ensuing election he received 404 of the 531 electoral votes, James Middleton Cox, of Ohio, the Democratic candidate, receiving 127.

Harding was the first President to be driven to his inauguration by motor car. The ceremony took place on Friday 4 March 1921, with Chief Justice Edward Douglass White administering the oath for the third and last time in his career. Harding was looked at with disdain by his predecessor, the scholarly Wilson, who described him as having 'a bungalow mind'. Nevertheless he enjoyed a certain amount of popularity with the general public throughout his two-and-a-half year presidency.

Things were far from well with his administration, however, and charges of graft and corruption were made against Harry Micajah Daugherty, the Attorney-General, and Albert Bacon Fall, the Secretary of the Interior, who was compelled to resign in March 1923 and later imprisoned. Harding became sick with worry over the mess which his government had become and in an attempt to recoup some of his waning popularity embarked on a strenous speaking tour on 20 June. He spoke in Missouri, Kansas, Colorado, Wyoming, Utah, Idaho, Oregon and Washington, and early in July sailed for Alaska where he undertook further engagements.

At the end of the month he visited Canada, spoke at a banquet in Vancouver, and then sailed for Seattle. After making two speeches in Seattle, Harding boarded

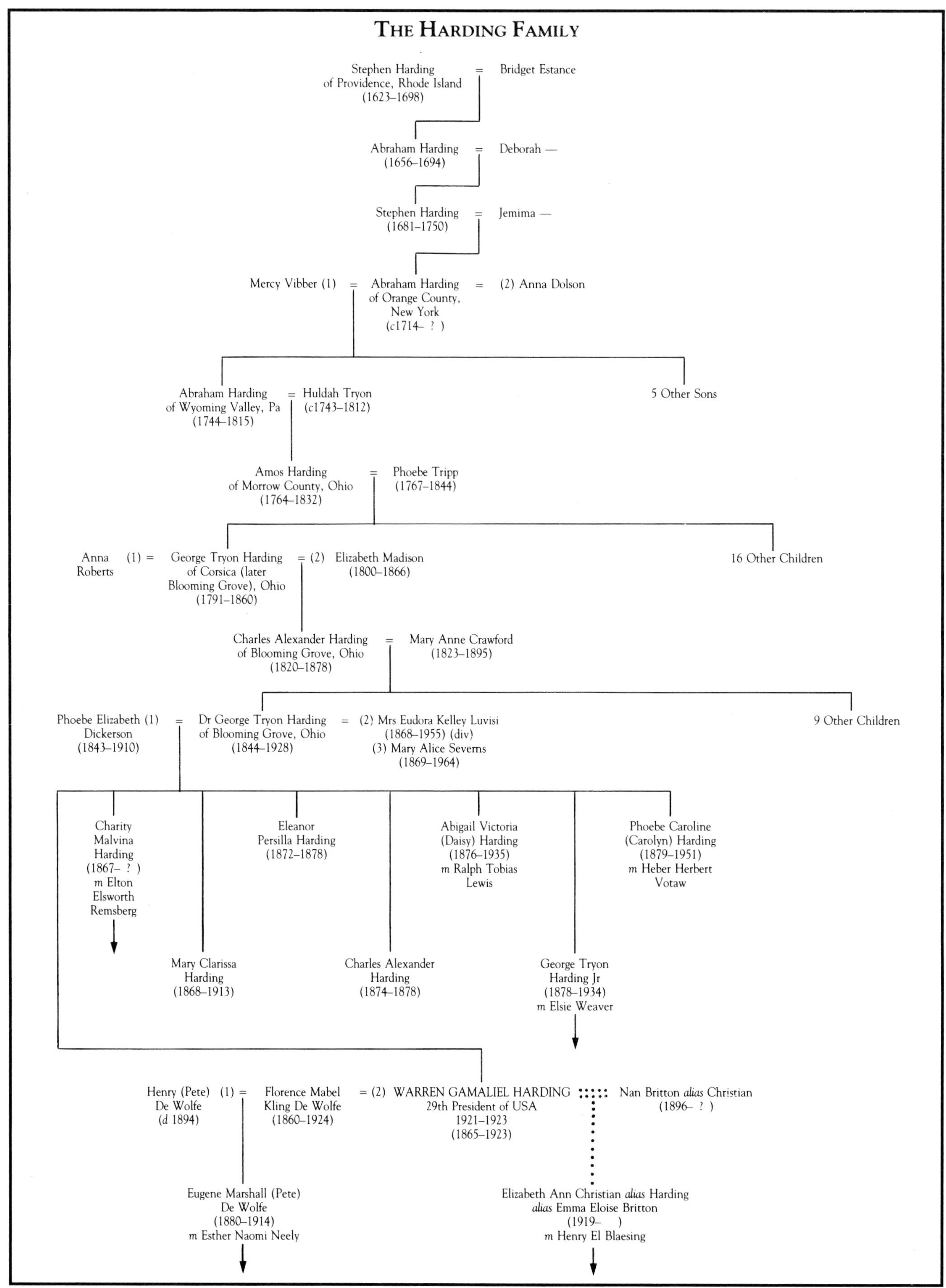
THE HARDING FAMILY
Stephen Harding of Providence, Rhode Island (1623–1698) = Bridget Estance
Abraham Harding (1656–1694) = Deborah —
Stephen Harding (1681–1750) = Jemima —
Mercy Vibber (1) = Abraham Harding of Orange County, New York (c1714– ?) = (2) Anna Dolson
Abraham Harding of Wyoming Valley, Pa (1744–1815) = Huldah Tryon (c1743–1812)
5 Other Sons
Amos Harding of Morrow County, Ohio (1764–1832) = Phoebe Tripp (1767–1844)
Anna Roberts (1) = George Tryon Harding of Corsica (later Blooming Grove), Ohio (1791–1860) = (2) Elizabeth Madison (1800–1866)
16 Other Children
Charles Alexander Harding of Blooming Grove, Ohio (1820–1878) = Mary Anne Crawford (1823–1895)
Phoebe Elizabeth (1) Dickerson (1843–1910) = Dr George Tryon Harding of Blooming Grove, Ohio (1844–1928) = (2) Mrs Eudora Kelley Luvisi (1868–1955) (div) (3) Mary Alice Severns (1869–1964)
9 Other Children
Charity Malvina Harding (1867– ?) m Elton Elsworth Remsberg
Mary Clarissa Harding (1868–1913)
Eleanor Persilla Harding (1872–1878)
Charles Alexander Harding (1874–1878)
Abigail Victoria (Daisy) Harding (1876–1935) m Ralph Tobias Lewis
George Tryon Harding Jr (1878–1934) m Elsie Weaver
Phoebe Caroline (Carolyn) Harding (1879–1951) m Heber Herbert Votaw
Henry (Pete) De Wolfe (d 1894) (1) = Florence Mabel Kling De Wolfe (1860–1924) = (2) WARREN GAMALIEL HARDING 29th President of USA 1921–1923 (1865–1923) Nan Britton alias Christian (1896– ?)
Eugene Marshall (Pete) De Wolfe (1880–1914) m Esther Naomi Neely
Elizabeth Ann Christian alias Harding alias Emma Eloise Britton (1919–) m Henry El Blaesing

a train *en route* to California. He suffered an attack of food poisoning on the night of 27 July and cancelled the arrangements for a stop in Oregon. The presidential party reached San Francisco on 29 July and put up at the Palace Hotel, where Harding took to his bed. He seemed to be well on the mend, but on 2 August 1923 while his wife was reading the newspaper to him, he suffered a sudden and fatal cerebral thrombosis, dying before medical assistance could be summoned. His death was so sudden and unexpected that there was a rumour that it had been precipitated by Mrs Harding in order to save him from facing a possible impeachment charge. Harding lay in state at the White House and then in the Capitol Rotunda before his body was taken to Marion for burial.

Mrs Harding, who was herself in failing health, survived him only fifteen months, but his old father, hale and hearty to the last and married to his third wife, survived until November 1928, when he died at the age of eighty-four. Three years after Harding's death Nan Britton published the story of her liaison with him in a sensational book entitled *The President's Daughter*.

Nan Britton, Harding's mistress, who gave birth to his daughter in 1919

(John) Calvin Coolidge 1923–1929

Born:	Plymouth, Vermont, 4 July 1872, only son of Col John Calvin Coolidge and his 1st wife Victoria Josephine Moor
Lieutenant-Governor of Massachusetts:	1916–1918
Governor of Massachusetts:	1919–1920
Elected Vice-President:	2 November 1920
Inaugurated:	4 March 1921
Succeeded as (30th) President:	2 August 1923
Took oath:	3 August 1923
Elected for 2nd term:	4 November 1924
Inaugurated:	East Portico of Capitol 4 March 1925
Retired from presidency:	4 March 1929
Married:	Burlington, Vermont, 4 October 1905 Grace Anna (*b* Burlington, Vermont, 3 January 1879; *d* Northampton, Massachusetts, 8 July 1957; *bur* Plymouth, Vermont), dau of Andrew Issachar Goodhue and Lemira Barrett.
Children:	(1) John, *b* Northampton, Massachusetts, 7 September 1906; *m* Plainville, Connecticut, 23 September 1929 Florence (*b* Plainville 30 November 1904), dau of Governor John H Trumbull and Maude Usher; 2 daus (2) Calvin, *b* Northampton, Massachusetts, 13 April 1908; *d* Washington DC 7 July 1924
Died:	Northampton, Massachusetts, 5 January 1933
Buried:	Plymouth, Vermont

Calvin Coolidge's taciturnity has become a legend. Many of the stories told about him are probably apocryphal. That of the young lady who sat next to him at dinner and bet a friend that she would get Coolidge to utter more than two words to her, foolishly told him of the wager, and received the laconic reply 'You lose!' before he turned to his other dinner companion, is typical of the genre. Coolidge himself was well aware of his 'lack of oratorical ability', but was one of the first to make good use of the new medium of radio to relay political messages.

The Coolidges trace their lineage back to Simon Cooledge of Cottenham in Cambridgeshire, England, whose will was dated 1591. Simon's grandson, John Coolidge, emigrated to Watertown, Massachusetts, about 1630, and he and his numerous descendants served as useful members of the community there and also spread elsewhere. Colonel John Calvin Coolidge, of Plymouth, Vermont, where he farmed, kept a store, and served as Justice of the Peace. He was married there in May 1868 to Victoria Josephine Moor and their first child and only son was the future President, John Calvin Coolidge, born on 4 July 1872.

The younger Coolidge, who soon discarded his first name, had a somewhat lonely childhood and youth. His mother died on her thirty-ninth birthday in March 1885, when he was twelve, and his only sister Abigail Gratia, whom he adored, five years later at the age of fifteen. In June 1890 Coolidge graduated from Black River Academy, Ludlow, Vermont, and hoped to enter Amherst College the same year, but failed the entrance

Calvin Coolidge with his sons John and Calvin, all looking surly and miserable; the younger boy died tragically from blood poisoning soon after this photograph was taken

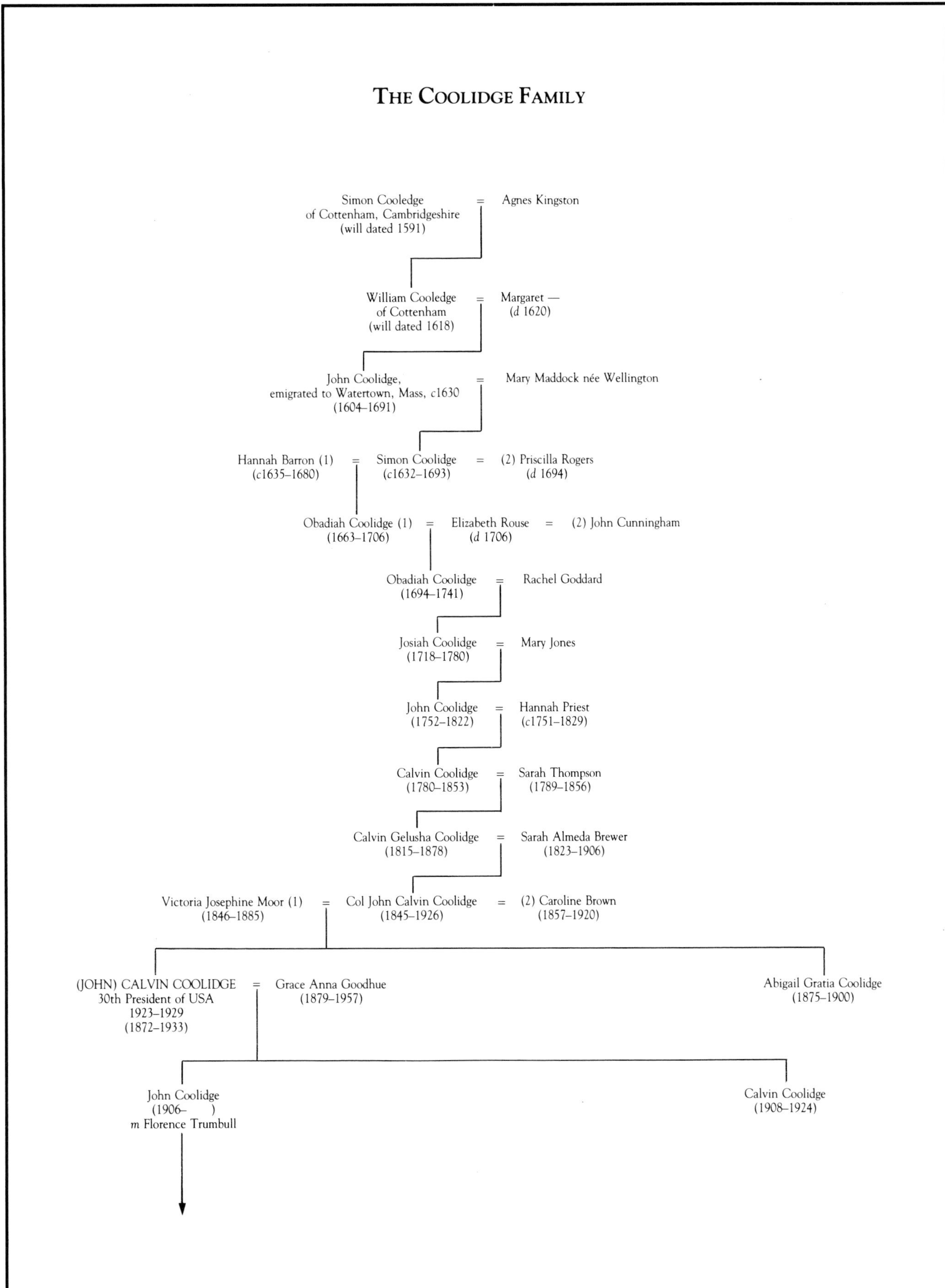
THE COOLIDGE FAMILY
Simon Cooledge of Cottenham, Cambridgeshire (will dated 1591) = Agnes Kingston
William Cooledge of Cottenham (will dated 1618) = Margaret — (d 1620)
John Coolidge, emigrated to Watertown, Mass, c1630 (1604–1691) = Mary Maddock née Wellington
Hannah Barron (1) (c1635–1680) = Simon Coolidge (c1632–1693) = (2) Priscilla Rogers (d 1694)
Obadiah Coolidge (1) (1663–1706) = Elizabeth Rouse (d 1706) = (2) John Cunningham
Obadiah Coolidge (1694–1741) = Rachel Goddard
Josiah Coolidge (1718–1780) = Mary Jones
John Coolidge (1752–1822) = Hannah Priest (c1751–1829)
Calvin Coolidge (1780–1853) = Sarah Thompson (1789–1856)
Calvin Gelusha Coolidge (1815–1878) = Sarah Almeda Brewer (1823–1906)
Victoria Josephine Moor (1) (1846–1885) = Col John Calvin Coolidge (1845–1926) = (2) Caroline Brown (1857–1920)
(JOHN) CALVIN COOLIDGE 30th President of USA 1923–1929 (1872–1933) = Grace Anna Goodhue (1879–1957)
Abigail Gratia Coolidge (1875–1900)
John Coolidge (1906–) m Florence Trumbull
Calvin Coolidge (1908–1924)

"All the News That's Fit to Print."

The New York Times.

EXTRA 6 A. M.

VOL. LXXII....No. 23,932. NEW YORK, FRIDAY, AUGUST 3, 1923. TWO CENTS

PRESIDENT HARDING DIES SUDDENLY; STROKE OF APOPLEXY AT 7:30 P. M.; CALVIN COOLIDGE IS PRESIDENT

COOLIDGE TAKES THE OATH OF OFFICE

His Father, Who Is a Notary Public, Administers It After Form Is Found By Him in His Library.

ANNOUNCES HE WILL FOLLOW THE HARDING POLICIES

Wants All Who Aided Harding to Remain in Office—Roused After Midnight to Be Told the News of the President's Death.

Statement by President Coolidge

Special to The New York Times.

PLYMOUTH, Vt., Aug. 3.—President Calvin Coolidge issued the following statement early this morning:

Reports have reached me, which I fear are correct, that President Harding is gone. The world has lost a great and good man. I mourn his loss. He was my chief and my friend.

It will be my purpose to carry out the policies which he has begun for the service of the American people and for meeting their responsibilities wherever they may arise.

For this purpose I shall seek the co-operation of all those who have been associated with the President during his term of office.

Those who have given their efforts to assist him I wish to remain in office that they may assist me. I have faith that God will direct the destinies of our nation.

It is my intention to remain here until I can secure the correct form for the oath of office, which will be administered to me by my father, who is a notary public.

CALVIN COOLIDGE
Thirtieth President of the United States by the Death of President Harding.

WARREN GAMALIEL HARDING
Twenty-ninth President of the United States, Who Died Yesterday in San Francisco.

Public Men Voice Tributes To Harding's Worth and Record

President's Death Shocks Capital, Which Had Expected Recovery

DEATH STROKE CAME WITHOUT WARNING

Mrs. Harding Was Reading to Her Husband When First Sign Appeared —She Ran for Doctor

BUT NOTHING COULD BE DONE TO REVIVE PATIENT

News of Tragic End Shocks Everybody, Coming After Day Said to Have Been the Best Since His Illness Began a Week Ago.

Special to The New York Times.

SAN FRANCISCO, Aug. 2.—President Harding died at 7:30 o'clock tonight [11:30 o'clock New York time] of a stroke of apoplexy.

The end came suddenly while Mrs. Harding was reading to him from the evening newspaper, and after what had been called the best day he had had since the beginning of his illness exactly one week ago.

A shudder ran through the President's frame and he collapsed.

Mrs. Harding and the two nurses in the sick room knew the end had come, and Mrs. Harding rushed out of the room and asked for Dr. Boone and the others to "come quick."

Dr. Boone and Brig. Gen. Sawyer reached the President before he passed away, but were not able to avert the inevitable.

This formal announcement following soon after told the story of the tragic end:

"The President died at 7:30 P. M. Mrs. Harding and the two nurses, Miss Ruth Powderly and Miss Sue Drusser, were in the room at the time. Mrs. Harding was reading to the President, when, utterly without warning, a slight shudder passed through his frame; he collapsed, and all recognized that the end had come. A stroke of apoplexy was the cause of his death.

"Within a few moments all of the President's official party had been summoned."

The New York Times of 3 August 1923 announces the death of Harding and the new, thirtieth, President, Calvin Coolidge

examination because of illness and instead enrolled in St Johnsburg Academy, Vermont, for a revision course. In September 1891, Coolidge's father remarried, but there were to be no further children. About the same time Coolidge finally entered Amherst College, Massachusetts, from which he graduated with a BA degree in June 1895.

Like many another President he began reading law and in 1896 won a gold medal for his essay on the principles of the American Revolution in the Sons of American Revolution essay contest. The following year he was admitted to the Massachusetts Bar at Northampton. Coolidge served as City Solicitor of Northampton from 1899 to 1902. On 4 October 1905 he married Grace Anna Goodhue, whose father was a steamboat inspector. She herself taught in a school for the deaf. There were two sons of the marriage and the death of the younger from blood poisoning in 1924 at the age of sixteen was to cause his father untold anguish.

In 1906 Coolidge was elected to the Massachusetts House of Representatives, in which he served two terms. From 1910 to 1911 he was Mayor of Northampton and in the latter year was elected to the Massachusetts Senate, serving four terms, the last two as President. He served three terms as Lieutenant-Governor of Massachusetts (1916, 1917 and 1918), and was elected Governor at the end of the last, taking office on 1 January 1919. In his capacity as Governor he welcomed President Wilson in Boston on his return from the Paris Peace Conference. After being re-elected Governor for a second term, Coolidge was nominated for Vice-President by the Republican National Convention at Chicago in June 1920 and duly elected, being inaugurated on 4 March 1921.

The sudden death of President Harding catapulted Coolidge into the presidency. He was at his father's home in Plymouth, Vermont, when the news came and he took the oath in his own house on 3 August 1923. It was administered by his father, acting in his capacity as a Justice of the Peace. He took it again in his suite at the Willard Hotel, Washington, on 21 August, when it was administered by Justice Adolph August Hoehling of the District of Colombia Supreme Court.

Coolidge's plain style and absolute integrity came as a welcome relief after the scandals of the Harding era. Alice Roosevelt Longworth, the daughter of President

Theodore Roosevelt, in spite of saying that Coolidge looked 'as if he'd been weaned on a pickle', contrasted life at the White House under the Hardings and the Coolidges as being 'as different as a New England front parlour is from a back room speakeasy'.

Coolidge was nominated for re-election at the Republican National Convention at Cleveland in July 1924 and in the ensuing election won 382 of the 531 electoral votes, 136 going to John William Davis, the Democratic candidate, and 13 to Robert Marion La Follette, the Progressive candidate. He was inaugurated for his second term on 4 March 1925, the oath being administered by the former President, now Chief Justice William Howard Taft. It was the first inauguration to be broadcast.

Coolidge retired from the presidency on 4 March 1929 and after attending the inauguration of Hoover, left with his wife for the semi-detached house at 21 Massasoit Street, Northampton, Massachusetts, which they had rented since they were first married in 1905. Soon after their return from Washington they bought The Beeches, a larger house with nine acres of ground on the town outskirts.

In 1931 and 1932 Coolidge contributed a daily column 'Thinking Things Over with Calvin Coolidge' to be syndicated in the New York *Herald Tribune* and other papers, but he grew tired of doing it and gave it up after a year. On 5 January 1933 Calvin Coolidge died of coronary thrombosis at the age of sixty, and was buried at Plymouth, Vermont. When the columnist Dorothy Parker received the news that he was dead, her comment was: 'How can they tell?'

HERBERT CLARK HOOVER 1929–1933

Born:	Downey Street, West Branch, Iowa, 10 August 1874, yr son of Jesse Clark Hoover and Hulda Randall Minthorn	Children:	(1) Herbert Charles, Under Secretary of State 1954–57; *b* London, England, 4 August 1903; *m* Stanford, California, 25 June 1925 Margaret Eva Watson (*b* San Francisco 28 March 1905); 1 son, 2 daus; *d* Pasadena, California, 9 July 1969
Secretary of Commerce:	1921–1928		
Elected (31st) President:	6 November 1928		
Inaugurated:	East Portico of Capitol 4 March 1929		(2) Allan Henry, *b* London, England, 17 July 1907; *m* Los Angeles, California, 17 March 1937 Margaret (*b* Tucson, Arizona, 7 March 1911), dau of William Baylor Coberly and Winifred Wheeler; 2 sons, 1 dau
Retired from presidency:	4 March 1933		
Married:	Monterey, California, 10 February 1899 Lou (*b* Waterloo, Iowa, 29 March 1874; *d* Waldorf Astoria Towers, New York, 7 January 1944; *bur* Hoover Cemetery, West Branch, Iowa), elder dau of Charles Delano Henry and Florence Ida Weed	Died:	New York 20 October 1964
		Buried:	Hoover Cemetery, West Branch, Iowa

Herbert Hoover, one of the most gifted and able men to hold the presidency this century, was a victim of the Depression in which he became identified with its worst features, precluding his re-election for a second term. His real worth was only to be appreciated later.

The Hoover family, originally Huber, can be traced back to Georg Huber, a miller at Oberkulm in the Canton of Aargau, Switzerland, who was Under Steward of Lenzburg in the same Canton and the father of Johann Heinrich Huber, a linen weaver at Oberkulm, who died there in 1706, leaving, among other issue, a son Gregor Jonas Huber, who settled at Ellerstadt, near Dürckheim, in the Rhenish Palatinate. His son, Andreas Huber, emigrated to America in 1738, anglicized his name as Andrew Hoover and settled first on Pipe Creek, Maryland, where he built a mill and farmed land acquired from government grants. Later he moved to Randolph County, North Carolina, where he died in 1794, having had a large family of eight sons and five daughters.

John Hoover, one of the sons, settled at West Milton, Miami County, Ohio in 1802, and his fifth son Jesse Hoover, moved to Hubbard, Iowa, in 1854, two years before his death. Jesse's eldest son, Eli, was the father of Jesse Clark Hoover, who set up as a blacksmith and farm-equipment salesman in West Branch, Iowa. He married Hulda Randall Minthorn, a native of Burgersville, Ontario, Canada, in March 1870 and they had two sons and one daughter. Herbert Clark Hoover, the future President, was the younger son and was born at West Branch on 10 August 1874. Unfortunately, the parents were not strong and Jesse Clark Hoover died at the age of thirty-four on 10 December 1880, to be followed by his wife a little over two years later on 24 February 1883.

The orphaned children lived for a time with their uncle Allan Hoover on his farm near West Branch and in 1884 moved to Newberg, Oregon, where their upbringing was undertaken by their mother's brother, Dr Henry John Minthorn. In 1885 they moved to

President Coolidge with Herbert Hoover (right), Secretary of Commerce and future President

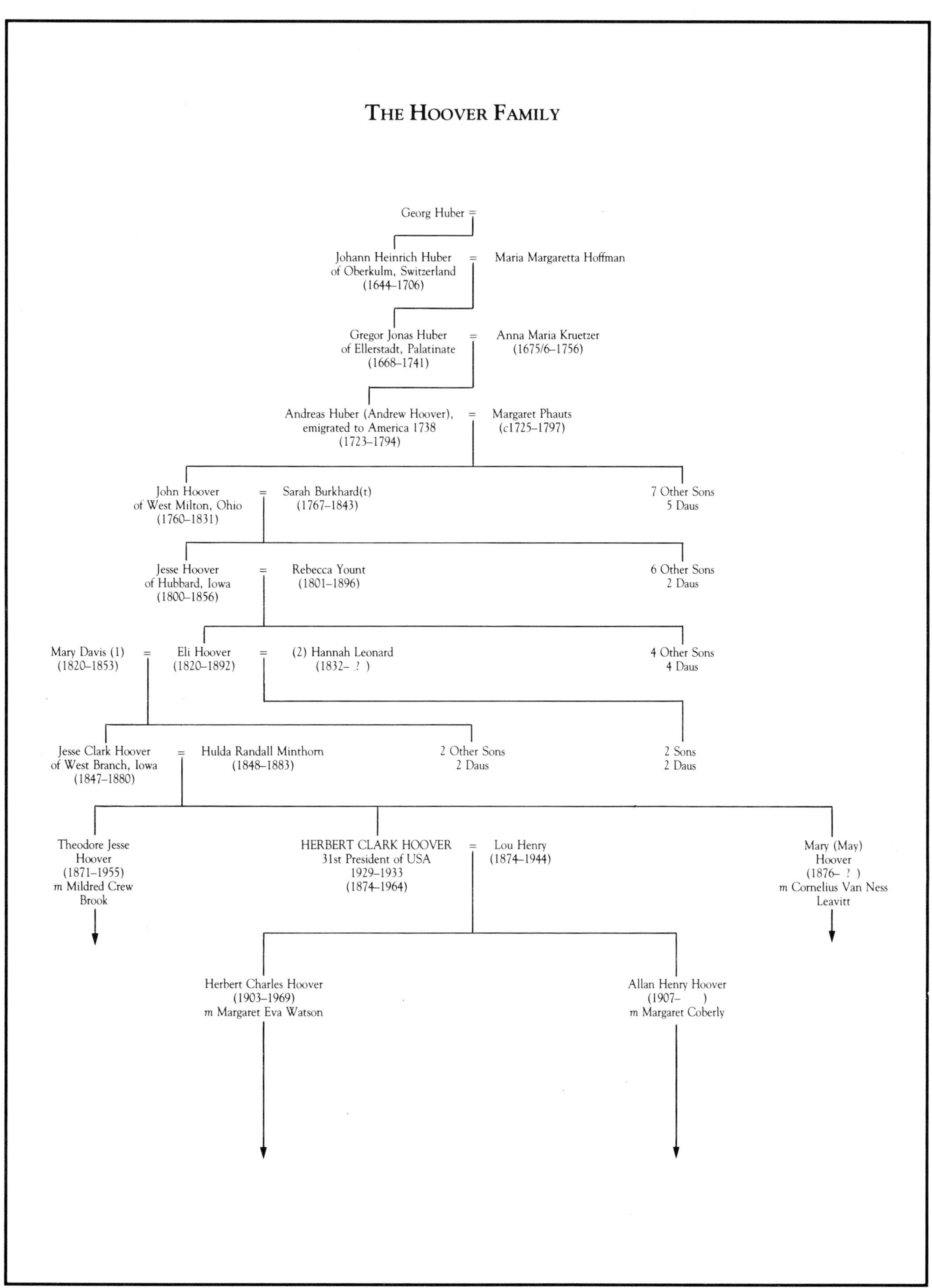
THE HOOVER FAMILY
Georg Huber =
Johann Heinrich Huber of Oberkulm, Switzerland (1644–1706) = Maria Margaretta Hoffman
Gregor Jonas Huber of Ellerstadt, Palatinate (1668–1741) = Anna Maria Kruetzer (1675/6–1756)
Andreas Huber (Andrew Hoover), emigrated to America 1738 (1723–1794) = Margaret Phauts (c1725–1797)
John Hoover of West Milton, Ohio (1760–1831) = Sarah Burkhard(t) (1767–1843)
7 Other Sons 5 Daus
Jesse Hoover of Hubbard, Iowa (1800–1856) = Rebecca Yount (1801–1896)
6 Other Sons 2 Daus
Mary Davis (1) (1820–1853) = Eli Hoover (1820–1892) = (2) Hannah Leonard (1832– ?)
4 Other Sons 4 Daus
Jesse Clark Hoover of West Branch, Iowa (1847–1880) = Hulda Randall Minthorn (1848–1883)
2 Other Sons 2 Daus
2 Sons 2 Daus
Theodore Jesse Hoover (1871–1955) m Mildred Crew Brook
HERBERT CLARK HOOVER 31st President of USA 1929–1933 (1874–1964) = Lou Henry (1874–1944)
Mary (May) Hoover (1876– ?) m Cornelius Van Ness Leavitt
Herbert Charles Hoover (1903–1969) m Margaret Eva Watson
Allan Henry Hoover (1907–) m Margaret Coberly

Mr and Mrs Herbert Hoover with their sons and daughter-in-law

Salem, Oregon, where the children attended high school. Herbert and his elder brother Theodore both went on to Stanford University, Palo Alto, California, from which they both graduated with an AB degree. Herbert gained experience working as a miner in California for two years and later found employment as a mining engineer in Western Australia, China, France, India, England, Hawaii, New Zealand, South Africa, Canada, Germany, Malaya, Russia and at home.

On 10 February 1899 Herbert married Lou Henry, the daughter of a banker, whom he had met when he was still at Stanford, and their two sons were born in London, England, when he was living and working there.

On the outbreak of the First World War in 1914, Hoover, a Quaker, undertook the organization of the American Relief Committee in London to aid those US citizens who had been stranded in Europe, and expedited the return home of 120,000. He later wrote in his memoirs that although he did not realize it at the time his engineering career was over forever and he 'was on the slippery road of public life'. In October 1914, Hoover formed a Committee for the Relief of Belgium and Northern France and was instrumental in obtaining relief for some ten million victims of the German occupation and Allied blockade with food, clothing and medical supplies. For this purpose he was allowed to move freely between London, Paris, Brussels and Berlin. When America entered the war on the Allies' side in 1917, President Wilson appointed Hoover US Food Administrator and shortly before the Armistice in the following year he was appointed Director-General of Relief and Reconstruction of Europe.

In the course of 1919 he served as member and alternate chairman of the Supreme Economic Council, as member of the committee of economic advisers to the American delegation to the Paris Peace Conference, and founded the Hoover Institution on War, Revolution and Peace at Stanford University. In March 1921, Hoover was appointed to the cabinet as Secretary of Commerce by President Harding and the appointment was retained by President Coolidge on his succession in 1923. The Republican National Convention at Kansas City, Missouri, nominated Hoover for President in June 1928. In the election he gained 444 of the electoral votes, an overwhelming victory over the Democratic candidate, Alfred Emanuel Smith, who only gained 87. Hoover was inaugurated on the East Portico of the Capitol on Monday 4 March 1929, the oath being administered for the second time by Chief Justice William Howard Taft, the former twenty-seventh President.

It was probably Hoover's Quaker simplicity as much as the need for economy which caused him to turn over the horses in the White House stables to the use of the army and decommission the presidential yacht *Mayflower*; but these measures were of little avail when the stock-market crash came in October 1929. Hoover was no believer in a welfare state and was loath to provide government relief to the unemployed, believing they should go out looking for work, oblivious of the fact that no work existed for them to do. His misunderstanding of the situation put paid to his chances of re-election in 1932, when, although nominated by the Republican National Convention at Chicago, he gained only 59 electoral votes as opposed to Roosevelt's 472. It was a complete reversal of the previous election. Hoover attended Roosevelt's inauguration on 4 March 1933 and then returned to his home at Palo Alto, California.

The rest of his long life was far from idle. He wrote many books, chaired commissions and was ever ready to help the government of the day with advice when called upon to do so. The popularity he had lost gradually came back to him and he became the country's revered elder statesman.

He died in New York on 20 Octoer 1964, two months after celebrating his ninetieth birthday and after lying in state in the Capitol Rotunda was taken to his birthplace for burial with his wife, who had predeceased him by twenty years. Hoover must rank with the small handful of American Presidents whose utter integrity is beyond question.

Franklin Delano Roosevelt 1933–1945

Born: Springwood, Hyde Park, Dutchess County, New York, 30 January 1882, son of James Roosevelt and his 2nd wife Sara Delano

Governor of New York: 1929–1932

Elected (32nd) President: 8 November 1932

Inaugurated: East Portico of Capitol 4 March 1933

Elected for 2nd term: 3 November 1936

Inaugurated: East Portico of Capitol 20 January 1937

Elected for 3rd term: 5 November 1940

Inaugurated: East Portico of Capitol 2 January 1941

Elected for 4th term: 7 November 1944

Inaugurated: South Portico of the White House 20 January 1945

Married: New York 17 March 1905 (Anna) Eleanor (*b* New York City 12 October 1884; *d* New York City 7 November 1962; *bur* Hyde Park, New York), only dau of Elliott Roosevelt (brother of President Theodore Roosevelt) and Anna Rebecca Hall

Children:

(1) Anna Eleanor, *b* 3 May 1906; *m* (1) 5 June 1926 (div 1934) Curtis Bean Dall, son of Charles Austin Dall; 1 son, 1 dau; *m* (2) New York 18 January 1935 (div 1949) John Boettiger Jr (*b* Chicago 25 March 1900; *d* Manhattan, New York, 31 October 1950); 1 son; *m* (3) Malibu, California, 11 November 1952 James Addison Halsted MD; no children

(2) James, member of House of Representatives, Col US Marine Corps, US Rep to UN Economic and Social Council, *b* New York City 23 December 1907; *m* (1) Brookline, Massachusetts, 4 June 1930 (div 1940) Betsey (*m* (2) John Hay Whitney, sometime US Ambassador to UK), dau of Dr Harvey Cushing; 2 daus; *m* (2) Beverly Hills, California, 14 April 1941 (div 1955) Romelle Theresa Schneider (*b* 1916); 2 sons, 1 dau; *m* (3) Los Angeles, California, 2 July 1956 (div 1969) Mrs Gladys Irene Owens (*b* 1917); 1 adopted son; *m* (4) Hyde Park, New York, 3 October 1969 Mary Lena Winskill (*b* Birkenhead, Cheshire, England, 5 June 1939); 1 dau

(3) Franklin Delano, *b* New York City 18 March 1909; *d* New York City 8 November 1909

(4) Elliott, *b* New York City 23 September 1910; *m* (1) 16 January 1932 (div 1933) Elizabeth Browning (*b* Pittsburgh 5 December 1911), dau of William Henry Donner; 1 son; *m* (2) Burlington, Iowa, 22 July 1933 (div 1944) Ruth Josephine Googins; 2 sons, 1 dau; *m* (3) Grand Canyon, Colorado, 3 December 1944 (div 1950) Faye Margaret Emerson, film actress (*b* Elizabeth, Louisiana, 8 July 1917; *d* Majorca 9 March 1983), formerly wife of William Wallace Crawford and dau of Lawrence Emerson; no children; *m* (4) Miami Beach, Florida, 15 March 1951 (div 1960) Minnewa (*b* 1911), formerly wife of Rex Ross and dau of Alonzo Bell; no children; *m* (5) Qualicum, British Columbia, November 1960, Patricia Whithead; 1 son (*d* in infancy)

(5) Franklin Delano Jr, member of the House of Representatives, Under Secretary of Commerce 1962–65, *b* Campobello Island, New Brunswick, Canada, 17 August 1914; *m* (1) Wilmington, Delaware, 30 June 1937 (div 1949) Ethel (*b* Wilmington 1915; *d* Grosse Pointe, Michigan, 24/25 May 1965), dau of Eugene du Pont; 2 sons; *m* (2) Manhattan, New York, 31 August 1949 (div) 1970), Suzanne, dau of Lee Perrin; 2 daus; *m* (3) New York 1 July 1970 (div) Felicia Schiff, formerly wife of Robert W Sarnoff and dau of Paul Felix Warburg; no children; *m* (4) Dutchess County, New York, 6 May 1977 (div) Patricia Louise Oakes (*b* Mexico City 17 March 1951), dau of Richard Marius Joseph Greene (Richard Greene, the actor) and Nancy Oakes; 1 son; *m* (5) Mrs Lynda McK Weicker née Stevenson; *d* Poughkeepsie, NY, 17 August 1988

(6) John Aspinwall, *b* Washington DC 13 March 1916; *m* (1) Nahant, Massachusetts, 18 June 1938 (div 1965) Anne Lindsay (*b* Concord, Massachusetts, 13 July 1916; *d* New York 28 May 1973), dau of Franklin Haven Clark and Francis Sturgis; 2 sons, 3 daus; *m* (2) New York 28 October 1965 Irene E (*b* New York 8 March 1931), formerly wife of Benjamin Brandreth McAlpine III and dau of James Hallam Boyd and Mary Elizabeth Watkins; no children; *d* New York 27 April 1981

Died in office: The Little White House, Warm Springs, Georgia, 12 April 1945

Buried: Hyde Park, New York

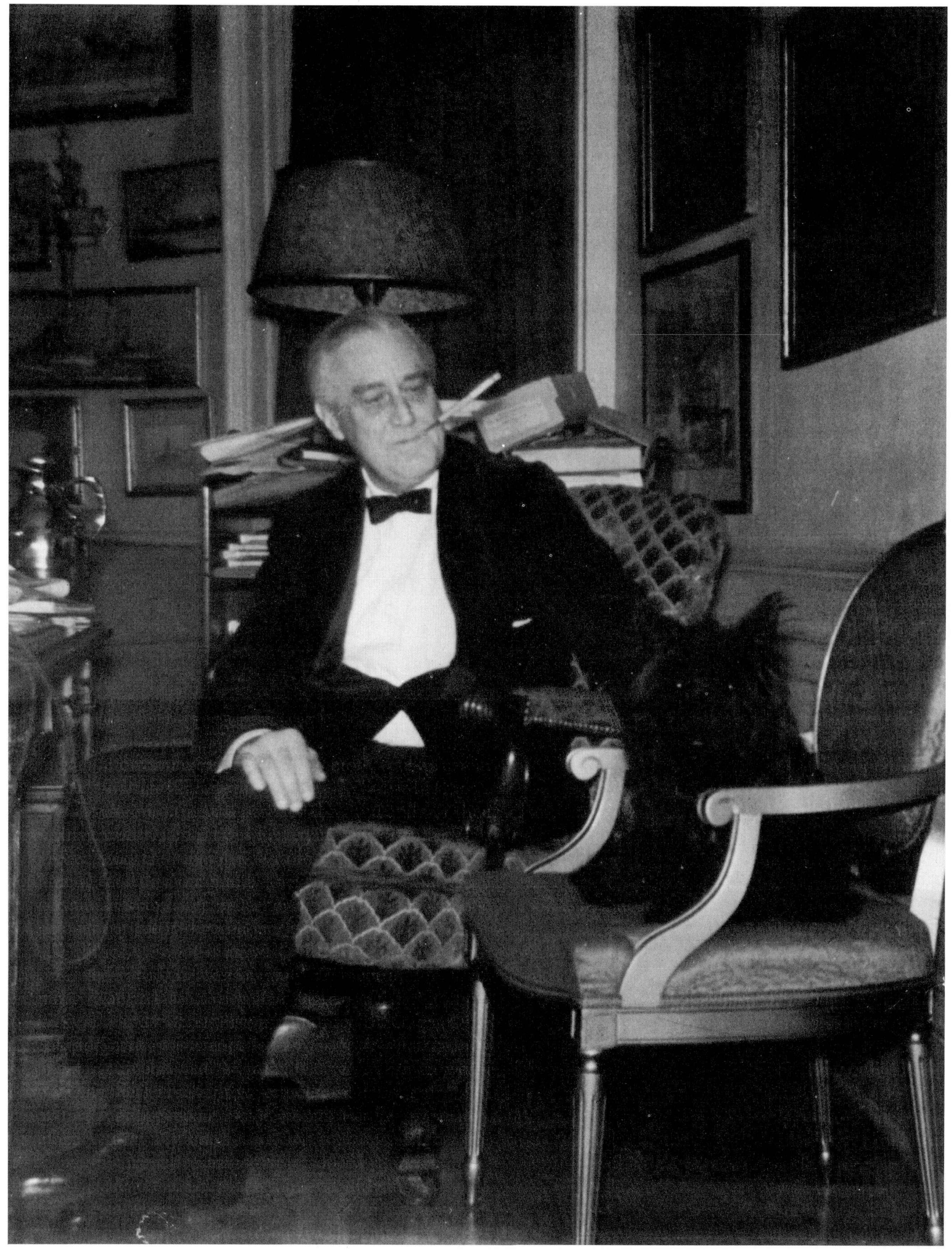

Franklin Delano Roosevelt in a characteristic pose, with his Scottie dog Fala (a personality in its own right), in his study at the White House on 20 December 1941

ABOVE Crum Elbow, formerly Springwood, Hyde Park, New York, the place where Roosevelt was born

RIGHT The talented Mrs Eleanor Roosevelt

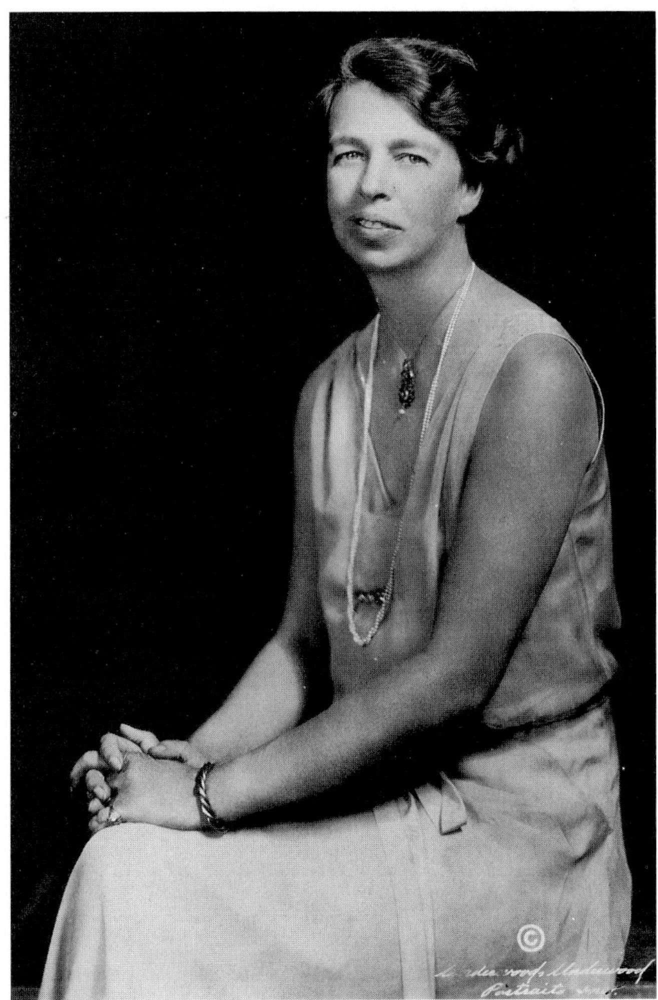

Franklin Delano Roosevelt – FDR – stands out among the list of Presidents, a dominating figure, the only man to be re-elected to office three times and to serve more than two terms, and a living legend as one of the 'Big Three' (with Winston Churchill and Stalin) who saved the world from the Nazi tyranny. It is however impossible to give a rounded account of the man within the limitations of this work.

If ever anyone was born with a golden spoon in his mouth, it was Franklin Delano Roosevelt. The only child of his mother, the formidable 'Mrs James', he was born when his father, James Roosevelt, a prosperous railway executive, was fifty-three and his one and only halfbrother nearly thirty and already the father of two children. The birth took place at the family mansion Springwood, Hyde Park, Dutchess County, New York, on 30 January 1882. The Roosevelts belonged to a junior branch of the same family as President Theodore Roosevelt and had long maintained a high position in New York Society. Franklin attended the exclusive Groton School at Groton, Massachusetts, went on to Harvard, where he graduated AB in 1903, and then to Colombia Law School in New York City. On 17 March 1905 he married his distant cousin, the distinctly plain Eleanor Roosevelt, who, an orphan, was given away by

The Roosevelt Family (2)

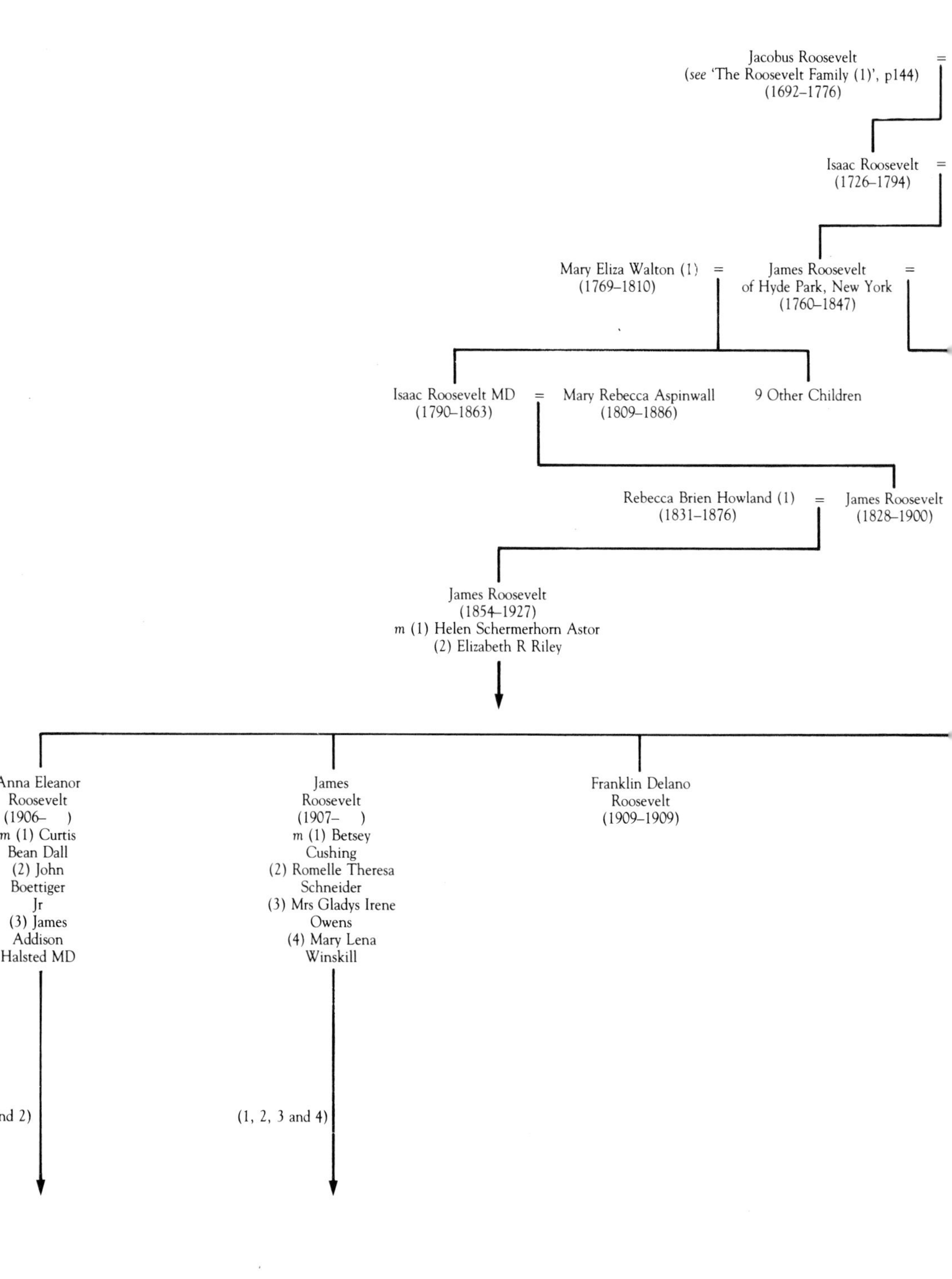

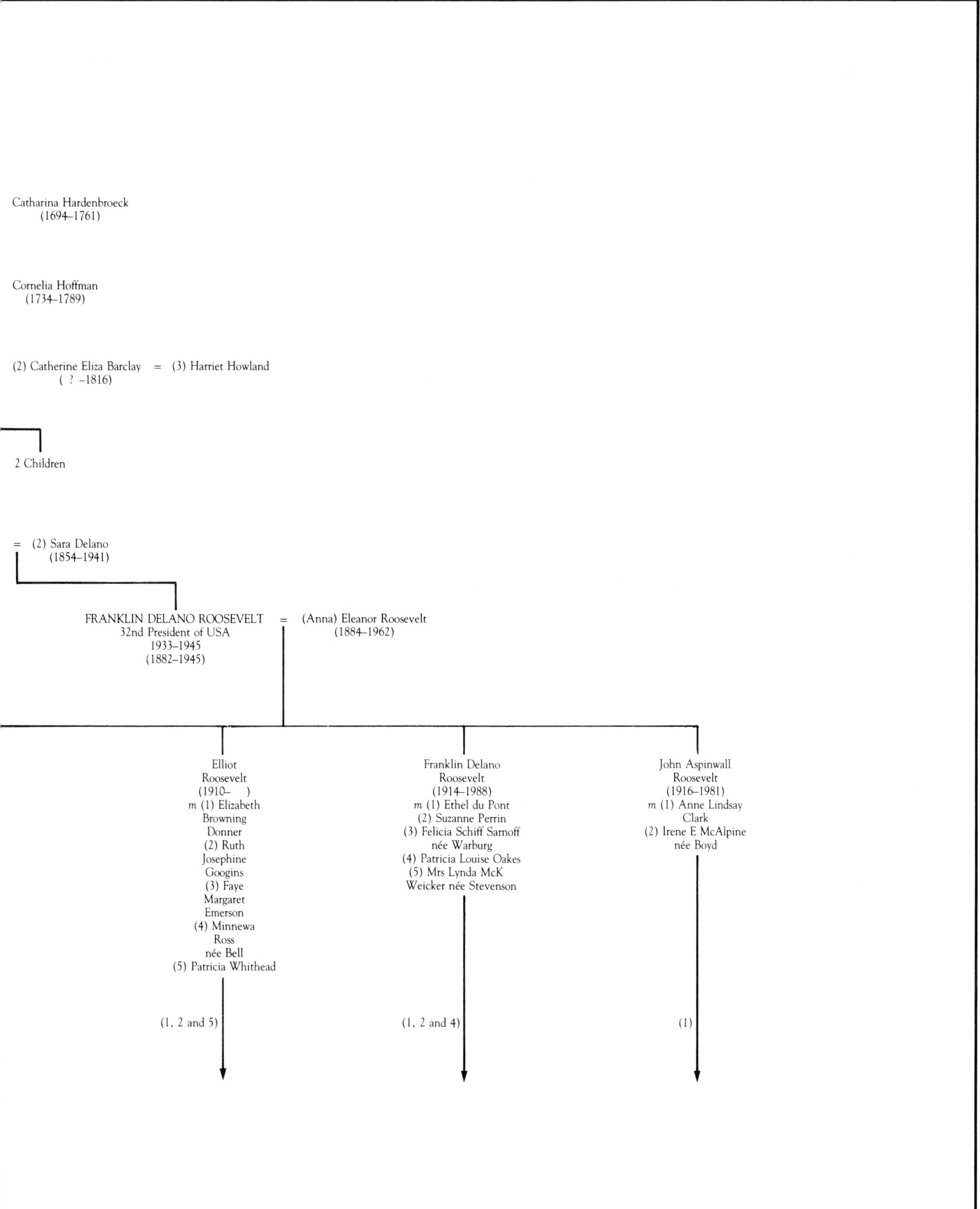
Catharina Hardenbroeck
(1694–1761)
Cornelia Hoffman
(1734–1789)
(2) Catherine Eliza Barclay = (3) Harriet Howland
(? –1816)
2 Children
= (2) Sara Delano
(1854–1941)
FRANKLIN DELANO ROOSEVELT = (Anna) Eleanor Roosevelt
32nd President of USA
1933–1945
(1882–1945)
(1884–1962)
Elliot
Roosevelt
(1910–)
m (1) Elizabeth
Browning
Donner
(2) Ruth
Josephine
Googins
(3) Faye
Margaret
Emerson
(4) Minnewa
Ross
née Bell
(5) Patricia Whithead
(1, 2 and 5)
Franklin Delano
Roosevelt
(1914–1988)
m (1) Ethel du Pont
(2) Suzanne Perrin
(3) Felicia Schiff Sarnoff
née Warburg
(4) Patricia Louise Oakes
(5) Mrs Lynda McK
Weicker née Stevenson
(1, 2 and 4)
John Aspinwall
Roosevelt
(1916–1981)
m (1) Anne Lindsay
Clark
(2) Irene E McAlpine
née Boyd
(1)

Churchill, Roosevelt and Stalin at the Yalta Conference 9 February 1945

her uncle President Theodore Roosevelt, who inevitably managed to steal the show. The honeymoon was a European tour.

Roosevelt was admitted to the New York Bar in 1907. In 1910 he was elected to New York State Senate and reelected in 1912. President Wilson appointed him Assistant Secretary of the Navy in 1913, a position which he held until 1920. In that year he was nominated for Vice-President at the Democratic National Convention at San Francisco but was defeated in the election.

In August 1921 Roosevelt suffered a severe attack of poliomyelitis which left him partially paralysed for the rest of his life, barely able to stand and walk more than a few steps, with his legs in irons. He found swimming a beneficial exercise and in 1924 paid his first visit to Warm Springs, Georgia.

In 1928 Roosevelt was elected Governor of New York, taking office on 1 January 1929. He was re-elected in 1930 with the largest majority in the history of the State.

The Democratic National Convention at Chicago nominated Roosevelt for President in July 1932 and in the ensuing election he received 472 of the 531 electoral votes, the incumbent President Hoover receiving 59.

The first of Roosevelt's four inaugurations took place on Saturday 4 March 1933 with Chief Justice Charles Evans Hughes administering the oath on the East Portico. The story of Roosevelt's twelve years in office as the only man to be re-elected to the presidency three times, belongs to the history of the world, not just that of the United States, encompassing almost the whole of the Second World War. His achievements are all the more outstanding when one considers his physical handicap, which he managed to conceal so successfully that many people never realized that he could barely stand or walk more than a few paces unaided.

He entered confidently into his fourth term in January 1945 and attended a summit conference at Yalta in Russia with Winston Churchill and Stalin in February. However, when staying at the Little White House in Warm Springs with his mistress Lucy Mercer, who had been his wife's secretary, a sudden cerebral haemorrhage led to his death on 12 April 1945. He was sixty-three years old. Mrs Roosevelt, a great personality in her own right and a talented writer and journalist, lived on until 7 November 1962.

HARRY S TRUMAN 1945–1953

Born:	Lamar, Missouri, 8 May 1884, elder son of John Anderson Truman and Martha Ellen Young
Senator:	1935–1944
Elected Vice-President:	7 November 1944
Inaugurated:	The White House 20 January 1945
Succeeded as (33rd) President:	12 April 1945
Took oath:	Cabinet room of the White House 12 April 1945
Elected for 2nd term:	2 November 1948
Inaugurated:	East Portico of Capitol 20 January 1949
Retired from presidency:	20 January 1953
Married:	Independence, Missouri, 28 June 1919 Elizabeth (Bess) Virginia (*b* Independence 13 February 1885; *d* Independence 18 October 1982; *bur* rose garden of Harry S Truman Library, Independence), dau of David Willock Wallace and Madge Gates
Daughter:	(Mary) Margaret, *b* Independence, Missouri, 17 February 1924; *m* Independence 21 April 1956 (Elbert) Clifton Daniel Jr (*b* Zebulon, North Carolina, 19 September 1912), son of Elbert Clifton Daniel and Elvah Jones; 4 sons
Died:	Kansas City, Missouri, 26 December 1972
Buried:	Rose garden of the Harry S Truman Library, Independence, Missouri

Of the Vice-Presidents who have succeeded to the office of President through death or assassination Harry S Truman towers above all the rest for having become one of the most outstanding and capable of all Presidents. When Roosevelt's death bought him into office he was virtually unknown throughout the world, but he very soon proved himself and won a respect and admiration which were to remain undiminished for the rest of his life.

It is not known when the first Truman ancestor arrived in America. William and Nancy Truman were the parents of another William Truman, born in Virginia on 15 January 1783. He later settled in Kentucky, where he married Emma Grant Shippe in August 1807 and raised a family of eight sons and four daughters. The fourth son, Anderson Shippe Truman, moved to Missouri in 1846 with his new wife Mary Jane Holmes. They had two sons and three daughters, the younger son being John Anderson Truman, who became a farmer and livestock salesman in Independence, Missouri. He married Martha Ellen Young and the eldest of their three children was Harry S Truman, born at Lamar, Missouri, on 8 May 1884. His middle initial, like that of Ulysses S Grant, did not represent a given name, although it has sometimes been said to stand for Shippe, the maiden name of his great-grandmother.

The family settled in Independence in 1890. Harry was a delicate boy, with weak eyesight, and he had to be fitted with thick-lensed spectacles before he could read his school textbooks. At the age of ten he suffered a bad attack of diphtheria from which he was slowly nursed back to health by his mother. The family finances were such that he was unable to enter college after leaving

Harry S Truman with his wife Bess and daughter Margaret

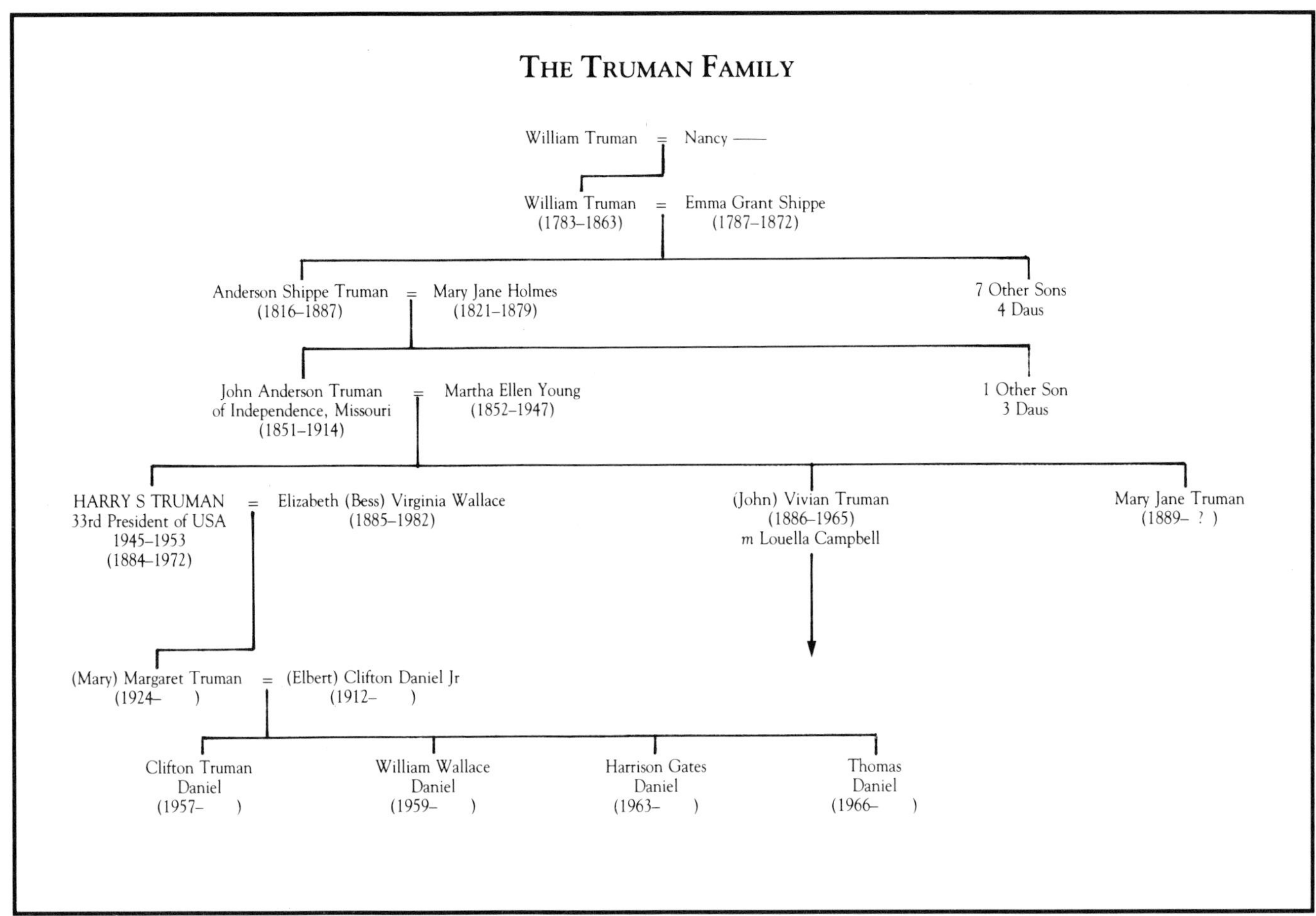

Independence High School in 1901 and he began work at a salary of $35 a month as timekeeper for a railroad construction contractor. In 1902 the family moved to Kansas City, Missouri, and Truman found work at $7 a week in the mailroom of the Kansas City *Star*. He held various clerking and book-keeping jobs until 1906, when he went to help manage the family farm at Grandview, which he did for more than two years. His father died in 1914 and the following year Truman was commissioned as Captain in the Field Artillery and saw active service in France. He was discharged from the army with the rank of Major in May 1919 and the following month married his boyhood sweetheart Elizabeth Virginia Wallace.

In November 1919 he went into partnership in a men's haberdashery shop in Independence but, after business deteriorated in the slump of 1921, the partners were obliged to close down in 1922, making agreements with their creditors to pay them off over a period of years.

Truman was elected County Judge of the Eastern District of Jackson County in November 1922. This was an administrative rather than a judicial position. He spent the years from 1923 to 1925 attending Kansas City School of Law, failed to be re-elected as County Judge in 1924, but was elected Presiding Judge of Jackson County in 1926. In 1925 he had boosted his income by taking a job as membership salesman for Kansas City Automobile Club and earned about $5,000. Truman became the Democratic leader of Eastern Jackson County in 1929 and the following year was re-elected Presiding Judge. On 6 November 1934 he was elected to the Senate and took his seat on 3 January 1935. He was re-elected in 1940 and in 1944 was nominated for Vice-President at the Democratic National Convention in Chicago. He was duly elected on 7 November 1944 and took the oath at the White House on 20 January 1945. On the 12 April he learnt that he had become President when Eleanor Roosevelt told him, 'Harry, the President is dead'. To follow such a giant as Roosevelt with the Second World War nearing its conclusion and the future of the world undiscernible would have been a daunting task for any man. Truman faced up to it fairly and squarely and did all that had to be done.

The famous notice he placed on his desk, 'The buck stops here', told it all. He was not a man to delegate authority and his energy and capacity for work and for attending to every detail himself were to be quite phenomenal. He did so well that when he was re-nominated for President in 1948 he gained 303 of the 531 electoral votes. He was inaugurated on 20 January 1949, Chief Justice Frederick Moore Vinson administer-

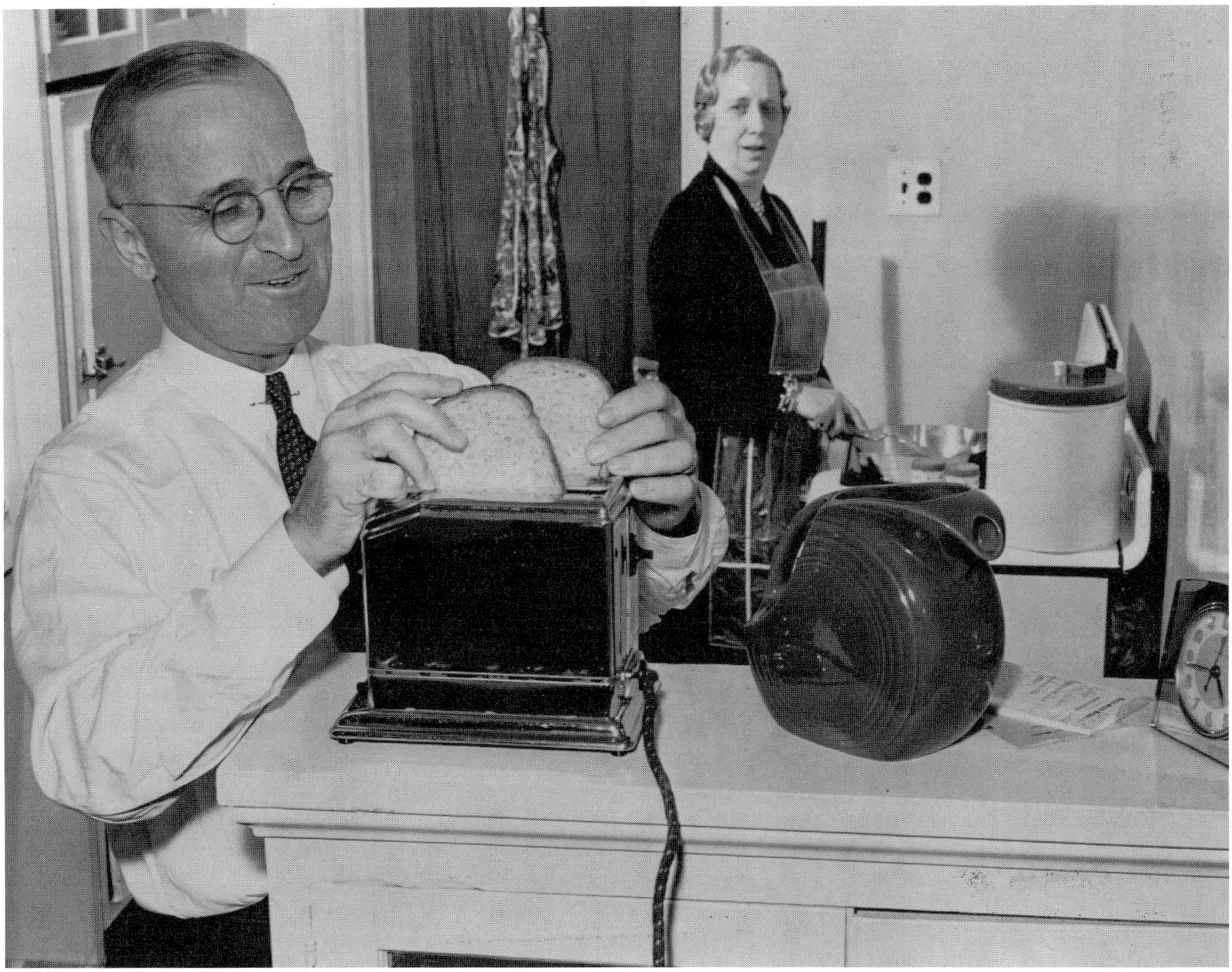

The Trumans at home, striking a pose of happy domesticity for the camera

ing the oath on the East Portico of the Capitol. The second term of office was a troubled one, seeing the outbreak of the Korean War which was to linger on for so long.

When Truman retired from office on 20 January 1953 and returned to Independence, Missouri, he still had twenty years of life left to him. He spent them by taking a keen interest in the foundation of the Harry S Truman Library at Independence, in travelling abroad, and in watching the growth and progress of his four grandsons, the children of his only daughter, Margaret. He also wrote two volumes of memoirs and was perhaps the most respected 'elder statesman' figure in the Western world. In 1971 he refused the Congressional Medal of Honour when it was offered to him, saying, 'I do not consider that I have done anything which should be the reason of any award, congressional or otherwise'. He died in Kansas City, Missouri, on 26 December 1972, aged eighty-eight.

DWIGHT DAVID EISENHOWER 1953–1961

Born:	Denison, Texas, 14 October 1890, 3rd son David Jacob Eisenhower and Ida Elizabeth Stover	Married:	Denver, Colorado, 1 July 1916 Mamie Geneva (*b* Boone, Iowa, 14 November 1896; *d* Walter Reed Army Hospital, Washington, 31 October 1979; *bur* Abilene, Kansas), dau of John Sheldon Doud and Elivera Mathilda Carlson
Supreme Commander of Allied Expeditionary Force:	1943–1945	Children:	(1) Doud Dwight (Icky), *b* Denver, Colorado, 24 September 1917; *d* Camp Meade, Maryland, 2 January 1921
Army Chief of Staff:	1945–1948		(2) John Sheldon Doud, Brig-Gen US Army Reserve, US Ambassador to Belgium 1969–71, *b* Denver, Colorado, 3 August 1922; *m* Fort Monroe, Virginia, 10 June 1947 Barbara Jean (*b* Fort Knox, Kentucky 15 June 1926), dau of Col Percy W Thompson and Beatrice Birchfield; 1 son (Dwight David Eisenhower II, who *m* Julie, yr dau of President Nixon, *qv*), 3 daus
Supreme Commander of European Defence:	1951–1952		
Elected (34th) President:	4 November 1952		
Inaugurated:	East Portico of Capitol 20 January 1953		
Elected for 2nd term:	6 November 1956		
Inaugurated:	(privately) The White House 20 January and (publicly) East Portico of Capitol 21 January 1957	Died:	Walter Reed Army Medical Center, Washington DC, 28 March 1969
Retired from presidency:	20 January 1961	Buried:	Abilene, Kansas

Dwight David Eisenhower, like Ulysses S Grant (*qv*) before him, was living proof that good generals do not necessarily make good Presidents. However, his prestige as a war leader remains undiminished and he will always be one of the nation's heroes.

To some it might appear ironic that Eisenhower, who was to gain fame as Supreme Allied Commander in the war against Germany, came from a family of German origin. The male line can be traced back to Hans Eisenhauer of Eiterbach in the Rhenish Palatinate, who was born about 1600. His grandson, Hans Nicholaus Eisenhauer, emigrated to America with his three sons and settled in Philadelphia in 1741. His eldest son, Peter, adopted the spelling Eisenhower and was the father of Frederick Eisenhower, who settled in Kansas, where he worked as manager of a gas company. His grandson, David Jacob Eisenhower, married Ida Elizabeth Stover in 1885 and they had a family of seven sons, of whom David Dwight Eisenhower (later to transpose his two first names) was the third and was born at Denison, Texas, on 14 October 1890, a year before the family moved to Abilene.

From Abilene High School, Eisenhower went on to West Point, from which he graduated in June 1915 and was assigned to the 19th Infantry at Fort Sam, Houston, San Antonio, Texas. On 1 July 1916, the day he was promoted First Lieutenant, he married Mamie Geneva

The General and Mamie stage a 'cook out' on the lawn of their house at Fort Lewis, Washington, in 1941

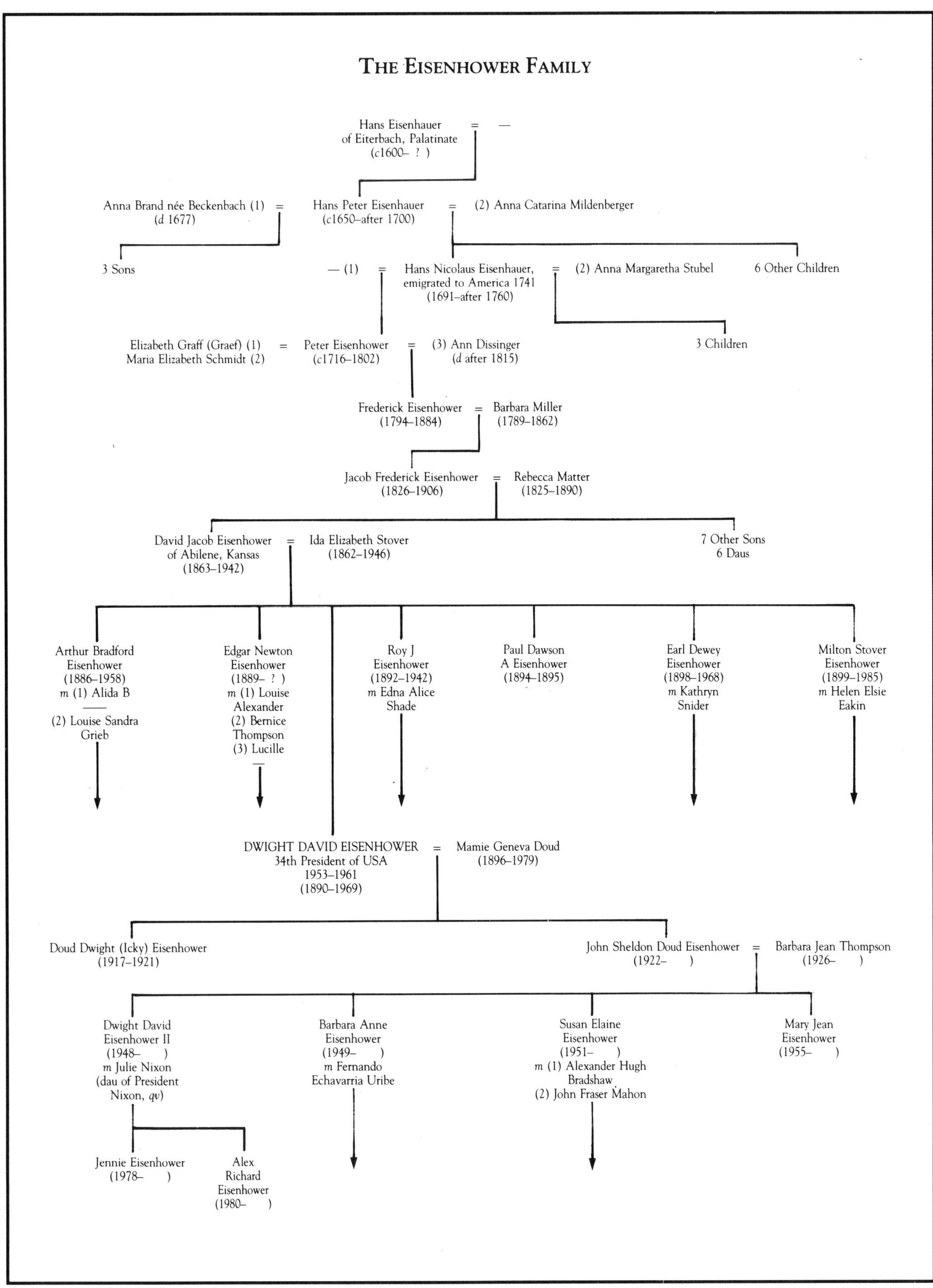
THE EISENHOWER FAMILY
Hans Eisenhauer of Eiterbach, Palatinate (c1600– ?) = —
Anna Brand née Beckenbach (1) (d 1677) = Hans Peter Eisenhauer (c1650–after 1700) = (2) Anna Catarina Mildenberger
3 Sons
— (1) = Hans Nicolaus Eisenhauer, emigrated to America 1741 (1691–after 1760) = (2) Anna Margaretha Stubel
6 Other Children
Elizabeth Graff (Graef) (1) Maria Elizabeth Schmidt (2) = Peter Eisenhower (c1716–1802) = (3) Ann Dissinger (d after 1815)
3 Children
Frederick Eisenhower (1794–1884) = Barbara Miller (1789–1862)
Jacob Frederick Eisenhower (1826–1906) = Rebecca Matter (1825–1890)
David Jacob Eisenhower of Abilene, Kansas (1863–1942) = Ida Elizabeth Stover (1862–1946)
7 Other Sons 6 Daus
Arthur Bradford Eisenhower (1886–1958) m (1) Alida B —— (2) Louise Sandra Grieb
Edgar Newton Eisenhower (1889– ?) m (1) Louise Alexander (2) Bernice Thompson (3) Lucille —
Roy J Eisenhower (1892–1942) m Edna Alice Shade
Paul Dawson A Eisenhower (1894–1895)
Earl Dewey Eisenhower (1898–1968) m Kathryn Snider
Milton Stover Eisenhower (1899–1985) m Helen Elsie Eakin
DWIGHT DAVID EISENHOWER 34th President of USA 1953–1961 (1890–1969) = Mamie Geneva Doud (1896–1979)
Doud Dwight (Icky) Eisenhower (1917–1921)
John Sheldon Doud Eisenhower (1922–) = Barbara Jean Thompson (1926–)
Dwight David Eisenhower II (1948–) m Julie Nixon (dau of President Nixon, qv)
Barbara Anne Eisenhower (1949–) m Fernando Echavarria Uribe
Susan Elaine Eisenhower (1951–) m (1) Alexander Hugh Bradshaw (2) John Fraser Mahon
Mary Jean Eisenhower (1955–)
Jennie Eisenhower (1978–)
Alex Richard Eisenhower (1980–)

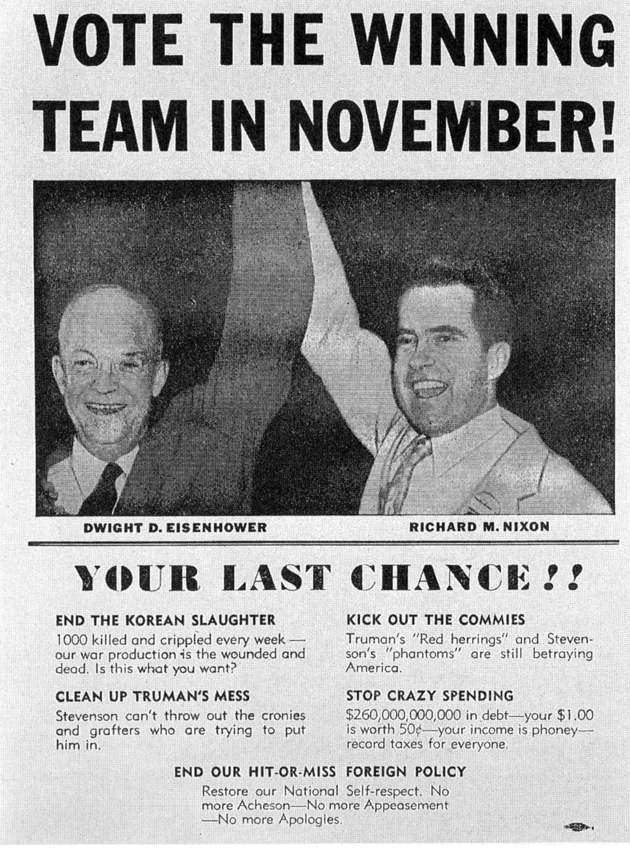

VOTE THE WINNING TEAM IN NOVEMBER!
DWIGHT D. EISENHOWER
RICHARD M. NIXON
YOUR LAST CHANCE!!
END THE KOREAN SLAUGHTER
1000 killed and crippled every week — our war production is the wounded and dead. Is this what you want?
KICK OUT THE COMMIES
Truman's "Red herrings" and Stevenson's "phantoms" are still betraying America.
CLEAN UP TRUMAN'S MESS
Stevenson can't throw out the cronies and grafters who are trying to put him in.
STOP CRAZY SPENDING
$260,000,000,000 in debt—your $1.00 is worth 50¢—your income is phoney—record taxes for everyone.
END OUR HIT-OR-MISS FOREIGN POLICY
Restore our National Self-respect. No more Acheson—No more Appeasement —No more Apologies.

An Eisenhower and Nixon campaign poster of 1952

Doud, a native of Boone, Iowa, whose parents now lived in Denver, Colorado.

In spite of America's entry into the First World War in April 1917, Eisenhower saw no service overseas and from 1922 to 1924 was stationed in the Panama Canal. He attended the Command and General Staff School at Fort Leavenworth, Kansas, from 1925 to 1926 and the Army War College at Washington DC in 1928. After serving from 1929 to 1932 on the staff of the Assistant Secretary of War, Eisenhower joined the staff of General Douglas A MacArthur, Army Chief of Staff in Washington from 1932 to 1934 and in the Philippines from 1935 to 1939. When the Japanese attacked Pearl Harbour on 7 December 1941, Eisenhower held the rank of temporary Brigadier-General. In February 1942 he was appointed assistant chief of staff on the War Plans Division, War Department and General Staff. Thereafter promotion was rapid and in November 1942 he became Allied-Commander-in-Chief for the invasion of North Africa. Promoted to the temporary rank of full General in February 1943, Eisenhower was designated Supreme Commander of the Allied Expeditionary Force on 24 December 1943 and as such planned the D-Day invasion of Europe on 6 June 1944. The Allied campaign went with such success that on 7 May 1945, Eisenhower accepted the surrender of the German army at Rheims.

After his return to America in triumph, Eisenhower served as army chief of staff from 1945 to 1948, when he retired and took up the post of President of Columbia University in October 1948.

In 1950 Eisenhower bought a farm at Gettysburg, Pennsylvania, as a residence for himself and his wife, and at the end of the year he was appointed Supreme Commander of European Defence by the foreign ministers of NATO countries. He took up the appointment in April 1952 but resigned it in July after being nominated for President at the Republican National Convention in Chicago. In the election he received 442 of the 531 electoral votes, the remaining 89 going to Adlai Ewing Stevenson, the Democratic candidate.

Eisenhower was inaugurated as 34th President on Tuesday 20 January 1953, Chief Justice Frederick M Vinson administering the oath on the East Portico of the Capitol.

Eisenhower's weakness became apparent throughout his presidency: his failure to take a firm stand against McCarthyism or in the civil rights controversies told against him. His lack of culture and avowedly middlebrow tastes, combined with recurring bouts of illness, did not help either, and Mrs Eisenhower did not shine as a hostess, having a drink problem to cope with, as was learnt later. Nevertheless, Eisenhower was nominated for President in 1956 and gained slightly more electoral votes than before, 457, while Stevenson, his opponent again, received 73.

As inauguration day fell on a Sunday, Eisenhower took the oath privately at the White House on 20 January 1957, followed by the now traditional public ceremony on the East Portico of the Capitol the following day, Chief Justice Earl Warren administering the oath. Alaska was admitted as the forty-ninth state in January 1959 and Hawaii as the fiftieth State in August, thus adding two more stars to the national flag. In June the President joined with Queen Elizabeth II of Great Britain in opening the St Lawrence seaway. He spent a great deal of the year in visits abroad, including a short stay in the apartment at Culzean Castle, Scotland, which the grateful Scottish people had given to him for life after the Second World War.

Eisenhower retired from the presidential office on 20 January 1961 and attended the inauguration of his successor President Kennedy, who on 22 March signed an act restoring his rank as General of the Army. 'Ike' and 'Mamie', as they were affectionately known, retired to their farm at Gettysburg, where they lived quietly for the next few years. Eisenhower then suffered a series of heart attacks of increasing severity and early in 1969 was operated on for acute intestinal obstruction. Five days later he contracted pneumonia and on 15 March suffered congestive heart failure, which proved fatal on 28 March. He was seventy-eight years old. Mrs Eisenhower survived another ten years, dying on 31 October 1979.

JOHN FITZGERALD KENNEDY 1961–1963

Born:	83 Beals Street, Brookline, Massachusetts, 29 May 1917, 2nd son of Joseph Patrick Kennedy and Rose Elizabeth Fitzgerald
Member of House of Representatives:	1947–1952
Senator:	1953–1960
Elected (35th) President:	8 November 1960
Inaugurated:	East Portico of Capitol 20 January 1961
Married:	Newport, Rhode Island, 12 September 1953 Jacqueline Lee (*b* Southampton, Long Island, New York, 28 July 1929; *m* (2) Skorpios, Greece, 22 October 1968, as his 2nd wife, Aristotle Socrates Onassis, who *d* in Paris, France, 15 March 1975), dau of John Vernou Bouvier III and Janet Lee.
Children:	(1) Daughter, stillborn 23 August 1956 (2) Caroline Bouvier, *b* New York 27 November 1957; *m* Centerville, Mass, 19 July 1987 Edwin Arthur Schlossberg; 1 dau (Rose, *b* New York, 25 June 1988) (3) John Fitzgerald Jr, *b* Washington DC 25 November 1960 (4) Patrick Bouvier, *b* Otis Air Force Base, Massachusetts, 7 August, *d* Boston 9 August 1963
Died (assassinated):	Dallas, Texas, 22 November 1963
Buried:	Arlington National Cemetery, Arlington, Virginia

The wave of hysteria which swept the world after the assassination of President Kennedy in 1963 almost amounted to canonization by acclamation. Its repercussions even moved the trustees of an old people's housing association in a borough of London, England, to name one of its new homes John F Kennedy House, much to the consternation of the residents, who had been expecting it to be named after a member of the British royal family.

The Kennedy family came straight out of the Irish bogs. Patrick Kennedy, a small tenant farmer in Dunganstown, County Wexford, had three sons, of whom the youngest, Patrick, emigrated to Boston in 1848 and followed the trade of cooper there until his death from consumption ten years later. His son, Patrick Joseph, a saloon keeper, was the father of Joseph Patrick Kennedy, who had a meteoric career, amassing a fortune as a real estate owner, financier and banker and rising to the position of Ambassador to the Court of St James's. Like many another self-made man he was hard driving and intent on furthering the careers of his many children with no expense spared. In 1914 he married, in spite of her parents' opposition, Rose Fitzgerald, the eldest daughter of 'Honey Fitz' Fitzgerald, Mayor of Boston. The couple had nine children, of whom the second, John Fitzgerald Kennedy, was born at Brookline, Massachusetts, on 29 May 1917.

Kennedy was educated expensively at private schools and then at the prestigious Choate School in Wallingford, Connecticut. He went on to Princeton in September 1935, but was forced to drop out in December because of recurring attacks of jaundice. By September 1936 he had recovered enough to enter Harvard. On his twenty-first birthday in May 1938 his father set up a million-dollar trust fund for him. Throughout 1939 Kennedy toured Europe, acting as private secretary to his father, then Ambassador to the United Kingdom. He graduated from Harvard as BSc *cum laude* in June 1940 and did a brief course of study at Stanford University Graduate School

President John F Kennedy

THE KENNEDY FAMILY

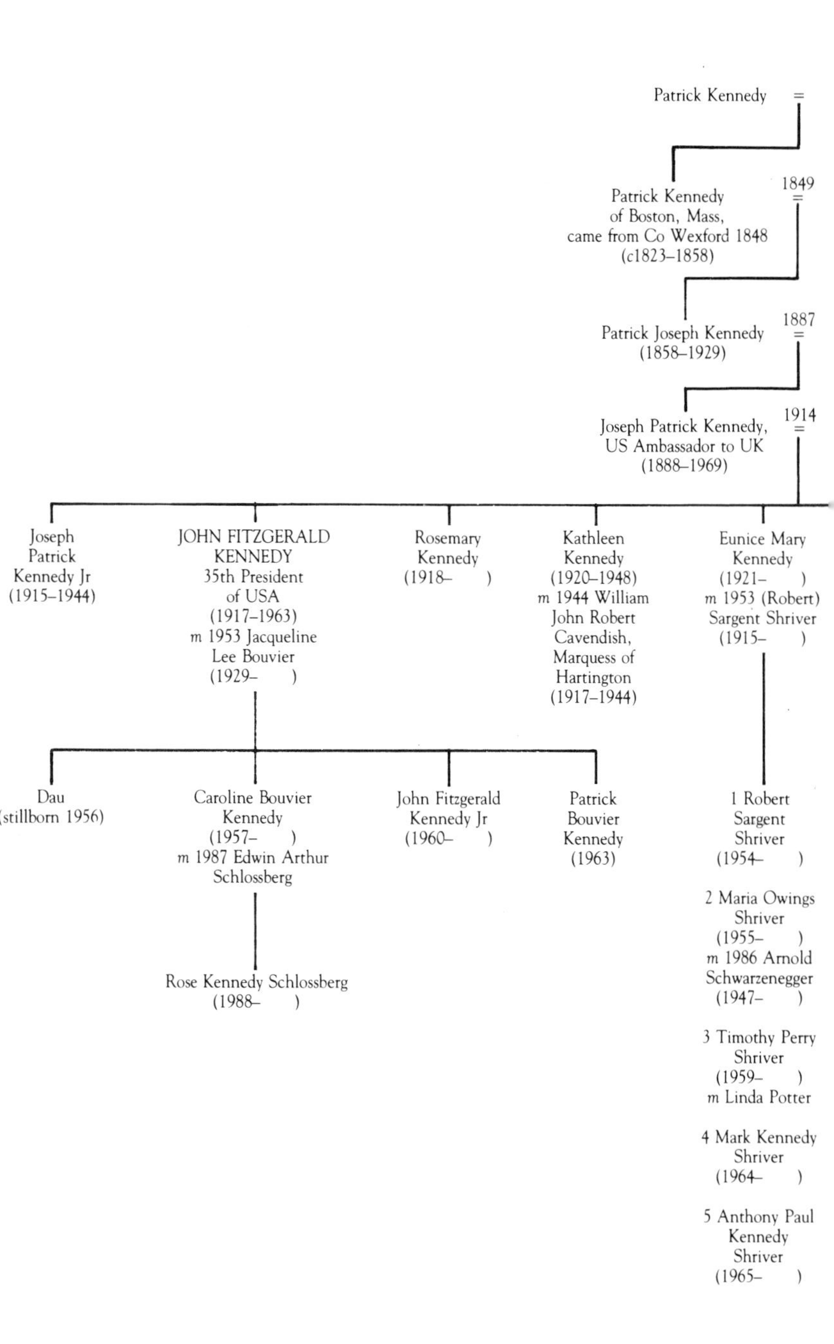
Patrick Kennedy =
1849 =
Patrick Kennedy
of Boston, Mass,
came from Co Wexford 1848
(c1823–1858)
1887 =
Patrick Joseph Kennedy
(1858–1929)
1914 =
Joseph Patrick Kennedy,
US Ambassador to UK
(1888–1969)
Joseph Patrick Kennedy Jr (1915–1944)
JOHN FITZGERALD KENNEDY
35th President of USA
(1917–1963)
m 1953 Jacqueline Lee Bouvier
(1929–)
Rosemary Kennedy (1918–)
Kathleen Kennedy (1920–1948)
m 1944 William John Robert Cavendish, Marquess of Hartington (1917–1944)
Eunice Mary Kennedy (1921–)
m 1953 (Robert) Sargent Shriver (1915–)
Dau (stillborn 1956)
Caroline Bouvier Kennedy (1957–)
m 1987 Edwin Arthur Schlossberg
John Fitzgerald Kennedy Jr (1960–)
Patrick Bouvier Kennedy (1963)
Rose Kennedy Schlossberg (1988–)
1 Robert Sargent Shriver (1954–)
2 Maria Owings Shriver (1955–)
m 1986 Arnold Schwarzenegger (1947–)
3 Timothy Perry Shriver (1959–)
m Linda Potter
4 Mark Kennedy Shriver (1964–)
5 Anthony Paul Kennedy Shriver (1965–)

Maria Johanna —

Bridget Murphy
(c1821–1888)

Mary Augusta Hickey
(1857–1923)

Rose Elizabeth Fitzgerald
(1890–)

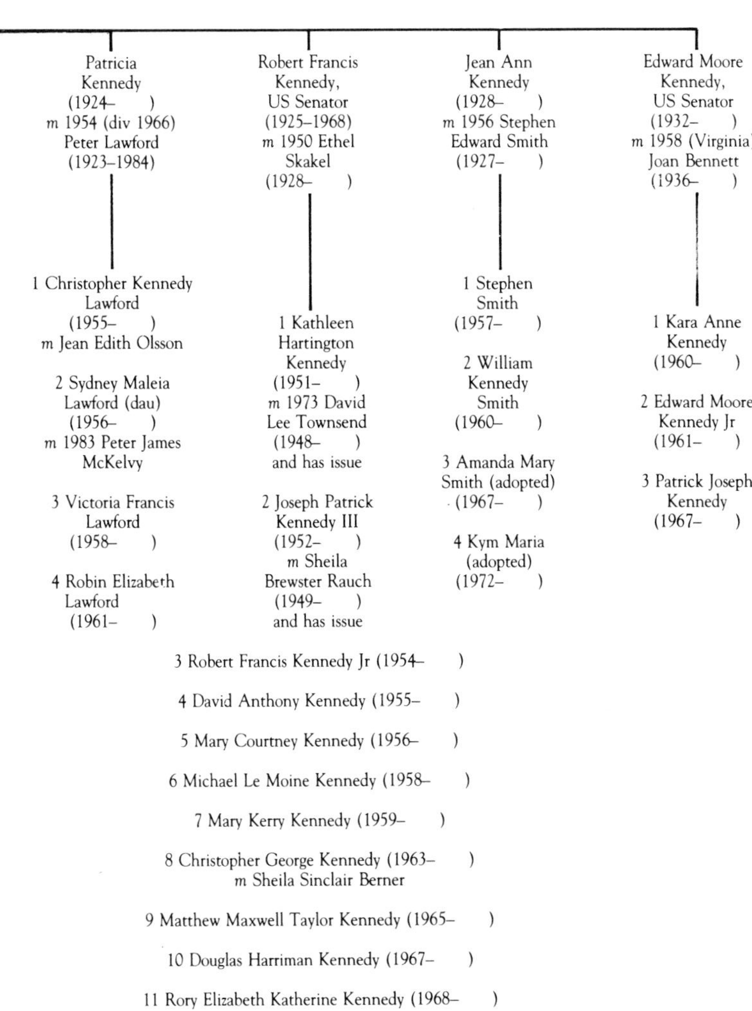

Patricia Kennedy (1924–) m 1954 (div 1966) Peter Lawford (1923–1984)
Robert Francis Kennedy, US Senator (1925–1968) m 1950 Ethel Skakel (1928–)
Jean Ann Kennedy (1928–) m 1956 Stephen Edward Smith (1927–)
Edward Moore Kennedy, US Senator (1932–) m 1958 (Virginia) Joan Bennett (1936–)
1 Christopher Kennedy Lawford (1955–) m Jean Edith Olsson
2 Sydney Maleia Lawford (dau) (1956–) m 1983 Peter James McKelvy
3 Victoria Francis Lawford (1958–)
4 Robin Elizabeth Lawford (1961–)
1 Kathleen Hartington Kennedy (1951–) m 1973 David Lee Townsend (1948–) and has issue
2 Joseph Patrick Kennedy III (1952–) m Sheila Brewster Rauch (1949–) and has issue
1 Stephen Smith (1957–)
2 William Kennedy Smith (1960–)
3 Amanda Mary Smith (adopted) (1967–)
4 Kym Maria (adopted) (1972–)
1 Kara Anne Kennedy (1960–)
2 Edward Moore Kennedy Jr (1961–)
3 Patrick Joseph Kennedy (1967–)
3 Robert Francis Kennedy Jr (1954–)
4 David Anthony Kennedy (1955–)
5 Mary Courtney Kennedy (1956–)
6 Michael Le Moine Kennedy (1958–)
7 Mary Kerry Kennedy (1959–)
8 Christopher George Kennedy (1963–) m Sheila Sinclair Berner
9 Matthew Maxwell Taylor Kennedy (1965–)
10 Douglas Harriman Kennedy (1967–)
11 Rory Elizabeth Katherine Kennedy (1968–)

Jacqueline Kennedy

of Business Administration in Palo Alto, California. The same year saw the publication of his book *Why England Slept*, an analysis of England's lack of preparedness for the Second World War.

Kennedy was commissioned as Ensign USN in October 1941 and called up for active service the following year. While serving in the Solomon Islands his ship was rammed and sunk by a Japanese destroyer and he and other survivors of the crew escaped to an island from which they were later rescued. In the course of the escape Kennedy injured his back and over the next few years underwent several operations to his spine. He never fully recovered and suffered back pains for the rest of his life, although he found the use of an old-fashioned rocking-chair afforded him some relief.

The legendary 'curse of the Kennedys' had begun with the death in action of Kennedy's elder brother Joseph P Kennedy Jr, who was shot down over England on 12 August 1944. A month later, on 10 September, their brother-in-law, the Marquess of Hartington, was killed in action in Belgium, leaving their sister Kathleen a widow after only four months of marriage. Kathleen, herself, was to be killed in a flying accident in France in May 1948.

Kennedy was discharged from the navy in April 1945. In November he was elected to the House of Representatives and took his seat in January 1947. He was twice re-elected and then in November 1952 elected to the Senate, taking his seat in January 1953. He was unsuccessful in winning the nomination for Vice-President in 1956; won the Pulitzer Prize for his book *Profiles in Courage* in 1957; and was re-elected to the Senate in 1958.

The Democratic National Convention at Los Angeles nominated Kennedy for President in July 1960, and he was elected with 303 electoral votes against 219 for Richard Nixon and 15 for Harry F Byrd. Kennedy was inaugurated on a platform erected on the renovated East Front of the Capitol on Friday 20 January 1961, the oath being administered by Chief Justice Earl Warren. His proud parents looked on, as also did Jacqueline, the socially prominent wife he had married in September 1953.

The couple set about redecorating and refurnishing the White House. A picture of Mrs Eisenhower which had hung in the entrance hall was one of the first things to be removed, but had to be hastily restored temporarily when the Eisenhowers came to dinner and it was realized they would miss it. Jacqueline organized a series of classical concerts and musical evenings at the White House.

Kennedy set out to be a dynamic young President, ready to fly to the corners of the earth in the cause of peace. The theme of his inaugural address had been 'Get America moving again', the machinery of state having run down under Eisenhower. His nepotism in appointing his brother Bobby Attorney-General and finding posts for other relations aroused some criticism, as did the Bay of Pigs invasion of Cuba; but on the whole it was roses, roses all the way for Kennedy. He reached the apogee of his presidency when he visited West Germany in June 1963 and, after honorary citizenship had been conferred upon him, made his theatrical declaration: '*Ich bin ein Berliner*'. He certainly knew how to play to an audience.

Five months later all was over. The ill-starred visit to Dallas, where the President was shot in the head by an assassin while riding with his wife in an open-topped automobile procession, has been written about again and again. Kennedy was forty-six years old, the fourth President to be assassinated and the eighth to die in office. He was accorded an impressive funeral and buried at Arlington National Cemetery, where two of his children were brought to lie beside him.

His widow, Jacqueline, made a much publicized second marriage with the multi-millionaire Greek ship-owner Aristotle Onassis. She is now again widowed and has recently become a grandmother with the birth of a daughter, Rose, to her daughter Caroline. Kennedy's mother, Rose, the great matriarch of the Kennedy clan, at the time of writing lives still, now in her ninety-ninth year.

LYNDON BAINES JOHNSON 1963–1969

Born:	Near Stonewall, Texas, 27 August 1908, elder son of Samuel Ealy Johnson Jr, and Rebekah Baines	Married:	San Antonio, Texas, 17 November 1934 Claudia Alta, called 'Lady Bird' (*b* Karnack, Texas, 22 December 1912), dau of Thomas Jefferson Taylor and Minnie Pattillo
Member of House of Representatives:	1937–1948	Children:	(1) Lynda Bird, *b* 19 March 1944; *m* the White House 9 December 1967 Major Charles Spittall Robb, US Marine Corps (*b* Phoenix, Arizona, 1940), son of James S Robb and Frances Woolley; 2 daus
Senator:	1949–1961		
Elected Vice-President:	6 November 1960		
Inaugurated:	20 January 1961		
Succeeded as (36th) President:	22 November 1963		(2) Lucy (Luci) Baines, *b* 2 July 1947; *m* Shrine of the Immaculate Conception, Washington DC, 6 August 1966 (div 1979) Patrick John Nugent (*b* 8 July 1943), son of Gerard P Nugent; 1 son, 3 daus
Took oath:	On board presidential jet *Air Force One* at Love Field, Dallas, Texas, 22 November 1963		
Elected for 2nd term:	3 November 1964		
Inaugurated:	East Portico of Capitol 20 January 1965	Died:	San Antonio, Texas, 22 January 1973
Retired from presidency:	20 January 1969	Buried:	LBJ Ranch, Stonewall, Texas

Lyndon Baines Johnson, better known as LBJ, who succeeded to the presidency on Kennedy's assassination, was to prove himself a capable if unspectacular President, and one not calculated to arouse any strong emotions either for or against him.

The Johnson family has been traced back to James Johnston of Currowaugh, in Nansemond and Isle of Wight Counties in Virginia, who was born about 1662 and was probably the son of an immigrant (the early records of Nansemond County no longer exist). His grandson John, who adopted the spelling Johnson, settled in Franklin County, North Carolina, about 1767, and was a hatter by trade. His descendants moved via Georgia and Alabama to Texas, where they prospered as cattle ranchers and dabbled in local politics, giving their name to Johnson City. Samuel Ealy Johnson Jr, who served as a member of the Texas House of Representatives for two periods (1904–9 and 1917–25), married Rebekah Baines, daughter of Captain Joseph Wilson Baines, of Blanco, Texas, and had two sons and three daughters.

Lyndon Baines Johnson, the elder son, was born near Stonewall, Texas, on 27 August 1908. After graduating from Johnson City High School in 1924, he went to California and did a variety of odd jobs for three years before returning home and entering Southwest Texas State Teachers College at San Marcos, from which he graduated with a BSc degree in August 1930. For the next year he taught public speaking and debate at Sam Houston High School in Houston.

In 1931 he was appointed Secretary to Representative

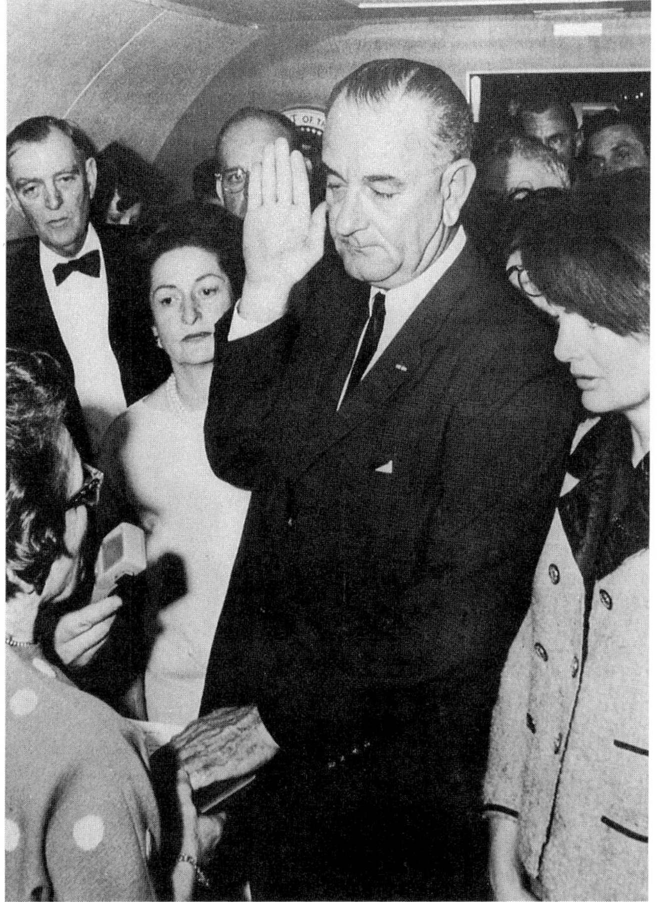

Following the assassination of President Kennedy, US District Judge Sarah T Hughes administers the oath to President Johnson on board *Air Force One*; Johnson is flanked by his wife and Mrs Kennedy

Johnson with his family: daughters Lynda Bird (left) and Luci Baines, and wife 'Lady Bird' (sitting)

Richard M Kleberg, a position which he held until 1935, when he resigned after he had been appointed Texas Director of National Youth Administration by President Roosevelt. In the meantime he had entered Georgetown University Law School for a short period and in November 1934 had married Claudia Alta Taylor, always known as 'Lady Bird', a socially accomplished young lady. Johnson remained Director of the National Youth Administration until 1937, when he was elected to the House of Representatives. He was to be re-elected five times.

He saw war service as a Lieutenant Commander in the US navy and was awarded a silver star for gallantry in action in New Guinea in June 1942, being decorated personally by General Douglas A MacArthur. Later that year he was ordered back to Washington when President Roosevelt ordered all members of Congress in the armed forces to return to their offices.

Johnson was elected to the Senate in 1948 and took his seat on 3 January 1949. He was elected majority whip of the Senate in January 1951 and in that year purchased 231 acres of land in Texas, the nucleus of the LBJ Ranch, from his aunt Mrs Clarence Martin.

In 1953, Johnson became minority leader of the Senate. He was re-elected to the Senate in 1954 and in 1955 became majority leader. In July that year he suffered a serious heart attack and was absent from the Senate until December.

At the Democratic National Convention in Los Angeles in July 1960, Johnson was defeated for presidential candidate by Kennedy on the first ballot, but nominated for Vice-President by acclamation the following day. On election day, 6 November, he was elected both Vice-President, and Senator for a third term. On 3 January 1961 he took the oath of office as Senator and immediately resigned. He took the oath as Vice-President on 20 January 1961. As Vice-President, Johnson made several trips overseas, visiting Europe, Asia and Africa. In November he accompanied President Kennedy on the fateful trip to Dallas, from which he was to return as President.

Johnson took the oath of office on board the presidential jet, *Air Force One*, at Love Field, Dallas, on Friday 22 November 1961. It was administered by Sarah T Hughes, US District Judge for the Northern district of Texas, the first time a woman had officiated. Johnson's quiet but whirlwind efficiency ensured his re-election as President in 1964. His catchy slogan 'All the way with LBJ' coupled with the campaign button reading 'Goldwater in '64; Hotwater in '65' played their part in the overwhelming defeat of Barry Morris Goldwater, the Republican candidate, the possibility of whose election was regarded with horror in most quarters. In the event, Johnson gained 486 of the 538 electoral votes, the other 52 going to Goldwater.

Johnson's second inauguration took place in traditional fashion on the East Portico on 20 January 1965, the oath being administered by Chief Justice Earl Warren. The second term was marred by the Vietnam War and Johnson's hopes of seeking nomination for a third term were dashed. On 31 March 1968 he announced that he would stand down, at the same time calling a halt to the air and naval bombardment of almost all North Vietnam in an attempt to bring hostilities to an end. Johnson retired from the presidency on 20 January 1969. He attended Nixon's inauguration and then left for the LBJ Ranch.

Four years of life remained to him. He made a few public appearances, delivered a few speches, but on the whole lived quietly and wrote his memoirs, which appeared in 1971. He suffered a heart attack at the ranch and died in the ambulance helicopter in which he was being conveyed to San Antonio, Texas, on 22 January 1973.

Mrs Johnson, whose book, *A White House Diary*, was published in 1970, still lives at LBJ Ranch occupying herself with good causes.

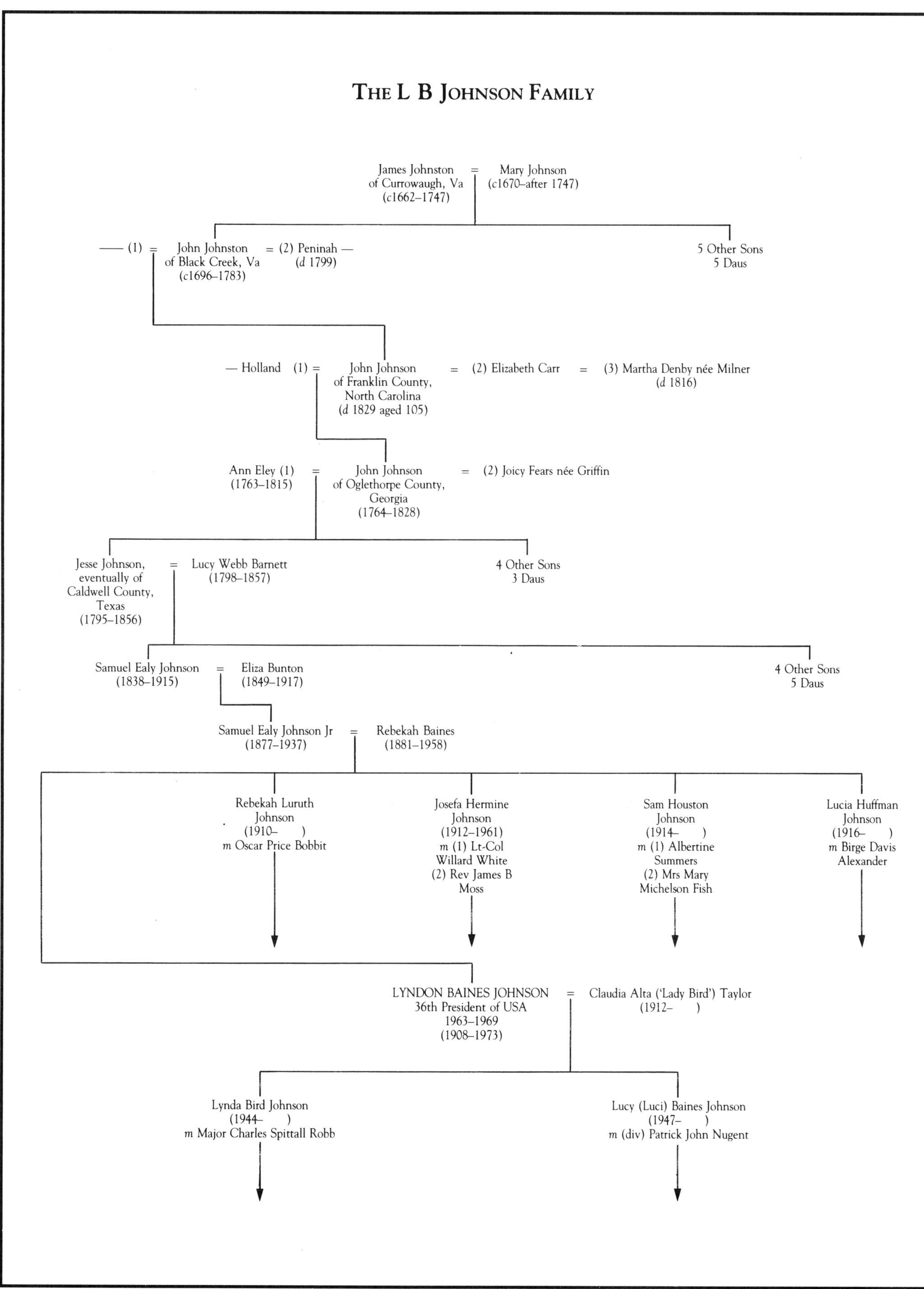
THE L B JOHNSON FAMILY
James Johnston of Currowaugh, Va (c1662–1747)
=
Mary Johnson (c1670–after 1747)
— (1) =
John Johnston of Black Creek, Va (c1696–1783)
= (2) Peninah — (d 1799)
5 Other Sons 5 Daus
— Holland (1) =
John Johnson of Franklin County, North Carolina (d 1829 aged 105)
= (2) Elizabeth Carr
= (3) Martha Denby née Milner (d 1816)
Ann Eley (1) (1763–1815)
=
John Johnson of Oglethorpe County, Georgia (1764–1828)
= (2) Joicy Fears née Griffin
Jesse Johnson, eventually of Caldwell County, Texas (1795–1856)
=
Lucy Webb Barnett (1798–1857)
4 Other Sons 3 Daus
Samuel Ealy Johnson (1838–1915)
=
Eliza Bunton (1849–1917)
4 Other Sons 5 Daus
Samuel Ealy Johnson Jr (1877–1937)
=
Rebekah Baines (1881–1958)
Rebekah Luruth Johnson (1910–) m Oscar Price Bobbit
Josefa Hermine Johnson (1912–1961) m (1) Lt-Col Willard White (2) Rev James B Moss
Sam Houston Johnson (1914–) m (1) Albertine Summers (2) Mrs Mary Michelson Fish
Lucia Huffman Johnson (1916–) m Birge Davis Alexander
LYNDON BAINES JOHNSON 36th President of USA 1963–1969 (1908–1973)
=
Claudia Alta ('Lady Bird') Taylor (1912–)
Lynda Bird Johnson (1944–) m Major Charles Spittall Robb
Lucy (Luci) Baines Johnson (1947–) m (div) Patrick John Nugent

RICHARD MILHOUS NIXON 1969–1974

Born:	Yorba Linda, California, 9 January 1913, 2nd son of Francis (Frank) Anthony Nixon of Whittier, California, and Hannah Milhous	Married:	Mission Inn, Riverside, California, 21 June 1940 Thelma Catherine (Pat) (*b* Ely, Nevada, 16 March 1912), dau of William Ryan and Katharina (Kate) Halberstadt Bender
Member of House of Representatives:	1947–1950	Children:	(1) Patricia, *b* 21 February 1946; *m* the White House, Washington, 12 June 1971 Edward Ridley Finch Cox (*b* 2 October 1946), son of Col Howard Elliott Cox and Anne C D Finch
Senator:	1951–1952		(2) Julie, *b* Washington 5 July 1948; *m* Marble Collegiate Church, New York City, 22 December 1968 Dwight David Eisenhower II (*b* West Point, New York, 31 March 1948), only son of Col Sheldon Doud Eisenhower, and grandson of Dwight David Eisenhower(*qv*), 34th President; 1 son, 1 dau
Vice-President:	1953–1961		
Elected (37th) President:	5 November 1968		
Inaugurated:	East Plaza of Capitol 20 January 1969		
Elected for 2nd term:	7 November 1972		
Inaugurated:	21 January 1973		
Resigned the presidency:	9 August 1974		

'Tricky Dicky', the only President to resign the office under a very heavy cloud, has still a long way to go before he is completely rehabilitated. The process has begun, however, and for some time now he has been making elder statesman comments on fairly uncontroversial subjects and thereby regained some of the respect which he lost in 1974 over the Watergate debacle. Already in 1974 there were many who felt sorry for him and believed he had been made a scapegoat for the defections of others.

The Nixon family is traced to James Nixon, who was born in Ireland about 1705 and is first recorded in Delaware in 1731. His descendants moved to Pennsylvania, Ohio, Illinois, Ohio again and finally California, where Francis (Frank) Anthony Nixon settled in 1907. The following year he married Hannah Milhous, the descendant of a Quaker family which came from County Kildare, Ireland, to settle in Chester County, Pennsylvania, in 1729. Hannah's father, Franklin Milhous, was also descended from King Edward III of England, while, through her mother, Almira Park Burdg, kinships to Presidents Taft and Hoover can be traced.

Frank and Hannah had a family of five sons, of whom Richard Milhous Nixon was the second. He was born at Yorba Linda, California, on 9 January 1913. His father's lemon grove failed in 1919 and the family moved to Whittier, California, where Frank Nixon started a grocery business with gas station attached.

Nixon graduated with honours from Whittier High School in June 1930, receiving a prize as the outstanding all-round student of his class. In September he entered Whittier College, which he left with a BA degree in June

Richard Milhous Nixon

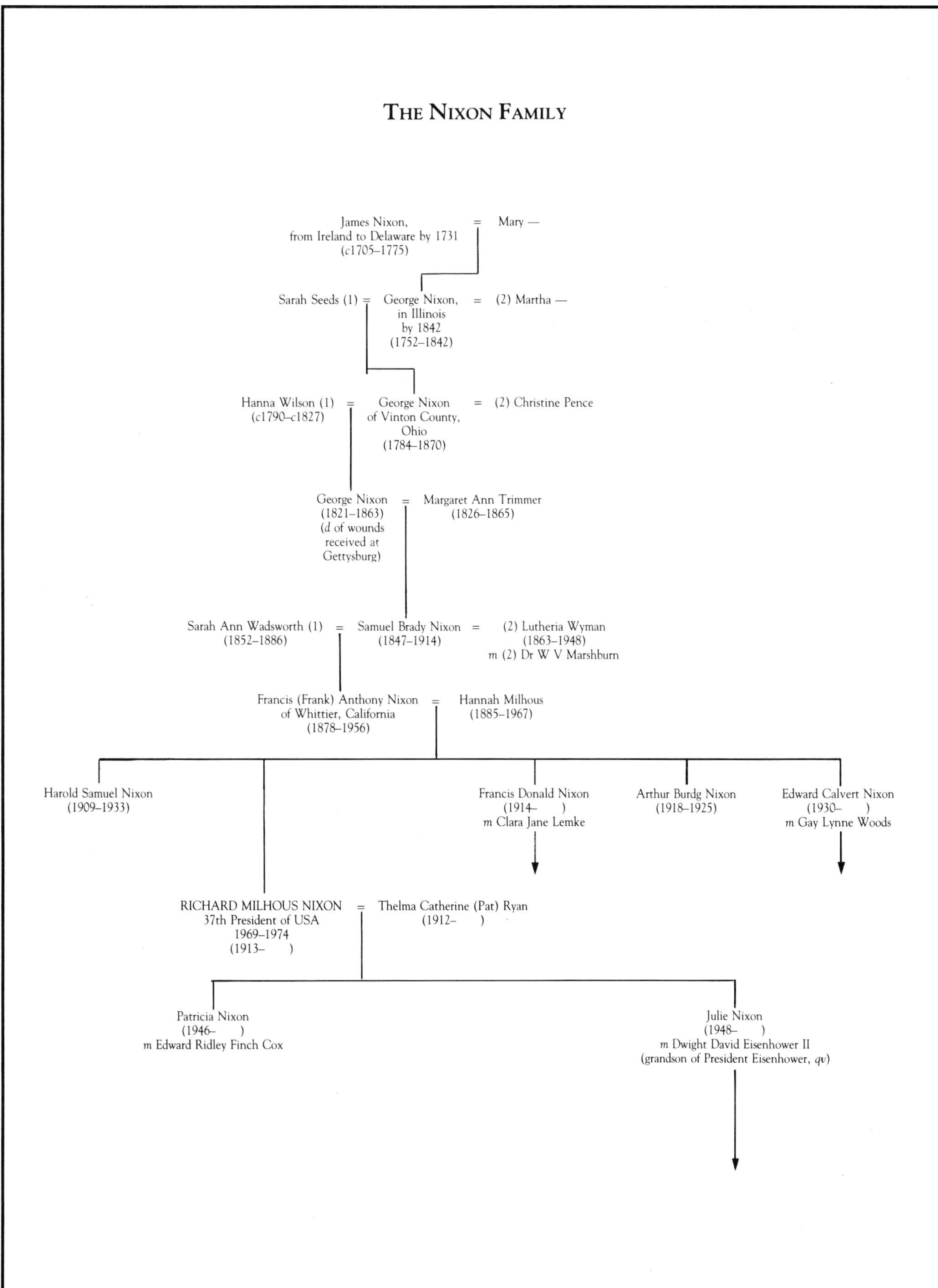
THE NIXON FAMILY
James Nixon, from Ireland to Delaware by 1731 (c1705–1775) = Mary —
Sarah Seeds (1) = George Nixon, in Illinois by 1842 (1752–1842) = (2) Martha —
Hanna Wilson (1) (c1790–c1827) = George Nixon of Vinton County, Ohio (1784–1870) = (2) Christine Pence
George Nixon (1821–1863) (d of wounds received at Gettysburg) = Margaret Ann Trimmer (1826–1865)
Sarah Ann Wadsworth (1) (1852–1886) = Samuel Brady Nixon (1847–1914) = (2) Lutheria Wyman (1863–1948) m (2) Dr W V Marshburn
Francis (Frank) Anthony Nixon of Whittier, California (1878–1956) = Hannah Milhous (1885–1967)
Harold Samuel Nixon (1909–1933)
Francis Donald Nixon (1914–) m Clara Jane Lemke
Arthur Burdg Nixon (1918–1925)
Edward Calvert Nixon (1930–) m Gay Lynne Woods
RICHARD MILHOUS NIXON 37th President of USA 1969–1974 (1913–) = Thelma Catherine (Pat) Ryan (1912–)
Patricia Nixon (1946–) m Edward Ridley Finch Cox
Julie Nixon (1948–) m Dwight David Eisenhower II (grandson of President Eisenhower, qv)

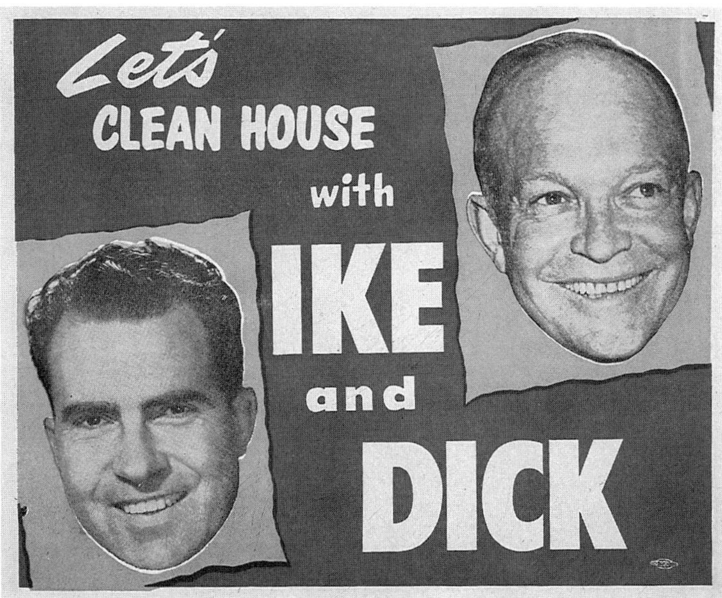

A Nixon and Eisenhower campaign poster for 1952

1934. He then entered Duke University Law School in Durham, North Carolina, where he obtained an LLB degree in 1937. He was admitted to the California Bar in November that year and entered a law firm in Whittier, being taken into partnership in 1939. On 21 June 1940, Nixon married Thelma Catherine (always known as Pat) Ryan, and they had two daughters. Nixon saw war service with the US navy and was assigned to the Fleet Air Command in the South Pacific. He reached the rank of Lieutenant-Commander and was discharged in March 1946. In November that year he was elected to the House of Representatives and took his seat on 3 January 1947. He served as chairman of the sub-committee on Un-American activities and was re-elected in 1948. Elected to the Senate in 1950, he took his seat in January 1951, and in 1952 was nominated by acclamation for Vice-President at the Republican National Convention in Chicago. He was elected on 4 November, resigned from the Senate on 11 November (effective from 1 January 1953), and took the oath as Vice-President on 20 January 1953.

Nixon was re-elected Vice-President on 1956 and took the oath privately in the East Room at the White House on 20 January (a Sunday) and publicly on the East Plaza of the Capitol on 21 January 1957. In 1960 he was nominated for President, but was beaten by Kennedy in the election and had the task, as Vice-President, of making the official announcement of the election of his opponent. The next few years were thwarting ones for Nixon. He was defeated for the Governorship of California in 1962 and campaigned for the spectacularly unsuccessful Barry Goldwater in 1964. Meanwhile he had moved to New York City, been admitted to the New York Bar, and become partner in the law firm of Nixon, Mudge, Rose, Guthrie and Alexander. He also did quite a lot of foreign travel, visiting Europe, South America and the Middle East.

The Republican National Convention at Miami nominated Nixon for President in 1968 and this time he won the day with 301 electoral votes out of 538, the rest being split between Hubert Humphrey, the Democratic candidate, and George Corley Wallace, of the American Independent party. Nixon was inaugurated on the East Plaza of the Capitol on Monday 20 January 1969. He has been described as 'Ordinary to the point of being a nonentity', and as an 'Uncommon man with common opinions'. The descriptions fit him very well.

Nixon's re-nomination for President in 1972 coincided almost exactly with the burglary of the Democratic National Convention Headquarters in the Watergate Building in Washington, which was to bring about his downfall.

At the election Nixon was returned to office with a record number of 520 votes, his opponents only gaining 18 between them. Before inauguration day on 21 January 1973 the Watergate trial had begun. It ended on 30 January with all defendants pleading guilty, but in May the Senate began hearings to investigate allegations of political espionage in the (1972) election in connection with the Watergate case. A subpoena was served on the President in June after he refused to release secret tape recordings of conversations he had held with those allegedly involved in the affair, and in August the select committee went into recess until the end of September. To add to Nixon's troubles, the Vice-President Spiro Agnew was accused of tax evasion when Governor of Maryland and resigned office on 10 October. Two days later the Federal Appeals Court ordered Nixon to hand over the tapes. He nominated Gerald Rudolph Ford as Vice-President in Agnew's place on 13 October and a week later was faced with calls for his impeachment from members of both parties in Congress. Nixon rejected all requests to produce the tapes and in May 1974 the House of Representatives met to consider whether grounds for his impeachment existed.

On 27 July they voted by 27 to 11 recommending the President's impeachment for obstructing the course of justice in the Watergate affair. On 9 August 1974 Nixon made history by becoming the first President to resign from office. A month later President Ford, in the face of severe criticism, granted the former President a full pardon for all offences against the country which he might have committed while in office.

Nixon retired to California where, inevitably, he wrote his memoirs (published in 1978). Now that nearly fifteen years have passed since his disgrace, people are beginning to wonder if he was not more victim than sinner, and his well-timed occasional pronouncements on the affairs of the day are again listened to with some respect.

Gerald Rudolph Ford 1974–1977

Born:	Omaha, Nebraska, 14 July 1913 as Leslie Lynch King Jr, son of Leslie Lynch King and his first wife Dorothy Ayer Gardner (later wife of Gerald Rudolf (*sic*) Ford). Name changed to Gerald Rudolph Ford Jr on legal adoption by stepfather 1916	Retired from presidency:	20 January 1977
Member of House of Representatives:	1949–1973	Married:	Grace Episcopal Church, Grand Rapids, Michigan, 15 October 1948 Elizabeth (Betty) Ann (*b* Chicago, Illinois, 8 April 1918), formerly wife of William G Warren (*m* 1942; div 1947) and dau of William Stephenson Bloomer and Hortense Nehr
Nominated Vice-President:	13 October 1973	Children:	(1) Michael Gerald, *b* 15 March 1950; *m* 5 July 1974 Gayle Ann (*b* 1951), dau of Edward A Brumbaugh (2) John (Jack) Gardner, *b* 16 March 1952 (3) Steven Meigs, *b* 19 May 1956 (4) Susan Elizabeth, *b* 6 July 1957
Took oath as Vice-President:	6 December 1973		
Succeeded as (38th) President and took oath:	9 August 1974		

Gerald Rudolph Ford, the only President of the United States never to have been elected to either the presidential or the vice-presidential office, has a most complex family background. He began life as Leslie Lynch King Jr at Omaha, Nebraska, on 14 July 1913, but his parents divorced when he was only two years old and his mother subsequently remarried Gerald Rudolf Ford, President of the Ford Paint and Varnish Company at Grand Rapids, Michigan. Ford adopted his stepson who then became Gerald Rudolph Ford Jr (The different spelling of the middle name has never been explained). Later the Fords had three more sons and Leslie Lynch King also remarried and had a further family of one son and two daughters, so Gerald ended up with six half siblings.

Gerald Ford grew up quite unaware that he had been adopted until the age of seventeen, when, eking out his pocket money as a part-time waiter in a Grand Rapids restaurant, he was approached by 'a tall, broad-shouldered, blue-eyed man', who, as the restaurant proprietor's widow Maria Skougis told a reporter after Gerald had become President, accosted him with the words: 'Young fellow, my name is Leslie King, and I'm your father. I was married and divorced from your mother many years ago. We used to call you Leslie, too. I wonder if we could talk somewhere for a few minutes.' With his employer's permission, Gerald left the restaurant with his father and was introduced to his stepmother and halfsister Patricia, who were waiting outside. The shock to a seventeen-year-old boy must have been considerable and one can well imagine the traumatic interview which took place that night when he confronted his mother and stepfather. One result of the meeting was that Gerald spent two summers at Riverton, Wyoming, with his real father

Gerald Ford campaigning

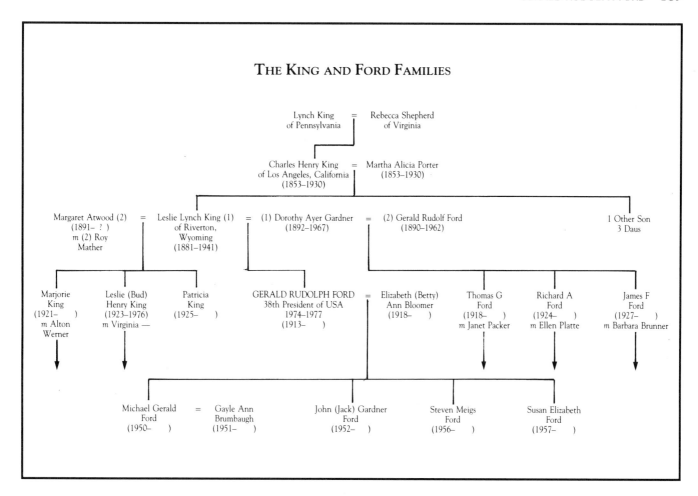

THE KING AND FORD FAMILIES

Lynch King of Pennsylvania = Rebecca Shepherd of Virginia

Charles Henry King of Los Angeles, California (1853–1930) = Martha Alicia Porter (1853–1930)

Margaret Atwood (2) (1891– ?) m (2) Roy Mather = Leslie Lynch King (1) of Riverton, Wyoming (1881–1941) = (1) Dorothy Ayer Gardner (1892–1967) = (2) Gerald Rudolf Ford (1890–1962)

1 Other Son
3 Daus

Marjorie King (1921–) m Alton Werner

Leslie (Bud) Henry King (1923–1976) m Virginia —

Patricia King (1925–)

GERALD RUDOLPH FORD 38th President of USA 1974–1977 (1913–) = Elizabeth (Betty) Ann Bloomer (1918–)

Thomas G Ford (1918–) m Janet Packer

Richard A Ford (1924–) m Ellen Platte

James F Ford (1927–) m Barbara Brunner

Michael Gerald Ford (1950–) = Gayle Ann Brumbaugh (1951–)

John (Jack) Gardner Ford (1952–)

Steven Meigs Ford (1956–)

Susan Elizabeth Ford (1957–)

(who found him a summer job in Yellowstone Park) and his family, with whom he appears to have got on very well.

Leslie King later moved to Tucson, Arizona, where he died in 1941 at the age of fifty-nine. His widow married Roy Mather, a copy editor on the Los Angeles *Times*, in 1949 and was again widowed in 1954. She was still living, aged eighty-three, when her stepson became President. 'Never! Never! in my wildest dreams,' she declared to the press, 'did I think that my stepson would ever become President of the United States.' She had not seen him for forty years.

Precisely when the King forebears emigrated to America has not been discovered. The earliest-known ancestor of President Ford was Lynch King of Pennsylvania, who married Rebecca Shepherd of Virginia, and became the father of Charles Henry King, a railroad pioneer in Wyoming, who amassed a small fortune and acquired a mansion in Los Angeles at 1423 South Manhattan Boulevard, where he died in February 1930. He was the father of Leslie Lynch King.

Gerald Ford's mother, Dorothy Ayer Gardner, had a rather more traceable ancestry, being descended, among others, from Ezra Chase, a minute man (volunteer) in the Massachusetts Militia, who served in the War of Independence.

The President with his wife Betty

After attending South High School in Grand Rapids, Gerald Ford went on to Michigan University, where he became the star of the football team. His limited intellectual abilities and a certain clumsiness of movement which rendered him accident-prone, were later to be attributed rather unkindly by former President Johnson to kicks on the head received during his footballing days. 'Jerry Ford played football too long without a helmet', was the actual comment.

In 1935 Gerald graduated AB and later attended Yale University Law School, where he obtained an LLB degree in 1941. He was admitted to the Michigan Bar the same year and began to practise law in Grand Rapids. His practice was interrupted by war service as a Lieutenant-Commander USNR with the Pacific fleet in aircraft carrier USS *Monterey* from 1942 until 1946. Gerald then continued the practice of law until 1949, when he took his seat in the House of Representatives. In October 1948 he married a thirty-year-old divorcee, Betty Bloomer Warren, by whom he was to have three sons and one daughter. As Congressman, Gerald Ford served on several committees and was a delegate to several conferences. In 1950 he received a Distinguished Service Award from the US Junior Chamber of Commerce as one of ten outstanding young men in the United States. President Johnson appointed him a member of the Warren Commission to investigate the assassination of President Kennedy in November 1963 and in 1965 he was elected minority leader of the House of Representatives and received a flood of honorary degrees.

On 10 October 1973 Vice-President Spiro Agnew resigned office following the revelation of tax evasion offences and Gerald Ford was nominated as Vice-President in his place by President Nixon, in accordance with the 25th Amendment to the Constitution. On the nomination being confirmed by Congress, he took the oath of office on 6 December. In eight months the Watergate scandal had led to the resignation of Nixon and Gerald Rudolph Ford found himself thirty-eighth President of the United States. He took the oath of office in the East Room of the White House on 9 August 1974.

Whatever his shortcomings, Ford always appeared sincere and honest and a good 'all-American guy'. His pardon of Nixon earned him some severe criticism during the early days of his presidency, but he weathered the storm and his popularity gradually increased. Mrs Ford's health, rather vaguely referred to as a 'pinched nerve' in the neck but later to be revealed as a case of chronic alcoholism over which she finally triumphed, provoked much sympathy.

In 1976 Ford put himself forward as the Republican candidate in the presidential election, but was beaten by James Earl Carter, the Democratic nominee, by 56 electoral votes and a margin of only two per cent of the popular vote. He left office on 20 January 1977 and retired to private life. His country should be grateful to him for his part in restoring integrity to the high office which came to him in such extraordinary and unsought fashion.

James Earl Carter 1977–1981

Born:	Plains, Georgia, 1 October 1924, elder son of James Earl Carter of Plains and (Bessie) Lillian Gordy	Married:	Plains, Georgia, 7 July 1946 Rosalynn (*b* Plains 18 August 1927), dau of W Edgar Smith of Plains and Allie Murray
Member of Georgia State Senate:	1962–1966	Children:	(1) John (Jack) William, attorney, *b* Plains 1947; *m* 1971 Juliette Langford; 1 son (Jason Carter *b* 1975)
Governor of Georgia:	1971–1974		(2) James Earl (Chip) III, *b* Plains 1950; *m* 1973 (*m* diss 1980) Caron Griffin of Hawkinsville, Georgia; 1 son (James Earl IV)
Elected (39th) President:	November 1976		(3) (Donnel) Jeffrey, *b* Plains 1952; *m* 1975 Annette Davis of Arlington, Georgia
Inaugurated:	Washington 20 January 1977		(4) Amy Lynn, *b* Plains 1967
Retired from presidency:	20 January 1981		

Jimmy Carter, the Georgia peanut farmer, whose greatest achievement during his single term presidency was the part he played in toppling the 2,500 year old Iranian monarchy, has sunk back into the oblivion from whence he came since retiring from office.

James Earl Carter Jr was born at Plains, Georgia, on 1 October 1924. His lineage can be traced to a Thomas Carter who emigrated from England and settled in Isle of Wight County, Virginia, in 1637. Thomas's origin is uncertain. There is some circumstantial evidence that he was a brother of John Carter of Carotoman, Virginia (whose son, Robert 'King' Carter, was the ancestor of several notable Virginians, including the two Harrison Presidents), and that both were the sons of John Carter, a London vintner, who named sons John and Thomas in his will dated 1630. Genealogists have attempted to connect the family with the Carters of Kings Langley, Hertfordshire, where records of persons bearing the name go back to 1361, but there is no satisfactory concrete proof.

Moore Carter, the grandson of Thomas who settled in Virginia, moved to Bertie County, North Carolina, and his grandson, Kindred Carter, moved to Georgia, where he acquired a wheat, cotton and livestock plantation of 307 acres on Little Germany Creek in Richmond County (now McDuffie County). Kindred's son, James, acquired a somewhat larger plantation in Warren County, which his son, Wiley Carter, sold in 1851, when he moved to Schley County and settled some twenty miles north of Plains. Before leaving Warren County, Wiley Carter had been tried and acquitted of the murder of a neighbour whom he had accused of slave stealing. The Carters were evidently a belligerent lot, as Wiley's son, Littleberry Walker Carter, was killed in a fight he had got into at a fair in 1873, and Littleberry's son, William Archibald Carter, died at Arlington in September 1903

James Earl Carter

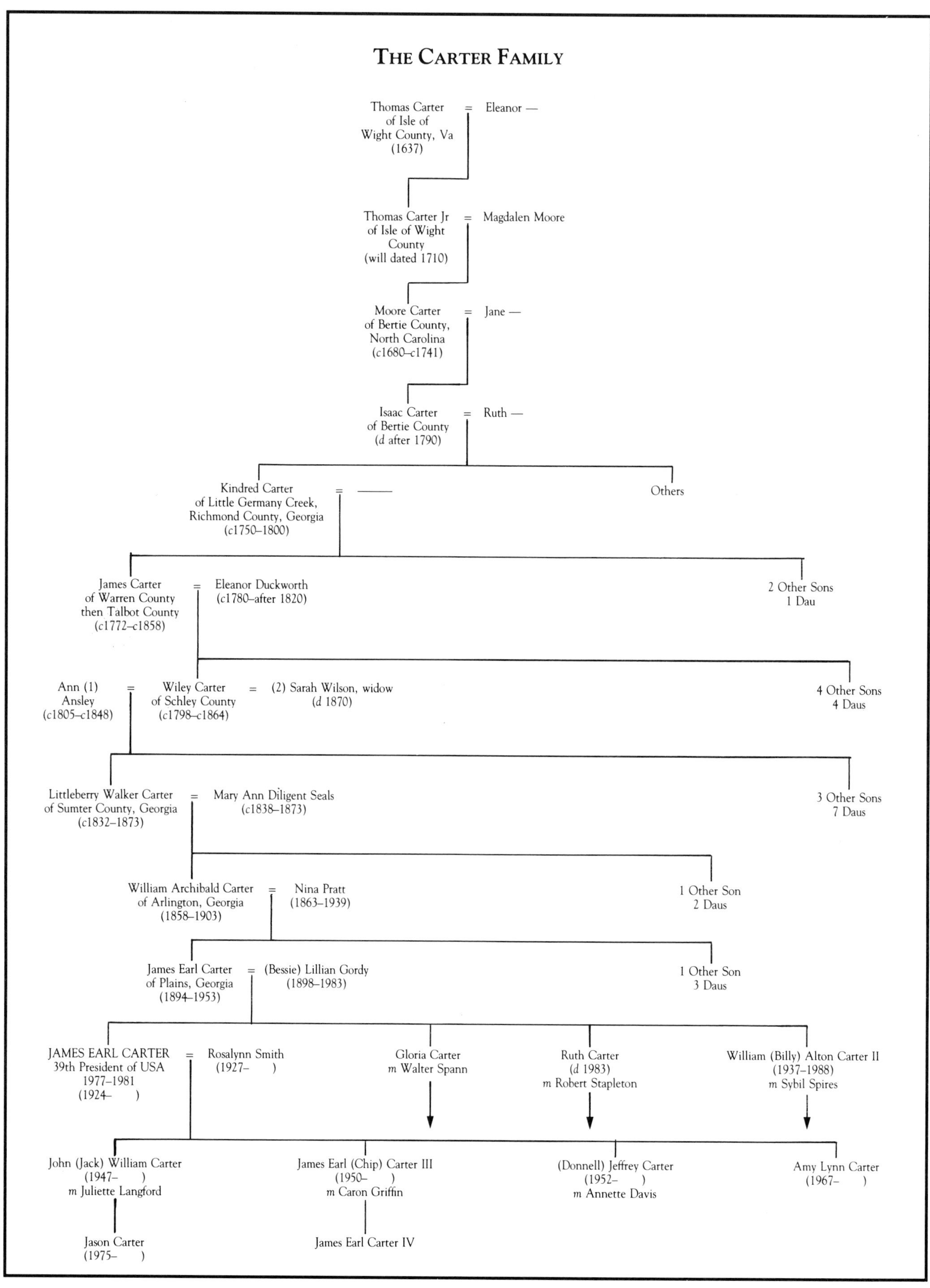
THE CARTER FAMILY
Thomas Carter of Isle of Wight County, Va (1637) = Eleanor —
Thomas Carter Jr of Isle of Wight County (will dated 1710) = Magdalen Moore
Moore Carter of Bertie County, North Carolina (c1680–c1741) = Jane —
Isaac Carter of Bertie County (d after 1790) = Ruth —
Kindred Carter of Little Germany Creek, Richmond County, Georgia (c1750–1800) = ——
Others
James Carter of Warren County then Talbot County (c1772–c1858) = Eleanor Duckworth (c1780–after 1820)
2 Other Sons 1 Dau
Ann (1) Ansley (c1805–c1848) = Wiley Carter of Schley County (c1798–c1864) = (2) Sarah Wilson, widow (d 1870)
4 Other Sons 4 Daus
Littleberry Walker Carter of Sumter County, Georgia (c1832–1873) = Mary Ann Diligent Seals (c1838–1873)
3 Other Sons 7 Daus
William Archibald Carter of Arlington, Georgia (1858–1903) = Nina Pratt (1863–1939)
1 Other Son 2 Daus
James Earl Carter of Plains, Georgia (1894–1953) = (Bessie) Lillian Gordy (1898–1983)
1 Other Son 3 Daus
JAMES EARL CARTER 39th President of USA 1977–1981 (1924–) = Rosalynn Smith (1927–)
Gloria Carter m Walter Spann
Ruth Carter (d 1983) m Robert Stapleton
William (Billy) Alton Carter II (1937–1988) m Sybil Spires
John (Jack) William Carter (1947–) m Juliette Langford
James Earl (Chip) Carter III (1950–) m Caron Griffin
(Donnell) Jeffrey Carter (1952–) m Annette Davis
Amy Lynn Carter (1967–)
Jason Carter (1975–)
James Earl Carter IV

President Carter greeting the Apollo II Commander Neil Armstrong on 1 October 1978

from injuries received when he was shot in the street at Rowena, Georgia. James Earl Carter, William Archibald's son, led a less hectic life as an insurance broker, farmer and fertilizer dealer, saw service in World War I and was a member of the County Board of Education and a State Representative. In 1923 he married Lillian Gordy, whose father, James Jackson (Jim Jack) Gordy, lived at Richland, Georgia. The future President, named James Earl after his father, was the eldest of their four children.

Jimmy Carter attended Georgia Southwestern University and Georgia Institute of Technology before going on to the United States Naval Academy, Annapolis, where he graduated BS in 1947 and was commissioned as Ensign USN. Promoted Lieutenant in 1950, he retired from the navy in 1952, took a postgraduate course at Union College and in 1953 on the death of his father took over the family business as a peanut farmer and warehouseman in his home of Plains. He served as a member of Georgia State Senate from 1962 to 1966 and in the latter year became a candidate for the Governorship of Georgia. It took four years of tireless campaigning to achieve that goal and Carter worked hard to establish his image as a caring human being. He had the support of his wife Rosalynn, whom he had married in 1946, and their four children, three stalwart 'all-American' sons and an ever-present and precocious daughter Amy. He also made political headway with his devout Baptist faith and his 'born-again' Christianity.

Jimmy Carter's bid to obtain the Democratic vice-presidential nomination in 1972 came to naught, but at the Democratic Convention in New York City in 1976 he won the presidential nomination on the first ballot. When the electoral votes were cast in November, Carter polled 297 and his only rival President Ford polled 241.

At his inauguration on 20 January 1977, Jimmy publicly demonstrated his humility by walking up Pennsylvania Avenue to the White House rather than riding from the Capitol in the customary 'motorcade'. He gave a further demonstration by forbidding the presidential anthem 'Hail to the Chief' to be played every time he made an official appearance.

The President jogging

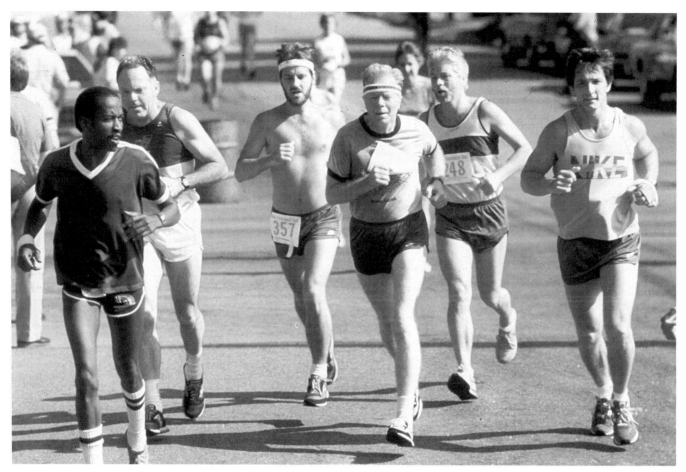

Apart from his wife and children, the President also made full use of his elderly mother 'Miss Lillian', appointing her to represent him overseas on sundry occasions, most notably at the state funeral of Marshal Tito in Belgrade in 1980. His only brother Billy, on the other hand, caused frequent embarrassments, as did his younger sister Mrs Ruth Carter Stapleton, whose extreme evangelical views exceeded the President's and included the practice of faith healing.

Alas the job proved too big for Jimmy and his incompetence to deal with the problems which beset him soon became apparent to all. His vacillations and disastrously bungling foreign policy lost him support and respect and by 1980 his popularity in the opinion polls was lower than that of any other President since Harding. When he offered himself for re-election he only polled 49 of the electoral votes as opposed to 489 for Ronald Reagan, the successful Republican candidate.

Ronald Wilson Reagan 1981–1989

Born: Tampico, Illinois, 6 February 1911, younger son of John Edward Reagan, of Tampico, later of Hollywood, California, and Nelle Clyde Wilson

Governor of California: 1967–1974

Elected (40th) President: 4 November 1980

Inaugurated: Washington 20 January 1981

Elected for 2nd term: 6 November 1984

Inaugurated: Washington 20 January 1985

Retired from presidency: 20 January 1989

Married: (1) Glendale, California, 24 January 1940 (*m* diss 28 June 1948) Sarah Jane Fulks, the actress Jane Wyman (*b* St Joseph, Missouri, 4 January 1914; *m* (3) 1952 (*m* diss 1954), re-*m* 1961 (*m* diss 1965) Fred Karger), formerly wife of Myron Futterman (*m* 1937; *m* diss 1938), and dau of Richard D Fulks, Mayor of St Joseph, Missouri, and his 2nd wife Emma Reise

Children: (1) Maureen Elizabeth, *b* Los Angeles, California, 4 January 1941; *m* (1) 1961 (*m* diss 1962) John Filippone, DC policeman (*b* New York City 1929); *m* (2) Beverley Hills, California, 8 February 1964 (*m* diss 1968) Davis Sills, attorney; *m* (3) 1981, Dennis Revell, law clerk (*b* 1953)

(2) (by adoption) Michael Edward, *b* 1945; *m* (1) 1970 (*m* diss 1971) Pamela (a dental surgeon), dau of Duane Putnam, former Los Angeles Rams footballer; *m* (2) 1975 Colleen Sterns; 1 son, 1 dau

(3) Dau, *b* 26 June 1947; *d* 27 June 1947

Married: (2) North Hollywood, California, 4 March 1952 Nancy Davis, formerly Anne Frances Robbins (*b* New York City 6 July 1923), dau of Kenneth Robbins of New Jersey, businessman, and Edith Luckett, and adopted dau of her stepfather Loyal Edward Davis, neurosurgeon

Children: (1) Patricia Ann, actress and songwriter as Patti Davis, *b* Los Angeles 21 October 1952

(2) Ronald ('Skip') Prescott, *b* Hollywood 20 May 1958; *m* Manhattan, New York, 24 November 1980 Doria Palmieri, literary researcher (*b* 1951)

Whatever the final judgement may be on Ronald Reagan, he will certainly not become a forgotten President like James K Polk, Millard Fillmore, or Franklin Pierce. Current views on the man and his stature are sharply divided: revered and hailed as the greatest President ever by a multitude of followers and admirers both at home and abroad; reviled and ridiculed as a bumbling, senile tool in the hands of others by an equal number. It remains for posterity to assess him fairly and produce a definitive portrait of Reagan the man and the President.

Ronald Wilson Reagan, like Kennedy, has a male-line Celtic-Irish ancestry. Some genealogists would have us believe that the O'Regans stem from Brian Boru, High King of Ireland, who perished at the battle of Clontarf in 1014. Be that as it may, the first traceable ancestor of the President is his great-grandfather Thomas O'Regan, a farm labourer at Doolis in the parish of Ballyporeen, County Tipperary, who married Margaret Murphy and had several children. The Catholic Registers of Ballyporeen only begin in 1817 and there is no record of any child of Thomas and Margaret before the baptism of Elena or Ellen was recorded on 5 July 1819, but they were almost certainly the parents of at least one older child, Nicholas, who emigrated to America and was living unmarried in Illinois in 1860. The baptism of Ellen was followed by those of John (1821), Margaret (1823), Elizabeth (1826), and Michael (1829). Michael left Ireland after the 'hungry forties' and emigrated to London, where he found employment as a soapmaker and a wife in the person of Catherine Mulcahy, also from Tipperary. They were married on 31 October 1852 at St George's Roman Catholic Church, Southwark (now Southwark Roman Catholic Cathedral). The couple already had a five-month-old son, Thomas, and two more children were born in London before they emigrated to the United States and settled at Fairhaven in Carroll County, Illinois, where their two youngest children were born.

It was their second son, John, who was to become the grandfather of the future President. Born at Peckham in south London on 29 May 1854, he was taken to America with his parents and later worked as a grain elevator operator. He married Jennie Cusick, the Canadian-born daughter of another Irish immigrant, in 1878 and both died of tuberculosis within three days of each other some ten years later, leaving three young children. John Edward Reagan, the youngest, was born at Fulton on 13

President and Mrs Reagan in the Blue Room of the White House

July 1883 and was brought up by his father's sister Margaret, who had married Orson G Baldwin, a dry-goods merchant in Bennett, Iowa. In later life John Edward became a shoe salesman and inebriate and lived at Tampico, Illinois. On 8 November 1904 he married Nelle Clyde Wilson at the Church of the Immaculate Conception in Fulton. She was the daughter of a Scottish-born father, Thomas Wilson, and his English-born wife Mary Ann Elsey, whose family came from Epsom, Surrey. Their two sons, Neil and Ronald, although baptized as Roman Catholics, were bought up in their mother's Presbyterian faith.

Ronald Wilson Reagan was born at Tampico, Illinois, on 6 February 1911. Having won a partial scholarship, he attended Eureka College, near Peoria, Illinois, and graduated AB in 1932. After working as a sports announcer with WHO in Des Moines, Iowa, he boke into motion pictures in 1937, making his first appearance in *Love Is On the Air*. For the next thirty years he starred in over fifty pictures, including *Dark Victory* (1939) with Bette Davis, *Brother Rat And A Baby* (1940) with Jane Wyman, his first wife, and *The Hasty Heart* (1949). He received so many requests for autographs from his fans that he paid his mother $75.00 a week to forge his signature on letters and photographs, a fact which only became known years later when the American Autograph Collectors Club made some investigations which revealed that official membership cards of the Ronald Reagan Fan Club were far less valuable than had been hoped. From 1942 to 1945 Reagan served as a Captain with the United States Air Force. He was also twice elected to serve as President of the Screen Actors Guild (1947–52 and 1959). On giving up acting in 1966, a year after the publication of his autobiography entitled *Where's The Rest Of Me*, Reagan decided to enter politics. He was elected Governor of the State of California in 1967 on the strength of his film star popularity, and served two terms until 1974. He first attempted to secure the Republican nomination for the presidency in 1968, but was too late. He supported Richard Nixon's re-election in 1972 and in 1976 campaigned for the Republican nomination against President Ford but was unsuccessful and had to wait until 1980, when his long run of primary successes secured him the nomination at the Republican Convention in Detroit. His election to the presidency followed, defeating the incumbent President Carter.

Before Reagan's election for a second term, he had survived an assassination attempt and become the oldest American President to hold office. Four years later, at the end of his second term, he appears as fit as he did at his first inauguration, in spite of several operations for intestinal cancer. Ronald Reagan's first wife, the film actress Jane Wyman, currently making a comeback in the television drama series *Falcon Crest*, has, to her great credit, avoided making any statements to the media

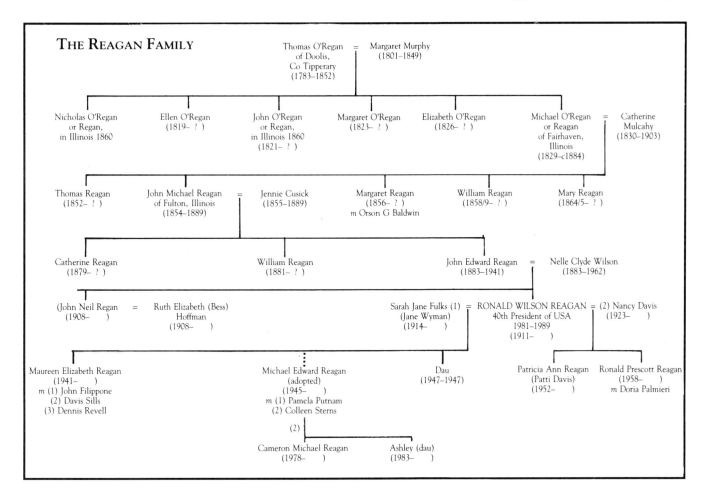

THE REAGAN FAMILY

Thomas O'Regan of Doolis, Co Tipperary (1783–1852) = Margaret Murphy (1801–1849)

Nicholas O'Regan or Regan, in Illinois 1860
Ellen O'Regan (1819– ?)
John O'Regan or Regan, in Illinois 1860 (1821– ?)
Margaret O'Regan (1823– ?)
Elizabeth O'Regan (1826– ?)
Michael O'Regan or Reagan of Fairhaven, Illinois (1829–c1884) = Catherine Mulcahy (1830–1903)

Thomas Reagan (1852– ?)
John Michael Reagan of Fulton, Illinois (1854–1889) = Jennie Cusick (1855–1889)
Margaret Reagan (1856– ?) m Orson G Baldwin
William Reagan (1858/9– ?)
Mary Reagan (1864/5– ?)

Catherine Reagan (1879– ?)
William Reagan (1881– ?)
John Edward Reagan (1883–1941) = Nelle Clyde Wilson (1883–1962)

(John Neil Regan (1908–) = Ruth Elizabeth (Bess) Hoffman (1908–)
Sarah Jane Fulks (1) (Jane Wyman) (1914–) = RONALD WILSON REAGAN 40th President of USA 1981–1989 (1911–) = (2) Nancy Davis (1923–)

Maureen Elizabeth Reagan (1941–) m (1) John Filippone (2) Davis Sills (3) Dennis Revell
Michael Edward Reagan (adopted) (1945–) m (1) Pamela Putnam (2) Colleen Sterns
Dau (1947–1947)
Patricia Ann Reagan (Patti Davis) (1952–)
Ronald Prescott Reagan (1958–) m Doria Palmieri

(2)
Cameron Michael Reagan (1978–)
Ashley (dau) (1983–)

about her married life with the co-star who was to become President. Offers she must have had aplenty, but she has steadfastly resisted them all. After their divorce in June 1948 Reagan remained unmarried for nearly four years. In March 1952 he married the twenty-eight-year-old starlet Nancy Davis, who had begun life as Anne Frances Robbins, but had been legally adopted in 1937 by her stepfather, Loyal Edward Davis, a neurosurgeon. Nancy's mother, Edith Luckett, who also had a show business career of sorts, had as Gibbon would have put it 'the singular felicity' of seeing her only daughter become First Lady. She died at Phoenix, Arizona, at the age of ninety-one on 26 October 1987.

The spun-glass, etiolated, ever-smiling figure of Nancy Reagan has never been far from Ronald's side throughout his presidency. Innumerable photographs of them kissing, gazing adoringly into each other's eyes, or walking hand-in-hand across tarmacs have appeared in the world's press almost daily. No other First Lady, even Jacqueline Kennedy, has received so much publicity or been rumoured to exercise so much power and influence behind the scenes. Nancy accompanied the President on his much vaunted summit talks with the Russian leader Gorbachev, and is said to have achieved an uncomfortable relationship with Mrs Gorbachev, who is obviously a woman of some intellect and not given to indulging in

Ronald Reagan: a still from one of his movies

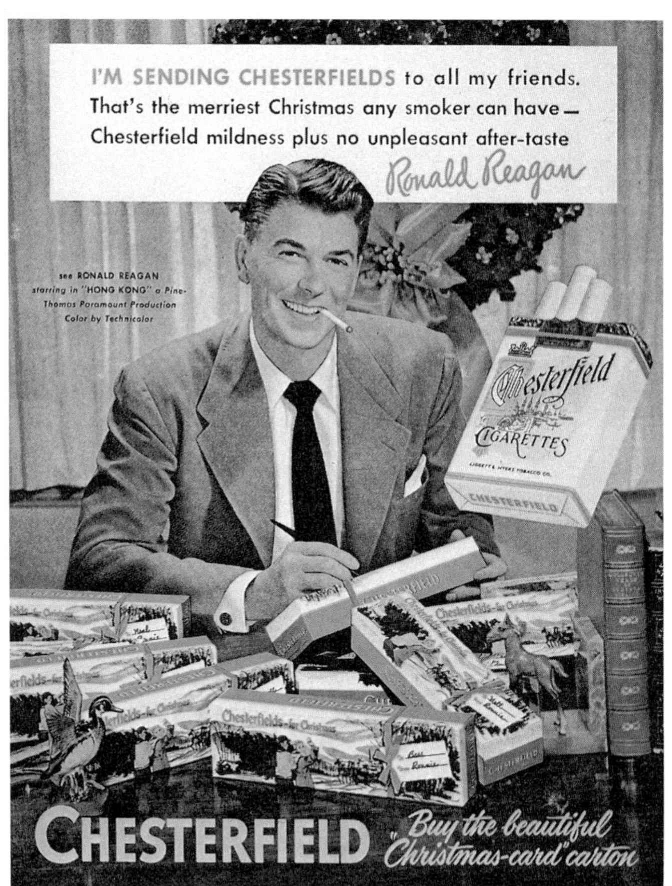

idle prattle or consultations with astrologers as America's First Lady was alleged to do.

I'M SENDING CHESTERFIELDS to all my friends.
That's the merriest Christmas any smoker can have—
Chesterfield mildness plus no unpleasant after-taste
Ronald Reagan
see RONALD REAGAN
starring in "HONG KONG" a Pine-
Thomas Paramount Production
Color by Technicolor
Chesterfield
CIGARETTES
CHESTERFIELD
CHESTERFIELD
"Buy the beautiful Christmas-card" carton

The Reagan children were far from being their father's greatest asset. Maureen, his daughter by Jane Wyman, has married three times, currently to a husband twelve years her junior, and has campaigned for her father in somewhat flamboyant fashion. Michael, the son Reagan and Jane Wyman adopted, has achieved little in life beyond falling out with his stepmother Nancy, making two marriages and providing Ronald with his only grandchildren to date. Nancy's elder child, Patricia Ann, has made a career for herself as the actress and songwriter Patti Davis, while her younger child, Ronald, known as 'Skip', gained unenviable notoriety during his father's first election campaign from the fact that he was a back-up dancer with the Joffrey II Dancers. To most red-blooded Americans a male dancer is synonymous with homosexual, but 'Skip' dispelled these fears by marrying in November 1980.

Ronald Reagan's controversial presidency ended in a blaze of glory when it appeared that his talks with the Russians were at last making some progress and the prospect of a peaceful co-existence lasting far into the foreseeable future seemed more likely to be achieved than it had done for many years past.

Ronald Reagan cheerily advertising Chesterfield cigarettes for Christmas 1950

GEORGE HERBERT WALKER BUSH 1989–

Born:	Milton, Massachusetts, 12 June 1924, 2nd son of Senator Prescott Sheldon Bush and Dorothy Walker
Member of House of Representatives:	1967–1971
Ambassador to UN:	1971–1973
Elected Vice-President:	4 November 1980
Inaugurated:	Washington 20 January 1981
Elected for 2nd term:	6 November 1984
Inaugurated:	Washington 20 January 1985
Elected (41st) President:	8 November 1988
Inaugurated:	East Portico of Capitol 20 January 1989
Married:	Rye, Westchester County, New York, 6 January 1945 Barbara (*b* Rye 8 June 1925), dau of Marvin Pierce and Pauline Robinson
Children:	(1) George Walker (2) John Ellis (Jeb) (3) Neil Mallon (4) Marvin Pierce (5) Dorothy Walker; *m* — Le Blond

George Bush is a conventional man. He has been a conventional Vice-President and shows every sign of being a conventional President.

In spite of various claims which have appeared in the press recently, the earliest proven ancestor of President Bush is Captain Timothy Bush, who served in the French and Indian Wars from 1755 to 1757 and lived at Hebron, Tolland County, Connecticut, and later at Norwich, Vermont. Timothy served in the Revolutionary War and died at Springport, New York, in 1815. One of his sons, Timothy Jr, was a blacksmith in Monroe County, New York, and the grandfather of the Rev

George Bush in August 1988

The Bush Family

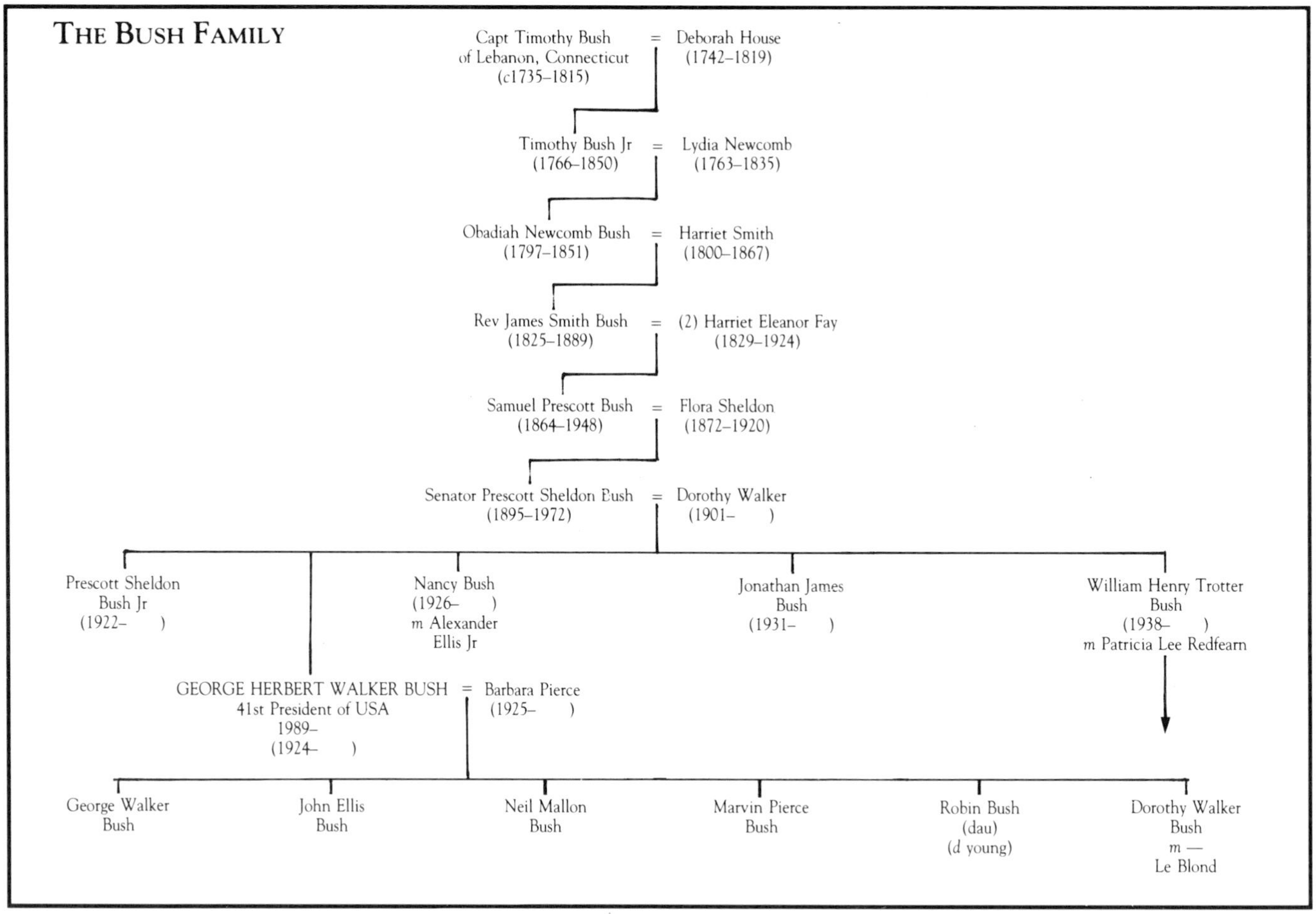

Capt Timothy Bush of Lebanon, Connecticut (c1735–1815) = Deborah House (1742–1819)

Timothy Bush Jr (1766–1850) = Lydia Newcomb (1763–1835)

Obadiah Newcomb Bush (1797–1851) = Harriet Smith (1800–1867)

Rev James Smith Bush (1825–1889) = (2) Harriet Eleanor Fay (1829–1924)

Samuel Prescott Bush (1864–1948) = Flora Sheldon (1872–1920)

Senator Prescott Sheldon Bush (1895–1972) = Dorothy Walker (1901–)

- Prescott Sheldon Bush Jr (1922–)
- GEORGE HERBERT WALKER BUSH 41st President of USA 1989– (1924–) = Barbara Pierce (1925–)
  - George Walker Bush
  - John Ellis Bush
  - Neil Mallon Bush
  - Marvin Pierce Bush
  - Robin Bush (dau) (*d* young)
  - Dorothy Walker Bush *m* — Le Blond
- Nancy Bush (1926–) *m* Alexander Ellis Jr
- Jonathan James Bush (1931–)
- William Henry Trotter Bush (1938–) *m* Patricia Lee Redfearn

Bush and his wife Barbara
in New Orleans for the 1988 Republican Convention

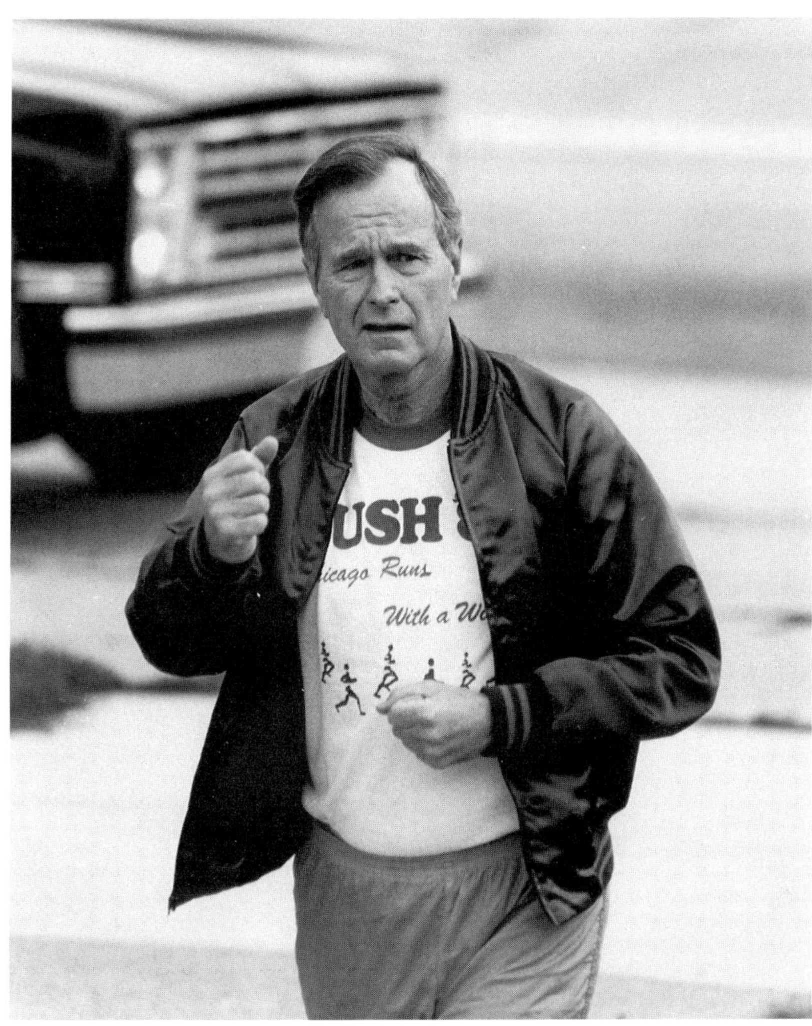

In Chicago to address the Veterans of Foreign Wars Association in August 1988, the Vice-President works on his 'dynamic candidate' image, jogging in one of the city's parks

James Smith Bush, an Episcopalian cleric, whose son, Samuel Prescott Bush, was a steel manufacturer and the father of Prescott Sheldon Bush, Senator from Connecticut from 1952 to 1963. Prescott Sheldon Bush married Dorothy Walker in 1921 and George Herbert Walker Bush, the future President, was the second of their five children, born at Milton, Massachusetts, on 12 June 1924.

From Phillips Academy, Andover, Massachusetts, Bush went on to war service as a naval carrier pilot, being shot down in combat and receiving a DFC and three air medals. After his discharge he entered Yale, from which he graduated BA in economics in 1948. From 1953 to 1966, Bush was engaged in the oil industry in Texas. He was an unsuccessful candidate for the Senate in 1964, but was elected a member of the House of Representatives for Houston, Texas, in 1966, being re-elected in 1968. He was again an unsuccessful candidate the Senate in 1970, and the following year was appointed US Ambassador to the United Nations, a position he held until 1973. He headed the Republican National Committee from 1973 to 1974, was chief of the US liaison office in Peking from 1974 to 1976, and Director of Central Intelligence from 1976 to 1977. Nominated for Vice-President in 1980, he was elected on 4 November 1980, taking office on 20 January 1981. He was re-elected in 1984. He was elected President in November 1988, defeating his opponent, Michael Dukakis, and inaugurated on the East Portico of the Capitol on Friday, 20 January 1989.

Bush was married at the age of twenty to the nineteen-year-old Barbara Pierce. Like him, she has maintained an extremely low profile throughout the vice-presidential terms. It is, of course, far too soon to predict how the Bush presidency may develop, but the signs are that it will endeavour to proceed calmly and unsensationally unless faced with catastrophic events at home or abroad.

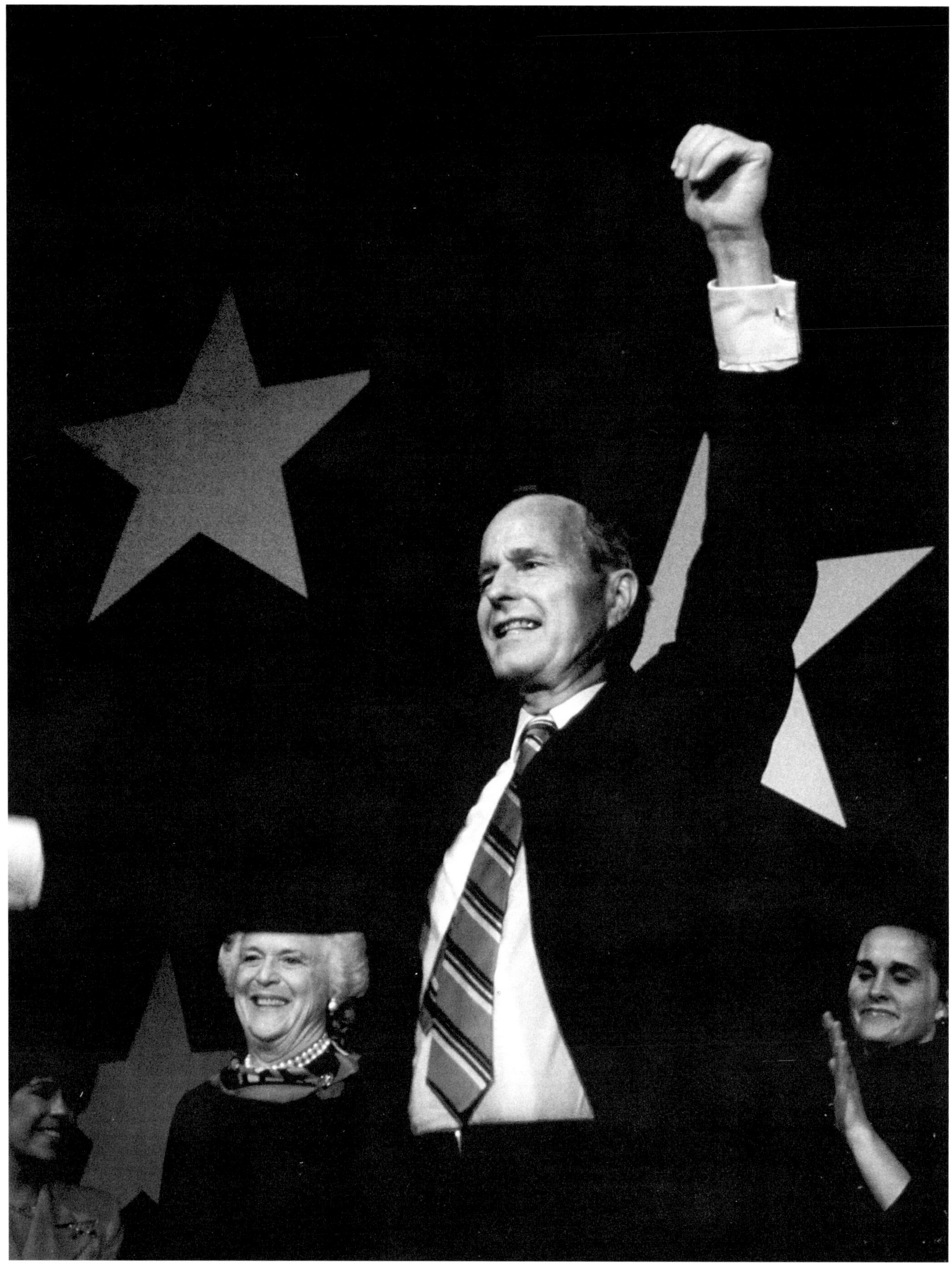

The victorious George Bush on election night, 8 November 1988

Appendix 1: The Vice-Presidents of the United States of America

1 **1789–1797** JOHN ADAMS, afterwards 2nd President (*qv*)
2 **1797–1801** THOMAS JEFFERSON, afterwards 3rd President (*qv*)
3 **1801–1805** AARON BURR
4 **1805–1812** GEORGE CLINTON
5 **1813–1814** ELBRIDGE GERRY
6 **1817–1825** DANIEL D TOMPKINS
7 **1825–1832** JOHN CALDWELL CALHOUN
8 **1833–1837** MARTIN VAN BUREN, afterwards 8th President (*qv*)
9 **1837–1841** RICHARD MENTOR JOHNSON
10 **1841** JOHN TYLER, afterwards 10th President (*qv*)
11 **1845–1849** GEORGE MIFFLIN DALLAS
12 **1849–1850** MILLARD FILLMORE, afterwards 13th President (*qv*)
13 **1853** WILLIAM RUFUS DEVANE KING
14 **1857–1861** JOHN CABELL BRECKINRIDGE
15 **1861–1865** HANNIBAL HAMLIN
16 **1865** ANDREW JOHNSON, afterwards 17th President (*qv*)
17 **1869–1873** SCHUYLER COLFAX
18 **1873–1875** HENRY WILSON
19 **1877–1881** WILLIAM ALMON WHEELER
20 **1881** CHESTER ALAN ARTHUR, afterwards 21st President (*qv*)
21 **1885** THOMAS ANDREWS HENDRICKS
22 **1889–1893** LEVI PARSONS MORTON
23 **1893–1897** ADLAI EWING STEVENSON
24 **1897–1899** GARRET AUGUSTUS HOBART
25 **1901** THEODORE ROOSEVELT, afterwards 26th President (*qv*)
26 **1905–1909** CHARLES WARREN FAIRBANKS
27 **1909–1912** JAMES SCHOOLCRAFT SHERMAN
28 **1913–1921** THOMAS RILEY MARSHALL
29 **1921–1923** (JOHN) CALVIN COOLIDGE, afterwards 30th President (*qv*)
30 **1925–1929** CHARLES GATES DAWES
31 **1929–1933** CHARLES CURTIS
32 **1933–1941** JOHN NANCE GARNER
33 **1941–1945** HENRY AGARD WALLACE
34 **1945** HARRY S TRUMAN, afterwards 33rd President (*qv*)
35 **1949–1953** ALBEN WILLIAM BARKLEY
36 **1953–1961** RICHARD MILHOUS NIXON, afterwards 37th President (*qv*)
37 **1961–1963** LYNDON BAINES JOHNSON, afterwards 36th President (*qv*)
38 **1965–1969** HUBERT HORATIO HUMPHREY
39 **1969–1973** SPIRO THEODORE AGNEW
40 **1973–1974** GERALD RUDOLPH FORD, afterwards 38th President (*qv*)
41 **1974–1977** NELSON ALDRICH ROCKEFELLER
42 **1977–1981** WALTER FREDERICK MONDALE
43 **1981–1989** GEORGE HERBERT WALKER BUSH, afterwards 41st President (*qv*)
44 **1989–** J DANFORTH QUAYLE

Appendix 2: Key to Abbreviations

AB/BA	Bachelor of Arts	div	divorced
b	born	*dsp*	died without issue
bapt	baptized	*k*	killed
BS/BSc	Bachelor of Science	*ka*	killed in action
bur	buried	Mass	Massachusetts
Conn	Connecticut	Pa	Pennsylvania
CSA	Confederate States of America	*unm*	unmarried
d	died	USN	United States Navy
dau(s)	daughter(s)	Va	Virginia
DC	District of Columbia	*yr*	younger
DD	Doctor of Divinity	*yst*	youngest
diss	dissolved		

Acknowledgements

The publishers would like to thank the following for permission to reproduce illustrations:

Colour: BPCC/Aldus Archive, pages 101 (below), 114, 116; Frank Spooner Pictures, pages 123, 126 (above), 126 (below), 128; MacDonald/Aldus Archive, pages 99, 112 (above), 121, 124; Michael Evans, White House/BPCC/Aldus, page 127; Peter Newark's Western Americana, pages 97, 98, 100 (above), 100 (below), 101 (above), 102, 103, 104, 105, 106 (above), 106 (below), 107, 108, 109, 110 (below), 111 (above), 111 (below), 113, 117, 118, 119, 120, 122, 125.

Black and white: BPCC/Aldus Archive, pages 78, 85 (left), 151, 158, 166; Frank Spooner Pictures, pages 188, 189, 194, 199, 200, 201, 202; MacDonald/Aldus Archive, pages 8, 24, 26, 28, 47, 58, 64, 69, 72, 76 (right), 82, 85 (right), 89, 93, 96, 115 (below), 129, 130, 133, 135, 138, 141, 143, 149, 155, 164, 167 (below), 171, 173, 174, 176, 180, 186, 193; Peter Newark's Western Americana, frontispiece, pages 14, 15, 16, 19, 21, 22, 25, 30, 31, 33, 34, 37, 38, 42 (above), 42 (below), 46, 49, 51, 54, 56, 62, 67, 70, 75, 76 (left), 80, 81, 84, 91, 115 (above), 136, 139, 145, 147, 149 (right), 152, 157, 160, 162, 167 (above), 170, 177, 181, 182, 184, 191, 196, 198, 202; US Embassy London, presidential seal.

Index

SEAL OF THE PRESIDENT OF THE UNITED STATES